Computing Information Technology: The Human Side

edited by

Steven Gordon
Babson College, USA

IRM Press
Publisher of innovative scholarly and professional information technology titles in the cyberage

Hershey • London • Melbourne • Singapore • Beijing

Acquisitions Editor: Mehdi Khosrow-Pour
Senior Managing Editor: Jan Travers
Managing Editor: Amanda Appicello
Developing Editor: Michele Rossi
Typesetter: Jennifer Wetzel
Copy Editor: Donna Kirker Morgan
Cover Design: Weston Pritts
Printed at: Integrated Book Technology

Published in the United States of America by
IRM Press (an imprint of Idea Group Inc.)
701 E. Chocolate Avenue, Suite 200
Hershey PA 17033-1240
Tel: 717-533-8845
Fax: 717-533-8661
E-mail: cust@idea-group.com
Web site: http://www.irm-press.com

and in the United Kingdom by
IRM Press (an imprint of Idea Group Inc.)
3 Henrietta Street
Covent Garden
London WC2E 8LU
Tel: 44 20 7240 0856
Fax: 44 20 7379 3313
Web site: http://www.eurospan.co.uk

Library of Congress Cataloging-in-Publication Data

Gordon, Steven R.
Computing information technology : the human side / Steven Gordon.
p. cm.
Issued also as an e-book.
ISBN 1-931777-52-7 (soft-cover) -- ISBN 1-931777-68-3 (e-book)
1. Computers. 2. Information technology. I. Title.
QA76.5.G635 2003
004--dc21

2002156238

eISBN: 1-931777-68-3

British Cataloguing in Publication Data
A Cataloguing in Publication record for this book is available from the British Library.

Other New Releases from IRM Press

Computing Information Technology: The Human Side

Table of Contents

SECTION III: END USER COMPUTING

SECTION IV: INFORMATION TECHNOLOGY AND THE ORGANIZATION

Preface

It is hard to think about computer information technology without considering its human side. Information technology is built by and for people. According to most definitions, information technology and human beings are two of the components of an information system. Computer information technology interacts with people in many ways as information systems process transactions or provide support for decision-making. This book — *Computing Information Technology: The Human Side* — examines the interaction and interface between people and information technology. Each of the 17 chapters presents cutting edge research on the human side of computer information technology.

The human side of computing information technology has a long history in information systems research. Among the journals dedicated to this topic are the *ACM Transactions on Computer Human Interaction* (http://www.acm.org/tochi/), *Information Technology & People* (http://www.emeraldinsight.com/itp.htm), and the *International Journal of Human-Computer Studies* (http://www.academicpress.com/ijhcs). Many other journals, such as Idea Group's own *Journal of End User Computing*, focus on various aspects of the human side of computing.

The field is also broad. It encompasses user-interface design and usability, end-user computing, the cultural and organizational impact of computer systems, user satisfaction with and adoption of information technology, various software products and technologies, such as groupware, knowledge management, and workflow, and many other sub-fields. In this volume, we explore many of these topics.

Seven of the 17 chapters, more than one third of this volume, focus on user interface design and usability. Four of these chapters deal specifically with the Web, comprising Section I — Web Site User Interface.

- Chapter I, "Navigational Tools in Hypertext Information Retrieval Frames and an Expandable Table of Contents," by Rawiwan Tenissara, addresses two elements of a Web page user interface — the table of contents and frames. Tenissara tests six hypotheses under controlled conditions and finds that users of expandable tables of contents performed worse and had less favorable attitudes towards their experience than users of traditional tables of contents. Tenissara also found that multiple frames do not lead to superior performance or speed in searching or browsing.

- Chapter II, "Website Interactivity and Amusement: Techniques and Effects," by Yuan Gao, reviews theory and research addressing how design decisions regarding interactivity and humor affect users' perceptions of a Web site's information and entertainment value. Gao concludes that more research is needed to uncover the causal factors that underlie the observed behaviors and assessments so that businesses can develop more effective Web sites.
- Chapter III, "Techniques for Visualizing Website Usage Patterns with an Adaptive Neural Network," by Victor Perotti, seeks to improve usability by offering Web designers' post-implementation techniques for examining how visitors use a Web site. Although previous studies have proposed alternative techniques for data mining of Web logs, Perotti presents a novel approach to both analysis and presentation, one that can be easily used and understood by Web designers without training in sophisticated analysis techniques.
- Chapter IV, "Using Usability Factors to Predict the E-Commerce User Experience," by Adrie Stander and Nata van der Merwe, identifies a number of factors that affect users' satisfaction with e-Commerce Web sites. Among these are depth of color, use of frames, existence of privacy statements, proportion of white space, background color and the value-added services provided by the site.

Section II, Interface Design and Usability, addresses these topics in contexts other than Web design. Chapter V deals with survey administration, Chapter VI with systems development, and Chapter VII with data analysis.

- Chapter V, "Social Issues in the Administration of Information Systems Survey Research," by Susan K. Lippert, compares manual with Internet-based (both Web and email) survey data collection methods. These methods are compared along a variety of performance parameters, including response rate, participation ease, attractiveness of survey, novelty effect, administrative costs, response flexibility, response time, population size, sample bias, instrument validity, the management of non-response data, and response error.
- Chapter VI, "User Interfaces and Markup Language Programming: The Effects of Interaction Mode on User Performance and Satisfaction," by Jeffrey Hsu, also concerns Web-based surveys, but only as a case example. Hsu addresses the question of whether a software wizard is a good user interface for developers programming in markup languages such as HTML or SGML. Hsu's case study compares the efficiency and satisfaction of experienced and novice developers in their creation of a Web-based survey using either a native markup language called SQML (Survey Questionnaire Markup Language) or a wizard that generates SQML commands through an intelligent user interface.
- Chapter VII, "Development of a Task Model for the Analysis and Retrieval of Statistical Data," by Peter N. Hyland, provides guidance to developers of systems designed to present and analyze statistical data. Hyland explores the sequence of tasks that analysts employ to make sense of data and answer specific questions when faced with tabular, OLAP, or value/rule-based user interfaces.

The vast majority of people who use computers can be considered end users, those who are not programmers, computer professionals, or systems designers. Section III, End User Computing, examines the problems and issues unique to end-users. Chapters VIII and IX are concerned with how end users seek and receive help with their computing problems. Chapter X explores how end users develop software for their own needs. Chapter XI addresses how to teach people to become proficient end users.

- Chapter VIII, "Media Selection and End-User Satisfaction: An Empirical Study of Help-Desk Using SERVQUAL," by Sang-Gun Lee, Sangjin Yoo and Zoonky Lee, examines how several dimensions of satisfaction with end user support vary depending on how that support is given. Face-to-face and telephone support provide more satisfaction on some dimensions, while the Internet, email, and hybrid methods of support provide more satisfaction on other dimensions. The authors conclude that organizations should consider automating help desks to provide more options to end-users.
- Chapter IX, "End User Support Usage," by Robin Munkvold, asks, "Why do end users choose different support services?" Munkvold shows that certain characteristics of end users, such as their technical skills, involvement with IT, and self-efficacy towards IT, determine whether or not they seek formal or informal sources of support and use internal or external documentation. Munkvold recommends that organizations should work to improve these end user qualities rather than providing only traditional support services.
- Chapter X, "Users as Developers — Conditions and Effects of User Systems Development," by Anders Avdic, answers the question, "How can end users best develop new information systems without the aid of information technology professionals?" Using spreadsheet creation as an example, Avdic shows that characteristics of end user development, such as the interactivity that arises as an end user switches between user and development roles, as well as integration and the ability to raise questions, result in superior outcomes, especially in uncomplicated applications.
- Chapter XI, "Solving Common Business Problems with Microsoft Office®," by Kathryn Marold and Gwynne Larsen, demonstrates the advantages of a problem-solving approach for training increasingly computer-savvy students in end-user computing tools such as Microsoft Office. The authors argue that students benefit from tackling operational problems, such as those they might experience on the job, in a relatively pressure free environment. They also find that the problem-solving approach works well in both Web-based and traditional learning environments.

The chapters in Section IV, Information Technology and the Organization, take a more macro view of the human/computer interface than preceding chapters do. For example, they address how technology affects organizations through changing culture and power relationships, and how existing cultures and political structures affect the adoption of new technology. Chapters XII and XIII focus on organizational adoption of new technology, while Chapters XIV and XV examine the effect of technology on inter-organizational relationships and alliances.

- Chapter XII, "Changing a Business School Corporate Culture: Teaching in the 21st Century on a Different Blackboard," by Jennifer Paige Nightingale, presents a case study of the introduction of SOBA-net, an Academic Management System for faculty, students, and staff at the Duquesne University School of Business in Pittsburgh, Pennsylvania. The case traces the history of adoption and use by members of the organization.
- Chapter XIII, "The Role of the Organizational Context in the Use of a Workflow System: Lessons From a Case Study," by Anabela Sarmento, is a longitudinal study of the introduction of a workflow system at an anonymous Portuguese company that consults on and implements electronic document storage systems. The case study shows how structural, political, human, technological and cultural factors can be enablers or constrainers of systems adoption. It also shows how these factors interact with one another and demonstrates how that interaction complicates the adoption decision.
- Chapter XIV, "Strategic Models for the Delivery of Personal Financial Services: The Role of Infocracy," by Steven Gordon and Paul Mulligan, develops the concept of "infocracy," a form of organization in which information provides the underpinning of structure and the basis of individual power. In the context of financial service integration, in an environment in which information technology can make inter-organizational alliances appear transparent to customers, the authors hypothesize that structure should depend upon the strategy of the firm.
- Chapter XV, "Role of Behavioral Factors in Strategic Alliances," by Chong Kim, Purnendu Mandal, and Dale H. Shao, highlights a number of human and organizational culture issues that play a major role in the development of a strategic alliance between a major telecommunications organization and several retail electricity organizations. The authors use this case study to develop a framework to help partners in new alliances understand each other's informational requirements and interdependencies.

No academic volume on the human side of computing information technology would be complete without attention to how research is done in this discipline. Section V, The Human Side in IT Research, presents two chapters that highlight contemporary research issues.

- Chapter XVI, "Building a Custom Client-Side Research Tool for Online Web-Based Experiments," by Stu Westin, describes the problems and techniques involved in building a research instrument to collect detailed data about a Web user's keystrokes and mouse movements. Such an instrument can collect more precise information than that which clickstream analysis or network sniffing can obtain. Such information is crucial to researchers' ability to understand and analyze how people actually perform Web-based activities, such as electronic commerce.
- Chapter XVII, "Towards a Sociopragmatic-Constructivist Understanding of Information Systems," by Boris Wyssusek and Martin Schwartz, argues that a philosophical foundation is needed for a better understanding of information systems. The authors develop a framework for information systems (IS) research and practice that they call

"sociopragmatic constructivism," which they believe will begin to question the basic assumptions taken for granted in contemporary IS research and will better integrate IS research with elements of cultural theory, philosophy of science and sociology.

The chapters of this book are extensions of manuscripts presented at the 2002 IRMA International Conference in Seattle, Washington, May 19-22. All were triple blind reviewed for acceptance at the conference. From among the approximately 350 conference presentations, acquisitions editor, Mehdi Khosrow-Pour, selected 17 for inclusion in this special volume, with the objective of transmitting knowledge that would be most valuable to academicians and practitioners. We hope and trust that you will find these chapters both valuable and enlightening.

Steven Gordon
Babson College, USA
January 2003

Section I

Web Site User Interface

Chapter I

Navigational Tools in Hypertext Information Retrieval Frames and an Expandable Table of Contents

Rawiwan Tenissara
Information Systems Education Center,
National Institute of Development Administration, Thailand

ABSTRACT

Difficulties with navigation are common in hypertext documents. Many studies have examined techniques and design strategies to find the proper structure of a hyperdocument whereas others have investigated navigational tools such as overview diagrams, maps, menus, and/or tables of contents that help users navigate through complex hyperdocuments. This study has investigated the effects of table of contents and frames as user interface on user performance and user satisfaction. The result suggests several guidelines for designing complex hypertext information retrieval systems and creating on-line documentation.

INTRODUCTION

Hypertext systems have found various practical applications that can range from on-line documentation, information retrieval systems, to sophisticated learning environments. These applications fall into four general classes: browsing systems, problem exploration tools, macro-library systems, and general hypertext systems (Conklin, 1987).

Hypertext systems, compared to traditional information retrieval systems, provide users with an easy and flexible access to a large amount of information. Hypertext proponents claim that the most salient advantages of these systems are the modularity of information and non-linear access to information through linking (Mohages, 1992).

The primary method for navigating through a hyperdocument is by browsing. However, the limitations of the browsing paradigm were soon revealed when it deals with large hypertext systems. The well-known problems of disorientation and cognitive overload in hypertext systems have been frequently reported and discussed in hypertext literature (Chen & Stanney, 1999; Conklin, 1987; Halasz, 1988; Nielsen, 1996; William, Eveland & Dunwoody, 2001). Marchionini (1988) states that the problem of disorientation will likely to diminish as the user gain experience with the system and as the designers apply common-sense interface designs. Consequently, designers must not only consider how to structure knowledge from a system performance standpoint, but must also consider what views and corresponding navigational tools are provided to the users.

Providing visual tools, such as overview diagrams or maps, is usually considered an efficient way of helping users navigate through complex hypertext structures (Halasz, Moran, & Trigg, 1987; Yankelovich, Meyrowitz & Druncker, 1988). However, as noted by many hypertext authors (Bernstein, Garzotto, Paoloni & Schwab, 1991), designing good overview diagrams for complex structures has proved to be difficult. Overview diagrams may facilitate navigation well in small hypertext systems, but for large systems, overview diagrams might introduce navigational problems of their own (Nielsen, 1990).

Hypertext usage depends on the mental models users have for the system. These mental models, in turn, depend on the conceptual model used by designers to create the system. The system views and navigational tools will be assimilated into a mental model for a system if they are familiar (Marchionini & Shneiderman, 1988). Therefore, designers must know how users seek information in traditional print systems and in the existing electric systems if they are to produce effective interfaces for new systems.

Many readers of books make extensive use of the table of contents and indexes to navigate through a book. They may transfer this experience to using hypertext systems. Table of contents (TOC) shows how the content of a book is related to its structure and provides the terminology of the book grouped in the context of its use (Jacques, Nonnecke, Preece & McKerlie, 1993). Table of contents is a valuable tool for presenting not only the structure of a hypertext system (Simpson & McKnight, 1990), but the relationships between items within the documents as well. If they are present in hypertext systems, they can provide tremendous help to users.

The interface design for table of contents can vary in hypertext systems. The TOC may be truncated if viewing the response to a query, and may use a fisheye view (Furnas, 1986). An expandable TOC, for example, presents the structure of a hypertext system by employing a fisheye-view method. The expandable TOC, while containing only the highest hierarchical level of headings when a document first displays, allows users to expand each section to its next lowest level and open as many different parts of the table of contents as desired at the same time. Types of interface chosen for table of contents can affect user behaviors, navigation patterns, and ultimately user performance and satisfaction with hypertext systems.

BACKGROUND LITERATURE

Hypertext systems are intended to help users more effectively retrieve information stored in database as Chen, Ekberg and Thompson (1990) describe. In traditional text, presentation of information assumes single location for each piece of information within a collection and an implicit linear order. Hypertext technology, on the other hand, offers new possibilities of document organization to the author and navigation to the user. However, with these new possibilities come new design challenges. The hypertext designer must create the structure flexible enough to express the flowing nature of hypertext system, while still clear enough to guide the user's navigation.

Navigation in Hypertext

How a user navigates through hypermedia space is affected by the linkages made by the hypermedia author (possibly better: the linkages made by the hypermedia author affects how a user navigates through hypermedia space) (Conklin, 1987). Similar in conception to Jonassen's (1986) levels of hypertext, Conklin (1987) distinguishes between two methods of linking two points in hypertext: referential links and organizational links. Referential links are non-hierarchical, while organizational links connect hierarchical information having both parent and child nodes. Having many referential links can make the hypertext document seem multi-dimensional (Anderson-Inman, 1989).

Although hierarchical and nonhierarchical links may appear to serve a purely organizational function, they may possess meaning that can influence the navigation of the user. As the complexity of a hypertext document increases, the potential for navigation problems also increase (McKnight, Dillon & Richardson, 1989). The most common navigational problem in hypermedia documents is disorientation or "getting lost" (Anderson-Inman, 1989; Botafogo & Shneiderman, 1991; Conklin, 1987; Nielson, 1990).

Disorientation

Conklin (1987) defines disorientation as the tendency to lose one's sense of location and direction in a nonlinear document, using the expression "lost in hyperspace" to describe it. Edwards and Hardman (1989) describe "getting lost in hyperspace" in hypertext applications as the result of users being unable to find desired information, or unable to gain an overview of information space. The user becomes "lost" because he does not know what actions he can perform. The problem of disorientation must be resolved. Bieber (1997) claims that proper implementations of advanced hypermedia features will alleviate these problems, as well as provide readers with a rich information environment.

Many researchers have investigated the navigation problem in hypermedia systems. Some led to techniques and design strategies for finding proper structure of a hyperdocument (Acksyn, McCracken & Yoder, 1988), while others led to visual tools such as overview diagrams or maps that help users navigate through complex hypermedia structures (Halasz, Moran & Trigg, 1987; Yankelovich, Meyrowitz & Drucker, 1988).

Navigational Tools

Graphical maps and browsers are quite useful in providing structural overviews of hypertext. Intermedia (Garett, Smith & Merowitz, 1986), Neptune (Delisle & Schwartz, 1986), Notecards (Halasz, 1988), Planetext (Conklin, 1987), gIBIS (Conklin & Begeman, 1988), and others use a graphical browser to help the users develop a mental model of the information in the system and maintain a sense of orientation as they navigate through it. This overview presentation provides a global view of a whole hyperdocument, as well as, local views of parts of the hyperdocument. These graphical representations are particularly good at representing the structure of small hyperdocuments with many cross-reference links, but are poor at representing hyperdocuments containing more than about 30 nodes because of the screen limitation. As systems grow beyond a browser's ability to depict concisely the information contained there, however, it becomes increasingly difficult to maintain a sense of orientation and context by looking at the browser. Techniques such as fisheye view (Furnas, 1986), and pruning help manage this problem.

There have been a number of studies investigating the use of maps, but very substantive evidence cannot be drawn from them. Hammond and Allinson (1989) compared the use of maps with no maps on performance of a database inquiry task. They found, although the performance was superior for subject using the maps, this difference was not statistically significant.

Stanton, Taylor and Tweedie (1992) conducted a study to determine if maps were an appropriate navigation aid for searching in hypertext documents. The researchers found that the high scores in the "no map" condition significantly outperformed the high scores in the "map" condition on the sentence completion tasks. They also found that those in the "no map" condition significantly outperformed those in the "map" condition on the cognitive mapping task. In addition, those in the "no map" condition felt as if they had more control over the lesson than those in the "map" condition. Stanton et al. (1992) concluded that in an information search and retrieval task, maps actually impaired performance.

Chen, Lin and Sun (2000) have investigated the effects of navigation maps on search performance, browsing behavior, and cognitive map development within hierarchical structured hypertext courseware. The results of the study showed that map type — the global map in particular — significantly affected students' search performance, and their browsing behavior. However, students with no map had the highest scores on the development of the cognitive map. Providing maps led not only to poor performance, but also to less perceived control and inferior development of cognitive maps when compared to a no-map group. This suggests that maps may hamper efficient use of a hypertext system.

Dee-Lucas (1996) studied the effects of overview structure on text review and the resulting internal representation when readers had a general and a specific learning goal. The results of the study showed that the hierarchical overview was easier to use in deciding what to review, as well as, for initial reading. The result of this experiment indicates that providing structure in a hypertext overview can enhance its usability by facilitating selection of a unit. Besides, regardless of the learning goal, readers spent less time selecting units from the hierarchical overview than from the list overview.

Providing a hierarchical skeleton, or tree structure, for hypertext organization can help users to develop a mental model of a system and maintain orientation (Akscyn, McCracken & Yoder, 1988).

Mental Models

Rovie and Morris (1986) have defined mental models as "... mechanisms whereby humans are able to generate descriptions of system purpose and form, explanations of the system functioning and observed system states and predictions of future system states" (p. 351). A user who is interacting with a system constructs a subjective causal model of this system in order to give reasons for the invisible structure of the system or for the process running in the system (Seel, 1999). However, mental models are often incomplete and do not necessarily reflect a technical correct image of the target system (Norman, 1983). In fact, sometimes users are not even aware of having such a model. Their mental model is only partially represented in conceptual structures. Mental models may comprise structural knowledge about the system, rules and procedural knowledge (e.g., on how to perform operations). They capture only aspects relevant to the user.

Users acquire and expand their mental models by observing the system's behavior in the course of its use, by training, instruction and documentation. The mental model is also expanded by deduction based on the existing model and is influenced by experience with other systems (Rupietta, 1990). During the design and development of a software system, Norman (1983) has suggested that designers need to create a conceptual model, which is a representation of the system on a conceptual level depending on the specific view of the designer, of the mental model. He suggests that designers should actively attempt to elicit mental models in users for the system being designed. The conceptual model should take into account the beliefs users are likely to bring to the system, the need for the concepts that make up the mental models to be observable in the system, and the need for the mental model to have predictive power.

Designers must not only consider how to structure knowledge from a system advantage, but also what views and corresponding navigational tools are provided for the users. The views and navigational tools will be assimilated easily into a mental model for a system if they are familiar. This reasoning lies behind the desktop and other metaphors (Marchionini & Shneiderman, 1988). Designers must know how a user seeks information in traditional print systems, if they are to provide effective interface for a new system.

Metaphors are well-recognized mechanisms for providing easy to use, interactive access to the complex functionalities of information systems. Metaphors are also employed for facilitating the forming and development of mental models. Examples are a storyteller, a navigator, a guide, a book, a map (Cartwright, 1999) and a travel metaphor.

Table of Contents

In the paper world, a table of contents is usually given at the beginning to provide a systematic list of headings identifying the items discussed in the documents; "it is an aid to both ways-finding and sense-making" (Carey, Hunt & Lopez-Suarez, 1990, p. 58). A table of contents orients the reader to the scope of the publication as the authors intend it to be viewed. In hypertext systems, a table of contents offers an overview of the document content, and overviews have often been recommended as useful navigation aids (Utting & Yankelovich, 1987).

A number of hypertext systems use a table of contents to aid navigation and represent the structure of a hyperdocument (Jacques, Nonnecke, McKerlie & Preece, 1993; Perrott & Smith, 1992). WebTOC (Heflin, Komlodi, Pasricha & Tan, 1998) is designed to diminish the difficulties for users to get an overview of the contents and the structure of the Web sites. A WebTOC provides a graphical description of the hierarchy of a Web through a hierarchical table of contents that employs a fisheye view method. The study comparing WebTOC, Textual TOC (a basic tables of contents interface), and ordinary Netscape found that the differences in task performance times were not statistically significant. However, users prefer having a table of contents of a Web site regardless of performances.

SuperBook (Landauer, Egan, Remde, Lesk, Lochbaum & Ketchum, 1993) is designed for accessing static documents, and its major concern is the improvement of retrieval efficiencies for each individual. The SuperBook browser provides computer-based enhancements to texts. It makes heavy use of the paper document's table of contents for hierarchical searching. SuperBook's dynamic expanded table of contents is not presented as a linear structure, but rather as an appropriation of a fisheye display (Furnas, 1986). When a document first comes up, only the highest hierarchical level of headings is displayed. Next to each heading, under which there are subheadings, is an asterisk, indicating the user can expand that section to its next lowest level by a mouse click. The user can open up as many different parts of the table of contents at the same time as desired.

Frames

Multiple-window environments have been used extensively for a decade in typical hypermedia documents as navigational aids. Frames, one may call windows, also have emerged as a feature of Netscape Navigator. The frames feature provides Netscape Navigator with sophisticated page-presentation facilities to display multiple, independently scrollable frames on a single screen.

A frame is a [rectangular] region in the window. It can have a name, so it can be addressed or targeted by being linked to documents. If a screen is divided into regions, each one is a frame, and a particular combination of frames is called the frameset. To use frames, one document must define the frameset, so that other documents can be displayed in each frame (Engelfriet, 1997).

According to Nielsen (1996), the fundamental design of the Web is based on having the page the atomic unit of information, and the notion of page permeates all aspects of the Web. The simplicity of the original Web contributed to its ease of use and its rapid update. Frames break the unified model of the Web and introduce a new way of looking at data that has not been well integrated into other aspects of the Web. With frames, the user's view of information on screen is now determined by a sequence of navigation actions rather than by a single navigation action. However, Nielsen (1996) claims that these problems with frames will go away over the next few years.

Currently, numerous home pages on the World Wide Web (WWW) use frames to present a table of contents. Unfortunately, no actual research studies are found either to support or to refute the use of these tools as generalized guidelines for hypermedia or Webpage designers. There are, however, no general guidelines for structuring and for the interface since their optimal design depends upon the task for which the information system is used (Vries & Jong, 1997). Thus, the hypermedia designers need to consider the types of tasks users will be undertaking in their design of hypermedia navigation system (Wright & Lickorish, 1990).

Information Seeking

Information seeking is a fundamental learning activity, a precursor to many others (Jonassen & Grabinger, 1990). It is also a pervasive human activity (Nickerson, 1986) and a special case of problem solving (Machionini, 1989). As problems can be classified into two broad categories — well-defined and ill-defined — in terms of the clarity of the starting point and goal, search targets are different in their complexity and specificity. Findings from studies that focus only on the retrieval of facts cannot be generalized to the wide range of information-seeking activities in which learners may be engaged in real information-searching situations.

Research has shown that information searchers prefer search facilities such as key word search or index mechanism (Joseph, Steingberg & Jones, 1989). But when search questions are vague, people tend to resort to the browsing or exploring strategies (Marchionini & Shneiderman, 1988). Marchionini (1992) proposed a framework of five functions involved in information seeking tasks. This framework reflects the iterative, nonlinear, and opportunistic characteristics typical of end-user information seeking patterns. Tonta (1991) has argued "...hypertext systems are not designed for fast and efficient fact retrieval. Rather they support unhurried and informal information searching" (p. 22). Therefore, when the search task is simple and specific, comparing different browsing systems is actually a comparison of search facilities and indexing schemes provided in each system rather than a comparison of the structure or interface design (Lai & Waugh, 1995). This is consistent with Vies and Jong (1997), who argue that information systems, and especially hypertext, can be used for tasks other than searching for information, such as information exploration. Information systems are thought to facilitate both problem structuring and problem solving (Begoray, 1990). In fact, on the task side, the development of hypertext systems coincides with a shift in interest from searching and locating a specific fact to tasks involving browsing and the exploring of subject areas.

Even though there is no actual research on the use of frames and the expandable table of contents on WWW applications, on the basis of previous research studies, the following hypotheses were generated for the present study.

H1: Users' performance in information searching and browsing with expandable table of contents will be more accurate than with traditional table of contents.

H2: Users' speed in searching and browsing with expandable table of contents will be higher than with traditional table of contents.

H3: The navigation will be more satisfy using expandable table of contents as opposed to traditional table of contents.

H4: Users' performance in information searching and browsing with multiple-frame will be more accurate than with single-frame.

H5: Users' speed in searching and browsing with multiple-frame will be higher than with single-frame.

H6: The navigation will be more satisfy using multiple-frame as opposed to single-frame.

RESEARCH METHODS

The objective of the study was to examine the effects of user interface — types of table of contents and frames — on user performance and user satisfaction. To accomplish this goal, a laboratory experiment was conducted using a Completely Randomized design in which two between-subjects factors were involved.

Procedures

Thirty-six students at Indiana University participated in the study voluntarily. When the subject arrived, he/she was randomly assigned to one of the four different experimental conditions, e.g., expandable table of contents with single-frame, traditional table of contents with single-frame, expandable table of contents with multiple-frame and traditional table of contents with multiple-frame. During the first 15 minutes, the subjects were given time to relax and familiarize themselves with the environment. Then, the subjects were guided to open the World Wide Web browser, and read written instruction for tasks. After that, the subjects were guided to open and browse through each experimental system in order to familiarize themselves with the navigation tools. Immediately after the introduction, the subjects were given 30 minutes to search and browse for information. Finally, the subjects were asked to complete a 22-item satisfaction questionnaire, and then to fill in the demographic information during the 10 minutes before their leaving the computer cluster.

DATA ANALYSIS AND RESULTS

To examine the effects of table of contents (TOC) and the use of frame on information searching and browsing, three different types of data were collected: scores on users' performance and speed in searching and browsing for information, along with the satisfaction questionnaire results.

The score on users' performance was calculated by counting the correct answers each user retrieved from an experimental system. The experimenter awarded one point for an unambiguously correct answer, a half-point for a partly answered response and no point for a wrong answer or abandoned question. Exceptionally, user's speed was calculated by counting unabandoned questions.

Results

The results are generalized according to the dependent measures: users' performance, users' speed and users' satisfaction.

Users' Performance

The users' performance in information searching and browsing with traditional TOC was statistically significant more accurate than with expandable TOC ($F(1,32) = 5.42$, $p < 0.05$). This finding did not support Hypothesis 1 that predicted users' performance with expandable TOC would be more accurate than with traditional TOC.

The mean score of the single-frame users was 11.208 and that of the multiple-frame users was 10. 875. However, the difference was not significant. This finding did not support Hypothesis 4 that predicted users' performance with multiple-frame would be more accurate than with single-frame.

However, there was a significance of the effects of interaction between table of contents and frames ($F(1,32) = 4.32$, $p < 0.05$). Users under expandable table of contents performed better under the single-frame treatment than the multiple-frame treatment. In contrast, users under traditional table of contents performed better under the multiple-frame treatment than the single-frame treatment.

Users' Speed

The users' speed in information searching and browsing with traditional TOC was statistically significantly higher than with expandable TOC ($F(1,32) = 7.28$, $p < 0.05$). This finding did not support Hypothesis 2 that predicted t users under expandable TOC treatment would have higher speed than those under traditional TOC treatment.

The mean speed of users under single-frame treatment was 8.00, which was exactly the same as that of users under multiple-frame treatment. This finding failed to support Hypothesis 5 that predicted that users' speed under multiple-frame treatment would have higher speed than those under single-frame treatment.

The effect of interaction between table of contents and frame was statistically significant ($F(1, 32) = 7.28$, $p < 0.05$). Users under traditional table of contents treatment possessed higher speed with multiple-frame treatment than with single-frame treatment. In contrast, users under expandable table of contents treatment possessed less speed with multiple-frame treatment than with single-frame treatment.

Users' Satisfaction

To test users' satisfaction, two dependent variables were employed: perceived degree of disorientation and perceived ease of use.

Perceived degree of disorientation. The mean scores on users' perceived degree of disorientation under the interaction between expandable table of contents and single-frame, traditional table of contents and single-frame, expandable table of contents and multiple-frame and traditional table of contents and multiple-frame treatments were between 2.28 and 3.37. Since seven category Likert scales were

Table 1: Source Information for 2×2 ANOVA of Mean Scores on Users' Perceived Degree of Description

Source	DF	Sum of Squares	Mean Square	F	P
TOC	1	8.3457	8.3457	7.56	0.0097
Frame	1	0.1372	0.1372	0.12	0.7268
TOC × Frame	1	2.5364	2.5364	2.30	0.1395
Residual	32	35.3388	1.1043		

used in the satisfaction questionnaire, it must be reasonable to conclude that users did not feel disoriented while navigating through the experimental systems.

Further analysis was made to determine the significant difference in users' perceived degree of disorientation. The results of this analysis are summarized in Table 1.

The results of the ANOVA in Table 1 indicate a significant difference in perceived degree of disorientation between the two groups of users in expandable TOC and traditional TOC ($F(1, 32) = 7.56, p < 0.01$). The mean score of expandable TOC users was 3.574 and that of traditional TOC users was 2.611. Thus, the users under traditional TOC treatment reported feeling significantly less disoriented than those under expandable TOC treatment. This finding did not support Hypothesis 3 that predicted navigation would be more satisfied using expandable TOC as opposed to traditional TOC. Users must be more satisfied if they feel less disoriented.

Table 1 indicates that the main effect of frame failed to reach significance ($F(1, 32) = 0.12, p = 0.7268$). This finding did not support Hypothesis 6 that predicted the navigation would be more satisfied with multiple-frame as opposed to single-frame. However, users under multiple-frame treatment reported feeling less disoriented than those users under single-frame treatment, because the means score of perceived degree of disorientation of users under multiple-frame treatment was 3.031, whereas that of users under single-frame treatment was 3.154.

The finding in Table 1 indicated as well that the interaction between table of contents and frame failed to reach significance ($F(1, 32) = 2.30, p = 0.1395$).

Perceived ease of use. The mean scores for users' perceived ease of use under the interaction between expandable table of contents and single-frame, traditional table of contents and single-frame, expandable table of contents and multiple-frame, and traditional table of contents and multiple-frame are 4.21, 5.03, 4.46, and 5.56 respectively. The score higher than 4.00 suggests that for users the hypermedia system was perceived as easy to use.

Further 2×2 ANOVA was employed to test the significant differences in users' perceived ease of use. The between-subjects were once again table of contents and frame (see Table 2).

Table 2: Source Information for 2×2 ANOVA of Mean Scores on Users' Perceived Ease of Use

Source	DF	Sum of Squares	Mean Square	F	P
TOC	1	8.2656	8.2656	7.04	0.0123
Frame	1	1.3611	1.3611	1.16	0.2898
TOC × Frame	1	0.1736	0.1736	0.15	0.7032
Residual	32	37.5903	1.1747		

The results in Table 2 indicate a significant difference between perceived ease of use means for the two levels of table of contents ($F(1, 32) = 7.04, p < 0.05$). The mean score of users' perceived ease of use under traditional table of contents treatment is 5.292, whereas the under expandable table of contents treatment is 4.333. In other words, users perceived the traditional table of contents treatment easier to use than expandable table of contents treatment. This finding did not support Hypothesis 3 that predicted that navigation would be more satisfied using expandable TOC as opposed to traditional TOC. The users who perceived more ease using navigation tools should be more satisfied with the navigation tools than those who perceived less ease using them.

The results of ANOVA in Table 2 indicate no significant difference was found between the two types of frame ($F(1, 32) = 1.16, p = 0.2898$). This finding did not support Hypothesis 6 that predicted the navigation would be more satisfying using multiple-frame as opposed to single-frame. However, users perceived multiple-frame (mean = 5.007) as easier to use than single-frame (mean = 4.618), which failed to differ significantly.

Similar to the previous finding, Table 2 revealed that no interactions between table of contents and frame were detected ($F(1, 32) = 0.15, p = 0.7032$). A comparison of means scores of all groups shows that for users traditional table of contents and multiple-frame was perceived as the easiest navigation tools to use. On the other hand, expandable table of contents and single-frame was perceived as the most difficult navigation tools to use.

The results of data analysis indicated several statistically significant effects. However, no hypothesis was supported by the experimental data.

DISCUSSION OF FINDINGS

Research findings over the past several years have led investigators to recognize the importance of table of contents as one of the effective navigation tools in hypertext system as well as to identify the various types of table of contents that must be considered in investigating the variable. In addition, the controversy over frame usage among World Wide Web application designers has not been clarified yet. The results of this study would have bearing on the pursuit of hypertext developing activities because they would suggest to the interface designers how to employ these variables in the design of WWW applications and hypertext as well.

Hypothesis 1

The first hypothesis was that users' performance in information searching and browsing with expandable TOC would be more accurate than with traditional TOC. Results of an analysis to test this hypothesis did not support it. However, a significant difference was found between users' performance under expandable TOC treatment and traditional TOC treatment. Users under traditional TOC treatment performed significantly better than those under expandable TOC treatment.

There are two possible explanations for the lack of significant effects of expandable TOC on users' performance over traditional TOC.

1. The average time spent interacting with the expandable TOC navigation tool was less than one hour for virtually all subjects. This short treatment period did not provide adequate exposure to this navigation tool. All subjects have reported themselves as intermittent or frequent users of WWW applications which can indicate that they tie-in with traditional TOC style rather than expandable TOC style. Subjects may have already developed a mental model of a WWW application in which all they had to do for the most operations was point, click, and scroll. It takes time for users to become familiar with the use of expandable TOC. The unfamiliarity of users with treatment has washed out most of the treatment effects. However, training could solve the unfamiliar nature of the tool. Having gained some familiarity with the various dimensions of a computerized environment, the user would become more comfortable with the design features of the interface. The researcher would expect this to happen if the individual continues to use and gain mastery of the same interface over some length of time frame.
2. Users employing expandable TOC complained about loading time. There were so many occasions on which users tried to expand or collapse the TOC and waited for a return set. Response time is one of the most critical issues in the friendliness of a hypertext system (Perrott & Smith, 1992). Akscyn, McCracken and Yoder (1988) suggest that a slow response time, for the selection of a link, can cause disorientation. Disorientation, in turn, can cause cognitive overload, and consequently degrades users' performance. A fast response time, for the selection of a link, would be an asset for a hypertext system because users would be more inclined to follow links and become experienced in the system. In order to optimize the response time, more sophisticated algorithm and effective and efficient programming language must be employed.

Hypothesis 2

The second hypothesis was that the users under expandable TOC treatment would have higher speed than those under traditional TOC treatment. The same rationale was followed in hypothesizing this hypothesis as in the first hypothesis. The results of an analysis did not support this prediction. However, a significant difference was found between users' speed under expandable TOC and that under traditional TOC treatment. A mean score of users' speed under traditional TOC treatment was significantly higher than that under expandable TOC treatment.

Two possible explanations for unexpected results are similar to those proposed for the first hypothesis.

Hypothesis 3

The third hypothesis was that the navigation would be more satisfied using expandable TOC as opposed to traditional TOC. To test this hypothesis, two dependent variables were employed: perceived degree of disorientation and perceived ease of use.

Perceived degree of disorientation. This hypothesis was predicted because Rada and Murphy's (1992) study presented that desirability rating was higher for SuperBook employing an expandable TOC. Lai and Waugh's (1995) postulation was also one of the bases for this hypothesis. They postulated that attitude towards the program should be negatively correlated to a sense of getting lost. It was, therefore, hypothesized that users under expandable TOC treatment would perceive less disoriented than those under traditional TOC treatment. Results of data analysis did not support this hypothesis. A significant difference between users' perceived degree of disorientation under expandable TOC treatment and under traditional TOC treatment was found, however. Users under expandable TOC treatment reported significantly more disorientation than those under traditional TOC treatment.

Similar to the first and second hypotheses, two possible factors influenced an unexpected result were slow loading time and users' unfamiliarity with the navigational tool. The findings of this current study support the suggestion of Akscyn, McCracken and Yoder (1988) who suggest that a low response time can cause disorientation. In addition, they also support Lai and Waugh (1995) who state that the unfamiliar interface in the hypertext system could increase users' sense of disorientation.

Perceived ease of use. In an attempt to exam users' satisfaction with the system, the users' perception of ease of use was employed. Davis, Bagozzi and Warshaw' s (1989) statement was one of the basis of this hypothesis. Davis et al. (1989) state that if the system is perceived as easy to use, it leads to the creation of positive attitudes about it. A system that is considered easy to use may be perceived as likely to save time and effort, thus increasing its perceived usefulness as well. It was, therefore, hypothesized that users under expandable TOC treatment will perceive easier to use the navigation tool than those under traditional TOC treatment.

Once again, results of the analysis on users' perceived ease of use did not support this hypothesis. However, a significant difference was found between users' perceived ease of use under expandable TOC treatment and that under traditional TOC treatment. Users under traditional TOC treatment reported perceived it significantly easier to use the navigation tool than those under expandable TOC treatment.

Similarly, two important factors that caused users' disorientation were the system's loading time and users' unfamiliarity with a navigational tool, increasing the difficulties to use a navigational tool.

Hypothesis 4

The fourth hypothesis predicted that users' performance in searching and browsing for information with multiple-frame would be more accurate than with single-frame. Results of an analysis to test this hypothesis did not support it. The rationale behind this hypothesis was based on the concepts of external memory and mental models. The window or frame may serve as an external memory. This external memory function reduces the need on the user's cognitive system caused by the increasing complexity of computer screen interfaces (Billingsly, 1988). Windows or frames can mitigate this overload by keeping important and frequently used information. In this current study, frames were organized so that the table of contents would be visible simultaneously with the text of the selected node. This external memory not only reduces the need for the user's actions to move back and forth between the text frame and a table of contents frame, but also keep the user reminded about the conceptual structure of a hypertext system presented in an hierarchical structure of a table of contents. That is, it is not enough simply to try to show the user how the system is functioning beneath its opaque surfaces. A useful representation must be cognitively transparent in the sense of facilitating the user's ability to grow a productive mental model of relevant aspects of the system (Brown, 1992). Previous research has shown that more advanced mental models benefit a user's search (Borgman, 1986; Elkerton & Williges, 1984). These sophisticated mental models have been adapted from the structure of the system being searched. Increased similarity between a user's cognitive structure and the hypertext structure should aid search performance (Brannon, 1993). Edwards and Hardman (1989) also note that a better cognitive conceptualization of the hypertext document allows one to search better.

The results of an analysis show that there was no significant main effect of frame. In addition, users under single-frame treatment outperformed those under multiple-frame treatment. This indicates opposite directed outcome to the predicted hypothesis. However, the results of an ANOVA test for significance indicate an overall interaction between table of contents and frame. The significance of the interaction of these two main effects suggests that the provision of multiple-frame with traditional TOC can make users' performance better than the provision of multiple-frame with expandable TOC. Besides, the users under multiple-frame and traditional TOC treatment performed better than all the other three groups. So, it is reasonable to conclude that the effect of multiple-frame has been masked and indeed the task performance was poorer under the provision of expandable table of contents.

Hypothesis 5

The fifth hypothesis predicted that users under multiple-frame treatment would have more speed than those under single-frame treatment. The same rationale was followed in hypothesizing this hypothesis as in the fourth hypothesis. There was no difference between these two treatment groups. Thus, this hypothesis was not supported.

The results can be explained by the same reasons used to interpret the result obtained in the fourth hypothesis.

Hypothesis 6

The sixth hypothesis was that the navigation would be more satisfied with multiple-frame as opposed to single-frame. Two dependent variables were employed to test this hypothesis: users' perceived degree of disorientation and users' perceived ease of use.

Perceived degree of disorientation. The same rationales were followed in hypothesizing this hypothesis as those in the third and fourth hypothesis. It was, therefore, hypothesized that users would perceive less degree of disorientation with multiple-frame than with single-frame. The results of an analysis did not support this hypothesis. Users under multiple-frame treatment reported perceiving less degree of disorientation than those under single-frame treatment, but the difference failed to reach a significant level. However, a marginal significance was found between the interaction of table of contents and frame ($p = 0.1395$). The unexpected result can be explained by the same reasons used to interpret the results obtained in the fourth hypothesis.

Perceived ease of use. The rationales supported the creation of this hypothesis were similar to those of the third and fourth hypothesis. It was, therefore, hypothesized that users under multiple-frame treatment would perceive the use a navigation tool as easier than those under single-frame treatment. Similarly, the users under multiple-frame treatment reported perceiving it easier to use the navigational tool than those under single-frame treatment, but the difference was not significant. Thus, the analysis to test this hypothesis did not support it. Once again, the same reasons used to interpret the results in the fourth hypothesis can be employed for the explanation to this unpredicted result, as well.

CONCLUSIONS

In general, in all of the dependent variables measured, the expandable table of contents users performed worse and had less favorable attitudes towards the system than the traditional table of contents users. The provision of multiple-frame does not lead to superior performance or speed in searching and browsing task. The lack of this significant main effect might be because the affect of an expandable table of contents overshadowed the good attribute of the multiple-frame. Finding significance in the interaction between table of contents and frame on users' performance, speed, and user satisfaction has led to the idea of holistic comparison in which the ensemble of software and hardware making the system is tested without decomposing its component variables (Wiedenbeck & Davis, 1997). In fact, Whiteside, Jones, Levy and Wixon (1985) argue that a reductionist experimental strategy is futile in investigating realistic systems because differences are due to an inextricably complex interaction of causes. Under these circumstance and the results of this study, it must be reasonable to identify the experimental goal in the largest sources of variance and investigate how they affect users. This suggests a need for further study of a holistic comparison to determine exactly how the combination of table of contents and frame affects users' performance and perceptions.

REFERENCES

Akscyn, R., McCracken, D.L., & Yoder, E. (1988). KMS: A distributed hypermedia system for managing knowledge in organizations. *Communications of the ACM*, 31(7), 820-835.

Anderson-Inman, L. (1989). Electronic studying: Organizers to help students study "better" not "harder" Part 2. *The Computing Teacher*, 6, 21-53.

Begoray, J.A. (1990). An introduction to hypermedia issues, systems and application areas. *International Journal of Man-Machine Studies*, 33, 121-147.

Bernstein, M., Garzotto, F., Paolini, P., & Schwabe, D. (1991). Tools for designing hyperdocuments. In E. Berk & J. Devlin (Eds.), *Hypertext/Hypermedia Handbook* (pp. 179-209). New York: McGraw-Hill.

Bieber, M. (1997). Advancing information comprehension through hypertext. In J. Mayfield & C. Nicholas, (Eds.), *Advance in Intelligent Hypertext*. Berlin: Springer-Verlag.

Billingsly, P.A. (1988). Taking panes: Issues in the design of windowing systems. In M. Helender (Ed.), *Handbook of Human-Computer Interaction*, (pp. 413-436). North-Holland: Elsevier Science Publishers B.V.

Borgman, C.L. (1986). The user's mental model of an information retrieval system: An experiment on a prototype on-line catalog. *International Journal of Man-Machine Studies*, 24(4), 47-64.

Botafogo, R.A., & Shneiderman, B. (1991). Identifying aggregates in hypertext structures. In R. Furuta & D. Stotts (Eds.), *Proceedings of the Third ACM Conference on Hypertext*, (pp. 63-73). New York: ACM Press.

Brannon, C.R. (1993). *Expert and novice children's navigation through and learning from hypertext.* Dissertation: University of California.

Brown, P.J. (1992). UNIX guide: Lessons from ten years' development. In D. Lucarella, J. Nanard, M. Nanard & P. Paolini (Eds.), *ECHT' 92: Proceedings of the fourth ACM Conference on Hypertext*, (pp. 63-70). New York: ACM Press.

Carey, T.T., Hunt, W.T., & Lopez-Suarez, A. (1990). Roles of table of contents as hypertext overviews. In D. Diaper, G. Gilmore, G. Cockton & B. Shackel (Eds.), *Human-Computer Interaction* — INTERACT' 90.

Cartwright, W. (1999). Extending the map metaphor using Web delivered multimedia. *International Journal of Geographical Information Science*, 13(4), 335-353.

Chen, C., Lin, H., & Sun, C.T. (2000). Navigation maps in hierarchical structured hypertext courseware. *International Journal of Instructional Media*, 27(2), 165-183.

Chen, J.C., Ekberg, T.W., & Thompson, C. (1990). Querying an object-oriented Hypermedia system. In R. McAleese & C. Green (Eds.), *Hypertext: State of the Art* (pp. 231-238). Oxford, England: Intellect.

Conklin, J. (1987). Hypertext: An introductory and survey. *IEEE Computers*, 20, 17-41.

Conklin, J., & Begeman, M. (1988). gIBIS: A hypertext tool for exploratory policy discussion. *Proceedings of the Conference on Computer Supported Cooperative Work*, (pp. 140-152).

Davis, F.D., Bagozzi, R.P., & Warshaw, P.R. (1989). User acceptance of computer technology: A comparison of two theoretical models. *Management Science*, 35, 982-1003.

Dee-Lucas, D. (1996). Effects of overview structure on study strategies and text representations for instructional hypertext. In J. Rouet, J.J. Levonen, A. Dillon & R.J. Spiro (Eds.), *Hypertext and cognition* (pp. 73-108). Mahwah, NJ: Lawrence Erlbaum Associates.

Delisle, N., & Hardman, L. (1989). Neptune: A hypertext system for CAD application. *Proceedings ACM SIGMOD'86*, (pp. 132-142).

Edwards, D.M., & Hardman, L. (1989). 'Lost in hyperspace': Cognitive mapping and navigation in a hypertext environment. In R. McAleese (Ed.), *Hypertext: Theory into practice* (pp. 105-125). Oxford, UK: Intellect.

Elkerton, J., & Williges, R.C. (1984). Information retrieval strategies in a file search environment. *Human Factors*, 26(2), 171-184.

Engelfriet, A.G. (1997). Frames design guidelines: Overview. Retrieved from the World Wide Web: *http://www.htmlhelp.com/design/frames/guidelines.*

Furnas, G.W. (1986). General fisheye views. *Proceedings of CHI'86 Human Factors in Computing Systems*, (pp. 12-23). New York: ACM Press.

Garett, N., Smith, K., & Meyrowitz, N. (1986). Intermedia: Issues, strategies, and tactics in the design of hypermedia document system. *Proceedings of the Conference on Computer Supported Cooperative Work*, (pp. 163-174).

Halasz, F.G. (1988). Reflection on notecards: Seven issues for the next generation of hypermedia system. *Communications of the ACM*, 31(7), 836-852.

Halasz, F.G., Moran, T.P., & Trigg, R.H. (1988). Notecards in a nutshell. *Proc. Human Factors in Computing Systems (CHI' 87),* (pp. 45-52). New York: ACM Press.

Hammond, N., & Allison, L. (1989). Extending hypertext for learning: An investigation of access and guidance tools. In A. Sutcliffe & L. McCauley (Eds.), *People and computers V.* Cambridge: Cambridge University Press.

Heflin, J., Komolodi, A., Pasricha, N., & Tan, T. (1998). WebTOC: Evaluation of a hierarchical browsing interface for the World Wide Web. Retrieved on the World Wide Web: *http://www.otal.umd.edu/SHORE/bs11/.*

Jacques, R., Nonnecke, B., Preece, J., & Mckerlie, D. (1993). Current design in HyperCard: What can we learn? *Journal of Educational Multimedia and Hypermedia*, 2(3), 219-237.

Jonassen, D.H. (1986). Hypertext principles for text and courseware design. *Educational Psychologist*, 21(4), 269-292.

Jonassen, D.H., & Grabinger, R.S. (1990). Problems and issues in designing hypertext, hypermedia for learning. In D.H. Jonassen & H. Mandl (Eds.), *Designing hypermedia for learning* (pp. 3-25). New York: Springer-Verlag.

Joseph, B., Steinberg, E.R., & Jones, A.R. (1989). User perceptions and expectations of an information retrieval system. *Behavior and Information Technology*, 8(2), 77-88.

Lai, Y., & Waugh, M.L. (1995). Effects of three different hypertextual menu designs on various information searching activities. *Journal of Educational Multimedia and Hypermedia*, 4(11), 25-52.

Landauer, T., Egan, D., Remde, J., Lesk, M., Lochbaum, C., & Ketchum, D. (1993). Enhancing the usability of text through computer delivery and formative evaluation: Super book project. In C. McKnight, A. Dillon & J. Richardson (Eds.), *Hypertext: A psychological perspective*, (pp. 71-136). New York: Ellis Horwood.

Marchionini, G. (1988). Hypermedia and learning: Freedom and chaos. *Educational Technology*, 29(11), 8-12.

Marchionini, G. (1989). Information-seeking strategies of novices using a full-text electronic encyclopedia. *Journal of the American Society for Information Science*, 40(1), 54-66.

Marchionini, G. (1992). Interface for end-user information-seeking. *Journal of the American Society for Information Science*, 43(2), 156-163.

Marchionini, G., & Shneiderman, B. (1988). Finding facts vs. browsing knowledge in hypertext systems. *IEEE Computer*, 21(1), 70-80.

Mohages, M.F. (1992). The influence of hypertext linking structures on the efficiency of information retrieval. *Human Factors*, 34(3), 351-367.

Nickerson, R.S. (1986). *Using computers: The human factors in information systems*. Cambridge, MA: The MIT Press.

Nielsen, J. (1990). *Hypertext and hypermedia*. New York: Academic Press.

Nielsen, J. (1996a). Why frames suck (most of the time). Retrieved on the World Wide Web: http://www.useit.com/alertbox/9612.html.

Nielsen, J. (1996b). *Multimedia and hypertext: The internet and beyond*. New York: Academic Press.

Norman, D.A. (1983). Some observations on mental models. In A.L. Stevens & D. Gentner (Eds.), *Mental models*, (pp. 1-14). Hillsdale, NJ: Lawrence Erlbaum Associates.

Perrott, R., & Smith, O. (1992). An experiment on the integration of hypertext within a multi-user text retrieval system. *Hypermedia*, 4(1), 31-52.

Rada, R., & Murphy, C. (1992). Searching versus browsing in hypertext. *Hypermedia*, 4(1), 1-30.

Rovie, W.B., & Morris, N.M. (1986). On looking into the black box: Prospects and limits in the search for mental models. *Psychological Bulletin*, 100(3), 349-363.

Rupietta, W. (1990). Mental models and the design of user manuals. In D. Ackermann & M.J. Tauber (Eds.), *Mental models and human — Computer interaction I*, (pp. 321-334). North-Holland: Elsevier Science Publishers B.V.

Seel, N.M. (1999). Educational diagnosis of mental models: Assessment problems and technology-based solutions. *Journal of Structural Learning & Intelligent System*, 14(2), 153-185.

Simpson, A., & McKnight, C. (1990). Navigation in hypertext: structural cues and mental maps. In R. McAleese & C. Green (Eds.), *Hypertext: State of the art* (pp. 73-83). Oxford, England: Intellect.

Stanton, N.A., & Baber, C. (1994). The myth of navigating in hypertext: How a "bandwagon" has lost its cost! *Journal of Educational Multimedia and Hypermedia*, 3 (3/4), 235-249.

Stanton, N.A., Taylor, R.G., & Tweedie, L.A. (1992). Maps as navigation aids in hypertext environments: An empirical evaluation. *Journal of Multimedia and Hypermedia*, 1(4), 431-444.

Tonta, Y. (1991). Indexing in hypertext databases. In S. Stone & M. Buckland (Eds.) *Studies in multimedia: State-of-the-art solutions in multimedia and hypertext*, (pp. 21-30). Medford, NJ: Learned Information.

Utting, K., & Yankelovich, N. (1987). Context and orientation in hypermedia networks. *ACM Transactions on Information System*, 7, 58-84.

Vries, E.D., & Jong, T.D. (1997). Using information systems while performing complex tasks: An example from architectural design. *International Journal of Human-Computer Studies*, 46, 31-54.

Whiteside, J., Jones, S., Levy, P.S., & Wixon, D. (1985). User performance with command, menu, and icon interfaces. *CHI'85 Conference Proceedings*, (pp. 185-191). New York: ACM Press.

Wiedenbeck, S., & Davis, S. (1997). The influence of interaction style and experience on user perceptions of software packages. *International Journal of Human-Computer Studies*, 46, 563-588.

William, P.E., & Dunwoody, S. (2001). User control and structural somorphism or disorientation and cognitive load? *Communication Research,* 28(1), 48-79.

Wright, P., & Lickorish, A. (1990). An empirical comparison of two navigation systems for hypertexts. In R. McAleese & C. Green, (Eds), *Hypertext: State of the art*, (pp. 84-93). London: Intellect.

Yankelovich, N., Meyrowitz, B.J., & Drucker, S.M. (1988). Intermedia: The concept and construction of a seamless information environment. *IEEE Computer*, 31(1), 81-96.

Chapter II

Website Interactivity and Amusement: Techniques and Effects

Yuan Gao
Ramapo College of New Jersey, USA

ABSTRACT

This chapter reviews recent studies in the use of Website presentation techniques for commercial Websites. In particular, it examines theoretical relationships between interactivity features and amusement techniques and their potential effects on enhanced visitor experience — more informative and entertaining Websites. Based on literature spanning research in traditional advertising media, Web advertising, user interface design, and human computer interaction, it proposes several theoretical relationships between the use of direct interactive techniques and perceived informativeness and entertainment, and between the use of amusement and humor features and perceived informativeness and entertainment. It suggests multiple future research directions and advocates further explorations that go beyond observational studies to uncover potential causal effects of certain hypermedia presentation techniques, and the combination thereof, on attitudinal and behavioral outcomes.

INTRODUCTION

Structural features such as text size, font, graphics, color, animation, video, and audio have been widely explored in the studies of the use of traditional media. Similar uses of such features have also been found in the online environment (Rodgers & Thorson, 2000). Factors related to consumer behavior, attitude, and perceptions related to Websites have begun to be examined in the academic literature (Chen & Wells, 1999; Coyle & Thorson, 2001; Ducoffe, 1996; Eighmey, 1997; Koufaris, Kambil & Labarbera, 2001). Recent literature has started exploring the effects of interactive features on Website appeal (Ghose & Dou, 1998), and that of e-store characteristics on e-store sales and traffic (Lohse & Spiller, 1998). Some experimental studies have also examined the effect of animation and image maps on perceived telepresence and consumer attitude (Coyle & Thorson, 2001), and that of the use of pop-up windows on consumer decision-making processes (Xia & Sadharshan, 2000). This chapter reviews the current literature on the use of interactive features for providing a more realistic experience, examines the potential use of humor for enhanced entertainment value of a Website, and proposes several theoretical relationships on the use of interactivity and amusement techniques in commercial Websites. This chapter also discusses the theoretical and practical implications, as well as future research opportunities on the use of related techniques in Websites, Web advertising, and user interface design.

PRESENTATION ATTRIBUTES

Analysis of information content of a communications message is a methodology proposed by Resnik and Stern (1977) in studying the informativeness of an advertisement. Recent literature has adapted this methodology to Websites in various studies examining information content and the presence of design features. These include modified versions of the Resnik and Stern approach (Philport & Arbittier, 1997; Ghose & Dou), and categories of Website content with regard to technology features (Huizingh, 2000; Palmer & Griffith, 1998). In these relatively recent studies, more aspects of a communication's message have been examined through content analysis criteria. In addition to information content, format or presentation attributes that contribute to the delivery of entertaining appeals have also been analyzed.

Philport and Arbittier (1997) studied the content of more than 2,000 commercial communications messages across TV, magazines, newspapers, and the Internet, and found that the number of unique ads for each brand varies by category, and that leading brands command a larger share of each media type than smaller brands. They included such content cues as customer or celebrity endorsement, facts and details, product display, availability of a Web address (for print or TV ads), 1-800 telephone numbers, customer service, and parent company references. They also considered whether a message presents any sort of sales incentive such as mentioning of a sale price, coupons, or favorable lease terms, etc. While they extended their coverage of media to Internet banner advertising, they found no distinguishing characteristics in Web advertising, i.e., banner ads were not particularly different in any dimension. Their study suggests marketing researchers are paying attention to advertising on the Web, yet the impact of a message delivered through a banner is fairly limited. This observation further solidifies our approach of looking at an entire Website, rather than a small banner ad, in the study of feature use in hypermedia commercial messages. We treat the integral collection of hypermedia-based documents, related image files, and systems functions as a whole in examining its effectiveness in Web communications.

Nonetheless, variables used in banner ads, such as product demonstration or display, special effect techniques like fantasies and virtual reality, and the employment of humor, reflect an attempt to assess message appeal enhanced by entertaining features (Philport & Arbittier, 1997).

Ghose and Dou (1998) performed an analysis linking the number of content attributes with site quality measured by being listed in Lycos's top 5 percent Websites. They find that greater degrees of interactivity, defined by the total count of interactive functions considered in their paper, relate positively to Website appeal, and the "customer support" component is most predictive of being included in the Lycos's top five percent list. In their study, presentation attributes include entertainment features such as electronic post card, surfer postings, and online games, and customer support features such as customer comments and inquiries section, online problem diagnostics, keyword search, personal-choice helper, dealer locator, user groups/chat room, and interactive job placement. Such interactive functions do not directly introduce product features or quality, but assist information retrieval and ease of browsing. For example, a personal-choice helper at www.ford.com is able to suggest an automobile based on user input and calculate monthly payments or present a comparison between buy and lease options. Though the entertainment features were not the feature group most predictive of inclusion in the Lycos top five percent, the presence of each feature increases the likelihood of being included. They adopted an appeal measure based on expert evaluations.

In a study of 651 companies from Yahoo! and Dutch Yellow Pages, Huizingh (2000) considers entertainment one of the content features, along with information and transactions, and has included elements like pictures, jokes, cartoons, games, and video clips. He finds that entertainment features appear in about one-third of all sites. Based on feature counts, he finds that larger sites tend to contain more forms of entertainment features.

Website designers for apparent reasons have examined presentation features in great length. A first-time visitor judges a site by its look: eye-catching graphics and animation, along with navigation buttons and company logos (Grotta, 2000). Software packages intended to enhance Website appeal have been developed by many vendors, e.g., Adobe Photoshop®, Adobe LiveMotion®, CorelDraw Graphics Suite®, Macromedia Flash®, and Macromedia Fireworks® (Pike, 2000). Technologies like Flash® and LiveMotion® have been used by many Websites as entrance pages. In a study on the effects of interactivity and vividness on consumer attitude, Coyle and Thorson (2001) find that a more vivid Website is related to a more positive attitude toward the site, where audio and animation were adopted to operationalize the vividness construct.

Along with the information being communicated, the formats through which product information is presented is undeniably an important dimension marketers need to explore because formats also communicate much non-product information that can affect company image and visitor attitude toward products and the Website. Together with information content, presentation attributes are important ingredients that impact the effective delivery of a commercial message because of their ability to enhance the interface between information content and consumers. Two effects may be of particular interest to both researchers and practitioners, on the use of presentation techniques in a Website: the means of delivering product information in a form perceived entertaining may enhance the communication of information, and may also create an affective response in the viewer.

In the hypermedia environment, marketers can also take advantage of the opportunities of incorporating certain system design features that further enhance a visitor's experience while visiting a Website. The significance of such an experience has been demonstrated in several studies.

For example, alongside entertainment and information, Chen and Wells (1999) identify a factor "organization" that consists of adjectives describing various feelings —confusing, distracting, irritating, cumbersome, and messy. Eighmey (1997) finds, in addition to information, structure and design of a Website are important factors contributing to better perceptions by the visitor. The following are some recent studies examining the effects of system design feature in Internet marketing sites.

Relating to site features, Lohse and Spiller (1998) performed a study measuring 32 user interface features at 28 online retail stores against store traffic and sales. They conclude online store traffic and sales are influenced by customer interfaces. In particular, they found that an FAQ page, promotional activities, and better organization of the product menu have significant influences on traffic and sales. Their study is one of a few to examine the impact of individual content features on the overall effectiveness of an e-store implementation. Recognizing content as the most important element of a Website, Nielsen (1999) provides several design principles based on his experience as a leading user interface design consultant in the field, e.g., speed, quality of a search mechanism, and structure and navigation.

Huizingh (2000) considers both the complexity of the navigation structure and search function design features. He finds that more complex structures are found in larger Websites, which are also more likely to have a search mechanism.

Research addressing the impact of different digital retailing interfaces by Westland and Au (1999) represents yet another attempt to study system design attributes as factors influencing user behavior and potentially attitude. They find that virtual reality storefronts increase a consumer's time spent searching for products but do not significantly increase sales. Such findings necessitate further explorations of the field.

In the area of human-computer interaction, significant research has been done relating network quality of service with usability and user satisfaction. One such factor affecting quality of service is system speed, which is a result of access speeds, processing delays, queuing delays, and propagation delays. These were manipulated in various studies to serve as independent variables, according to Sears and Jacko (2000). Such studies are gradually migrating to the study of Websites. Nielsen (1997) argued, based on a combination of human factors and computer networking, "speed must be the overriding design criterion." He asserts that research has shown that users need a response time of less than one second, moving from one page to another, based on traditional human factors research.

In a study linking the use of interruption implemented via pop-up windows, Xia and Sudharshan (2000) manipulated the frequency of interruptions and found that interruptions had a negative impact on consumer-shopping experiences. Intrusive formats of advertising like interstitials are found to have "backlash risks" in this new medium (Jupiter Research, 1999).

INTERACTIVITY

An important attribute of the use of a Website to disseminate product information and conduct e-commerce is the ability of the customer to interact with the site, through certain features in support of such functions (Palmer & Griffith, 1998). These functions include both text-based email inquiries and feedback forms and entertaining features that attempt to retain customers at the site for longer visits (Ghose & Dou, 1998). Entertaining features in this particular hypertext medium include pictures, virtual reality display of products, multimedia shows, online games, and use of cartoons and humor (Ghose & Dou, 1998; Huizingh, 2000; Philport & Arbittier, 1997).

A Website is a mix of direct selling and advertising with characteristics of both general product display and interactive involvement with customers (Berthon, Pitt, & Watson, 1996). In addition to providing product information, through hypermedia, a Website can engage visitors in dialogues such as inquiries, suggestions, order status tracking, new product proposal, and online problem diagnostics (Ghose & Dou, 1998). This medium affords a rich collection of formats that are available to the marketer in the presentation of products.

From a broader perspective, interactivity is an important dimension of features that distinguish the Internet from other media. Steuer (1992) gives a concise definition of this concept related to the Internet. He considers interactivity to be "the extent to which users can participate in modifying the form and content of a mediated environment in real time" (p. 84). Interactive functions allow the user to participate actively in the exchange and persuasion process through direct manipulation of the structural elements of a site (Rodgers & Thorson, 2000).

Like television, the interactivity of this medium provides the potential to deliver information in an entertaining form.

Hypermedia is multimedia. Animation, video, and audio complement traditional text and graphics when used judiciously. The behavior of Website visitors can be either goal-directed, i.e., searchers, or can be experiential, i.e., surfers (Hoffman & Novak, 1996; Singh & Dalal, 1999). Entertainment supports experiential flow of surfers because they are more likely to engage in "shallow, sensory-level, peripheral processing of the executional aspects of the message" (Singh & Dalal, 1999, p. 95). Hence, entertainment features are more likely to have an impact on exploration behavior and attitude of surfers.

In traditional advertising literature, the following ad features have been studied and linked to subjective measures derived from user profile studies (Rodgers & Thorson, 2000): color, size, typeface, product class, appeal type, animation, audio, sound level, sound clarity, and movement. They argue additional features like vividness, realism, and interactivity can be studied because the Internet encompasses and expands the complexities of print and broadcast media. Ultimately, the purpose of identifying objective and subjective measures of a commercial message is to enable predictions of consumer perceptions and responses to messages that contain those features.

In an experimental study, Li and Bukovac (1999) find the objective structure of size and animation on a banner ad makes a difference in viewer responses. They find large animated banners are more attention getting than smaller and static banners and thus assist recall of the ad. Coyle and Thorson (2001) argue interactivity and vividness are the two main factors affecting perceived telepresence, and, consequently, attitude toward the site. They find the presence of image maps, audio, and animation influence perceived telepresence and attitude toward the site (Coyle & Thorson, 2001).

According to Steuer (1992), telepresence is the perception of direct experience through virtual reality, which in turn is a simulated environment in which the user feels present. Such a telepresence fulfills the needs of escapism, diversion, or aesthetic enjoyment (Ducoffe, 1995, p. 3), where the value of entertainment lies (McQuail, 1983).

Unlike continuous animation in a banner ad or on a Web page, whose only purpose is to gain attention, some animations are intended to display a product from a multi-dimensional perspective and are only active upon request or when the mouse pointer is moved upon. Many shopping sites present a larger image, some full screen, to let the user view the details of a product, if the user so desires, by clicking on a miniature version of the product picture. The same benefit derives from use of animation upon request. For example, Nissan's Website allows the user to look at its newly introduced model through animation of a car turning around slowly after the visitor requests it. This interactive capability allows the user to choose what she wants to see (Rodgers & Thorson, 2000).

A picture is worth a thousand words. A literal interpretation of this old saying is appropriate in our current context. A "true picture" of a product is information a consumer values (Ducoffe, 1996; McQuail, 1983). Animated product displays not only provide the consumers an opportunity to see the product from multiple angles, but also enhance the directness of their product experience, which has been found to produce more confidently held and more enduring attitudes (Coyle & Thorson, 2001; Smith & Swinyard, 1982, 1983). Such direct product experience is informative due to its truthfulness, relevancy, and completeness.

Nielsen (1995) believes that product demos through animation or video clips are good for showing things that move. In particular, he believes that demos of physical products are well suited for the Internet medium. Judicious use of text, graphics, animation, video, and audio enhances the presentation of products and alerts visitors to promotions and special offers. Product detail can be presented from more angles than still pictures.

The user or visitor is the ultimate judge of the attractiveness of a site presentation. In a low-engagement information-processing mode — typically when a user stumbles across a site of marginal interest — pure text and plain background will not arouse much interest in the surfer. Graphics, animations, and video clips might be some of the elements that prevent a visitor from simply clicking away from a site.

The presentation of such product animation at a customer's request also signals the customer's willingness to process the information. The benefits derived from such exchanges conform to the substantiality of an "informative commercial" that warrants processing, as defined by Aaker and Norris (1982).

Seeing control as a major benefit of shopping online, customers favor sites that provide them with more perceived control (Koufaris et al., 2001). Additionally, a clickable image also leads to perceived interactiveness of a Website that Coyle and Thorson (2001) argue would further lead to a consumer's favorable attitude. The adoption of animation in this setting provides the consumer with more product information in an entertaining form, without causing irritation.

AMUSEMENT

The use of amusement features such as humor in traditional advertising has been a complex topic due to mixed findings from over a quarter century's research on humorous ads (Weinberger & Gulas, 1992). However, research has shown humor does attract attention and seems to be most effective in ads promoting low-risk routine purchases (Weinberger, Spotts, Campbell & Parsons, 1995). In a series of field studies, Scott, Klein, and Bryant (1990) find humorous fliers increase attendance at social events like neighborhood picnics and clambakes but have little effect on attendance of business gatherings.

Wells, Leavitt and McConville (1971) find — along with vigor, personal relevance, and irritation — humor is a major perceptual dimension in their profiling of user responses to TV commercials. The adjectives that accounted for this factor include jolly, merry, playful, humorous and amusing. They believe humor contributes to perceived entertainment, even though it does not necessarily score high on personal relevance.

Additionally, when a Web surfer is engaged in low-risk message processing, peripheral cues like humor may be used and can succeed in gaining visitor attention as they do in traditional media (Weinberger et al., 1995). A more likable interface will also encourage visitors to visit more pages and stay longer, and hence nurture a more positive attitude.

Ducoffe's (1996) entertainment factor is based on audience needs for escapism, diversion, aesthetic enjoyment, or emotional release. Humor fulfills most, if not all of these needs: a diversion because of its incongruous nature, emotional releases like laughing, temporary escapism, and enjoyment. The conceptualization of this dimension is closely in line with some earlier user profiling studies in advertising. From a pool of 600 adjectives, Aaker and Bruzzone (1981) identify four factors that explain the majority of variance in predicting informative, enjoyable, annoying, or offensive ads. In particular, amusing/humorous did not break out as a separate factor but contribute to 37.6 percent of the variance explained by the factor "entertainment." Examination of the 25 most entertaining commercials, each of which scored two standard deviations above the average, reveals that "amusing/humorous" is the predominant part of the factor. In particular, none of the most amusing commercials scored low on the "entertainment" factor. These amusing commercials involve a comedian interacting with children, animated characters, and conversations that had a "touch of warmth and quiet humor" (p. 21).

Humor's intention is to amuse and entertain people, to make them laugh, and to convey light-hearted enjoyment (Morkes, Kernal & Nass, 1999). Morkes et al. (1999) define humor to be "an incongruous comment that is recognized by the receiver as an attempt to amuse and that succeeds at amusing" (p. 403). Humor is found to enhance the likability of the computer interface and has a positive effect on user cooperation (Morkes et al., 1999). Based on the above discussion, we ague the use of humor contributes positively to the entertainment value of Websites.

In addition to entertainment, humor also helps gain attention and comprehension, especially when humor is related to the products presented (Speck, 1991). Many studies have been devoted to the effect of thematic and structural relatedness of humor to a message (Weinberger et al., 1995). Here "thematic" refers to humor's relationship with product themes and "structural" refers to the integration of humor with product claims (Speck, 1991). When ad effectiveness was measured through reader or viewer recall and comprehension, both related and unrelated humor have been found to have a positive effect (Ziv, 1988; Chapman & Crompton, 1978; Scott et al., 1990; Zillmann, Willians, Bryant, Boynton & Wolf, 1980). However, related humor was found to be superior to unrelated humor when direct comparison studies were conducted (Kaplan & Pascoe, 1977). Measures of recall and comprehension reflect the ad's effectiveness at getting product-related messages across to the viewer, which implies a more informative message to the visitor. Weinberger et al. (1995) found a positive relationship between related humor and attention and comprehension in low risk products. Attention and comprehension contribute to the delivery of information contained in a message and lead to more informative perceptions of advertised products. No use of humor in Web advertising or Web pages have been studied in the past. This study will extend advertising from the traditional media to the Web, and study the impact of humor on attention and comprehension (perceived informativeness) of products. Thus, we also argue that the amusement effect contributed by product-related humor also enhances the perceived informativeness of a Website about its products.

FUTURE TRENDS AND RESEARCH DIRECTIONS

Web marketing research in profiling user reactions to Websites or home pages has been largely observational (Chen & Wells, 1999; Eighmey, 1997; Lohse & Spiller, 1998).

To answer the question what "effect" a certain presentation's attribute has on attitudinal outcomes in the hypermedia environment requires controlled experiments that can be used in cross group comparisons. This line of research is gradually appearing in the literature recently (Coyle & Thorson, 2001; Gao, 2002; Li & Bukovac, 1999). This chapter advocates the line of research that explores the effects of different combinations of elements in this new medium. Such effects are in general considered hard to predict yet necessary for Web designers to test in order to achieve whatever goal they have in mind (Coyle & Thorson, 2001). Both interactivity and humor have been considered in the traditional advertising and marketing research to influence their respective dependent variables by implicit assumptions or research results. For example, effects of humor have been studied in past research of marketing and advertising (Weinberger & Spotts, 1989).

The advantage of experimental studies is their ability to validate causal relationships between the treatment effects and the dependent variables. Experimental research, though limited in scope, goes beyond the predictive powers of observational research. In completely randomized design fixed-factor experiments, the differences in dependent variables can be reasonably attributed to the participants' membership in different treatment groups and thus a causal effect between the treatment factor and the dependent variable can be validated (Hildebrand, 1986; McCall, 2001).

Future research should explore various combinations of presentation attributes like interactive features and humor as fixed factors. Future studies can also explore the effect of information content design features in varying degrees of information saturation at the site. Data collection should be broadly based. Researchers should also take advantage of the convenience of Web surveys techniques, and consider non-intrusive means of collection usage and exploration data through click streams. This chapter tries to contribute to the theories and constructs in e-commerce in a practical way. Research findings will add value to providing guidance to Internet marketers and technical designers alike, in future commercial Website design and Web marketing and promotions.

CONCLUSION

In summary, this chapter reviews the current state of research in the area of Website presentation attributes in general, and interactivity and amusement features in particular. It proposes a set of theoretical relationships between the effective use of such hypermedia features and their potential outcomes in terms of perceived entertainment and informativeness by the visitor. It advocates a research paradigm that goes beyond mere observational research and user profiling, and suggests potential future research directions in the area.

Doing business online is still in its infancy. It is necessary to take a rigorous and scientific look at the various components that go into this environment, in order to help electronic business to develop in a structured, efficient, and effective way (Koufaris et al., 2001). Research in both marketing and human computer interaction has begun to explore the effects of presentation and design attributes on consumer perceptions and attitude, which in turn may impact the bottom line of firms who conduct electronic business. The line of research seeking to understand ways to maximize the effectiveness of the e-business environment is promising.

REFERENCES

Aaker, D.A., & Bruzzone, D.E. (1985). Causes of irritation in advertising. *Journal of Marketing*, 49, 47-57.

Aaker, D.A., & Norris, D. (1982). Characteristics of TV commercials perceived as informative. *Journal of Advertising Research*, 22(2), 61-70.

Berthon, P., Pitt, L.F., & Watson, R.T. (1996). The World Wide Web as an advertising medium: toward an understanding of conversion efficiency. *Journal of Advertising Research,* 36(1), 43-54.

Chapman, A.J., & Crompton, P. (1978). Humorous presentations of material and presentations of humorous material: A review of the humor and memory literature and two experimental studies. In M.M. Gruneberg, (Ed.), *Practical aspects of memory.* New York: Academic Press.

Chen, Q., & Wells, W.D. (1999). Attitude toward the site. *Journal of Advertising Research*, 39(5), 27-38.

Coyle, J.R., & Thorson, E. (2001). The effects of progressive levels of interactivity and vividness in Web marketing sites. *Journal of Advertising*, 30(3), 65-77.

Ducoffe, R.H. (1995). How consumers assess the value of advertising. *Journal of Current Issues and Research in Advertising,* 17(1), 1-18.

Ducoffe, R.H. (1996). Advertising value and advertising on the Web. *Journal of Advertising Research,* 36(5), 21-34.

Eighmey, J. (1997). Profiling user responses to commercial Website. *Journal of Advertising Research*, 37(3), 59-66.

Gao, Y. (2002). Effects of humor and realism in hypermedia. In M. Khosrow-Pour, (Ed.), *Issues and trends of information technology management in contemporary organizations*. Hershey, PA: Idea Group Publishing.

Ghose, S., & Dou, W. (1998). Interactive functions and their impact on the appeal of the Internet presence sites. *Journal of Advertising Research*, 38(2), 29-43.

Grotta, S. W. (2000, June 27). State of the art. *PC Magazine*, 201-209.

Hildebrand, D.K. (1986). *Statistical thinking for behavioral scientists*. Boston, MA: Duxbury Press.

Hoffman, D.L., & Novak, T.P. (1996). Marketing in hypermedia computer-mediated environments: Conceptual foundations. *Journal of Marketing*, 60(3), 50-68.

Huizingh, E.K.R.E. (2000). The content and design of Websites: An empirical study. *Information & Management*, 37, 123-134.

Jupiter Research. (1999). Inside the mind of the online consumer — Increasing advertising effectiveness. By Johnson, M., Slack, M., and Keane, P. *Jupiter Research* at http://www.jupiter.com, Vol. 18. Accessed online August 19, 1999.

Kaplan, R.M., & Pascoe, G.C. (1977). Humorous lectures and humorous examples: Some effects upon comprehension and retention. *Journal of Educational Psychology*, 69(1), 61-65.

Koufaris, M., Kambil, M.A., & Labarbera, P.A. (2001). Consumer behavior in Web-based commerce: An empirical study. *International Journal of Electronic Commerce*, 6(2), 131-154.

Li, H., & Bukovac, J. L. (1999). Cognitive impact of banner ad characteristics: An experimental study. *Journalism and Mass Communication Quarterly*, 76 (2), 341-353.

Lohse, G.L., & Spiller, P. (1998). Electronic shopping. *Communications of the ACM*, 41(7), 81-86.

McCall, R. (2001). *Fundamental statistics for behavioral sciences (8th ed.)*. Belmont, CA: Wadsworth/Thomson Learning.

McQuail, D. (1983). *Mass communication theory: An introduction*. London: Sage Publications.

Morkes, J., Kernal, H.K., & Nass, C. (1999). Effects of humor in task-oriented human-computer interaction and computer-mediated communication: A direct test of SRCT theory. *Human-Computer Interaction*, 14, 395-435.

Nielsen, J. (1995). Multimedia guidelines. *Jakob Nielsen's Alertbox.* Retrieved December 1995 from the World Wide Web: http://www.useit.com/alertbox/.

Nielsen, J. (1997). The need for speed. *Jakob Nielsen's Alertbox*. Retrieved March 1997 from the World Wide Web: http://www.useit.com/alertbox/.

Nielsen, J. (1999). User interface directions for the Web. *Communications of the ACM*, 42(1), 65-72.

Palmer, J.W. & Griffith, D.A. (1998). An emerging model of Website design for marketing. *Communications of the ACM*, 41(3), 45-51.

Pike, S. (2000, June 27). A new face for the Web. *PC Magazine*, 207.

Philport, J.C., & Arbittier, J. (1997). Advertising: brand communications styles in established media and the Internet. *Journal of Advertising Research*, 37(2), 68-76.

Resnik, A., & Stern, B.L. (1977). An analysis of information content in television advertising. *Journal of Marketing*, 41(1), 50-53.

Rodgers, S., & Thorson, E. (2000). The interactive advertising model: How users perceive and process online ads. *Journal of Interactive Advertising* (accessed online).

Scott, C., Klein, D.M., & Bryant, J. (1990). Consumer response to humor in advertising: A series of field studies using behavioral observation. *Journal of Consumer Research*, 16(1), 498-501.

Sears, A., & Jacko, J.A. (2000). Understanding the relation between network quality of service and the usability of distributed multimedia documents. *Human-Computer Interaction*, 15, 43-68.

Singh, S.N. & Dalal, N.P. (1999). Web homepages as advertisements. *Communications of the ACM*, 42(8), 91-98.

Smith, R.E., & Swinyard, W.R. (1982). Information response models: An integrated approach. *Journal of Marketing*, 46, 81-93.

Smith, R.E., & Swinyard, W.R. (1983). Attitude-behavior consistency: The impact of product trial versus advertising. *Journal of Marketing Research*, 20, 257-267.

Speck, P.S. (1991). The humorous message taxonomy: A framework for the study of humorous ads. In J.H. Leigh & C. R. Martin, Jr. (Eds.), *Current Issues and Research in Advertising*. Ann Arbor, MI: The University of Michigan.

Steuer, J. (1992). Defining virtual reality: Dimensions determining telepresence. *Journal of Communication*, 42(4), 73-93.

Weinberger, M.G., & Gulas, C.S. (1992). The impact of humor in advertising: A review. *Journal of Advertising*, 21(4), 23-59.

Weinberger, M.G., & Spotts, H.E. (1989). A situational view of information content in TV advertising in the U.S. and U.K. *Journal of Marketing*, 53(1), 89-94.

Weinberger, M.G., Spotts, H., Campbell, L., & Parsons, A.L. (1995). The use and effect of humor in different advertising media. *Journal of Advertising Research*, 35(2), 44-56.

Wells, W.D., Leavitt, C., & McConville, M. (1971). A reaction profile for TV commercials. *Journal of Advertising*, 11(6), 11-17.

Westland, J.C., & Au, G. (1998). A comparison of shopping experience across three competing digital retailing interfaces. *International Journal of Electronic Commerce*, 2(2), 57-69.

Xia, L., & Sudharshan, D. (2000). An examination of the effects of cognitive interruptions on consumer on-line decision processes. Paper presented at *the Second Marketing Science and the Internet Conference*, USC, Los Angeles, CA, April 28-30.

Zillmann, D., Willians, B.R., Bryant, J., Boynton, K.R., & Wolf, M.A. (1980). Acquisition of information from educational television as a function of differently paced humorous inserts. *Journal of Educational Psychology*, 72(2), 170-180.

Ziv, A. (1988). Teaching and learning with humor: Experiment and replication. *Journal of Experimental Education*, 57(1), 5-15.

Chapter III

Techniques for Visualizing Website Usage Patterns with an Adaptive Neural Network

Victor Perotti
Rochester Institute of Technology College of Business, USA

ABSTRACT

At any given Website, the flow of users' visitations represents a valuable source of information for Web professionals. However, the identification and interpretation of Web usage patterns is not necessarily an easy task. The sheer volume and complexity of the browsing patterns captured in the Website server logs makes understanding users a difficult, time-consuming task. The present chapter explores the use of an adaptive neural network to visualize the Website usage patterns. This visual representation supports the identification of clusters of Web pages that are frequently visited together by users. A Website designer can see, at a glance, the primary groups of Web pages that visitors browse. Further, the site structure can be readily compared to the usage clusters to measure how well the links at the Website support the actual use of the site.

INTRODUCTION

As the importance of the Internet rises, the need to create more adaptive and more usable Websites also grows. Most improvements to a Website require some knowledge of the site's users and how they are interacting with the pages. However, Web professionals today have relatively few good options for capturing this information. Certainly, there are software and services to help summarize the basic information from the Website logs. This could mean keeping track of the frequency of visits for the individual Web pages that make up a site, counting how many times the overall Website is visited from a specific Web location, or other basic statistics.

Web usage mining refers to the application of data mining techniques to the Web server log in order to recover patterns in the use of a Website. For example, Mobasher, Cooley and Srivastava (2000) describe an automated recommender system that dynamically suggests appropriate pages for a user based on the overall Website usage patterns. The system presented in Spiliopoulou (2000) answers questions about the Website usage, when asked in an SQL-like language. An experienced user could interactively use this system to identify the Web page sequences that meet any criterion that the user specifies. Such a general tool is very powerful, but requires considerable expertise from the user.

Perotti and Burke (2001) presented a technique and visualization that offers Web developers an opportunity to easily see the pattern of usage at a Website. Unlike earlier depictions, their Web Usage Plot emphasizes the relationship between the various pages at a Website by displaying them in a topographic organization; sites that are visited together frequently appear close together, while those that are seldom visited together in the same session appear far apart. Their process to create the Web Usage Plot visualization has several steps, as depicted in Table 1.

The final visualization step relies on a multivariate statistical technique called Multidimensional Scaling (MDS). This technique allows the reduction of the high dimensional data into lower dimensional coordinates that can be more easily visualized. The Web Usage Plot created with MDS does have many advantages over earlier representations of Website usage patterns.

Unfortunately, using MDS for Web usage visualization can be tedious because the algorithms for reducing the data dimensionality are computationally expensive.

Table 1: A Simple Process for Visualizing Web Usage (Adapted from Perotti & Burke, 2001)

1. Cleaning and organizing the Web server logs
2. Creating an aggregate representation of all users Web page visits, the co-occurrence matrix
3. Visualizing this representation

For example, the authors used the SPSS software package, which limits the user to visualizing no more than 100 Web pages. Clearly, many Websites have more Web pages than this arbitrary limit. The present research explores an alternative and potentially superior approach using a Neural Network to capture the usage patterns at a Website. In this technique, a neural network would be trained with the patterns of usage at a Website, and then would automatically organize a low dimensional representation of these patterns.

Kohonen Self Organizing Map

Kohonen's self organizing map (SOM) is a well-known neural network technique to do data dimensionality reduction. In this technique, a neural network is created in the desired low dimensionality, say two dimensions for the sake of explanation. This network is then trained with a set of input patterns that correspond to the high dimensional data to be reduced. As the network adapts, one of the network nodes becomes highly associated with each input pattern, so that when the correct input pattern is presented, it will be the most highly active node in the network. After training, the neural network represents a simple (two dimensional) map with nearby nodes representing similar input patterns in the multidimensional input data.

Self-organizing maps have been already used for a great variety of problems, including browsing a picture database, data exploration, representing large text collections and classifying Web documents based on their textual content (Kohonen et al., 2000).

The goal for the present research is to create and visualize a self-organizing map neural network representation of Website usage patterns. As in the Web Usage Plot, the self-organizing map visualization should be useful for Web page developers to identify clusters of Web pages that are visited together frequently. However, the new techniques go well beyond a simple substitution of the SOM for the Multidimensional Scaling in the procedure outlined above.

One of the key issues in using a SOM is how the data is represented for training. We have found that the co-occurrence matrix (in Table 1) is not well suited for training a neural network. To understand why, consider the structure of the co-occurrence matrix. For every Web page at the given Website, both a row and a column are created. So, if there were n total Web pages at the Website, then the resulting co-occurrence matrix would be of size n^2. Inside a specific cell in the matrix is the number of times that the two pages (represented by the row and column) were visited together in the same session. So, for example, if Web page 16 was visited frequently with Web page 42, then we would see a high number in the cell for column 16 and row 42. Of course, only half of the matrix is really needed, since the usage of two pages in the same session is symmetrical.

To use the co-occurrence matrix, as input to the SOM, simply requires the treatment of each row in the matrix as an input pattern, since each row is a vector that describes the aggregate usage for one Web page with all other Web pages. The problem with this is the goal for the SOM is to have pages that are visited together frequently map to nearby nodes in the two dimensional network. Unfortunately, the vectors representing two highly associated pages may be very different. Consider the example given above, where the row for Web page 16 will have a high number in column 42, while the row for Web page 42 will have a high number in column 16. These two vectors are thus very different!

A potentially superior representation of the same information for input to the SOM could be called the **session membership matrix**. As before, each row corresponds to a specific Web page. However, each column now corresponds to a particular user session that was recovered from the Web log file. For a given row, each column will have a one (1) in it, if the Web page represented by the row is visited the session corresponding to the column, and a zero (0) otherwise. Thus, to continue the example above, because Web pages 16 and 42 are visited together in the same sessions, they should have a similar pattern of ones and zeros along their corresponding rows. Because Web pages that are visited together in the same session will have similar vectors, the session membership matrix is more appropriate to train the SOM than the earlier co-occurrence matrix.

Visualization of the Self Organizing Map

Another unique contribution of the present research is in the visualization of the SOM. While there are several existing techniques to create a depiction from the self-organizing map, the resulting pictures are often much more difficult to interpret than the simple map-like presentation in the Web Usage Plot. For example, a common SOM depiction requires the viewer to infer the presented relationships from a complex image of gray-scale or color levels. Since the goal of the research is to make an effective tool for Web administrators and developers, a simpler image is desirable.

One existing way to visualize an SOM is to simply note which node in the matrix responds the most when presented with a given input pattern. The matrix can then be visualized by plotting a point at every grid location whose node responded the most during the presentation of the input. In our case, a point located at a grid location would represent each Web page. However, this approach has two problems. For one, multiple pages frequently map to the same network node. So, the viewer would only see one point, when in fact several associated Web pages may be represented there. A second problem is that the distance between points is somewhat arbitrary, since it simply corresponds to the regular distance between the SOM nodes in their grid.

Figure 1 demonstrates a novel "jittered" visualization of the self-organizing map neural network, which overcomes the two problems mentioned above. Using this procedure, the visualized location of each Web page is jittered by a small amount to displace it from the regular grid location. The displacement of each point is proportional to the error reported by the SOM network, when responding to the specific input pattern. Thus, multiple Web pages can be visualized at the same node

Figure 1: A Jittered Grid Depicting Clusters of Web Pages

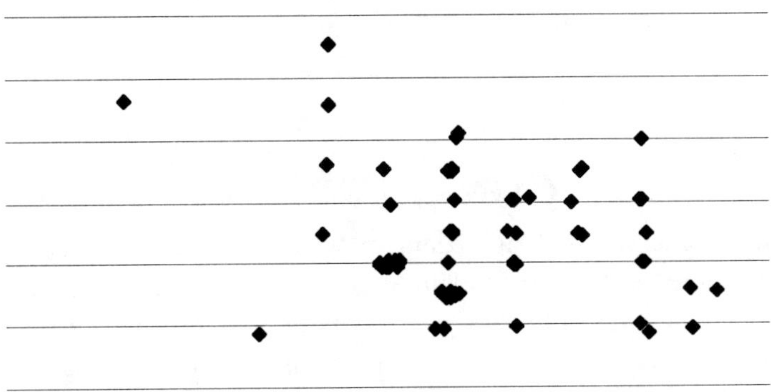

location, and the viewer can see the association between the two of them as a cluster. Also, the distance of any point from the regular grid location is a measure of how well that grid location's node succeeded in distinguishing that input pattern from the rest. Such a depiction is easy to interpret, and a viewer can quickly get a sense for the primary usage patterns that are present at the Website.

FUTURE TRENDS

The Self Organizing Map has great potential as a tool for creating useful visualizations of Websites. The present research has begun to develop the techniques necessary to get meaningful and useful results from the SOM neural network. In doing so, a visualization can be created that is as useful as the Web Usage Plot, but more robust in its computation. The SOM technique is relatively fast to compute, and has no restriction on the number of Web pages that can be considered.

However, there is still much more research necessary to successfully use the SOM as part of a professional visualization system. One difficulty in using the SOM is a problem with dealing with sparse data sets. In a small Website sample, it is quite possible that most of the Web pages are never visited, or are visited in one session. This means that of the hundreds of sessions available, a given Web page will have only a single column active. The SOM network will frequently overlook the subtle difference between such pages, in considering the vast similarity in their pattern of not being accessed in so many sessions. Finding a set of parameters and appropriate training regimen for dealing with this problem can be quite time consuming. At present, a variety of different parameters must be experimented with using trial and error in order to find a useful visualization.

Perhaps even more important than the enabling of intuitive visualizations, capturing a Website's usage pattern in a neural network could provide a remarkably versatile component in new Web-based applications. Recommendations could be made to the user on the fly, since when a user goes to a particular Web page, it will be clear which other pages the other users have visited from there. Also, it would be possible to recreate some user behaviors from the network itself, so that novel Website structures can be readily evaluated or compared.

CONCLUSIONS

For many businesses, the trail of data left by users visiting the company Website is an untapped resource. Each visit to the Website generates several lines in the Web log file, each of which has only a few pieces of relevant information. New tools are actively being developed to help Web professionals interpret this large, complex data set. The present research explores the application of a new tool, the self-organizing map neural network to the problem of Web usage mining.

The visualization of the self-organizing map presented here is unlike earlier work because it enables the interpretation of Website usage by individuals who do not have extensive training. Earlier Web usage mining procedures automate the analysis so that no human is involved (Mobasher et al., 2000), or use special data mining languages for interacting with the system (Spiliopoulou, 2000). By using the natural grouping of the self-organizing map, the present visualization allows an inexperienced individual to identify usage clusters, and to understand which pages are visited together frequently. Such a simple, specialized tool should enable a wide variety of practitioners to gain a better understanding of their Website users.

REFERENCES

Kohonen, T., Kaski, S., Lagus, K., Salojärvi, J., Paatero, V., & Saarela, A. (2000). Self Organization of a Massive Document Collection. *IEEE Transactions on Neural Networks*, Special Issue on Neural Networks for Data Mining and Knowledge Discovery, 3(11), 574-585.

Mobasher, B., Cooley, R., & Srivastava, J. (2000). Automatic Personalization Based on Web Usage Mining. *Communications of the ACM, 43*(8).

Perotti, V., & Burke, A. (2001). The Visualization of Usage Patterns for Web Customization, Managing Information Technology in a Global Economy. *Proceedings of the 2001 IRMA Conference*. Toronto, Canada.

Spiliopoulou, M. (2000). Web Usage Mining for Web Site Evaluation. *Communications of the ACM, 43*(8).

Chapter IV

Using Usability Factors to Predict the E-Commerce User Experience

Adrie Stander
University of Cape Town, South Africa

Nata van der Merwe
University of Cape Town, South Africa

ABSTRACT

This chapter introduces the use of usability factors as a means of predicting the e-commerce user experience. It argues objectively measurable usability factors, such as page layout, navigation techniques, privacy statements and color can be used to predict how a user of an e-commerce Website will experience the interaction with the site. In support for this argument, it reports on the results of a small pilot study that was done to determine the feasibility of a more extensive study aimed at building a model for the prediction of the user experience. The authors hope a better understanding of the intricate relationship between usability factors and the subjective user experience will lead to the design of more successful e-commerce Websites.

INTRODUCTION

A large base of research on the usability of computer systems exists. Traditionally this was aimed at optimizing the task performance of expert users (D'Hertfelt, 2000), but the introduction of e-commerce has caused a widening of the focus of human computer interaction (HCI) to include aspects typically found in marketing and sociology. New fields such as user experience strategy, the design of consumer trust and captology, the design, theory and analysis of persuasive technologies, are emerging (de Groot, Eikelboom & Egger, 2001), with the actual interaction with the customer becoming of paramount importance.

To date there has been a lack of genuine knowledge about what contributes to effective interactions with online customers, although intuition and previous research (Dholakia & Bagozzi, 1999), suggest that creating a compelling online environment for Web consumers will have numerous positive consequences for commercial Web providers.

Usability techniques can be used to reduce software and e-commerce costs and improve marketability (Gilb, 1988). Websites that are hard to use frustrate customers, forfeit revenue, and erode brands (Forrester, 1998). Lohse and Spiller (1999) found that poor interfaces and store navigation negatively influence online sales, while Li, Kuo and Russel (1999) found significant positive relationships between online buying behavior and online channel characteristics such as interactivity. The intention to revisit a Website is in part a function of Website characteristics (Hoffman, Novak & Chattejee, 1995), and empirical support for usefulness and enjoyment as drivers of Website usage exist (Atkinson & Kydd, 1997). This suggests that Website characteristics at least partly determine the frequency and duration of a Website visit.

Hurst (2000) predicted that e-commerce sites in the USA would lose several billion dollars in sales during the 2000 Christmas season due to difficulties with the checkout process of these sites, while Gartner (1999) points out studies in the United Kingdom and Europe have shown many users are put off by the failure of Websites to provide a satisfactory buying process.

CONCEPTS

User satisfaction is seen as the user's perception that Website has met or exceeded their expectations and is created through the careful design of information content, site usability, security and privacy, while also taking the characteristics of the intended users into account (Hill, 1997). User satisfaction is used to measure the subjective quality of the user experience.

The user experience encompasses all aspects of the end-user's interaction with the site. The most important requirement for the user experience is to meet the exact needs of the customer with simplicity and elegance in order to produce e-commerce

Websites that are a pleasure to use. True user experience goes far beyond giving customers what they say they want, or providing checklist features. In order to achieve high-quality user experience, there must be a seamless merging of multiple disciplines, including engineering, marketing, graphical and industrial design, and interface design (Nielsen, 2000).

Usability, often defined as the system's ease-of use and throughput (Egger, 1999), is attributed to numerous design factors. Typical factors include items such as page layout, site navigation, color, the use of frames and the use of graphics. Many studies have investigated these factors, but often looked at only a few or even one factor in isolation and with small well-defined user groups. Often the guidelines developed from these studies are not very useful in normal usability engineering practices (Nielsen & Molich, 1990).

Perceived usefulness, "the degree to which an individual believes that using a particular system would enhance his or her job performance," is a construct of the Technology Acceptance Model (Davis, 1989), often used in research to predict the acceptance of technology.

PILOT STUDY

This study looked at how page layout and design, navigation techniques, security and privacy and perceived usefulness influences the user experience of e-commerce Website users.

Research Instrument

The method used by the study entails performing a preliminary classification of usability factors such as color, navigation technique and functionality for a number of South African e-commerce Websites. A Web portal then acts as a launching pad for users to access these sites. Upon exit from the site, users are asked to complete a short evaluation to determine the subjective user experience of the Website they accessed. This method holds the advantage that the user's experience is measured immediately after using the site.

Problem Areas

It is difficult to define the norm for the user experience and how it relates to other factors. The user interface, machine factors, cultural factors, individual factors and usability factors are likely to influence the experience. Many user characteristics such as age, experience and gender can also influence the interaction with the Website.

A number of instruments such as the Questionnaire for User Interface Satisfaction (QUIS) and the Webqual questionnaire are available for the determination of user satisfaction. The length of these instruments makes them unsuitable for high volume data collection and a shorter questionnaire will have to be designed for the study.

The chosen method of data collection employs non-probabilistic sampling and self-selection; therefore, it may not be representative of the general population of e-commerce users.

RESULTS

A total of 101 responses, including 72 from university students, covering 17 Websites from the banking, recruitment, travel, retail and automotive sectors were collected.

Page Design and Layout

It was found that users seem to prefer less saturated colors. While a number of suites used both red and blue, only one got a relatively high rating. This could be attributed to the fact that the colors were less saturated, and so less obtrusive, and that there was less of the colour, rather using the colour to highlight more important areas.

There seem to be a general dislike for background colors. One site had a light blue background, and another had a yellow background. Neither got high ratings. On the other hand, a site with an off-white background did not get low ratings, which suggests t users do not like colored backgrounds.

Those sites packed with information, with little background space showing, did not get high ratings. Two sites with a high percentage of content and little background got low ratings, while two sites with a high percentage of blank space showing, got higher ratings. This suggests that users prefer sites to have some free space so that they are not too busy or full with information.

The one aspect of design that is strongly warned against by many authors is the use of frames, but the researchers did not find any evidence that users do not like them.

Navigation

Websites that have a high level of clarity and a well-defined layout are rated much higher than those sites with a "busy" layout. A greater use of white space, i.e., blank spaces on the page, translates into more favorable navigation ratings opposed to those with little blank space.

The pages whose navigation bars were both text and graphics based, also resulted in a favorable perception by the user of the site's navigation capabilities. Those Websites that had no navigation bars were rated average or below average by the respondents as these sites used plain links on the page. A possible explanation for this is the fact that the user does not have a feeling of a standard and structured navigation layout and therefore their experience, and thus, consequent satisfaction are detracted from.

Finally the use of well positioned and clearly defined sub-menus have a good effect on a user's satisfaction with the Website, as this provides the user with information in a neat and structured format.

Security and Privacy

Only one site, a bank, got a high ranking for security. This may be attributed to the fact that the design of the Website was extremely professional in comparison to the other sites, creating a sense of security, even though it may not have been one of the most secure Websites. The general sense of uncertainty could be attributed to the fact that South Africa has an emerging e-commerce market, and consumers have not yet adapted to the idea of their safety on the Internet.

There seemed to be no evidence that privacy statements and digital certificates had any affect whatsoever on the perceived security of the sites.

Usefulness

The sites preferred for usefulness had accuracy, reliability and relevance as common characteristics with regards to their information content.

Specifically, value added services provided by sites tended to translate into a favorable response from users. This included all the various possibilities and variations that a user might opt for or require whilst using the Website. Much attention was given to the accuracy, reliability and the relevance of the information on these sites in relation to their core business activities.

Conversely, the remaining sites were rated lower, due to the fact that these value added services were not present or were present but had no relevance to the Website's core business activities. Specifically, this could be seen on some sites that have these so called extras on the site, but are unrelated to any of the core activities performed by the businesses.

Often users did not find the information due to the poor design of the site's navigation.

The User

Since the sample consisted mostly of university students, it did not offer a wide range with regards to age, language and computer experience; therefore, no conclusions regarding this could be drawn.

CONCLUSION

Even though based on a limited sample, this study shows that users prefer a user interface with enough white space and a neutral, light colored background. Standardized navigation bars were preferred over unstructured links for navigation. Privacy statements and digital certificates did not seem to improve the perceived security of the sites — while accuracy, reliability and relevance of value added services — helped to create a perception of usefulness.

REFERENCES

Atkinson, M.A., & Kydd, C. (1997). Individual characteristics associated with World Wide Web use: An empirical study of playfulness and motivation. *Database for Advances in Information Systems, 28*(2), 53-62.

Davis, F.D. (1989). Perceived usefulness, perceived ease of use, and user acceptance of information technology. *MIS Quarterly, September,* 319-340.

De Groot, B., Eikelboom, P., & Egger, F.N. (2001). User or consumer? Bringing together HCI and marketing. *CHI2001: Conference on Human Factors in Computing Systems*, Seattle, WA, March 31 – April 5, 2001.

De'Hertefelt, S. (2000). Emerging and future usability challenges: Designing user experiences and user communities. Retrieved February 2, 2000 on the World Wide Web: http://www.interactionarchitect.com.

Dholakia, U., & Bagozzi, R.P. (1999). Consumer behaviour in digital environments. Working Paper.

Egger, F.N. (1999, June). Human factors in electronic commerce: Making systems appealing, usable & trustworthy. *Graduate Students Consortium, 12th Bled International E-Commerce Conference.* Bled, Slovenia.

Forrester Research. (1998). *Why Most Websites Fail. 1998.* Retrieved April 18, 2002, from http://www.forrester.com/ER/research/report/excerpt/0,1338,1285,FF.html.

Gartner Research. (1999). Consumers are ready for e-commerce; Websites are not. *Research Note*. Retrieved November 30, 1999 on the World Wide Web: http://www.gartner.com.

Gilb, T. (1988). *Principles of software engineering management*. Reading, MA: Addison Wesley.

Hill, N. (1997). *Handbook of customer satisfaction measurement*. UK: Grower Publishing Ltd.

Hoffman, D.L., Novak, T.P., & Chattejee, P. (1995). Commercial scenario's for the Web: Opportunities and challenges. *Journal of Computer-mediated Communication, 1*(3).

Hurst, M. (2000). Special report: Design usability getting past go. Retrieved December 15, 2000 on the World Wide Web: http://www.internetworld.com.

Li, H., Kuo, C., & Russel, M. G. (1999). The impact of perceived channel utilities, shopping orientations, and demographics on the consumer's online buying behaviour. *Journal of Computer-mediated Communication, 5*(2).

Lohse, G.L., & Spiller, P. (1999). Internet retail store design: How the user interface influences traffic and sales. *Journal of Computer-mediated Communication, 5*(2).

Nielsen, J. (2000). A definition of user experience. Retrieved April 14, 2002 on the World Wide Web: http:www.useit.com.

Nielson, J. & Molich, R. (1990). Heuristic Evaluation of User Interfaces. *CHI'90 Proceedings, SIGCHI Bulletin, Special Issue*, (pp. 249-256).

Section II

Interface Design and Usability

Chapter V

Social Issues in the Administration of Information Systems Survey Research

Susan K. Lippert
Drexel University, USA

ABSTRACT

Survey responses differ between direct paper and pencil (manual) administration and Internet-based (electronic) survey data collection methods. Social dynamics (issues) play an important role in influencing respondent participation. A review of the existing literature suggests that the medium and administration context affect differences in instrument performance parameters, i.e., response rate, participation ease, attractiveness of survey, novelty effect, administrative costs, response flexibility, response time, population size, sample bias, instrument validity, the management of non-response data, and response error. This chapter attempts to identify, describe and map the differences between survey data collection media as a function of selected social variables.

INTRODUCTION

The purpose of this chapter is to compare and contrast survey research administration between direct paper and pencil (manual) and Internet-based (electronic) survey data collection methods (Lippert, 2002). Social dynamics play an important role in influencing respondent participation. A review of the existing literature suggests that the medium and administration context affect differences in survey instrument performance parameters, i.e., response rate, participation ease, attractiveness of survey, novelty effect, administrative costs, response flexibility, response time, population size, sample bias, instrument validity, the management of non-response data, and response error. This chapter attempts to identify, describe and map the differences between survey data collection media as a function of selected social variables.

Differences exist between electronically based and manually administered surveys. Responses to survey questions can be affected by the survey medium (Ayidiya & McClendon, 1990), and can result in response rate differences (Heberlein & Baumgartner, 1978). Response rates by different data collection methods exhibit high variance. Internet-based surveys can produce double-digit response rates (McCooey, 2000). Ease of use, as reported by Cook, Heath and Thompson (2000), is cited as a response enabler when answering Web-based surveys. Novelty effects of Internet-based surveys encourage participant response by attracting users to investigate available features (Dillman, Torora, Conradt & Bowker, 1998). Administrative costs for Internet-based surveys are less than those associated with paper administration (Parker, 1999). Greater response flexibility as a function of respondent options is increased in paper-based administrations (Matz, 1999). Web-based surveys offer reduced response time from initial distribution to time of reply (Oppermann, 1995). Large and geo-spatially dispersed populations of respondents are more efficiently accessed through Web-based surveys (Mehta & Sivadas, 1995; Schmidt, 1997a). Respondents of Web-based surveys exhibit self-selection bias due to participation of only technology-active individuals (Gorman, 2000). Content validity maybe reduced through Internet data collection formats (Dillman & Bowker, 1996). Internet-based data collection permits greater response reliability (Quality Progress, 1999). Higher frequencies of non-response data are found with Web-based formats (Schmidt, 1997a). Response error represents a class of variables that includes various data response problems (Fiske, 1971; Subman & Bradburn, 1974).

Stanton (1998) examined three parameters or problems in Web-based applications of survey research — participant motivation, response consistency and sampling problems. Participant motivation is a series of phenomena that address a respondent's willingness or rationale for participating in a data collection effort. Response consistency is the internal reliability of responses for a fixed population — e.g., sampling all women with doctorates born after 1962 suggests that there will be similarity among the participants' responses. Sampling problems include the ability and convenience to collect data under controlled sampling conditions — e.g., the solicitation of a specific individual through the creation of criteria related listservs.

As an extension of the Stanton (1998) classification parameters for Web-based survey administration, this chapter introduces 12 instrument performance parameters. Figure 1 depicts the 12 parameters as they cross-link to the Stanton (1998) criteria. A descriptive summary and comparison of the differences between paper and Internet-based survey administrations as a function of social dynamics are discussed.

A limited number of comparative analyses exist which contrast effects of one survey medium to another (Ayidiya & McClendon, 1990). Through examining the advantages and disadvantages of the two primary survey data collection media — electronic and manual administration — information systems researchers can be better informed on expected variances in response parameters. This enables more systematic data format selections and decisions. Narrative, tabular, and graphic summary representations are provided.

Further differences in instrument performance output parameters can be identified for various survey methods, such as electronic mail, Internet-based,

Figure 1: Survey Instrument Performance Parameters

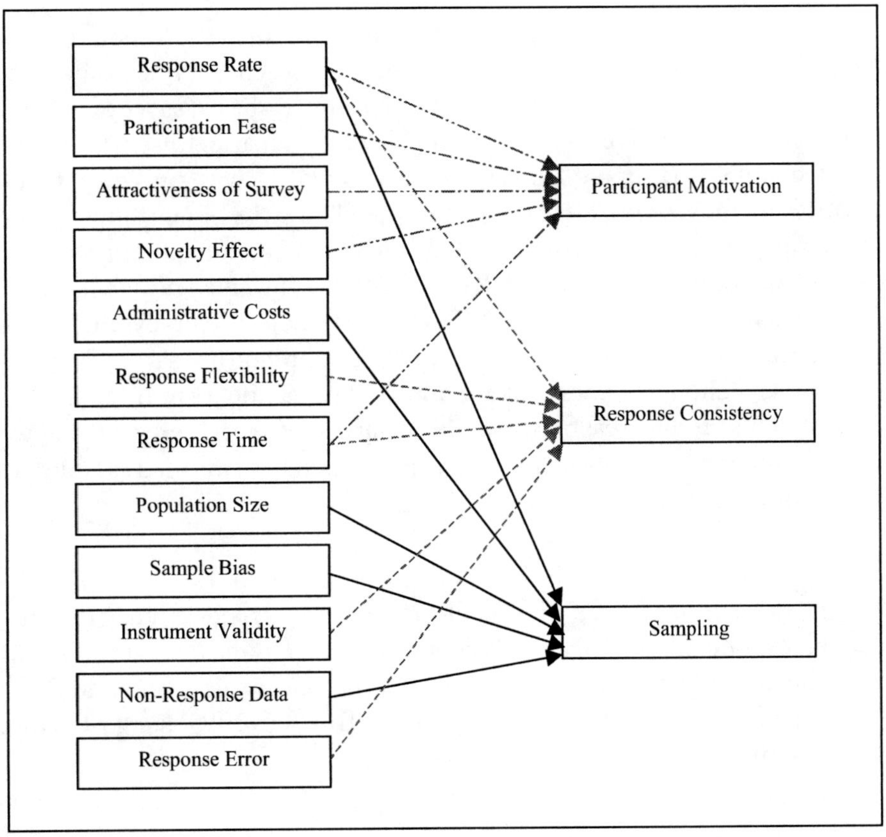

telephonically recorded, paper and pencil, and postal mail administrations. Researchers should consider response inconsistencies, which might result from employing different survey administration media. Understanding and controlling for the administration variance should be considered prior to using any survey instrument.

BACKGROUND

Electronic Administration

Web-Based Surveys

Web-based surveys involve computer-to-computer communication via the Internet (Dillman, 2000), where information requests are made of individual users or groups of users. Bradley (1999) suggests a three-category classification for Web-based questionnaires:

- *"Open"* — The survey is available to any user since access is non-restricted.
- *"Closed"* — The survey is only available to invited respondents with knowledge of the instrument's URL.
- *"Hidden"* — A 'pop-up' survey appears when triggered by a user's selection of linked information.

An example of an open survey is the Microsoft Network (MSN) polls available to any and all visitors choosing to respond. A closed survey example was implemented in a recent research study. The closed Web-based survey design was used to collect data from five independent organizations on user trust in information systems technology (Lippert, 2001). A unique URL was provided to each organization, thereby, segmenting the sample populations by organization. . Closed Web-based questionnaires enable a researcher to control administration and access to the survey instrument. Dedicated URLs can control unwanted respondent access through selected invitation. Malhotra (1999) suggests 'pop-up' surveys offer a better response rate than a simple banner invitation. Hidden or 'pop up' surveys appear on portals such as Yahoo or Lycos and are aimed at obtaining a specific end user's immediate attention and response. Hidden surveys are triggered by keyword searches or banner links initiated by the user and generate a stratified sample based on the HTML connection.

Email Attached Surveys

Email attached surveys involve an electronic survey request made to a group of potential respondents within a given population. Electronic mail questionnaires appeared concurrently with the advent of the Internet and email for communication purposes (Bachmann, Elfrink & Vazzana, 1996). Bradley (1999) suggests a three-category classification for email questionnaires:

- *Simple email* — An email message containing a list of questions, which appear within the email text body.
- *Email attachment* — An email message containing a cover email message with the questionnaire provided as a file attachment.
- *Email URL embedded questionnaires* — An embedded URL within an email message requesting recipient participation through a hyperlink.

The email survey approach can be disseminated via the Internet or on a closed network through an Intranet or Extranet. Email and Web-based surveys both involve computer-to-computer communication. Email surveys, while easier to compose than Web-based surveys, are more limited in their visual stimulation and interaction capabilities (Dillman, 2000).

Manual Administration

Paper Based Surveys

Non-electronic surveys are divided into two broad classifications: questionnaires and interviews (Singleton, Straits & Straits, 1993). Paper and pencil questionnaires seek information from the respondent on a hardcopy document using a marking implement. Interviews are completed via telephone or face-to-face by an individual or group of researchers. Paper based surveys are limited to text questions and lack the dynamic capabilities of response bridges found in Web-based administration. A response bridge facilitates the sequencing from an initial question to the appropriate follow-on segment. For example, user trust of the technology may function as the initial question. Based on the individual's response — low trust or high trust — the response bridge will automatically redirect to an appropriate follow-on question.

Like Internet surveys, both open and closed ended questions can be employed in paper-based administrations. Researchers primarily used mailed questionnaires to obtain respondent information until the late 1970s (Dillman, 1978). Blattberg and Glazer (1993) suggest that through the development of advanced electronic technology, two-way data exchanges dramatically increased efficiency.

Schmidt (1997b) suggests that Web-based surveys offer the ability to implement interactive or dynamic instruments — a unique characteristic of this data collection medium. The variety of question formats and presentation styles enables flexibility in questionnaire design matched to specific research goals (Schmidt, 1997b).

Definitions of Instrument Performance Parameters

Instrument performance parameters discussed in this chapter are defined in Table 1. These parameters form the basis for comparing administration media by output performance measures. Current trends in administration usage are directed toward electronic surveys. Researchers should consider all output parameters prior to selection of a data collection medium.

Table 1: Survey Instrument Performance Parameters

Parameter	Definition
Response Rate	The ratio of completed and usable instruments divided by the total number of distributed instruments.
Participation Ease	The subjective perception that the survey instrument is user friendly to the respondent.
Attractiveness of Survey	A subjectively pleasant and visually stimulating presentation.
Novelty Effect	The appeal of a new or unusual feature, which impacts the respondent's willingness to participate.
Administrative Costs	The costs associated with instrument development, survey dissemination, questionnaire follow-up, data entry and organization of results.
Response Flexibility	The degree of individual control available in the design and completion of a survey instrument.
Response Time	The time from the initial dissemination to the arrival of completed instruments, including the time necessary for actual administration.
Population Size	The boundary or totality representing the limit of all potential respondents.
Sample Bias	A type of sampling error that decreases generalizability of results.
Instrument Validity	The quality of a survey instrument to measure the intended phenomena.
Management of Non-Response Data	The data provided by a survey respondent in which no response, a spurious response or a clearly false one is offered.
Response Error	The class of all potential responses that are either incorrect, inaccurate, intentionally deceiving, misguided, or methodologically misclassified.

Parametric Comparison of Web-Based Versus Paper-Based Administrations

Response Rate

Response rate is generally defined as the ratio of completed and usable instruments divided by the total number of distributed instruments. Scholars exploring response rate variance differ in findings regarding whether electronic-based or paper-based administrations yield higher response rates. Often response rate variance is attributable to sampling frame limitations rather than actual differences in survey media (Couper, 2000). Sampling frame limitations are the inequity to access the entire sampling frame as a function of technology accessibility issues. A 1996 survey by Bachmann, Elfrink and Vazzana of business school deans and chairpersons reported no significant difference between responses to email and regular mail instruments. Miller, Daly, Wood, Brooks and Roper (1996) found response differences between the email and paper surveys of professional computer scientists, which they attributed to sampling issues, rather than actual differences in survey media. Shaw and Davis (1996) reported significant differences in responses between their electronic and paper groups — attributable to demographic differences rather than differences in survey media.

Response rates for most American national surveys, regardless of type, have fallen over the last 40 years (Cook et al., 2000). Response rates for email surveys have significantly decreased between 1986 and 2000 (Sheehan, 2001). The decline in response rates may also be a function of the general over saturation of surveys within society (Marits, 1998). Response rates for sampled populations may vary, based on a combination of factors (Turley, 1999). Turley suggests that response rates may differ depending upon topic relevance to the respondent and/or the respondent's socio-demographic characteristics. Men tend to respond more to Web-based formats than women (Tomsic, Hendel & Matross, 2000). In general, response rates tend to increase over time for Web-based administrations (Tomsic et al., 2000).

Response rates appear to be lower for Web-based surveys than for equivalent mail surveys (Allen & Fry, 1986; Cook et al., 2000; Crawford, Couper & Lamias, 2001; Handwerk, Carson & Blackwell, 2000; Manfreda, Vehovar & Batagelj, 2001). Web-based surveys conducted from listservs produce lower response rates than mail administrations (Couper, 2001). In a general study, postal mail produced three times the response rate of email (Schuldt & Totten, 1994). Although different in experimental treatments, subjects, and type of electronic medium employed, a summary of nine studies (see Figure 2), shows agreement across eight of the nine studies that paper-based response rates exceed electronic response rates. In a recent study to develop standard techniques for email surveys, Sheehan and McMillan (1999) discovered a slight improvement in email survey response rates.

Response rates for paper and pencil instruments increase through proctored administration because respondents are monitored throughout the survey completion process (Krysan, Schuman, Scott & Beatty, 1994). Response rates for Web-based

Figure 2: Response Rate Comparisons Between Electronic and Paper and Pencil Surveys

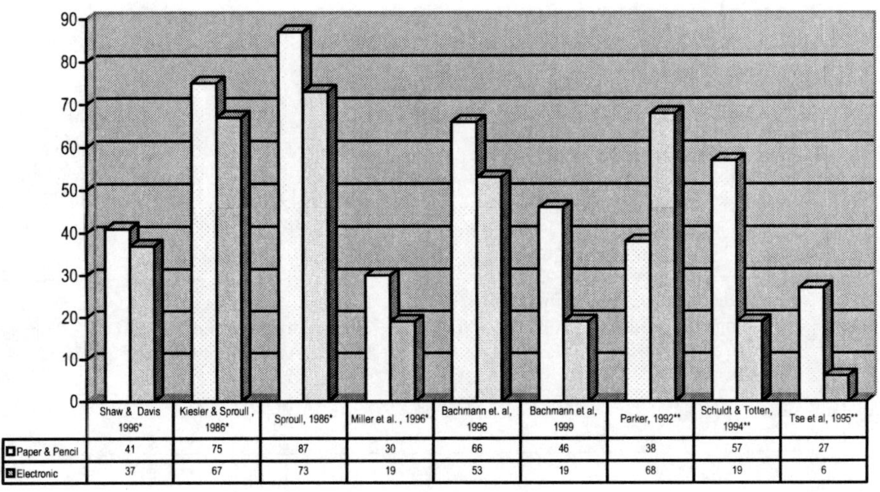

	Shaw & Davis 1996*	Kiesler & Sproull, 1986*	Sproull, 1986*	Miller et al., 1996*	Bachmann et. al, 1996	Bachmann et al, 1999	Parker, 1992**	Schuldt & Totten, 1994**	Tse et al, 1995**
Paper & Pencil	41	75	87	30	66	46	38	57	27
Electronic	37	67	73	19	53	19	68	19	6

surveys can be increased through instrumentation design that accommodates ease of use and attractiveness.

Dillman (2000) suggests that many of the techniques used to increase paper-based survey response rates will not produce the same results with Web-based surveys. He further suggests using multiple contacts for email surveys as a mechanism for increasing response rates. Similar strategies to improve response rates can be employed with paper and pencil administration. Personal contact through pre-notification, reminder emails or notices, and/or voicemail messages may contribute to higher rates (Fox, Crask & Kim, 1988). Higher rates are clearly found to exist for Web-based administrations when incentives are utilized (Tomsic et al., 2000) and/or when samples are selected from targeted populations on interest sites (Cheyne & Ritter, 2001).

Turley (1999) suggests there are three influences to mail survey response rates: sponsorship, subject matter, and population. Sponsorship refers to the perceived influence of the individual or institution requesting respondent participation. Subject matter refers to the content specific theme of the data collection. Population refers to the unit of analysis under investigation. Table 2 provides response rate advantages and disadvantages between Web-based and paper and pencil administrations.

Cook et al. (2000) report recent research indicates lower response rates may be more accurate than surveys yielding higher response rates. This suggests an inconsistency with a survey research standard that data quality (both validity and reliability) is improved through higher response rates.

Table 2: Response Rate – Advantages and Disadvantages Comparing Web-based and Paper and Pencil Surveys

Response Rate – Advantages and Disadvantages		
	Web-Based	**Paper and Pencil**
Advantages	• Response rates have been found to increase as an inverse proportion to the volume of junk email (Weible & Wallace, 1998) • Increased data reliability for proportional response rates without increasing costs (Quality Progress, 1999) • Progress indicators (triggers to offer a respondent's survey completion position) reduce respondent abandonment (the respondent's leaving the survey prior to completion) (Couper et al., 2001)	• Response rates tend to improve through the preservation and control of the confidentiality of respondents' identity, both real and perceived (Kuhnert & McCauley, 1996) • Responses tend to be higher overall when compared to electronic administrations (Crawford et al., 2001; Cook et al., 2000; Allen & Fry, 1986; Manfreda et al., 2001; Handwerk et al., 2000)
Disadvantages	• Respondent lack of familiarity with technology may reduce response rates for Web-based administration (Dillman & Bowker, 1996)	• Long self-administered questionnaires produce lower response rates (Heberlein & Baumgartner, 1978; Dillman, Sinclair & Clark, 1993)

Response rate does not function as an independent, isolated, or linear variable; rather, it is affected by many direct and indirect intervening variables. A simple association between response rate and administration media is probably naive. Given the existing data, response rate, as a single performance variable, may not be an adequate comparison variable between paper and pencil and Web-based surveys (Underwood, Kim & Matier, 2000).

Participation Ease

Participation ease is the subjective perception that the survey instrument is user friendly to the respondent. User friendliness may include ease of completing the questions under inquiry. A review of existing research on ease of participation generally favors Web-based over manual survey administration. Web-based instruments enable keyboard based response devices or point and click mouse actions. The attractiveness of quick single keystroke entries, the ease of working with radio buttons, check boxes, or drop down lists are key features facilitating participation ease. Audio components or instructions permit a dual sensing source of survey questions. The potential multi-sense stimuli associated with Web-based administration supports simultaneous kinetic, auditory and visual understanding. Specialized feedback offered to Web-based respondents (Schmidt, 1997a) may assist participants in survey completion. The addition of help menus or tool tips can facilitate respondent inquiries in the absence of a proctor or principal researcher. While many respondents are computer literate, a segment of the population lacks basic keyboard entry skills or suffers from computer anxiety (Igbaria & Parasuruman, 1989). Participation is inhibited because the use of technology becomes a greater obstacle to the respondent than the perceived value of survey completion.

A disadvantage associated with some Web-based survey administration is the difficulty of returning to a previously unanswered question (Dillman & Bunker, 1996), or the need to complete the survey in a single sitting (Lippert, 2001; Tomsic et al., 2000). Serial-order constraints may impede participation ease and affect response rates. Time issues may encumber Web-based participation. For example, system boot-up times become a factor for individuals with older machines. Dial-up access speeds and limited bandwidth may inhibit participation ease. In one study, university students preferred paper and pencil formats because they had a greater assurance of the confidentiality of their responses (Tomsic et al., 2000). Table 3 provides participation ease differences between Web-based and paper and pencil survey administrations.

Participation ease may function based on a sequential decision matrix. Figure 3 depicts the possible sequencing. Experience with technology, as the underlying factor, may determine a respondent's overall perception that a Web-based survey is easier to answer. When instant access to technology is available, a stronger relationship exists between participation ease and response rate (Tomsic et al., 2000). Easy access to computers and Internet links favored Web-based surveys (Handwerk et al., 2000).

Table 3: Participation Ease – Advantages and Disadvantages Comparing Web-Based and Paper and Pencil Surveys

Participation Ease – Advantages and Disadvantages		
	Web-Based	**Paper and Pencil**
Advantages	• Web-based administration has been found to be more enjoyable, thus resulting in an increased perception of participation ease (Dillman et al., 1998) • Radio buttons and check boxes provide greater control over how respondents answer questions (Matz, 1999) • Interactive surveys may offer the respondent specialized feedback throughout the administration process (Schmidt, 1997a) • Help menus and tool tips are readily available	• A standard and familiar format requiring minimal instructions for survey completion • A high set of potential response categories based in presentation media (Rockwood, Sangster & Dillman, 1997) • Respondents' perception of a higher level of confidentiality in responses (Tomsic et al., 2000)
Disadvantages	• Diminished degree of user trust in IS technology (Lippert, 2001) • Lack of Internet familiarity or computer experience may result in user frustration associated with Web-based surveys (Dillman & Bowker, 1996) • Web-based surveys often require a forced response choice, even when no choice appears appropriate (Dillman & Bowker, 1996) • Respondents with older systems may experience system problems or crashes resulting in lost survey responses (Dillman et al., 1998) • The need to scroll up or down the page to view all answer choices (Dillman & Bowker, 1996) • Disabled response features may appear within the online questionnaire (Dillman et al., 1998) • A single response sometimes requires multiple entry actions – e.g., clicking an answer choice and scrolling down to reveal the next instruction (Dillman & Bowker, 1996)	• Penmanship issues can impact the legibility of survey responses

Attractiveness of Survey

Attractiveness is generally accepted as a subjectively pleasant and visually stimulating presentation. Attractiveness of survey instruments combines clarity of content, balanced graphics and reading ease. What constitutes attractiveness, however, varies by respondent. A few general attractiveness features, such as message personalization and screen attractiveness, possess broad appeal. Message personalization facilitates Web-based survey attractiveness to many who might otherwise not respond to a survey instrument. This is accomplished through personalized email attachments or even, in the case of sophisticated designs, the use of IP identification when a respondent logs on to participate in an administration. Screen attractiveness or 'wiz bang' (panache) also was cited as an attractiveness

Figure 3: Participation Ease Sequencing Activities

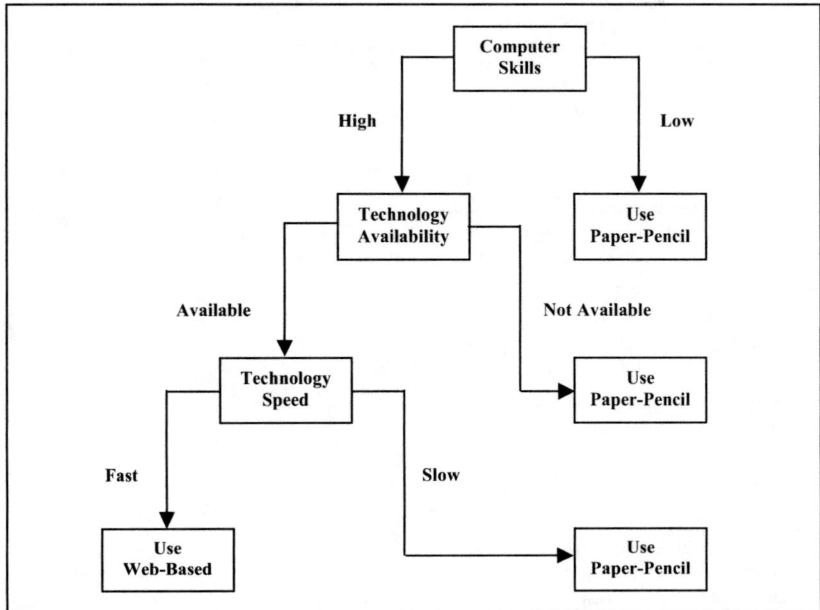

feature for Web-based administration. Limited graphics and professional layout have been identified as attractiveness variables. Paper-based instruments can be designed with special response technology that uses 'special marking pens' or 'rub-outs.'

In general, Web-based surveys have a greater potential to enable attractiveness. Web surveys may contain a more refined appearance than email surveys (Dillman, 2000). Redline and Dillman (2000) found that visual design elements, such as color, graphics, and interactive features, can facilitate or distract from the task of completing the survey — hence, the relationship between attractiveness and distraction. Couper (2000) suggests that a Web-based survey can vary from respondent to respondent based on different browser usage and/or settings. Web surveys enable dynamic interactions between the respondent and the survey (Dillman, 2000). Web questionnaires can incorporate invisible response bridges (Dillman, 2000).

Self-administered surveys, whether presented on paper or on the Web, rely on both verbal and visual information to communicate with respondents (Redline & Dillman, 1999). Smith (1995) found that differences in layout format affect both self-administered and proctored surveys. Formatting issues, such as typeface, the use of lines, and black ink, affect a survey participant's willingness to respond (Carroll, 1994). Table 4 provides attractiveness of survey advantages and disadvantages of both media.

Table 4: Attractiveness of Survey – Advantages and Disadvantages Comparing Web-based and Paper and Pencil Surveys

Attractiveness of Survey – Advantages and Disadvantages		
	Web-Based	**Paper and Pencil**
Advantages	• Visual design elements such as color and graphics can serve as attractors or detractors (Redline & Dillman, 1999) • Web surveys enable dynamic interactions, such as HTML and Java-applets, between the respondent and the survey (Dillman, 2000; Dillman et al., 1998) • Availability of various media types (text, sound, graphics, animation and video) facilitates format diversity • Sequence and question skips are easily integrated into the survey with little impact on the respondent (Dillman, 2000) • Greater potential for respondent personalization (McCooey, 2000) • Presentation format variance enables the development of questionnaire designs matched to specific research goals (Schmidt, 1997b) • The end user can manipulate screen formats – font, font size, color, and resolution	• Survey length/size is immediately visible • No knowledge of computer technology is required
Disadvantages	• Greater transmission time for graphic intensive questionnaires (Dillman & Bowker, 1996)	• Dynamic interactions between the respondent and the survey are not possible (Dillman, 2000) • Unable to accommodate audio, animation and video media elements

A greater potential for visual attractiveness exists within Web-based surveys. The opportunity for inclusion of multimedia, particularly the use of sound, graphics, and video is facilitated in electronic formats. Hyperlink activities, enabled in Web-based surveys, permit wide variance in questionnaire design, visual presentation, and provide the potential for a multi-sensing experience.

Novelty Effect

Novelty effect is defined as the appeal of a new or unusual feature, which impacts the respondent's willingness to participate. For some respondents, participating in a Web-based survey for the first time may constitute a novel experience. Novelty effect has a short half-life and is only a factor when a new response technology is introduced or prototyped. The novelty of using a Web-based interactive administration appeals to those with moderate familiarity of electronic

Table 5: Novelty Effect – Advantages and Disadvantages Comparing Web-based and Paper and Pencil Surveys

Novelty Effect – Advantages and Disadvantages		
	Web-Based	**Paper and Pencil**
Advantages	• A relatively new means of data collection provides respondents with a novel alternative to traditional paper and pencil administrations	• Involves a single marking device, e.g., a pencil or pen, for question response • User motivation is modulated by subject matter interest (Rogleberg, Fisher, Maynard, Hakel & Horvath, 2001)
Disadvantages	• User frustration from lack of Internet familiarity or computer experience (Dillman & Bowker, 1996) • New response features – drop-down menu access, selecting a single radio button versus clicking multiple check boxes – make questionnaires more difficult for some respondents to access and complete (Dillman & Bowker, 1996; Dillman et al., 1998)	• A resistance to participate due to societal over saturation of paper and pencil surveys (Marits, 1998)

media, both email and Internet. Web-based surveys have higher response rates as a function of novelty effect (Cheyne & Ritter, 2001). By contrast, Sheehan (2001) found that over time the novelty effect of electronic email surveys has diminished. The result of the reduced novelty effect is a decrease in response rate (Sheehan, 2001). The over saturation of surveys within society (Marits, 1998) may offer a reverse novelty effect associated with paper and pencil surveys. Table 5 offers novelty effect advantages and disadvantages of Web-based and paper and pencil administrations.

Administrative Costs

Costs vary greatly for survey instrument management. Administrative costs include instrument development, survey dissemination, questionnaire follow-up, data entry and costs associated with organizing the results. Web-based surveys may contain multiple media elements — audio, video and animation — resulting in development costs, which far exceed those of paper-based instruments. The most cost efficient administration method (advantage) for large samples is Web-based, because of the speed and ease of accessing large and geographically dispersed populations. Web surveys offer opportunities for low-cost self-administered surveys (Bachmann et al., 1999/2000; Cook et al., 2000; Couper, 2000; Matz, 1999; Parker, 1999; Schmidt, 1997a; Solomon, 2001; Weible & Wallace, 1998).

Email based administration is also cost effective and fast, in both dissemination and data analysis (Sheehan & McMillan, 1999). When compared to telephonic survey techniques, Web-based administration continues to be more cost effective, although far less flexible. Activities to increase response rates are more cost effective when conducted via email (Cook et al., 2000), rather than through telephone or postal mail follow-up (Matz, 1999; Weible & Wallace, 1998). Automatic data compilation obtained through Web-based collection means can dramatically reduce research costs (Dillman et al., 1998). Sample size decisions may influence the type of administration selected. Cost trade-off will always be a consideration in decisions on the use of Web-based vs. paper and pencil administration.

Web-based administration may incur additional costs related to survey design, coding, and development. Server hosting costs do not exist for paper and pencil surveys. Web management costs, depending upon the hosting site, may add additional costs for Web-based administration. The trade off may be the volume of survey activity, which can be efficiently handled through online administration. Table 6 suggests administrative cost differences between Web-based and paper and pencil administrations.

Data entry can be generally classified in three forms: manual — keypunch entry into a database for processing; semi-automated — optical scanning which enables automated data entry for inclusion into a database for processing; and, automated — entries automatically entered into the database at time of keyboarding. The per unit cost decreases the more automated the administration. In a small sample survey, a manual administration may be overall less expensive, but the per unit cost will be greatest for paper and pencil administration (Manfreda et al., 2001).

Table 6: Administration Costs — Advantages and Disadvantages Comparing Web-Based and Paper and Pencil Surveys

Administration Costs – Advantages and Disadvantages		
	Web-Based	**Paper and Pencil**
Advantages	• Offers opportunities for low-cost self-administered surveys (Couper, 2000; Weible & Wallace, 1998; Bachmann et al., 1999/2000; Matz, 1999; Cook et al., 2000; Schmidt, 1997a; Solomon, 2001) • Can reach large audiences with minimal expense permitting rapid replies (Cook et al., 2000) • No copy or postage fees (Matz, 1999) • Enables automatic result compilation (Dillman et al., 1998; Stanton, 1998), thus dramatically reducing research costs	• Less costly to create if electronic surveys contain multimedia elements
Disadvantages	• High cost of code design and development • Server hosting costs • Increased Web management costs	• More costly in terms of financial, administrative, and researcher effort • High costs of survey postage (Dillman, 2000) • High follow up costs (Weible & Wallace, 1998; Matz, 1999)

Response Flexibility

Response flexibility is the degree of individual control available in the design and completion of a survey instrument. Web-based administration provides for a variety of response formats — check boxes, radio buttons, slider bars, scroll bars, text boxes, and drop down alternatives — in the design of survey instruments. These response formats provide greater design control, thus limiting potential data type mismatches. The limiting of mismatch errors further reduces result compilation time, effort and costs.

Paper and pencil administration provides flexibility through a uni-mechanistic response process achieved via a marking implement. Individuals, with limited computer familiarity, may find a greater sense of respondent control over paper and pencil administrations. Expert computer users may find the notion of pencil and paper administration less flexible since many of their communication interactions are conducted electronically. In Web-based administration, forced choice responses can be controlled through non-response defaults, in which the respondent is not permitted to go forward or to submit, when a question remains unanswered. In paper and pencil administrations, this control mechanism is unavailable. Response flexibility is an important variable in instrument design and a due consideration in the choice of survey administration. Table 7 provides response flexibility advantages and disadvantages between Web-based and paper and pencil administrations.

Response Time

Response time refers to the time from the initial dissemination to the arrival of completed instruments, including the time necessary for actual administration.

Table 7: Response Flexibility – Advantages and Disadvantages Comparing Web-Based and Paper and Pencil Surveys

	Response Flexibility – Advantages and Disadvantages	
	Web-Based	**Paper and Pencil**
Advantages	• Availability of programming languages to support flexible presentation display (Schmidt, 1997b) • Easy integration of sequence and response bridges into the survey (Dillman, 2000) • Increased flexibility in data collection structures, i.e., radio buttons, check boxes, etc. (Matz, 1999)	• Availability of additional space for respondent comments throughout the instrument • Greater perceived control for respondents with limited computer familiarity
Disadvantages	• Screen presentation formats can vary across respondents based on the browser used and the established settings (Couper, 2000)	• Researcher control is diminished as a function of unrestricted response formats

Table 8: Response Time – Advantages and Disadvantages Comparing Web-Based and Paper and Pencil Surveys

	Response Time – Advantages and Disadvantages	
	Web-Based	**Paper and Pencil**
Advantages	• Rapid return of completed surveys is enabled (Matz, 1999; Weible & Wallace, 1998; Schmidt, 1997a; Sheehan & McMillan, 1999; Solomon, 2001)	• Total response time decreases for single sitting administrations
Disadvantages	• Increased download time associated with multimedia intensive survey designs (Dillman et al., 1998)	• Slower administration times as a function of postal distribution systems (Oppermann, 1995)

Response time is more efficient with Web-based deployment when delivery time is included. Internet surveys enable rapid return of completed surveys (Matz, 1999; Schmidt, 1997a; Sheehan & McMillan, 1999; Solomon, 2001; Weible & Wallace, 1998). However, when response time is broken down into actual respondent time for completion of the survey, paper-pencil and Web-based are virtually identical (Handwerk et al., 2000). When using the postal system, mail surveys are significantly slower than email based surveys (Oppermann, 1995). Cobanoglu, Warde and Moreo (2001) found that mail surveys (paper and pencil) were 3.5 times slower than Web-based surveys. Overall response time increases as a function of the complexity of survey design (Dillman et al., 1998). Table 8 provides response time advantages and disadvantages associated with Web-based and paper and pencil survey administrations.

Population Size

Large sample surveys strongly favor Web-based administration. However, Dillman et al. (1998) suggest a Web culture has emerged that ignores the scientific underpinnings of survey design in favor of larger potential population access. An advantage of Web-based surveys for large-scale administration includes ease of administrative management and direct recording of results. Automatic analysis routines associated with Web-based surveys further facilitate the data analysis process. Additionally, geographically dispersed populations are better addressed in Web-based or email based (electronic format) administration. Electronic formats permit survey researchers to define larger and more diverse populations because of the ease of distribution, administration and analysis. The same disadvantage may exist in both Web-based and paper-based data collections because respondent address lists may be outdated. Table 9 provides population size advantages and disadvantages associated with Web-based and paper and pencil survey administrations.

Table 9: Population Size – Advantages and Disadvantages Comparing Web-Based and Paper and Pencil Surveys

Population Size – Advantages and Disadvantages		
	Web-Based	**Paper and Pencil**
Advantages	• Access to large populations of individuals with concurrent time and cost savings (Schmidt, 1997a; Dillman & Bowker, 1996) • Availability of mass populations formerly limited to governments and large corporations (Couper, 2000)	• Facilitates administrations in which populations are small and intact • Useful when administration time is fixed
Disadvantages	• Ignoring systematic survey processes in favor of easy access to large populations (Dillman et al., 1998) • Requirement to access respondent address lists or specific URLs. Oftentimes, access data are difficult to locate or are maintained on proprietary databases	• Difficulties in accessing large populations

Sample Bias

Sampling bias is a type of sampling error that decreases the generalizability of results. Sample bias can have a profound impact on survey administration. Different forms of sampling bias exist. Volunteerism — the respondent's option to select in or out — is reduced when paper and pencil administration occurs under the supervision of a data collector or monitor.

In Web-based administration, only computer literate users with technology access are reachable. Therefore, populations are parameterized without regard to respondents who choose not to use or access electronic media. Internet based surveys are likely to contain sampling errors since not all members of the frame population are measured (Basi, 1999; Couper, 2000). Couper (2000) suggests Web-based surveys are plagued with external validity issues through a potential target population-frame population mismatch. Generalizability of study results may limit the effectiveness of Internet-based surveys.

Figure 4: Example of Website Survey Solicitation

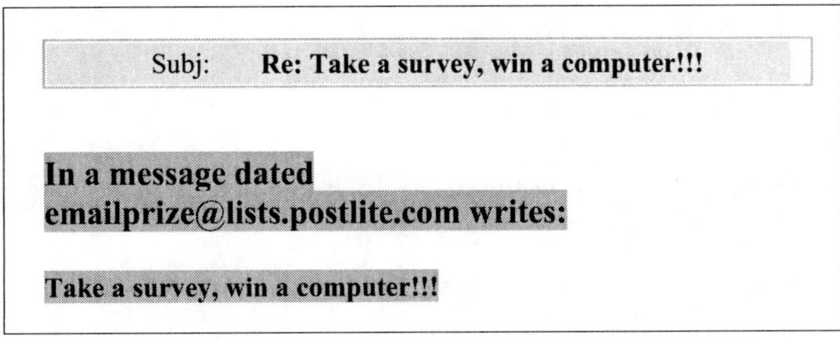

Surveyphiles are individuals who find surveys/polls appealing. Incentives used to lure Website viewers to an online survey may influence the type of respondents surveyed, thus biasing the responses (Tierney, 2000). An example of a Website survey solicitation is provided in Figure 4.

Frequently, surveyphiles are sophisticated in their ability to respond. They may be attracted to Web-based surveys; however, the identification of these individuals is often difficult and expensive. Complex routines to classify and treat sampling bias are required. Research on self-administered surveys suggests that the design of the instrument may be important in obtaining unbiased answers from respondents (Couper et al., 2001). Table 10 describes sample bias differences between Web-based and paper and pencil survey administrations.

Web-based administrations entail many more control requirements than paper based surveys. Far greater attention is required in Web-based administrations to minimize sampling error.

Instrument Validity

Instrument validity is equivalent between Web-based (electronic) and paper and pencil (manual) survey administration, since content and construct validity are

Table 10: Sample Bias – Advantages and Disadvantages Comparing Web-Based and Paper and Pencil Surveys

Sample Bias – Advantages and Disadvantages		
	Web-Based	**Paper and Pencil**
Advantage	• Potential of a large number of completed surveys improve sample validity (Tierney, 2000) • Reduced sampling bias (Solomon, 2001)	• Greater control over sampling bias (Epstein, Klinkenberg, Wiley & McKinley, 2001)
Disadvantages	• Not all members of the frame population are measured (Couper, 2000; Basi, 1999) • The mismatch between target and the frame populations (the largest generalizability issue) (Couper, 2000) • Non representative survey populations are common (Matz, 1999) • Incentives to lure survey participants influence the demography of final respondents (Tierney, 2000) • Two types of respondents are most attracted: those who like to answer surveys (surveyphiles) or those who have a public agenda (Parker, 1999) • A need for greater control of response reliability (Stanton, 1998) • Greater concern for participant motivation (Stanton, 1998)	• Voluntary participation by members within a sampling frame may produce sampling bias

based on survey design (Cronbach, 1990). Threats to internal validity are easier to control for Web-based surveys (Davis, 1999). Most survey designs can be accommodated in Web-based, email or paper and pencil formats. Improved instrument validity is marginally in favor of Web-based administration as a function of better response and completion rates (Buchanan & Smith, 1999). (See *Response Rates*, Table 2). Table 11 provides advantages and disadvantages of instrument validity issues associated with Web-based and paper and pencil survey administrations.

Management of Non-Response Data

Non-response data are those data in which a survey respondent either provides no response, a spurious response or a clearly false one. Survey research convention typically ignores non-response data by discarding obvious erroneous or sabotaged answers. Lack of clarity of a respondent's intent is also a potential issue of survey data management. Through the use of electronic techniques and the use of automatic analysis routines, non-responses can be measured and provided as usable data. Errors produced by non-responses are better controlled in Web-Based surveys (Couper, 2001). Electronic data collections can incorporate forced pauses, which will not advance until a response is provided (Schmidt, 1997a).

In a recent study comparing online and Opscan (paper and pencil) for a U.S. Government agency, non-response items were found to be greater for online administration (Church, 2001). "Don't know" responses were slightly greater for Opscan (paper and pencil) than for the online administration (Church, 2001). Table 12 provides management of non-response data advantages and disadvantages between Web-based and paper and pencil survey administrations.

Table 11: Instrument Validity — Advantages and Disadvantages Comparing Web-Based and Paper and Pencil Surveys

Instrument Validity – Advantages and Disadvantages		
	Web-Based	**Paper and Pencil**
Advantages	• Better control of instrument validity through availability of respondent tracking mechanisms • Easier control of internal validity issues (Davis, 1999)	
Disadvantages	• Measurement of instrument validities is time consuming, costly and subject to greater error (Marits, 2002)	• Measurement of instrument validities is time consuming, costly and subject to greater error (Marits, 2002)

Table 12: Management of Non-Response Data — Advantages and Disadvantages Comparing Web-Based and Paper and Pencil Surveys

Management of Non-Response Data – Advantages and Disadvantages		
	Web-Based	**Paper and Pencil**
Advantages	• Can include a no response choice to differentiate respondents' intent • The underlying code can catch unacceptable responses through real-time error checking (Schmidt, 1997a) • Programs can guard against multiple submissions by the same respondent (Schmidt, 1997a) • Significantly lower levels of missing data (Stanton, 1998)	
Disadvantages	• Increased variability of missing data associated with differences in data collection mechanisms – entry box versions produce more missing data than radio buttons (Couper et al., 2001) • Missing, unacceptable, incorrect or duplicate data and increased security risks (Schmidt, 1997a)	• Respondents can quickly skip through questions and provide spurious data to expedite survey completion • Increased frequencies of routing and skipping errors (Marits, 2002)

Response Error

Response error is defined as the class of all potential responses that are either incorrect, inaccurate, intentionally deceiving, misguided, or methodologically misclassified. Incorrect responses represent answers that are different from that which are being asked. An incorrect response may include an inaccurate response such as the percentage of time a respondent utilizes the computer for daily activities. The respondent inaccurately indicates a level that is either above or below the actual amount. This is sometimes classified as a misguided response, distorted response (Potosky & Bobko, 1997), or mischievous response (Schmidt, 1997a; Smith & Leigh, 1997), based on intention — either intentional or unintentional. Response error is equivalent, between Web-based and paper and pencil administrations, in short answer surveys (Liefeld, 1988), while for longer or more complex response requirements, computer or Web-based surveys showed greater inaccuracies (Liefeld, 1988; Manfreda et al., 2001).

Response error can be generated from social desirability phenomena, whereby individuals have the propensity to answer in a manner thought to be most socially acceptable rather than how he/she actually performs (Schwab, 1999). While response error through social desirability is generally unintentional, there is also response error from intentional deception — a response intended to skew data in a given direction — mischievous response (Schmidt, 1997a; Smith & Leigh, 1997). Response error may occur when the readability index exceeds the reading level of

Table 13: Response Error – Advantages and Disadvantages Comparing Web-Based and Paper and Pencil Surveys

Response Error – Advantages and Disadvantages		
	Web-Based	**Paper and Pencil**
Advantages	• Ease of generating subroutines to capture some inaccurate responses • Internal consistency is easily dealt with at the time of data collection • Computer-administered surveys tend to have less response error (Martin & Nagao, 1989; Rosenfeld, Giacalone, Knouse, Doherty, Vicino, Kantor & Greaves, 1991; Solomon, 2001)	• Ease of correcting a response at any time during the survey completion process • Paper and pencil administrations tend to contain lower response error (Allen & Fry, 1986)
Disadvantages	• Computer administered surveys tend to contain greater inaccuracies for longer or more complex response requirements (Liefeld, 1988) • Inability to backtrack, preview or change responses (Lautenschlager & Flaherty, 1990)	• In optical scanning data entry, response error increases for paper and pencil survey responses as a function of the sensitivity of the optical scanning equipment

the respondent. Methodologically misclassified responses are those in which the types of data are miscoded. Response error can be partially controlled through expanded explication of responses, either through follow-up or the use of multiple questions aimed at assessing the same construct.

Martin and Nagao (1989) showed that a degree of respondent honesty exists when comparing computer-administered, paper and pencil, and face-to-face interviews, but the difference was not statistically significant. Less response error was found in the computer-administered scenarios. Table 13 provides management of response error advantages and disadvantages between Web-based and paper and pencil survey administrations.

Comparative Summary of Web-Based and Paper-Based Survey Administrations

Table 14 offers a comparison between Web-based and paper-based administrations. Academic and public media sources are included. A comprehensive review of the literature suggested the treatment of 12 parameters for consideration in comparing and contrasting Web-based administrations to paper and pencil administrations. The table below was generated through examination of the literature sources for the parameters and its focus on either Web-based, paper and pencil or mixed mode. In some cases, parameters were not tagged because treatment was peripheral to the ancillary investigation.

Table 14: Summary Parametric Comparison of Web-Based and Paper and Pencil Surveys

Source	Response Rate	Participation Ease	Attractiveness of Survey	Novelty Effect	Administrative Costs	Response Flexibility	Response Time	Population Size	Sample Bias	Instrument Validit	NonResponse Dat	Response Error
Allen and Fry (1986)	▲■											▲
Ayidiya and McClendon (1990)	▲					▲						▲■
Bachman (1999)	▲■											
Bachmann, Elfrink and Vazzana (1996)	▲■						▲■			▲■	▲■	▲■
Bachmann, Elfrink and Vazzana (1999/2000)	▲■				■	■	▲					
Basi (1999)	■	■							■	■		■
Bradley (1999)									■			
Buchanan and Smith (1999)										■		
Carroll (1994)	▲■		▲■									
Cheyne and Ritter (2001)	■			■								
Church (2001)											▲■	
Cobanoglu, Warde and Moreo (2001)							▲■					
Cook, Heath and Thompson (2000)	■	■						▲■	▲■	▲■		
Couper (2001)	▲■											
Couper (2000)	■	■	■	■	■	■	■	■	■	■	■	■
Couper, Traugott and Lamias (2001)	▲■		■			■				■		■
Cronbach (1990)										▲■		
Crawford, Couper and Lamias (2001)	▲■											
Davis (1999)										■		
De Leeuw (1992)												▲■
Dillman (2000)	▲■	▲■	▲■	▲■	▲■	▲■	▲■				▲■	▲■
Dillman and Bowker (1996)	■	■	■	■			■		■	■	■	■
Dillman, Sinclair and Clark (1993)	▲	▲	▲	▲								
Dillman, Torora, Conradt and Bowker (1998)	■	■	■			■	■					
Epstein, Klinkenberg, Wiley and McKinley (2001)									▲			
Fox, Crask and Kim (1988)	▲	▲			▲							
Gorman (2000)	■				■			■	■	■		■
Handwerk, Carson and Blackwell (2000)	▲■	■					▲■					
Heberlein and Baumgartner (1978)	▲									▲		
Krysan, Schuman, Scott and Beatty (1994)	▲	▲				▲	▲					▲
Kuhnert and McCauley (1996)	▲											
Lautenschlager and Flaherty (1990)												■
Liefeld (1988)												▲■
Lippert (2001)	▲■	▲■	▲■	▲■				▲■	▲■			
Lippert (2002)	▲■	▲■	▲■	▲■	▲■	▲■	▲■	▲■	▲■	▲■	▲■	
Malhotra (1999)	■											
Manfreda, Vehovar and Batagelj (2001)	▲■				▲■							▲■
Marits (1998)	■			▲		▲■	▲■			▲■		
Martin and Nagao (1989)												▲■
Matz (1999)	▲■	■	▲■		▲■	■	▲■		▲■			
McCooey (2000)	■		■		■	■	■					
Mehta and Sivadas (1995)	▲■	▲■	▲■				▲■					▲■
Miller, Daly, Wood, Brooks and Roper (1996)	■											
Oppermann (1995)	▲■						▲■					
Parker (1999)				■	■	■			■			
Potosky and Bobko (1997)												▲■
Quality Progress (1999)	■				■		■		■			■
Redline and Dillman (1999)			▲	▲							▲	
Rockwood, Sangster and Dillman (1997)		▲	▲			▲					▲	▲
Rogleberg, Fisher, Maynard, Hakel and Horvath (2001)	▲■	▲■	▲■	▲■			▲■					▲■
Rosenfeld, Giacalone, Knouse, Doherty, Vicino, Kantor and Greaves (1991)												▲■
Schmidt (1997a)		■			▲■		▲■	■		▲■	■	■
Schmidt (1997b)			■	■		■						
Schuldt and Totten (1994)	▲■											
Schwab (1999)												▲■
Schwarz, Hippler and Noelle-Neumann (1992)												▲■
Shaw and Davis (1996)	▲■											
Sheehan (2001)	■			■								
Sheehan and McMillan (1999)	■				■		■					
Smith (1995)		▲■	▲■	▲■								
Smith and Leigh (1997)												■
Solomon (2001)					■		■		■			■
Stanton (1998)					■				■		■	
Subman and Bradburn (1974)												▲
Tierney (2000)	■	■			■				■		■	
Tomsic, Hendel and Matross (2000)	■	▲■										
Turley (1999)	▲■				▲			▲	▲			
Underwood, Kim and Matier (2000)	▲■											
Weible and Wallace (1998)	▲■		▲■		▲■	▲■	▲■	▲■				

▲ = Paper and Pencil Survey ■ = Web-Based Survey

FUTURE TRENDS

The future trend within information systems research is toward electronically based survey administrations. Included within this family of electronic administrations are Web-based or Internet, Intranet, and Extranet applications. Internet based survey data collection has a broad series of potential uses, with a wide variety of parameters that are subject to research management and control. Intranet applications enable collection of data within a restricted organizational setting. The use of such applications facilitates short, immediate, and frequent collection of data. Extranets applications enable organizations to solicit immediate feedback from customers, vendors or employees, using targeted samples or respondent communities.

Paper and pencil surveys are still available and attractive to those individuals, groups or organizations having limited technical knowledge, technology availability or other specialized contexts, which would make electronically based data collection difficult, costly or inefficient.

The future trend is toward the reduction of email surveys, except where short or simple administrations are required. The use of long email-administered surveys appears less likely to continue due to advances in the technology, increasingly uncomplicated survey design structures, ease of data collection and processing and proliferation of Web-based activities. Email surveys, while useful, do not permit the same degree of confidentiality as other Web-based methods. Additionally, the handling and analysis of data related to email surveys is far more time consuming and costly than electronic methods that enable direct data processing. As more individuals become computer literate, and as technology continues to proliferate — both hardware and software — the availability of Web-based designs and collection procedures to larger segments of the general population will increase. Postal mail surveys, a form of paper-pencil administration, will still be useful and efficient for specialized populations and applications. With the availability of Web-based administrations as the medium for data collection, researchers need to be conscious of the technical requirements for survey design, as well as, the parameters of the technology affecting administration, analysis and reporting.

CONCLUSION

In general, the advantages of Internet based surveys outweigh the disadvantages (Allen, 1987). Web-based surveys are more attractive for researchers using self-report inventories due to the ability to select large heterogeneous samples (Pasveer & Ellard, 1998). The best sample representation is when a multi-administration mode — the use of two or more of Web, email, mail, paper and pencil direct application — is utilized (Yun, 2000). The use of multi-administrations accommodates the strengths of each administration type (Yun, 2000). However, several researchers (De Leeuw, 1992; Dillman, 1999; Schwarz et al., 1992) found in independent studies that mixed mode surveys, for the same population, produced an increase in response error.

This chapter is designed to:

- Increase awareness and sensitivity of IS researchers to differences in survey administration.
- Summarize the differences in instrument performance parameters that can be expected by survey medium.
- Inform the research community about the existing literature comparing the differences in the two basic administration media — manual paper direct and electronic-Internet-based administration.

The human-to-human interaction present in the paper-direct administration provides a significant operating dynamic. Internet-based survey administration tends to lack personalization and sometimes is characterized as remote, indirect or impersonal. In electronic surveys, the administration and most interactions with respondents are achieved using electronic technology. The presence or absence of the human intervention may ultimately influence user behaviors and also responses to survey queries. Further empirical research into the effects of administration differences is warranted.

Members of the information systems community of practice seek to understand human behaviors regarding use of, and user trust of, information systems technology. As such, social dynamics offer insight and understanding to user performance in survey research. The medium of survey administration has a direct relationship to user trust in technology. The human-dimension is worth further exploration to understand the social dynamics of data collection. This chapter attempted to identify, describe and map the differences between survey data collection media as a function of selected social variables.

REFERENCES

Allen, D.F. (1987). Computers Versus Scanners: An Experiment in Nontraditional Forms of Survey Administration. *Journal of College Student Personnel*, 28(3), 266-273.

Allen, D.F., & Fry, R.E. (1986). Survey Administration: Computer-Based vs. Machine Readable. Paper presented at the *Annual Meeting of the American Educational Research Association*, San Francisco, CA.

Ayidiya, S., & McClendon, M. (1990). Response Effects in Mail Surveys. *Public Opinion Quarterly*, 54(2), 229-247.

Bachmann, D., Elfrink, J., & Vazzana, R. (1996). Tracking the Progress of E-Mail versus Snail-Mail. *Marketing Research*, 8(2), 31-35.

Bachmann, D., Elfrink, J., & Vazzana, R. (1999-2000, Winter/Spring). E-mail and snail mail face off in rematch. *Marketing Research*, 11(4), 10-15.

Bachman, K. (1999) Diaries: Not So Dear. *Mediaweek*, 9(45), 4-5.

Basi, R. (1999). WWW Response Rates To Socio-Demographic Items. *Market Research Society*, 41(4), 397.

Blattberg, R.C., & Glazer, R (1993). Marketing in the Information Revolution. In R.C. Blattberg, R. Glazer & J.D.C. Little (Eds.), *The Marketing Information Revolution.* Boston, MA: Harvard University Press.

Bradley, N. (1999). Sampling for Internet Surveys. An Examination of Respondent Selection for Internet Research. *Journal of the Market Research Society*, 41(4), 387-395.

Buchanan, T., & Smith, J.L. (1999). Using The Internet for Psychological Research: Personality Testing on the World Wide Web. *British Journal of Psychology*, 90(1), 125-144.

Carroll, S. (1994). Questionnaire Design Affects Response Rates. *Marketing News*, 28(1), 14.

Cheyne, T.L., & Ritter, F.E. (2001). Targeting Audiences on the Internet. *Communications of the ACM*, 44(4), 94-98.

Church, A.H. (2001). Is There a Method to Our Madness? The Impact of Data Collection Methodology on Organizational Survey Results. *Personnel Psychology*, 54, 937-969.

Cobanoglu, C., Warde, B., & Moreo, P.J. (2001). A Comparison of Mail, Fax and Web-Based Survey Methods. *International Journal of Market Research*, 43(4), 441-452.

Cook, C., Heath, F., & Thompson, R. (2000). A Meta-Analysis of Response Rates in Web- or Internet-Based Surveys. *Educational and Psychological Measurement*, 60(6), 821-836.

Couper, M.P. (2000). Usability Evaluation of Computer Assisted Survey Instruments. *Social Science Computer Review*, 18(4), 384-396.

Couper, M.P. (2001). The Promises and Perils of WebSurveys. Paper presented at the *ASC Conference: The Challenge of the Internet.*

Couper, M.P., Traugott, M.W., & Lamias, M.J. (2001). WebSurvey Design and Administration. *Public Opinion Quarterly*, 65, 230-253.

Crawford, S.D., Couper, M.P., & Lamias, M.J. (2001). *WebSurveys: Perceptions of Burden. Social Science Computer Review*, 19(2), 146-162.

Cronbach, L.J. (1990). *Essentials of Psychological Testing* (5th ed.). New York: Harper Collins.

Davis, R.N. (1999). Web-Based Administration of a Personality Questionnaire: Comparison With Traditional Methods. *Behavior Research Methods, Instruments & Computers*, 31(4), 572-577.

De Leeuw, E.D. (1992). *Data Quality in Mail, Telephone and Face-to-Face Surveys*. Amsterdam: TT Publications.

Dillman, D.A. (1978). *Mail and Telephone Surveys: The Total Design Method.* New York: John Wiley and Sons.

Dillman, D.A. (2000). *Mail and Internet Surveys: The Tailored Design Method (2nd Ed.).* New York: John Wiley and Sons.

Dillman, D.A., & Bowker, D. (1996). *The WebQuestionnaire Challenge to Survey Methodologists.*

Dillman, D.A., Sinclair, M.D., & Clark, J.R. (1993). Effects of Questionnaire Length, Respondent-Friendly Design, And a Difficult Question on Response Rates for Occupant-Addressed Census Mail Surveys. *Public Opinion Quarterly*, 57(3), 289-304.

Dillman, D.A., Torora, R. D., Conradt, J., & Bowker, D. (1998). Influence of Plain Versus Fancy Design on Response Rates for WebSurveys. Paper presented at the *Joint Statistical Meetings of the American Statistical Association*, Indianapolis, IN.

Epstein, J., Klinkenberg, W.D., Wiley, D., & McKinley, L. (2001). Insuring Sample Equivalence Across Internet and Paper-and-Pencil Assessments. *Computers in Human Behavior*, 17, 339-346.

Fiske, D.W. (1971). *Measuring the Concepts of Personality.* Chicago, IL: Aldine.

Fox, R., Crask, M., & Kim, J. (1988). Mail Survey Response Rates: A Meta-Analysis of Selected Techniques for Inducing Response. *Public Opinion Quarterly*, 52(4), 467-491.

Gorman, J.W. (2000). An Opposing View of Online Surveying. *Marketing News*, 34(9), 48.

Handwerk, P.G., Carson, C., & Blackwell, K.M. (2000). On-Line vs. Paper-and-Pencil Surveying of Students: A Case Study. Paper presented at the *Annual Forum of the Association for Institutional Research*, Cincinnati, OH.

Heberlein, T., & Baumgartner, R. (1978). Factors Affecting Response Rates to Mailed Questionnaires: A Quantitative Analysis of the Published Literature. *American Sociological Review*, 43(4), 447-461.

Igbaria, M., & Parasuruman, S. (1989). A Path Analytic Study of Individual Characteristics, Computer Anxiety and Attitudes Toward Microcomputers. *Journal of Management*, 15, 373-388.

Internet Technology Aids Market Research Efforts. (1999). *Quality Progress*, 32(6), 17.

Kiesler, S., & Sproull, L. (1986). Response Effects in the Electronic Survey. *Public Opinion Quarterly*, 50(3), 402-413.

Krysan, M., Schuman, H., Scott, L., & Beatty P. (1994). Response Rates and Response Content in Mail versus Face-to-Face Surveys. *Public Opinion Quarterly*, 58(3), 381-399.

Kuhnert, K., & McCauley, D.P. (1996). Applying Alternative Survey Methods. In A.I. Kraut (Ed), *Organizational Surveys* (pp. 233-254). San Francisco, CA: Jossey-Bass.

Lautenschlager, G.J., & Flaherty, V.L. (1990). Computer Administration of Questions: More Desirable or More Social Desirability? *Journal of Applied Psychology*, 75, 31-314.

Liefeld, J.P. (1988, November). Response Effects in Computer-Administered Questioning. *Journal of Marketing Research*, 405-409.

Lippert, S.K. (2001). An Exploratory Study into the Relevance of Trust in the Context of Information Systems Technology. *Doctoral Dissertation*. The George Washington University, Washington, D.C.

Lippert, S.K. (2002). Social Dynamics in Information Systems Survey Research: A Comparison of Administration Media. *Proceedings of the International Resources for Information Management*, Seattle, WA.

Malhotra, N.K. (1999). *Marketing Research: An Applied Orientation.* (International Edition, 3rd ed.). London: Prentice Hall.

Manfreda, K.L., Vehovar, V., & Batagelj, Z. (2001). WebVersus Mail Questionnaire for an Institutional Survey. In A. Westlake et al. (Eds.), *The Challenge of the Internet*, Association for Survey Computing.

Marits, E.G. (1998). UGH, Not Another Survey. *Program Manager Magazine of the Defense Acquisition University*, 10(5), 24-30.

Marits, E.G. (2002). Personal Conversation, George Washington University regarding survey design.

Martin, C.L., & Nagao, D.H. (1989). Some Effects of Computerized Interviewing on Job Applicant Responses. *Journal of Applied Psychology*, 74, 72-80.

Matz, C. M. (1999). *Administration of WebVersus Paper Surveys: Mode Effects and Response Rates.* Masters Research Paper, University of North Carolina, Chapel Hill.

McCooey, E. (2000). Making an Impact. *Adweek*, 41(16), 68-70.

Mehta, R., & Sivadas, E. (1995). Comparing Response Rates and Response Content in Mail Versus Electronic Mail Surveys. *Journal of the Market Research Society*, 37(4), 429-439.

Miller, J., Daly, J., Wood, M., Brooks, A., & Roper M. (1996). Electronic Bulletin Board Distributed Questionnaires for Exploratory Research. *Journal of Information Science*, 22(2), 107-115.

Oppermann, M. (1995). E-mail Surveys – Potentials and Pitfalls. *Marketing Research*, 7(3), 28.

Parker, K. (1999). Got Questions? All You Have To Do Is Ask. *American Demographics*, 21(11), 36-39.

Pasveer, K.A., & Ellard, J.H. (1998). The Making of a Personality Inventory: Help From the WWW. *Behavior Research Methods, Instruments & Computers*, 30(2), 309-313.

Potosky, D., & Bobko, P. (1997). Computer Versus Paper-and-Pencil Administration Mode and Response Distortion in Noncognitive Selection Tests. *Journal of Applied Psychology*, 82(2), 293-299.

Redline, C.D., & Dillman, D.A. (1999). The Influence of Auxiliary, Symbolic, Numeric, and Verbal Languages on Navigational Compliance in Self-Administered Questionnaires. *International Conference on Survey Nonresponse*, Portland, OR.

Rockwood, T.H., Sangster, R.L., & Dillman, D.A. (1997). The Effect of Response Categories on Questionnaire Answers Context and Mode Effects. *Sociological Methods and Research*, 26(1), 118-140.

Rogelberg, S.G., Fisher, G.G., Maynard, D.C., Hakel, M.D., & Horvath, M. (2001). Attitudes Toward Surveys: Development of a Measure and Its Relationship to Respondent Behavior. *Organizational Research Methods*, 4(1), 3-25.

Rosenfeld, P., Giacalone, R.A., Knouse, S.B., Doherty, L.N., Vicino, S.M., Kantor, J., & Greaves, J. (1991). Impression Management, Candor, and Microcomputer-Based Organizational Surveys: An Individual Differences Approach. *Computers in Human Behavior*, 7, 23-32.

Schmidt, W. (1997a). World Wide WebSurvey Research: Benefits, Potential Problems, and Solutions. *Behavior Research Methods, Instruments, & Computers*, 29(2), 274-279.

Schmidt, W. (1997b). World Wide WebSurvey Research Made Easy With WWW Survey Assistant. *Behavior Research Methods, Instruments, & Computers*, 29(2), 303-305.

Schuldt, B.A., & Totten, J.W. (1994). Electronic Mail vs. Mail Survey Response Rates. *Marketing Research*, 6(1), 36-39.

Schwab, D.P. (1999). *Research Methods for Organizational Studies*. Mahwah, NJ: Lawrence Erlbaum Associates.

Schwarz, N., Hippler, H.J., & Noelle-Neumann, E. (1992). A Cognitive Model of Response-Order Effects in Survey Measurement. In N. Schwarz & S. Sudman (Eds.), *Context Effects in Social and Psychological Research*, (pp. 187-199). New York: Springer-Verlag.

Shaw, D., & Davis, C.H. (1996). The Modern Language Association: Electronic and Paper Surveys of Computer-Based Tool Use. *Journal of the American Society for Information Science*, 47(12), 932-940.

Sheehan, K.B. (2001). E-mail Survey Response Rates: A Review. *Journal of Computer Mediated Communication*, 6(2). [Online]. Available: http://www.ascusc.org/jcmc/vol6/issue2/sheehan.html.

Sheehan, K.B., & McMillan, S.J. (1999, July/August). Response Variation in E-Mail Surveys: An Exploration. *Journal of Advertising Research*, 45-54.

Singleton, R.A., Straits, B.C., & Straits, M.M. (1993). *Approaches to Social Research* (2nd ed.). New York: Oxford University Press.

Smith, M.A., & Leigh, B. (1997). Virtual Subjects: Using the Internet as an Alternative Source of Subjects and Research Environment. *Behavior Research Methods, Instruments, and Computers*, 29, 496-505.

Smith, T.W. (1995). Little Things Matter: A Sampler of How Differences in Questionnaire Format Can Affect Survey Responses. *Proceedings of the American Statistical Association, Survey Research Methods Section*, 1046-1051, Alexandria, VA.

Solomon, D.J. (2001, December). Conducting Web-Based Surveys. *Office of Educational Research and Improvement*, U.S. Department of Education, (ED458291). Washington, DC.

Sproull, L. (1986). Using Electronic Mail for Data Collection in Organizational Research. *Academy of Management Journal*, 29(1), 159-169.

Stanton, J.M. (1998). An Empirical Assessment of Data Collection Using the Internet. *Personnel Psychology, 51(3),* 709-725.

Subman, S., & Bradburn, N.M. (1974). *Response Effects in Surveys*. Chicago, IL: Aldine.

Tierney, P. (2000). Internet-Based Evaluation of Tourism WebSite Effectiveness: Methodological Issues and Survey Results. *Journal of Travel Research*, 39(2), 212-219.

Tomsic, M.L., Hendel, D.D., & Matross, R.P. (2000). A World Wide Web Response to Student Satisfaction Surveys: Comparisons Using Paper and Internet Formats. *Annual Meeting of the Association for International Research*, Cincinnati, OH.

Tse, A.C.B., Tse, K.C., Yin, C.H., & Ting, C.B. (1995). Comparing Two Methods of Sending Out Questionnaires: E-mail Versus Mail. *Journal of Market Research Society,* 37(4), 441-446.

Turley, S. (1999). A Case of Response Rate Success. *Market Research Society*, 4(3), 301-309.

Underwood, D., Kim, H., & Matier, M. (2000). To Mail or To Web: Comparisons of Survey Response Rates and Respondent Characteristics. *Annual Forum of the Association for Institutional Research*, Cincinnati, OH.

Weible, R., & Wallace, J. (1998). Cyber Research: The Impact of the Internet on Data Collection. *Marketing Research*, 10(3), 19-24.

Yun, G.W. (2000). Comparative Response to a Survey Executed by Post, E-mail, & WebForm. *Journal of Computer Mediated Communication*, 6(1). [Online]. Available: http://www.ascusc.org/jcmc/vol6/issue1/yun.html.

Chapter VI

User Interfaces and Markup Language Programming: The Effects of Interaction Mode on User Performance and Satisfaction

Jeffrey Hsu
Fairleigh Dickinson University, USA

ABSTRACT

The role of the user interface (interaction mode) is of considerable importance, since the method of interaction can have an impact on both performance and satisfaction with regards to using a programming language. While markup languages are now widely used for Web page and site design and electronic publishing applications, they have not been studied adequately compared with other kinds of languages. The impact of interaction mode, in this case command-based coding, versus using a form-fill-in wizard, is examined, with respect to performance and satisfaction while performing a survey-oriented task. Skill level, which classified users as being either a novice or experienced, was another factor, which was taken into account in this study. The results showed the use of wizards brought about better performance than using the command language, and the difference between modes was far greater for novices rather than experienced users. In addition, using the wizard tended to equalize performance across skill levels. With regards to system satisfaction, there were significant differences between interaction modes, however no differences were reported between skill levels. These differences in performance and satisfaction should be noted and considered when designing interactive systems for programming-related applications.

INTRODUCTION

Interaction mode has long been a key factor in user interfaces, and the choice of mode — whether command, direct manipulation, menu, or other kinds — can impact performance, learning, satisfaction, and other variables. In particular, the type of interaction mode can frequently have a significant impact on how quickly or effectively a task is completed, and also on how satisfied the user is with the language and task. There can also be significant differences when the effects of skill level are considered (Shneiderman, 1992, 1997). In this study, two main interaction modes are examined: command language (manual coding) and menu/form fill-in (wizard).

COMMAND LANGUAGES

Command languages, as a method for communicating with computers, has as its basis in the development of languages for written and verbal communications between humans. Centuries ago, cave writings and Egyptian hieroglyphics were the basis for the modern languages of today. In our modern age, there are not only a multitude of human languages, but also languages for math, music, and the sciences. So, it is not surprising that a system of languages was developed for working with computers (Shneiderman, 1997, 1992, 1987).

Command languages are quite common in the computing world. Operating systems such as MS-DOS, UNIX, and DCL are examples of command languages for dealing with the hardware of computer systems. Programming languages allow for the creation of application and systems programs for various users. Database query languages, such as SQL are also widely used (Shneiderman, 1997, 1992, 1987).

The advantages of command language are most apparent when dealing with systems where users are very familiar with the computer and its structure and tasks. They are also useful when, long menus or direct manipulation objects are a hindrance rather than an asset, memorization of commands can improve performance, and time constraints make the compactness of the commands useful (Shneiderman, 1997, 1992, 1987).

The disadvantages of command languages are that they require extensive memorization of commands and syntax, their complexity can often make them difficult to decipher and understand, and frequently — in an effort to make the system as comprehensive and powerful as possible — designers create excess functionality. Excess functionality is the overabundance of commands, features, and "bells and whistles" which create a vast number of possible commands, only a small fraction of which are used on a regular basis. The result of this is increased error, increased learning time, and creates both confusion and dissatisfaction with the system (Shneiderman, 1997, 1992, 1987). A feature analysis list is a useful tool for working with command languages, according to Roberts (1980).

There are various kinds of command languages that can be created, and the potential diversity is as great as that for human languages. One important need is for an underlying metaphor to help in learning, use, and remembering the command language (Carroll & Thomas, 1982). For instance, an electronic mail language could contain references to drawers, files, messages, letters, etc. (Shneiderman, 1997, 1992, 1987).

Command language interfaces, generally speaking, require a user to write and use specific commands, often requiring a specific syntax. Using operating systems such as DOS or UNIX, or writing programming code, are examples of command language interaction. These have tended to bring about better performance for experienced users, but can be a stumbling block for novice users due to the complexities of understanding and creating the detailed commands. As a result, novice users tend to be less satisfied with the command approach, while many experienced users tend to prefer it (Shneiderman, 1997, 1992).

The principles of good command language design should always be followed when designing a language. This include the following principles used to design the SQML language used in this research:

- Consistent order of command and arguments.
- English-like commands.
- Perceptual cues aid in learning and use.
- Concrete images or metaphors to be associated with the language aid in learning.
- Similarities between the name and the usage aids in learning and use.

Closely associated with good command language design is the learnability of the language. Green and Payne (1984) studied the learnability of computer languages, whether they are command languages or programming languages. The overall goal is to achieve ease of learning, while at the same time being powerful. One set of key principles are referred to by the authors as "guiding principles," which have been obtained from several works examining this problem and area. These principles are as follows:

a. The order of arguments should be consistent (Barnard & Hammond, 1981a, 1981b).
b. The order of the language, if not consistent, should be similar to the patterns and organizations of English (Barnard & Hammond, 1981a, 1981b).
c. Perceptual cues to a grammatical structure of a command language can affect learnability (Ledgard, Whiteside, Singer, & Seymour, 1980).
d. Concrete images or metaphors should be used to help learning (Du Boulay, O'Shea, & Monk, 1981; Mayer, 1979).
e. Encourage similarity and suggestiveness between the command and its name (Tversky, 1977).
f. Congruency is a useful technique to implement in command languages (Carroll, 1982).

The organization of command languages is an important concept, and the use of "marker words" which help to indicate the class of the command, were found to be useful. Even a large language with a clear organization was found to be easier to learn than a small language without a clear structure (Green, 1979). The use of descriptive models in learning command language (metaphors, flow charts) was studied by Simpson and Pellegrino (1993), and the metaphor was found to be particularly effective. Another study examined the effects of using unfamiliar languages on an experienced programmer (Scholtz & Wiedenbeck, 1993). Doane et al. (1990) studied the development of expertise on a command-language operating system.

The avoidance of "excess functionality" will help to make a language easier to use and understand. In the case of the Survey Questionnaire Markup Language (SQML), these principles are applied to create the most easy to learn and effective language possible. The language defined here is designed to closely follow the structure of other markup languages such as HTML and SGML. This language is profiled in Hsu and Turoff (1996).

MENU/FORM FILL-IN INTERFACES

Menu/form fill-in interfaces, which are the main element of wizards, simplify the process of writing code, since users need only respond to inputs such as choosing the type of command desired and filling in the appropriate boxes to have the system create the code (Shneiderman, 1997, 1992).

Menu systems have the benefits of ease of interaction (especially when working with novice users), reduce learning time, require fewer keystrokes, and provide structure to the interaction and decision-making process. Disadvantages include the problems of slow speed for experienced users (and for the system in general), excessive use of screen space, and the problem of being cumbersome if many menus are used. Menu systems seem to be most useful in the preliminary stages of problem solving and interaction, when the user desires some structure rather than just being greeted with a forbidding prompt for commands (Shneiderman, 1997, 1992, 1987).

Another advantage of menu-based systems is that it eliminates the extensive memorization (and related training) necessary when using command languages. However, menu systems also need to be carefully designed so that the resulting system will be as easy to use and effective as possible (Shneiderman, 1997, 1992, 1987).

Menu and Form-Based Structures

There are a number of menu/form-based structures that exist:

- *Single Menu Structure* is the simplest form of menu structure. While there can be two or more choices available, as well as more than two screens, the basic organization is as a single menu. There are options within this category, including binary menu (yes/no choice), multiple item menus (one menu with more than two items), as well as extended menus (two or more screens with the same basic structure), pop-up/pull-down menus, multiple selection (choose more than one option at a time), and permanent (always on screen) menus (Shneiderman, 1997, 1992, 1987).
- *Tree Menu Structures* are used whenever a listing of items becomes so large and unwieldy that it is no longer easy to use. Therefore, menu systems are formed which use a tree structure, which involves the hierarchical classification or categorization of items (Brown, 1982; Clauer, 1972). This form of menu system is quite common and popular, and is used on various kinds of systems.
- *Acyclic Menu Structures* are more complicated than the tree structure, since they allow a certain menu in the "network" to be reached by more than one path. This type of menu "network" is more complex than the tree, and can result in greater disorientation and difficulty as a result of this. (Shneiderman, 1997, 1992, 1987).
- *Cyclic Menu Structures* allow the user to return to or repeat a previous or "higher up" menu, even though it has been used before. Instead of only moving in a straightforward manner, it also allows the user to "go back" to a previous, perhaps more general frame. This type of structure is even more complex than the acyclic, and can result in greater confusion on the part of the user (Shneiderman, 1987). For both this and the acyclic, the conclusion made by Mantei (1982) holds true: "the structure of the interface... causes disorientation if this structure is not obvious to the user" (Shneiderman, 1997, 1992, 1987).
- *Depth vs. Breadth of Menu Structures* is another important factor to consider, especially when menu systems involve more complex levels of nesting and hierarchy. There has been work done in this area, which attempts to explain the relationships between depth (total number of levels) versus breadth (number of items per level). Kiger (1984) looked at this problem and

created several groupings of menu tree forms, with varying numbers of items and levels. The results showed that the menu with eight items and two levels seemed to produce the best results for accuracy and speed. On the other hand, the deep narrow menu tree had the worst results. Dray, Ogden and Vestewig (1981) compared one and two level menus, with the one level menu having greater breadth. It was found the one level menu was easier to learn. Miller (1981) also found that the speed of performance was best when there were four or eight items per menu screen, and eight seemed to result in the least errors. Doughty and Kelso (1984) reported that a menu tree having great depth, but very little breadth, required search times twice as long as those with more breadth but less depth. The results seem to suggest users are more efficient with menu systems that have breadth, however a great deal of depth seems to hinder performance. Results by Landauer and Nachbar (1985) also support this general conclusion.

- *Form Fill-In Structure* is another kind of menu design structure that has use in certain kinds of applications. It is especially useful in instances where a large number of keyboard entries are needed. The close resemblance to paper forms makes users comfortable with the format, and it also gives users the impression of being "in control." Detailed instructions are also not as necessary, as for other kinds of menu systems (Shneiderman, 1997, 1992, 1987). This type of interface system has been found to result in greater speed over command languages (Ogden & Boyle, 1982). There are a number of vital elements to effective form fill-in interfaces, including the use of meaningful titles, the inclusion of comprehensible instructions, maintaining a logical grouping and sequencing of fields. These ensure a visually appealing layout of the form, field labels, consistent technology and abbreviations, use of space, convenient cursor movement, easy error correction, error messages, optional fields, explanatory messages for fields, and providing some kind of signal for completion (Shneiderman, 1987). Research on form fill-in was conducted by Brown (1986), Pakin and Wray (1982), and Galitz (1980).

Wizards are now featured on many of the software we use daily, including components of the Microsoft Office suite, for example. They automate the process by leading the user through a series of input screens, after which the system will write the command or code for the user.

In addition to examining the role of interaction modes, it is also important to examine what markup languages are, and why they should be the subject of further study. Markup languages have become increasingly important in the computing community, because of their wide use in both Internet Web page design/development and electronic publishing. Simply put, a markup language consist of a set of tags, tokens, characters, or specialized commands which are placed in a body of text in order to provide information about the text or other data being processed (Coombs, Renear & Rose, 1987; Goldfarb, 1991).

Markups are sets of tags, tokens, characters, or specialized commands, which are placed into a body of text in order to provide information about the text or other data being processed. A markup could be as simple as a space or line feed, or a complex set of symbols for setting all the formatting details for a text document (Coombs et al., 1987; Goldfarb, 1981).

Markups enable one to "unlock" the data content of a document. In other words, a document is not just a stream of characters, but rather is a data structure that encompasses a great deal of content (Cronk, 1993).

The concept of a markup is simple — whenever you write something, you also "mark it up." Markups can be used to specify the boundaries between words, sentences, and paragraphs, and also indicate the typographical and structural features of a text, such as chapter headings, titles, and indented sections. Some forms of markup allow one to specify the various components of a specific document type, whether it is a book, article, or paper. There are several different kinds of markup, which are used.

One commonly used form of markup is *punctuational markup*. This basically involves adding punctuation to the text, such as commas, periods, question marks, and exclamation points (Coombs et al., 1987).

Presentational markup is another widely used form, which uses formatting commands to enhance the presentation of text. For instance, horizontal and vertical spacing, underlining, indenting, and page breaks are added directly into the text to make it more understandable and easy to read. Presentational markup clarifies presentation of the text (Coombs et al., 1987).

Procedural markup is another form of markup where commands placed in the text indicate how text should be formatted. Basically, it provides instructions to the text formatter, and might include commands to set line spacing, format text, justify (left, right, full) a paragraph, and the like. Usually a certain word processor or formatter has its own set of procedural markup commands (Coombs et al., 1987).

Probably the most important and significant type of markup is *descriptive markup*. This specifies what text element a unit of data is, and allows you to describe and classify it. A descriptive markup (command) language approach allows the creator of a document to define a number of "element types" or "data structures," which identifies a text portion as a member of a certain class. For instance, you can specify if a piece of text is a long quotation, table, paragraph, or a footnote (Blake, 1989; Coombs et al., 1987; MacLeod, 1990; Tuck, 1989)

The power of markup languages is becoming more apparent for the efficient formatting and processing of text, especially with the increased interest in electronic text manipulation, desktop publishing, the Internet, and the World Wide Web. Descriptive markup is of particular importance, because it allows a description of a document or text element that is independent of its final form and output. One important component of any markup language standard should be the inclusion of markups for survey question types. These descriptive markup functions would be very useful in providing support for survey applications and for extending the usefulness of markup languages.

A practical example of an existing markup language standard is SGML. SGML is an international standard for describing marked-up electronic text. SGML is less of a language in itself, but instead is a metalanguage, which is used to define a markup language. In order to create a formal specification for a SGML document, it is necessary to produce what is called a document type definition, or DTD. The elements of this need to be specified in a defined format, which includes elements such as angle brackets, element keywords, minimization rules, and content models. This standard for marking up text has been utilized by various publishers of information and is an important component of electronic publishing (Association of American Publishers, 1992; Wright, 1992; W3C Web page, 1998). A widely used instance (or application) of SGML is HTML (Hyper Text Markup Language), which is used to create hypertext-based documents (Web pages) on the Internet World Wide Web (Darnell, 1997; Mullen, 1998). Someone can easily create text, graphical, and forms-based "pages" which can then be placed on the Internet World Wide Web and presented to a global audience. The markup language developed here in this study can easily be added to the SGML and HTML standards, both for use on text processing systems and on the Internet (Hsu & Turoff, 1996).

Recent advances in markup languages include Dynamic HTML (DHTML), which includes as one important component cascading style sheets (CSS), as well as XML (eXtensible Markup Language). These represent some of the advanced HTML markup features that are available.

Dynamic HTML is an enhancement of HTML, in that the use of dynamic HTML can bring about such effects as dynamic styles, dynamic content, and dynamic positioning. Dynamic styles allow for changes in content without the need to re-load the entire page content back in each time. The use of dynamic content would allow for the graphics or text on a page to change, upon receipt of input from a keyboard or mouse. Graphics and text can also be moved around on a page using the dynamic positioning features of DHTML (Pardi & Schurman, 1998; Powers, 1998; St. Laurent, 1997). An important element of this is the use of cascading style sheets (CSS), which allows for the definition of style specifications which can improve document presentation and layout (Busch, 1998; Lie & Bos, 1997; Mace, Flohr, Dobson & Graham, 1998).

XML could be considered a less comprehensive version of SGML, in that it is more powerful than HTML, yet less complicated than full SGML, and is designed to be easier to use. It allows someone to define his/her own markup language and move beyond the fixed tags, which are found in a SGML application such as HTML. However, the use of XML requires the use of a special XML browser, which is different from the HTML-based browsers commonly used (Holzner, 1997; Leventhal & Lewis, 1998; Light & Bray, 1997; Mace, Flohr, Dobson & Graham, 1998; St. Laurent, 1997).

There are other new types of markup languages, especially for use with the Internet and World Wide Web, such as VRML (Virtual Reality Markup Language), which have been developed. They allow someone to develop three-dimensional virtual reality-oriented pages for the World Wide Web. There are a number of books that have been published on the use of markup languages (SGML, HTML, VRML), and this is a type of language, which has become widely accepted and used.

Using a descriptive markup language (Coombs et al., 1987) approach to creating surveys appears to be a viable alternative to the manual direct manipulation or WYSIWYG (what you see is what you get) approach which is currently the basis of most text editing systems commonly used for creating surveys.

The descriptive markup (command) language approach allows the creator of a survey to select from a number of "element types" or "data structures," which classify a text stream as a member of a certain type. A document that has been tagged with descriptive markup can be processed by different kinds of systems, and is independent of its final form and the specific system it is being processed on. Instead of specifying the intricacies of formatting and text presentation, it allows the focus to be entirely on the questions and structure of the questionnaire as a whole (Coombs et al., 1987).

One of the most important benefits of a descriptive markup approach to survey design is its ability to minimize cognitive demands. Rather than recalling, selecting, and remembering codes for the creation of entry and coding of procedural markup, there is only one step involved in descriptive markup after recognizing the element type — to use the appropriate markup command together with the text to be "marked up." This frees the survey creator from formatting concerns inherent in traditional direct manipulation or WYSIWYG methods.

The use of descriptive markup also has the benefits of better maintainability and portability. In terms of maintainability, in the case where the actual formatting or structure of a question (element) type needs to be modified, this can be done by changing the processing program or system, without affecting the markups or text. This allows the same data to be used across different applications and platforms, resulting in greater portability (Blake, 1989; Coombs et al., 1987; MacLeod, 1990; Tuck, 1989).

Going to a more general level, the benefits of markup could be related to the difference between command languages (markup) and direct manipulation (manual means). For a survey task, a markup language is best because users are familiar with the task, the number of element types is relatively small, dealing with survey questions as direct manipulation objects is slow and cumbersome, and the compactness of a command language makes it simpler to work with (Shneiderman, 1997, 1992, 1987).

Using a markup language allows a system to potentially aid the user by better expressing what the specific objectives or task is. The semantic approach inherent in the markup command language can be more effective than the direct manipulation approach, especially if incremental feedback, visual interpretation, or other learning aids are also used (Shneiderman, 1997, 1992, 1987).

While there have been studies conducted on command languages such as DOS or procedural programming languages, there have been few which have been on markup languages. The implications of this study, given the fact that many millions of people are getting onto the Internet and the World Wide Web, is that more effective help systems and learning aids can be developed which can help people to learn and work with markup languages such as HTML and SGML.

User background is another important factor, which was examined in this experiment. The previous programming background of the subjects is an important factor, which should be examined when it comes to evaluating interaction mode and performance/satisfaction. In general, experienced users tended to have a better "mental model" of a system or a language. There are a number of ways to obtain this kind of mental model—through usage, through analogy, and through training (Sein & Bostrom, 1989). A person can learn how a system is put together by using it; it is a function of the user interface, knowledge of other systems, and various individual traits. Analogies are also useful to help someone develop this kind of mental model, which can be heavily influenced by their use of similar systems or by previous experiences.

Payne (1988) found that one of the main differences between novices and experienced users was found in the kinds of mental models, which they have. Many novices having incorrect or ill-conceived models which lead to difficulty in actually conducting the task or writing the code. Since experienced users have much better mental models of programming and the use of markups, it is expected they would have better performance compared with novice users. In connection with this, knowledge and experience with the complexities of programming would tend to improve satisfaction for these same experienced subjects, as compared with novices.

This paper describes the background, results, and summary/conclusions for a research experiment which examines performance and satisfaction as it relates to the usage of a survey questionnaire markup language. The language used, which has specific markup tag types designed for the creation of questionnaire question types, was designed to be an enhancement to markup language standards such as HTML and SGML (Hsu & Turoff, 1996).

SURVEY QUESTIONNAIRE MARKUP LANGUAGE (SQML)

The markup language used in this program is adapted from the SGML concept, however, it has been modified with respect to syntax to make it easier to input and use. SGML is a complete language for specifying mark-up codes — how they are to be interpreted, and how the codes relate to each other (Tuck, 1989). This language is also described in Hsu and Turoff (1996).

Survey Generation Language Specifications

The following are the specifications, in detail, of the markup language created for this survey system. This gives the general form of each specific markup, an example of how it would be used, and an example of the output produced by using that markup. The question types included represent the major types of questions that comprise survey questionnaires (Alreck & Steele, 1995). The advantages of this language are as follows:

- Easy to use,
- Consistent and clear format,
- Full question names supported,
- Generally consistent with HTML and SGML standards,
- Includes three components: type tag, question text, and options.

QUESTION TYPE: ALLOCATION OF RESOURCES

This type of question is designed to allow the user to allocate resources between various choices. Examples of this include the allocation of funds, a certain limited resource, or some other material, which can be measured in dollars or units. Basically, the respondent is given the choices, the amount of the resource, and some guidelines or restrictions on how it can be allocated. Then, he or she is asked to allocate the resource between various choices.

The following is the general form of the allocation markup:

General Form

```
<allocation>
<text —allocation question text -- >
<limit 999>                        // specifies allocation limit
<list/choice1/choice2/choice3/choice4/choice5....>
</allocation>
```

They will allow the user to type in the entries to allocate some resource.

There is **<allocation>**, which is the question type identifier. This should be at the beginning of the markup and be on a line by itself.

The <**text** [question text] > should be placed after text keyword, in brackets.

The allowed allocation limit comes next. This should be in brackets, such as <**limit** 2000>.

The <**list**.....> should follow the previous commands, which consists of an opening bracket, the keyword list, followed by a list of allocation choices, separated by forward slashes (/). The closing bracket completes the command, while </ **allocation**> closes the markup.

This text example:

```
<allocation>
<text ALLOCATION OF RESOURCES: You have a total of $500.00>
<limit 500>
<list /clothes/vacation/computer/stereo>
</allocation>
```

will produce the following output:

```
ALLOCATION OF RESOURCES: You have a total of $500.00
clothes      ?
vacation     ?
computer     ?
stereo       ?
Total     ????
```

EXPLICIT RESPONSE

Frequently, it is desirable to get responses, which are of a certain type or format. For instance, you might want a binary choice (yes or no), or to ask for the response to a true/false question, or to ask someone's gender (male/female). This kind of item asks for a specific response, such as 'Y' or 'N' or 'T' or 'F.'

General Form

```
<explicit>
<text  [question text]>
<valid a/b/c/d>
</explicit>
```

The following are the components of the explicit response question:

The <explicit> is the keyword for the explicit response question.

The <text [text] > is for the text question. The question text is placed after the keyword in brackets.

<valid c1/c2/c3/c4> Place the valid choices separated by forward slashes.

</explicit> Closes the markup.

Example

```
<explicit>
<text Are you older than 21?>
```

<valid Yes/No>
</explicit>

FREE RESPONSE

Often, the need arises to allow the respondent to provide more information than just a single response (as in multiple choice or Likert/Semantic Differential), and instead allows the respondent to enter lines or paragraphs of text.

This allows for a response question similar to the following: What are your feelings about world peace?

General Format

Each free response item or group of response items must have the following general markup:

<free response>
<text [text of the question] >
</free response>

When this markup is executed, it will display the question, together with an editing screen that allows the user to create a free-form text response to the question. The user enters the data into the editing screen much like he or she would when using a text or line editor. This text is saved as a response to the question. The following is an explanation of the tags:

<free response> is the keyword tag for the question type.
<text [text]> is the question text for the free response.
</free response> closes the free response markup tag.

Example

<free response>
<text What are your feelings about world peace?>
</free response>

LIKERT SCALE

Frequently, the need arises to express various levels of agreement or disagreement with a statement or idea. This is where the Likert scale is appropriate. For instance, someone could agree, disagree, be neutral, or strongly disagree or disagree with a statement.

The markup set up for this system allows for both the nominal (such as Strongly Agree...Strongly Disagree), and the interval scale type questions (with numbering 1 to 7 and the anchor points Strongly Agree...Strongly Disagree). This markup allows for complete flexibility in that the question designer can enter any kind of scale descriptors, as well as how many choices for the interval scale and specifying the anchor points.

The respondent is given choices on a scale, using English descriptors. A commonly used set of descriptors is the following: Strongly Agree (SA)/Agree (A)/ Neutral (N)/ Disagree (D)/ Strongly Disagree (SD). The scales and questions are set up to suit the particular survey being created.

General Format

```
<likert>                                  //required function name
<[nominal/interval]>                     //type specifier
< text [text of the question] >          //question text
<endpoints /endpoint1/endpoint2>
<list /choice1/choice2/choice3/choice4 ----->
</likert>
```

There are several basic elements to the Likert question markup:

<likert> is the required function name, which specifies what type of question it is.

There is also <[nominal/interval]>. This specifies the type of question that will be produced. This includes both the nominal and interval types of questions. The nominal type will allow selected choices to be chosen, while interval will allow intermediate values to be selected. For instance, nominal will allow you to select SA, A, N, D, SD, while interval allows one to make a selection between SA and A.

<text [text of the question] >. This is the text of the Likert question.

<endpoints /e1/e2> will specify the particular endpoints which will be placed on each end of the scale. Typical choices might be “Strongly Agree” on one end and “Strongly Disagree” on the other.

<list /c1 /c2 /c3 > allows you to specify the individual choices which you are allowed to make in regards to the Likert question.

</likert> closes the markup.

Example

```
<likert>
<interval>
<text Winter is my favorite season.
SA=Strongly Agree, A=Agree, N=Neutral, D=Disagree,
```

SD=Strongly Disagree>
<endpoints /strongly agree /strongly disagree>
<list /SA/A/N/D/SD>
</likert>

This will produce an output similar to the following:

Winter is my favorite season.
SA=Strongly Agree, A=Agree, N=Neutral, D=Disagree, SD=Strongly Disagree

: SA : A : N : D : SD :

Strongly Agree ... Strongly Disagree

MULTIPLE CHOICE

One of the most commonly used types of survey questions asks the respondent to choose between various options. Whether it is age, income level, or any one of a myriad of topics, multiple choice is a necessary element of many surveys. The markup provided here allows for the creation of both alphabetic and numeric multiple choice. This is useful for cases where the response to a question can be one of several choices and for alternating between presentations.

General Form

Specification:
<multiple choice> --required function name
<text [text of the question] >
<option **[alpha/numeric] [single/multiple] [horizontal/vertical]**>
<list /choice1/choice2/choice3......>
</multiple choice>

The following are the options for this markup:

<multiple choice> is the required keyword identifier for this question type.
<text [text] > of the question, in brackets, follows the keyword identifier.
The third set of commands specifies the multiple-choice options, which includes:
<option ....> see below for details:

a. *alpha* has alphabetic choices, meaning that the user can select from one or more in a sequence of letter choices (a,b,c,d...).
b. *numeric* allows for choices using numbers, such as one or more in the sequence (1,2,3,4...).

c. *single* means that only one choice can be chosen from the list when answering the question.
d. *multiple* means that more than one can be chosen from the list, up to N choices when answering the question.
e. *horizontal* format means that the choices will be listed side by side on the screen or on paper.
f. *vertical* format means that the choices are listed on separate lines.

<list / / /...> specifies the choices for each of the selections in the list. The individual choices should be separated by forward slashes.

</multiple choice> closes the markup.

The syntax for the various choices needs to be specified in the order presented above. Selection choices listed in the "list" markup should be placed exactly as they are to appear in the final version. The second line of any markup is the question text.

Example/Alphabetic. An example of how this markup can be used is as follows:

```
<multiple choice>
<text What is your favorite color?>
<option alpha single vertical>
<list /blue/red/green>
</multiple choice>
```

which will produce output as follows:

What is your favorite color?
a. blue
b. red
c. green

Choice: []

Example/Other Formats. Numeric will bring about the selections with numeric entries: 1, 2, 3, etc. The multiple option will allow selection of the desired (N) number of choices. Vertical presents the choices in a vertical list format, while horizontal does it in a horizontal side-by-side format. These are generally similar in appearance and do not need to be illustrated.

RANK ORDER

Another important type of question concerns rank ordering of items, in terms of preference, necessity, or some other criterion. The markup presented here allows respondents to rank order the choices given on the screen.

General Form

The general form of the markup is as follows:

<rank order>
<text [text of the question] >
<option [ties/noties]>
<list /choice1/choice2/choice3/choice4 ----->
</rank order>

<rank order> is the required keyword for rank order question markups.

<text [text] > the text of the question follows the questions, and is placed in brackets.

<option [ties/noties]> is designed to specify whether you want to allow tied values in this rank ordering sequence.

<list /./.....> specifies the choices which you want to specify for the rank ordering. Each of the choices must be clearly separated from another using a forward slash (/).

</rank order> closes the markup.

Example

<rank order>
<text Which present would you like best?>
<option ties>
<list /car/computer/diamond ring/vacation>
</rank order>

where the type of question is presented in the top line, followed by the question, and after that, a list of the choices that the system will then present for rank ordering. After interpretation by the system, the survey respondent will be presented with output similar to the following:

Which present would you like best?
car { }
computer { }
diamond ring { }
vacation { }

SEMANTIC DIFFERENTIAL SCALE

Another widely used question type is the semantic differential, which typically involves descriptive endpoints and a numerical scale in which to select how strongly one feels about something. The semantic differential scale is supported in the system as follows:

General Format

<semantic>
<text [question text] >
<endpoints /endpoint1 /endpoint2>
<list /choice1/choice2/choice3/choice4/choice5...>
</semantic>

<semantic> is the required keyword for the semantic differential question text.

<text [question text]> the question text follows the keyword.

<endpoints /./..> specifies the two endpoint descriptions which are displayed on the screen for that question.

<list /././.…..> specifies the individual choices which the respondent will select from when answering the survey.

</semantic> closes the markup.

Example

<semantic>
<text Shoveling snow is lots of fun.
1=Agree, 4=Neutral, 7=Disagree>
<endpoints /agree /disagree>
<list /1/2/3/4/5/6/7>
</semantic>

This will produce the following output:

Shoveling snow is lots of fun.
1=Agree 4=Neutral 7=Disagree

1	2	3	4	5	6	7
Agree						Disagree

The study of the interaction with this specially designed markup command language using various interface tools (menus, help systems) is one of the components of this research.

MLSS INTERACTION MODES

Command Language Mode. Subjects are asked to build the survey markup text on a text editor, which is part of the MLSS Integrated Development Environment

Figure 1: Command Language Mode

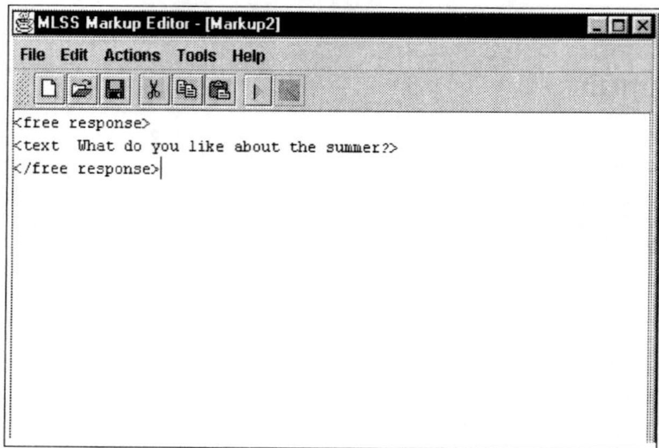

(IDE). The subject was provided with materials to assist them in completing the task, but it basically involved the creation of code character by character. This interaction method may provide for better performance and efficiency by experienced users, who through this mode must solve the problem with interpretive instructions and who are working with a familiar task (Norman, 1986).

Wizard (Menu-Form) Mode. A subject creates an online survey using a sequence of menu screens, which "walks" or "holds the person's hand" through the interaction process. This menu consists of both selection and fill-in-the-blank type items. The system correspondingly builds the markup language, line by line until the entire markup question structure is completed. The advantage of this method is it allows users to build the markups without needing to be concerned with the syntax and details of coding each line of the markup language tags and elements. From a theoretical perspective, it could be said the menu-based method provides for specific instructions for a non-familiar task, which may make it ideal for novice users. On the other hand, it may result in slower, less efficient performance for experienced users (Norman, 1986). The menu structure, built in the MLSS software, and designed specifically for this research is designed to aid the novice user in building markups using a combination of "multiple choice" and "form fill-in" input items. It is a form of "training wheels" learning system (Carroll & Carrithers, 1984) whereby someone can enter the inputs and see on the screen how the markups are being built automatically.

In particular, the issues of menu performance and the depth/breadth tradeoff were given attention when designing the menu-driven system for the MLSS software. The ideal menu structure should have four to eight items per page, and would not have too many levels. This more depth/less depth structure is found to bring about better efficiency and performance. One element of the research would be to look at how experts and novices perform using both the menu-driven system and the command interface.

Figure 2: Wizard Mode

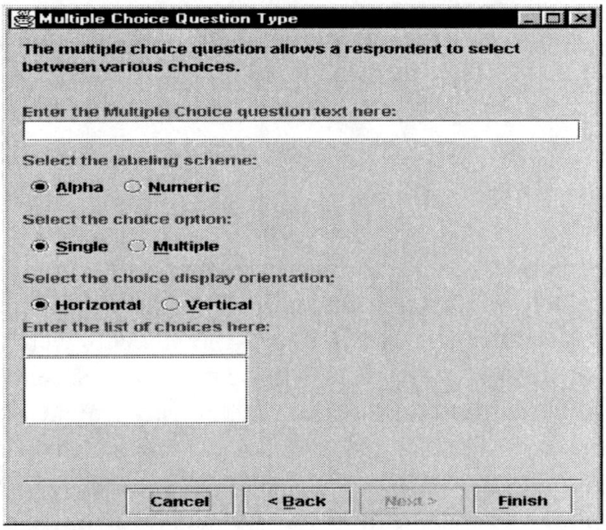

The combination of a broad/shallow menu structure and form fill-in input allow for the quick and easy input of data and the corresponding building of markups without actual coding of the language code are the benefits of the MLSS system.

The effects of the use of a specially designed menu structure on the learning and usability of command markup languages is a focus of this research.

MATERIALS

The following materials were used in this study:

Pre-Test Questionnaire. Filled out by all subjects who participated. A key section of the questionnaire addressed previous background, and was used to determine skill level.

MLSS Software. Each participant was provided with a customized copy of the experimental software, which was a custom-designed Java-based PC application which incorporated the following:

- Editor for writing the markup code.
- Interpreter who reads and creates output from the markup code.

Experimental Task. The task entailed taking a printed 15-item survey questionnaire, and coding it using the markup language. The resulting code, if written correctly, should produce an online version of the questions to be displayed on the screen. The questionnaire used is an adapted (shortened and simplified) form of the EIES Virtual Classroom questionnaire , which has been used in previous research to test users' reactions and responses to online Virtual Classroom courses and systems.

Post-Test Questionnaire. This questionnaire, administered after the completion of the experimental task, included items that measured the user's satisfaction with the language and the task.

SUBJECTS

A total of 268 undergraduate students participated in this experiment. The students were volunteers recruited among students majoring in computer science, engineering, architecture, and accounting. The students were given credit for participating in the study. Subjects were categorized as either "novice" or "experienced" subjects, according to their previous background, as reflected in their responses to items in the Pre-Test Questionnaire, administered to the subjects prior to conducting the actual task. The subjects who participated in the study were primarily undergraduate students from the New Jersey Institute of Technology in Newark, NJ.

PROCEDURE

This experiment, which examined the performance, as well as system satisfaction of users in completing a markup language task, as it relates to interaction mode and user experience level, is in effect a 2x2 factorial design, with two forms of interaction and two types of experience level. The procedure for this experiment was conducted in three main stages: Pre-Test, Test, and Post-Test.

The Pre-Test stage involved the distribution of Pre-Test Questionnaires to prospective subjects, with the intention of analyzing them and categorizing them according to skill level. The determination of skill level was determined according to the following formula:

Experienced were defined as those subjects who rated themselves as having either:

- Medium or high or very high programming experience

or

- Medium or high or very high markup knowledge/experience.

Novices were defined as those subjects who did not meet either of the above conditions.

The Task Stage required subjects to build an online questionnaire using the markup language, using the markup tags/code. In essence, the subject would build an "electronic" version of the paper questionnaire, which displays survey questions onto the screen after interpretation of the markup language code.

The Post-Test stage involved submittal of all task-related information, followed by the completion of a Post-Test Questionnaire, which included a quiz and items that focused on subjects' perceptions of learning.

The scores for the two groups (Command, Wizard) crossing with the two levels of experience (Novice, Experienced) were analyzed using GLM ANOVA, using SPSS v9.0 at a 0.05 level of significance.

RESULTS

Online time is a measure of how long a subject spent online, using the MLSS system, in working on the task. This was measured in minutes using the MLSS system's built-in log file system, and was the total time spent online working on the task.

As clearly shown in the above table (see Table 1), there were significant differences between subjects of differing skill levels and interaction modes. Both of these were highly significant at $p < .01$. Command language interaction by novices clearly took the longest time (216.37), followed by command language by experienced users (137.78). However, there was little difference between the results across skill levels, for users of the wizard (67.09 for novice and 67.45 for experienced).

System satisfaction is a measure of how satisfied subjects were with the system they used, which in this case was the MLSS software. System satisfaction was measured using a composite system satisfaction scale. The questionnaires and scales used in this research were generally consistent with those used in past NJIT research, which include both research projects and dissertation research (Benbunan, 1997; Dufner, 1995; Fjermestad, 1995; Ocker, 1995).

Table 1: GLM Analysis of Performance/Online Time: Means by Condition (Minutes)

Symbol	Condition	Novice	Experienced	All Conditions
CMD	COMMAND	216.37	137.78	177.55
WIZ	WIZARD	67.09	67.45	67.27
	All Subjects	**141.70**	**103.12**	**122.41**

GLM Results			Significance
Model	F =99.90	p = .000	***
SKILL	F = 18.97	p = .000	***
MODE	F = 154.96	p = .000	***
SKILL * MODE	F=19.33	p = .000	***

** = Significant at p < .1; ** = Significant at p< .05; *** = Significant at p< .01*

Table 2: GLM Analysis of System Satisfaction: Means by Condition

Symbol	Condition	Novice	Experienced	All Conditions
CMD	COMMAND	24.24	18.85	21.55
WIZ	WIZARD	15.34	19.67	17.51
	All Subjects	**19.72**	**19.26**	**19.53**

GLM Results			Significance
Model	F = 238.20	p = .000	***
SKILL	F = .497	p = .481	
MODE	F = 29.01	p= .000	***
SKILL * MODE	F= 41.88	p= .000	***

* = *Significant at p < .1;* ** = *Significant at p< .05;* *** = *Significant at p< .01*
Note: Smaller values indicate higher system satisfaction

The results, shown in Table 2, indicate there were significant differences between subjects of differing interaction modes (p < .01), but there were no significant differences between skill levels (p > .1). There was a significant difference when the interaction of skill level and interaction mode was considered (p<.01). In general, wizard users showed a higher level of system satisfaction, and while novice users preferred the wizard, experienced users preferred the command language. It appears, however there is a greater difference for the novice users, as compared with the experienced users.

DISCUSSION, CONCLUSION, AND FUTURE RESEARCH

The results presented here focus on two main dimensions: performance, as measured by online time spent on the task, and satisfaction, as measured by a system satisfaction scale.

To start, performance was generally better overall for experienced users (103.12), as opposed to novices (141.70), and the difference was significant. However there was a large and considerable difference between users of the command language (177.55) versus the wizard (67.27). Also of interest is the fact that the wizard tended to equalize performance across skill levels; in other words, both novice and experienced users spent roughly the same amount of time to complete the task. It is of course expected that experienced users would complete the task in less time than novices, and the wizard would bring about faster performance. However, it would have seemed logical that experienced users would have still complete the task faster than novices using the wizard, but that did not turn out to be true.

From the perspective of system satisfaction, there was no significant difference between novice and experienced users (F = .497, p = .481). However, there was a difference when it came to system satisfaction as it related to interaction mode (F = 29.01, p = .000). In general, wizard users were far more satisfied overall than command language users (17.21 versus 21.55).

In addition, it appears there is a greater difference in satisfaction between interaction modes for novices than for experienced users. Clearly, users with experience in programming and markups would find the interaction mode to be less critical in terms of their satisfaction with the system — simply different ways of doing the same thing. However, novices may find the wizard approach to be user-friendly and enjoyable, while the experience of using the command language and editor may prove to be rather trying and difficult.

In general, it could be concluded that if the goal is to complete a task quickly, the wizard is definitely the mode to use. Both experienced users and novices were able to complete the task significantly faster than using the command mode. However, if command language coding is used, experienced users were able to complete it in twice the time needed, compared with the wizard. In the case of novices, it took approximately three times as long.

Experienced users were roughly equally satisfied regardless of the interaction mode used, a reflection of their previous experience in programming and markup languages. Novices, on the other hand, were quite affected by interaction mode, expressing great satisfaction with the wizard and far lower levels of satisfaction with the command language mode.

System designers who are looking to design programming or Web development systems should apply these findings to systems they are looking to design or enhance. For tasks where prompt execution and fast completion is desired, the best choice would be to offer a wizard feature so that users of any skill/experience level could use it easily. The addition of the wizard feature could help to enhance acceptance of the system and encourage users to work with it frequently. On the other hand, it appears that while novices greatly appreciate wizard-based systems, experienced users do not show the tendency to the same degree, and it is possible that some experienced users would actually prefer using the command language interaction. Further research which examines the relationships between these interaction modes and learning, as well as the effects upon other measures of performance, could yield more insights into the impacts of interaction mode, on using and learning markup languages.

There are a number of research questions and issues, which are deserving of further research in command languages. These include the following areas:

- Combined menu/command language approaches. The combination of menu techniques together with traditional command language approaches is worthy of further study, especially in the case of learning command languages. How can command languages be presented to help someone learn the language more quickly and effectively?
- Formatting of commands to conform to certain metaphors. When teaching a command language, what kinds of formats and organization structure can be emphasized to enable someone to more easily learn the language? Can they be designed to fit specific metaphors or structures?
- New methods of organizing command languages to make command languages easier.
- There are a number of areas relating to menus/form fill-in where further research and study would be both interesting and fruitful. These are in the areas of:
  - Nonlinear menus. These are menus which are not laid out in a traditional linear organization. Instead, menus can be patterned using a more meaningful ordering of items. For instance, a menu can be arranged in a tabular format, as a circular form as on a clock, or in a pie, geographical map, or color wheel formats. Do these alternate formats improve performance, satisfaction, and usability?
  - Interdependent menus. Menus can be designed so there are relationships and dependencies between items. Instead of selecting "a, b, c, d," there can be menus that follow an organizational chart, process/function, or "tree" structure. The structure of the interdependent menu can be defined in a graphical display instead of a linear list.
  - Analog menus. These menus, using pointing devices, allow for the entry of continuous values.
  - Improving the performance on "deep menus." Most research points to broad and shallow menus are more efficient than deep ones. Are there methods of improving performance on narrow, deep menu structures?

These are just some of the issues and questions, which can be explored in further research of menus.

This study produced a number of useful and meaningful results in better understanding human-computer interaction as it relates to markup languages. There are a number of interesting and meaningful research directions, which can be explored with this study, as a starting point. They include logical extensions to the research conducted here, including the use of different kinds of subjects, or perhaps, doing this kind of study on different kinds on new languages which are currently being developed and used, especially for the Internet and Web development.

Infrequent/Casual Users and Markup Languages. There is a body of literature (Martin & Fuerst, 1987; Trumbly, 1988), which examines the behavior and performance of intermittent users, such as doctors, lawyers, and other kinds of professionals. They use computers on an irregular, intermittent basis, and are neither true novices nor true experienced, using computing systems. While they likely would not perform well on an involved programming application (like C or C++), it would be useful to study their performance, learning, and satisfaction on a task such as using markup languages. In fact, many professionals probably would want to understand how to build Web and Websites for their businesses and practices. In a future study, where subjects of this type are available, this would be an interesting investigation to pursue.

Adaptive Interfaces for Novices and Experienced. Another extension of this research, which would require greater resources for advanced programming and coding of the experimental software, would be to create an innovative kind of "adaptive" interface which would be able to adjust to the level of the subject in providing the proper interface and help systems for the user.

Dynamic/Adaptive Menus are menus which "adapt to the current user by compensating for weaknesses, providing help appropriate to the context, and decreasing the mental and physical workload of the particular user" or more simply put, should conform to the idea that "the interface should adapt to the user rather than the user adapt to the system." The system should be able to provide appropriate help when necessary, compensate for user weaknesses, as well as decrease the mental load placed onto the user (Norcio & Stanley, 1989).

There are two main types of adaptive interfaces. This includes both dynamic adaptation by the system, as well as interfaces which can be modified by the user. The first type is what is generally referred to as an adaptive interface. Some of the options available for adaptive interfaces include user selectable and definable options/choices, dynamic menus, which adapt to the user automatically, or moving the cursor to the next needed item rather than at the beginning of the menu. These options can be run at the user's desire and discretion, or made continuously running. The important issues involved in adaptive menus, or adaptive interfaces in general, include the user models, which support these kinds of systems, as well as the dialogue between the system and its users (Norcio & Stanley, 1989).

There is a debate concerning whether these kinds of adaptive menu interfaces are desirable. Those who support it cite the user's knowledge of the task, the need for different interfaces for different people, reduction in learning time, user satisfaction, and reducing mental workload. Opponents claim static interfaces are better, because the user prefers to learn and use one interaction style, makes skills portable across systems, reduces learning time due to a standardized arrangement, reduces cost of implementation, creates the feeling of a "loss of control," as well as results in the inability for a user to develop a model of the system due to constant changes (Norcio & Stanley, 1989; Mitchell & Shneiderman, 1989).

Adaptive interfaces, while simple to define, are not simple to build, as it requires a knowledge base, which consists of four types of domain knowledge. These follow those classifications suggested by Rissland (1984) and Croft (1984): knowledge of the user, knowledge of the interaction, knowledge of the task/domain, and knowledge of the system.

For instance, knowledge of the user is important for adaptive interfaces, especially in the creation of a "user model." A user model is "the description and knowledge of the user maintained by the system." The user model in an adaptive interface varies according to user, and is modified by the system if the user changes. What factors are important when designing a user model for an adaptive system? Potosnak (1984) suggests that they might be computer experience, computer knowledge, and program-specific knowledge. The differentiation between "novice" and "expert," based on levels of experience, is commonly used. Of course, even classifying users, using this system is difficult. How can novices and experts be differentiated? This might be the types of commands used, number of times on the system, times requesting help, or something else. A problem with the "novice-expert" set of user models is that when a user reaches the point where the system is directed to upgrade him or her to "expert" status, then the changes made can be disturbing to the user. Errors, declines in performance, and excessive help requests can all come about, when the system is changed to "expert mode." Instead, the process should be a continuous and gradual one (Norcio & Stanley, 1989; Maskery, 1984).

Aside from this, there are various other variables that can be considered. Some of these include differences in information processing skills, cognitive styles, interaction preferences and styles, as well as spatial and verbal abilities. Yallow (1980) did some research in this area and found the amount of retention of material was based upon the individuals' low/high spatial ability, and the format of the information provided (verbal vs. graphic). If the abilities of users are known, then it is easier to create specific modules, either to remedy or to maximize the individual abilities involved. Another example concerns the use of windowing in an adaptive system. Since people differ in their attention capabilities, and windowing allows for multiple windows of information, tasks, and programs at the same time, it seems appropriate that different windowing layouts would be required to assure that all information displayed is received (Robertson, 1985). The user's mental model of the system is also important (Norcio & Stanley, 1989).

Knowledge of the interaction and dialogue is also important, especially if natural language is used. A knowledge of the domain and task is also important, and the creation of models for the task, goals, and plans (Norcio & Stanley, 1989).

An experiment with a dynamic menu that changed its structure to place the most frequently used commands always at the top was tested against a static menu system. The results showed that users tended to learn the structure of a menu system rather quickly, and that the changes in order were disturbing. The dynamic menus slowed down novice users and, even after practice, dynamic menus did not bring about improved performance over the static arrangement.

The overall reaction to the dynamic menu was negative; however, giving users more control (change order, not change order, amount of order changed) over the changes might have improved satisfaction. In general, the results showed dynamic menus, although a good idea, may not be as effective as originally thought, although no definite conclusions can yet be drawn at this point (Mitchell & Shneiderman, 1989).

Despite the negative findings presented in the previous research, Norman and Chin (1989) call for further work into the creation of self-adapting menus, which create the optimal arrangement of the menu, based on what the user has selected before frequently, described by Berke and Vidal (1987), as the Most Frequent Use (MFU) metric. While this claims to close the gap between the designer's and the user's conceptions of the system, poorly designed adaptive menus can cause confusion, due to the changes in the arrangements of the menu items. User-adaptable menus (Chin, 1988) allow the use to change and arrange the existing menu structure (or names of the options), to make it more personalized and fit his or her interaction style more effectively. Hypercard pulldown tearoff menus are examples of this (Norman & Chin, 1989).

Possible functionality of the experimental software might be a kind of "pre-use questionnaire" which queries the user on his/her background and preferences, and then presents (and sets up) a suggested "customized" interface and help system for that user. Users could be tested in various ways: being forced to use this interface, and/or have the choice to choose the type of interface and help system he/she wants to use by making choices from the check boxes/radio buttons on the screen. The results obtained from the use of this "adaptive" form of screen would be interesting, and would extend the work which has been previous done in terms of adaptive interfaces.

Another option might be to have a longer experiment (perhaps a kind of repeated measures design) which asks novice users to start with a novice interface and help system, and then have him/her repeat the task again using an experienced interface, with the expectation that the second time around he/she would be more familiar with the system and task.

Survey Experts and Markup Languages for Surveys. One area, which can be examined in more detail, given a subject pool of marketing research professionals, survey designers, and other related experienced staff, would be to participate in an experiment such as this, to see if there are any significant impacts or effects for survey experts.

Experimental Testing of Other, New Internet/Web Languages. There are many other kinds of new languages, which are being introduced, especially for the Internet and Web development. In particular, while the results of this study can be generalized to all forms of markup languages, it would be interesting and instructive to see what results would come about in studying languages for Internet scripting, such as JavaScript, VBscript, or Perl. It would be interesting to examine user interaction in terms of learning, satisfaction, and performance, using languages such as these. The continually advancing developments in the area of markup languages, including DHTML, VRML, HTML 4, and XML ensures there will be many opportunities for further research in the area of markup command languages.

REFERENCES

Alreck, P.A., & Settle, R.B. (1995). *The Survey Research Handbook.* Homewood, IL: Irwin.

Association of American Publishers, Electronic Manuscript Project, Reference Manual on Electronic Manuscript Preparation and Markup, 1992.

Barnard, P.J., & Hammond, N.V. (1981). Consistency and Compatibility in Human-Computer Dialogue. *International Journal Man-Machine Systems,* 15, 87-134.

Benbunan, R. (1997). *Effects Of Computer-Mediated Communication Systems On Learning, Performance and Satisfaction: A Comparison of Groups and Individuals Solving Ethical Scenarios.* Ph.D. Dissertation, Rutgers University.

Blake, M. (1989, December). Archiving of Electronic Documents. *The Electronic Library*, 7, (6), 376-385.

Brown, C.M. (1986). *Human-Computer Interface Design Guidelines.* Norwood, NJ: Ablex.

Brown, J.W. (1982, July). Controlling the Complexity of Menu Networks. *Communications of the ACM*, 25(7), 412-418.

Busch, D. (1998). *Cascading Style Sheet Complete.* New York: McGraw-Hill.

Carroll, J.M., & Carrithers, C. (1984). Training Wheels in a User Interface. *Communications of the ACM*, 27(8), 800-806.

Carroll, J.M., & Thomas, J.C. (1982, March/April). Metaphor and the Cognitive Representation of Computing Systems. *IEEE Transactions on Systems, Man, and Cybernetics*, 12(2), 107-115.

Coombs, J.H., Remear, A.H. & Rose, S. J. (1987). Markup Systems and the Future of Scholarly Text Processing. *Communications of the ACM*, 30(11), 933-947.

Croft, W.B. (1984). The Role of Context and Adaptation in User Interfaces. *International Journal Man-Machine Studies*, 21, 283-292.

Cronk, R. D. (1993, September). Unlocking Data's Content. *BYTE*, 18(10), 111-120.

Darnell, R. (1997). *HTML 4 Unleashed.* Indianapolis, IN: Sams.

Doane, S.M., Pellegrino, J., & Klatsky, R. (1990). Expertise in a Computer Operating System. *Human-Computer Interaction*, 5, 267-304.

Doughty, R.K., & Kelso, J. (1984). An Evaluation of Menu Width and Depth on User Performance. Unpublished Paper. Washington DC: George Washington University.

Dray, S.M., Ogden, W.G., & Vestwig, R.E. (1981, October). Measuring Performance with a Menu-Selection Human-Computer Interface. *Proceedings of the 25th Annual Meeting of the Human Factors Society*, (pp. 746-748).

Dufner, D. (1995). *The Effects of Group Support (Listing and Voting Tools) and Sequential Procedures on Group Decision Making, Using Asynchronous Computer Conferences.* Doctoral Dissertation, Graduate School of Management, Rutgers University, Newark, 1995.

Fjermestad, J. (1994). *Group Strategic Decision Making in a Computer-Mediated Communications Environment: A Comparison of Dialectical Inquiry and Constructive Consensus Approaches.* Doctoral Dissertation, Rutgers University, Newark.

Goldfarb, C. (1991). *The SGML Handbook*. New York: Oxford University Press.

Green T.R., & Payne, S. (1984). Organization and Learnability in Computer Languages. *Int'l Journal Man-Machine Studies*, 21, 7-18.

Green, T.R.G. (1979). The Necessity of Syntax Markers. *Journal of Verbal Learning and Verbal Behavior*, 18, 481-496.

Holzner, S. (1997). *Xml Complete.* New York: McGraw-Hill.

Hsu, J., & Turoff, M. (1996). A Markup Approach to Surveys and Questionnaires. *Journal of End User Computing*, 8(4), 20-27.

Kiger, J.I. (1984). The Depth/Breadth Tradeoff in the Design of Menu-Driven User Interfaces. *Int'l Journal Man-Machine Studies*, 20, 201-213.

Landauer, T.K., & Nachbar, D.W. (1985, April). Selection from Alphabetic and Numeric Trees Using a Touch Screen: Breadth, Depth, and Width. *Proceedings Human Factors in Computing Systems*, (pp. 73-78) New York: ACM SIGCHI.

Ledgard, H., et al. (1980). The Natural Language of Interactive Systems. *Communications of the ACM*, 23, 556-563.

Leventhal, M., & Lewis, D. (1998). *Designing Xml Internet Applications (Charles F. Goldfarb Series).* Upper Saddle River, NJ: Prentice Hall.

Lie, H.W., & Bos, B. (1997). *Cascading Style Sheets: Designing for the Web.* Reading, MA: Addison Wesley.

Light, R., & Bray, T. (1997). *Presenting Xml.* Indianapolis, IN: Sams.

Mace, S., Flohr, U., Dobson, R., & Graham, T. (1998, March). Weaving a Better Web. *BYTE*, 23(3), 58-68.

Macleod, I. (1990). Storage and Retrieval of Structured Documents. *Information Processing and Management*, 26(2), 197-208.

Mantei, M. (1982). Disorientation Behavior in Person-Computer Behavior. Dissertation, University of Southern California.

Martin, M.P., & Fuerst, W. (1987). Using Computer Knowledge in the Design of Interactive systems. *International Journal Man-Machine Systems*, 25, 515-528.

Miller, D.P. (1981). The Depth/Breadth Tradeoff in Hierarchical Computer Menus. *Proceedings Human Factors Society.*

Mullen, R. (1989). *The Html 4 Programmer's Reference.* RTP: Ventana.

Norcio, A.F., & Stanley, J. (1989, March, April). Adaptive Human-Computer Interfaces: A Literature Review and Survey. *IEEE Transactions on Systems, Man, and Cybernetics*, 19(2), 399-408.

Norman, D. (1986). Cognitive Engineering. In D.L. Norman & S.W. Draper (Eds.), *User-Centered System Design* (pp. 31-61). Hillsdale NJ: Lawrence Erlbaum.

Norman, K.L., & Chin, J.P. (1989). The Menu Metaphor: Food for Thought. *Behavior and Information Technology*, 8(2), 125-134.

Ocker, R. (1995). *Requirements Definition Using a Distributed Asynchronous Group Support System: Experimental Results on Quality, Creativity and Satisfaction.* Dissertation, Rutgers University.

Ogden, W.C., & Boyle, J.M. (1982). Evaluating Human-Computer Dialog Styles: Command Versus Form Fill-In for Report Modification. *Proceedings Human Factors Society, 26th Annual Meeting*, (pp. 542-545) Santa Monica, CA.

Pakin, S.E., &. Wray, P, (1982, July). Designing Screens for People to Use Easily. *Data Management*, 36-41.

Pardi, W.J., & Schurman, E.M. (1998). *Dynamic HTML in Action.* Redmond: Microsoft Press.

Payne, S.J., & Green, T. (1989). The Structure of Command Languages. *International Journal Man-Machine Studies*, 30, 213-234.

Potosnak, K.M. (1984). Choice of Interface Modes by Empirical Grouping of Computer Users. *Proceedings IFIPS*, (pp. 27-32).

Powers, S. (1998). *Dynamic HTML.* Foster City, CA: IDG.

Rissland, E.L. (1984). Ingredients of Intelligent User Interfaces. *International Journal Man-Machine Systems*, 21, 377-388.

Roberts, T.L. (1980). Evaluation of Computer Text Editors. Dissertation, Stanford University.

Robertson, I.T. (1985). Human-Information Processing Strategies and Style. *Behavior and Information Technology*, 4(1), 19-29.

Scholtz, J. & Wiedenbeck, S. (1993). Using Unfamiliar Programming Languages: The Effects on Expertise. *Interacting with Computers*, 5(1), 13-30.

Sein, M.K., & Bostrom, R.P. (1989). Individual Differences and Conceptual Models in Training Novice Users. *Human Computer Interaction*, 4, 197-229.

Shneiderman, B. (1987). *Designing the User Interface.* Reading, MA: Addison Wesley.

Shneiderman, B. (1992). *Designing the User Interface 2/E.* Reading, MA: Addison Wesley.

Shneiderman, B. (1997). *Designing the User Interface 3/E.* Reading, MA: Addison Wesley.

Simpson, H.K., &. Pellegrino, J.W. (1993). Descriptive Models in Learning Command Language. *Journal of Educational Psychology*, 85(3), 539-550.

St. Laurent, S. (1997). *Dynamic HTML: A prime.* Foster City, CA: IDG.

St. Laurent, S. (1997). *XML: A primer*. Foster City, CA: IDG.

Trumbly, J.E. (1988). *An Investigation of User Performance Enhancement for Computer Based Management Information Systems Using an Adaptive User Interface.* DBA Thesis, Mississippi State University.

Tuck, B. (1989). Desktop Publishing: What It Is and What It Can Do For You. *ASLIB Proceedings*, 41(1).

Tversky, A. (1977). Features of Similarity. *Psychological Review*, 84, 327-352.

Wright, H. (1992, June). SGML Frees Information. *BYTE*, 263-268.

Yallow, E. (1980). Individual Differences in Learning from Verbal and Figural Materials. ARPT Rep. 13, School of Education, Stanford University, Palo Alto, CA.

Chapter VII

Development of a Task Model for the Analysis and Retrieval of Statistical Data

Peter N. Hyland
University of Wollongong, Australia

ABSTRACT

This chapter explores the task of retrieving and analysing statistical data from external sources, such as national statistical agencies, government departments, the World Bank, etc. Although external statistical data (ESD) is widely used in planning, decision-making and project evaluation, the process of gathering and analysing such data is poorly understood. This chapter describes the usability testing of a prototype Statistical Information System (SIS) and uses the data gathered during that testing to develop an initial task model for retrieving and analysing ESD. The proposed task model would be useful in the development of improved Statistical Information Systems, particularly those intended for use by casual or ad hoc users.

INTRODUCTION

Every year, public and private sector organisations spend millions of dollars, gathering and publishing statistical data intended for use by people outside of those organizations. From the point of view of these outside users, the data is external statistical data (ESD), because it is provided by an external source over which end users have little or no control. Typical sources of ESD include international agencies, such as the United Nations, national statistical agencies, such as the Australian Bureau of Statistics, both state and national government departments and many businesses, particularly financial institutions.

ESD is made available to users outside of the organization in which the data originates because it is considered to be of interest to a wider group of users, such as researchers, students, business analysts or members of the community at large. These users include both experienced users of ESD, such as professional business analysts, and casual users, such as business managers, executives, researchers and members of the wider community who may only use ESD infrequently. Little research has been done about these types of users of ESD, but studies suggest there are many casual users of ESD in the community (Hyland & Hasan, 1997).

Casual users face a number of distinctive problems in their use of ESD, partly due to their lack of familiarity with the task of retrieving and analysing ESD and partly because the tools provided for retrieving and analysing ESD are more suited to the needs of more experienced users. To begin with, much of the ESD in use has traditionally been provided in print form. This may be problematic for many users because printed tables or charts may not contain all the variables that a user requires or they may contain some or all of the variables at an inappropriate level of aggregation, i.e., in too much or too little detail. When using printed summaries, the user cannot combine variables from different tables or charts and any aggregation of data must be done manually. Because the raw data is not available in printed summaries, it is impossible to disaggregate data, i.e., calculate values for lower levels of aggregation. All of these are significant problems for users of ESD in print form.

It is our contention the problems being experienced by casual users of ESD are due to a lack of understanding of the tasks performed by ESD users and a consequent lack of appropriate tools to support those tasks. Research into the use of ESD is particularly pressing in light of some emergent social and technological trends, such as:

- The increasing availability of statistical data, particularly via the World Wide Web.
- The increasing competence of casual users of statistical data and the consequent increase in the complexity of tasks that they may wish to perform.
- The ongoing development of new technologies to improve access to statistical data.

In an attempt to understand the tasks carried out by casual users of ESD, a computer prototype has been developed to address many of the problems experienced by casual users of ESD. The *Abacus* prototype has been tested with a number of typical casual users and that testing has given rise to an initial model of the task of retrieving and analysing ESD.

BACKGROUND

The study in this chapter concerns the *task* of retrieving and analysing ESD by casual users of *Statistical Information Systems* (SIS). Both these key concepts will now be described.

Statistical Information Systems (SIS)

The term SIS is not widely used in the literature and systems described as SIS often differ quite significantly from one another. Malmborg and Sundgren (1994) provide a description that is consistent with the general usage, namely: an SIS is an information system that takes statistical data as its inputs and produces statistical information as its outputs. The tasks associated with SIS are to locate, organize and present statistical data in ways that are meaningful to users. This description is consistent with that found in the literature (Gassler, Frohlich & Kopcsa, 1996; Rogers, 1987).

The term SIS has not been widely used in the literature because the similarities that exist between SIS were often overshadowed by the differences that exist between the functionality and technologies found in different types of SIS. A Geographical Information System (GIS), for example, presents the results of statistical calculations on a map of a geographical region. Such a GIS takes statistical data as its inputs and produces statistical information as its outputs and, hence, satisfies the definition of an SIS. Similarly, software like SAS, Minitab or JMP can be shown to meet the definition of an SIS but are usually described as "statistics packages" or "statistical software." Finally, statistical databases could also be described, quite appropriately, as SIS but this is seldom, if ever, the case. Despite these differences, all of these types of systems do share the defining characteristics of SIS. Two more recent technologies that have been used to disseminate ESD are Online Analytical Processing (OAP) and the World Wide Web (Web). It is these two technologies that were integrated to produce the *Abacus* prototype. Both of these will be described in more detail.

Online Analytical Processing (OLAP)

Thomsen (1997, p. xvii) describes OLAP as *"the process of creating and managing multi-dimensional enterprise data for analysis* and *viewing by the user* who seeks *an understanding of what the data is really saying*." Three aspects of Thomsen's description need further explanation. First, Thomsen says OLAP systems **create and manage** multi-dimensional data because, typically, OLAP systems generate either a permanent or temporary multi-dimensional database from original source data. Second, he notes that OLAP systems do more than simply allow the user to view that multi-dimensional data set, they allow the user to **analyse** it. They do this by allowing the user to select the dimensions that will be involved, the level of aggregation of each of the dimensions and the members of dimensions to be included in their custom view of the data. Finally, Thomsen says that OLAP allows the user to see **what the data is really saying**. By this, he means that OLAP allows the user to bring together disparate sets of data, to detect trends in that data and to explore the underlying causes of those trends by drilling down into the data.

The main features associated with OLAP in the literature include:

- Providing a simple means of analysing multi-dimensional data, which is usually historical data drawn from a number of sources.
- Supporting complex analysis such as calculations and modelling applied across dimensions, through hierarchies and/or across members.
- Carrying out analyses in an interactive setting and with a response time of five to 20 seconds.

Providing several common functions including being able to:

- Add or remove entire dimensions from an analysis of a population (rotation).
- Aggregate (roll up) or disaggregate (drill down) data for any dimension having a hierarchical structure.
- Filter particular members of a dimension out of an analysis.
- View a sub-population of the data (slicing) (Thomsen, 1997; Pendse, 1999).

An initial set of requirements for the manipulation of ESD, by casual users of ESD, was gathered via pilot studies conducted by Hyland and Hasan (1997). The functions provided by OLAP appear to match these requirements very closely. For this reason, OLAP would seem to be a useful technology to incorporate in a system for casual users of ESD.

World Wide Web and the Internet

One problem associated with the retrieval and analysis of ESD is the difficulty in getting access to sources of data in electronic form. This problem has been significantly addressed in recent years by the use of the Internet and the Web. The Web has been described as a global information service that is available on almost all hardware platforms and which subsumes virtually all the previous Internet tools (Ford, 1995). The Web provides a common interface to virtually the entire Internet and in which the technological aspects of navigating the network are virtually invisible to the user. From a user's perspective, the Web provides a method for moving from one resource to another by simply clicking on a link.

There are a growing number of references in the literature to the use of the Web and the Internet by ESD providers. The growing use of the Web by community organizations and local councils (Latamore, 1996; McQueen, 1996; Zorn, 1996) would strongly support the idea that the Web could play an important part in the provision of ESD to the community at large. In regard to the casual users of ESD, the Web provides an excellent means of accessing the data because the hypertext interface is straightforward and unintimidating (Ford, 1995).

The *Tasks* Carried Out by Users of ESD

The literature does not appear to provide any model of the task of using ESD. This is not surprising and supports the proposition that many of the problems encountered by users of ESD stem from the lack of adequate models of the tasks users perform. Malmborg and Sundgren (1994) imply an initial set of sub-tasks in their definition of an SIS, namely, to locate, organise and present statistical data in ways that are meaningful to users.

Task models do exist for **related** tasks, such as information gathering for managerial decision-making (Goodhue, 1998) and these models may serve as a useful starting point for a task model for the use of ESD. There is a close parallel between the three sub-tasks suggested by Goodhue and those suggested by Malmborg and Sundgren. Goodhue (1998) posits that the task of decision-making consists of three sub-tasks and suggests some of the factors that may affect the success of these three sub-tasks. These are summarized below:

1. Identification of the data needed:
   - Identification of the dimensions, structure and level of detail required.
   - Selection of a source or sources from which the data can be acquired.
2. Acquisition of data:
   - Query formulation, selection of useful data, paring of unwanted data.
3. Interpretation of that data:
   - Assessment of the currency, credibility and compatibility of the acquired data.

The models suggested by Goodhue and by Malmborg and Sundgren are shown in Figure 1.

Figure 1: Comparison of Goodhue's Model and a Proposed Model for ESD Use

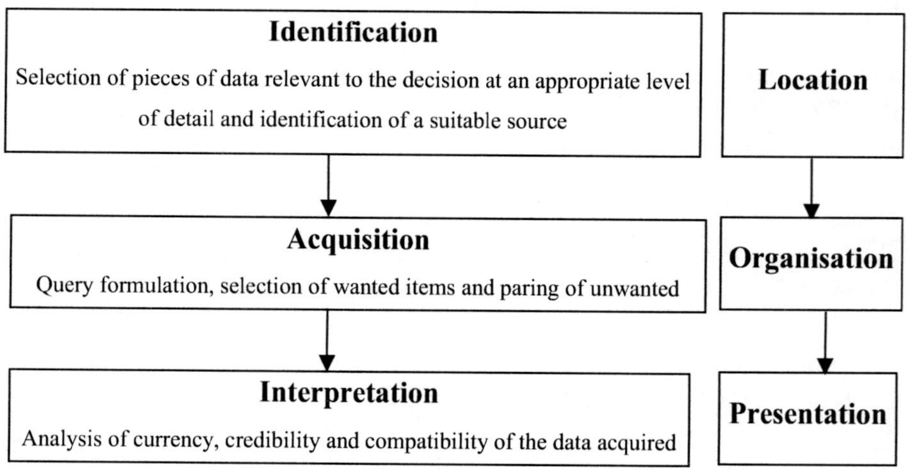

Figure 1 shows a possible relationship between these sub-tasks and the sub-tasks suggested for ESD use by Malmborg and Sundgren (1994). The use of ESD is frequently associated with decision-making, which accounts for the similarity between the proposed model of ESD use and Goodhue's model of information gathering to support managerial decision making.

At this stage, it is unclear exactly what is involved in the three subtasks proposed by Malmborg and Sundgren (1994). However, the availability of the *Abacus* prototype provides an excellent opportunity to observe typical users of ESD carrying out the task of manipulating ESD and so add further detail to the skeleton model proposed in Figure 1. The results of user observation and the resultant model of the task are discussed later in the chapter.

UNDERSTANDING HOW *ABACUS* WORKS

To understand the strategies used by participants, it is necessary to understand how *Abacus* works. The data used in *Abacus* was a one percent sample of the 1991 census of Australia, and included data about dwellings, families and people. The data was quite complex, having over 50 variables and up to 160,000 records. For each of the primary entities, there were three separate data sets, e.g., People A, People B and People C. Although these data sets described the same population, the population in each set was described in terms of different variables, e.g., People B used the variables occupation and location while People C used the variables sex and age. *Abacus* provided two distinct modes of interaction – *Value Mode* and *Table Mode*.

Value Mode

When users enter *Value Mode*, a highly directed dialogue takes them through the steps of finding a single value. The screen displays a row of navigation buttons, a single button, labeled "Define a Rule," and a default table showing the total number in the population for the chosen data set. The table contains the time dimension as the column and the measure dimension as the row. When the user selects the "Define a Rule" button, *Abacus* provides a list of available dimensions and asks the user to select the dimension to which the rule will be applied. *Abacus* then presents the list of members for that dimension and asks the user to select one. Once the member has been selected, a rule of the following form is displayed:

The value "member name" will be included for the variable "dimension name."

For example, a rule about People might be: The value '40 to 64' is included for the variable 'Age,' as shown in the centre of Figure 2.

Once a rule is defined, new buttons are displayed on the screen. Two of the new buttons can be seen below the rule in Figure 2. These allow the user to change the sense of the rule, from include to exclude, or to apply the rule. A third button, located above the rule display, allows the user to cancel the current rule before it is applied.

Figure 2: A Screen from Value Mode Showing the Process of Defining a Rule

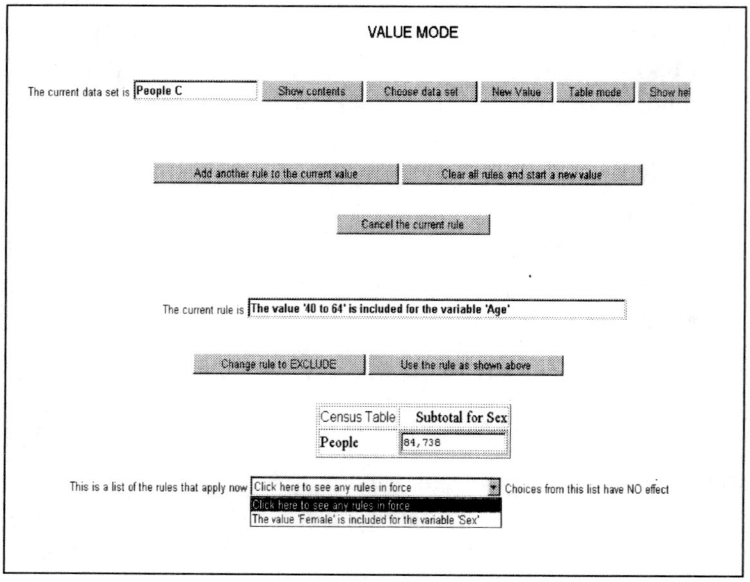

Once a rule is applied, the selected member is filtered from the value being displayed in a one-celled table. Filtering is done either positively or negatively, depending on the choice of "Include" or "Exclude," reflected in the wording of the rule. The user can apply additional rules until the desired sub-set of the population has been fully described, e.g., all females between the ages of 40 and 64 who speak Greek. A drop down list shown at the bottom of Figure 2 shows the rules that are currently in force. The table in Figure 2 has a column heading of "Subtotal for Sex," showing the rules currently in force are related to the sex dimension. If additional dimensions were constrained, additional column headings would indicate which dimensions had been constrained. If, for example, the user applied the rule displayed in Figure 2, the heading "Subtotal for Age" would appear above the heading "Subtotal for Sex," indicating that two dimensions had been constrained. The total displayed would then be the population of females between 40 and 65.

Table Mode

In contrast to *Value Mode*, *Table Mode* provides an extensive range of OLAP functions in an undirected manner, i.e., users can choose to use any function whenever they want, (with some minor restrictions). As with *Value Mode*, the user is presented with a single-celled table showing the total for the population in the chosen data set. The user can then add new dimensions (variables) to the table and, once added, the user can drill down or roll up the variables by clicking on the heading in the table itself. A typical screen from *Table Mode* is shown in Figure 3.

Figure 3: A Screen Showing Table Mode

TABLE MODE

The current data set is People C | Show contents | Choose data set | New Table | Value mode | Show help

Add new variable | Move out | Hide slicer | Change to the other axis | Print display

Remove variable | Move in | Define a rule | Swap a row and column | Chart or Table

All English proficiency | All indigenous and non-indigenous | All personal incomes | All marital status | People | Use this choice

Census Table		Both sexes	Male	Female
1991 - 1991	All ages	168,540	83,802	84,738
	Up to 5	12,787	6,561	6,226
	5 to 12	19,933	10,354	9,579
	13 to 18	15,518	7,939	7,579
	19 to 24	16,105	8,169	7,936
	25 to 39	40,286	19,930	20,356
	40 to 64	45,021	22,755	22,266
	65 and over	18,890	8,094	10,796

The user can also define a rule (as in *Value Mode*) and have this applied as a filter to the data in the table. The user can also define slices for any dimension not in the table and move dimensions from one axis to the other. In the case of multi-level tables, the user can move a dimension to a lower or higher level on its present axis. For example, if a table had both sex and age on the column axis, with column being the outer heading and age the inner heading, the system allows the user to move sex to the outer heading and age to the inner heading. The buttons in the upper row are navigation functions while the central block of buttons provides the OLAP functions. The first two buttons on the left of the OLAP block let the user add or remove a dimension from the table, as either a row or column. The next two buttons let the user move a dimension inwards or outwards on multi- level tables. The lower of the next two buttons starts the same "Define a Rule" process used in *Value Mode* while the upper one hides or shows the slicer — the slicer is visible in Figure 3, as a set of drop down lists below the OLAP buttons. The next two buttons control processes for moving dimensions from one axis to the other, e.g., moving a row to a column.

Figure 3 shows a two-way table by age and sex. Both the age and sex dimensions have been disaggregated one level (drilled down). Row headings for age, such as "Up to 5" and "5 to 12," are bold-faced and underlined, indicating they can be disaggregated further, while "Male" and "Female" are shown in plain text to indicate that they cannot be drilled down any further. The headings "Both Sexes" and "All Ages" are shown in bold-faced, underlined, italics, indicating that lower level members can be rolled up into these aggregate values.

TESTING OF THE *ABACUS* PROTOTYPE

Thirty-six academics, university students and local government employees who were known to be users of ESD, took part in the study. Of these, five were deemed to be experts with ESD and, although the study was concerned with casual users of ESD, the experts were included in the usability testing for the purposes of comparison with the casual users. A sample of 36 participants is comparable to those in studies described by Nielsen and Levy (1994).

The Usability Testing Procedure

Usability tests were conducted with one volunteer at a time under identical conditions. After a scripted introduction, all participants were given the same three sets of printed material:

- A set of training activities to be carried out using the prototype.
- A set of typical tasks to be carried out using the prototype.
- An evaluation sheet.

Each participant's interactions with the prototype were video recorded.

It was necessary to familiarize the participants with the prototype prior to their carrying out a set of representative tasks. To minimize both variability and bias in the training regime, it was decided neither to instruct participants verbally nor to allow them to experiment, at length, with the prototype. Instead, all participants were given the same set of written instructions to follow in a hands-on training session with the prototype.

One of the objectives of the usability testing was to learn whether participants could apply different OLAP functions to complete tasks. For this reason, the training materials did not present participants with one or two simple strategies that could be used to complete all the tasks. Such a training approach would only allow us to determine whether participants could select the appropriate strategy for a particular type of task. Instead, the training materials only showed the participants how to select a database and how to use the various OLAP functions, not how to combine these functions to complete tasks. Thus, the development of strategies was left to the participants.

A set of 18 tasks was developed and organized as follows:

- Seven tasks in *Table Mode.*
- Seven tasks in *Value Mode.*
- Four *Mixed Tasks* — tasks for which the participant could select either mode.

A typical task would be to "find the number of single people in NSW who earn over $80,000."

The *Mixed Tasks* were intended to test whether: (a) participants had a preference for one mode of interaction over another and (b) whether participants could distinguish between tasks that were more suited to one mode than another. Consequently, *Mixed Tasks* were always done last, to ensure participants were already familiar with both *Table Mode* and *Value Mode*.

The tasks in both *Value* and *Table Mode* were organized as follows. The first two tasks required the participant to define only single rules or create only a simple, two-way table. These were followed by four progressively more difficult tasks. In *Value Mode*, the number of rules required for each task was increased and two tasks required the use of negative rules – where a member was excluded from the population. In *Table Mode*, the number of dimensions required for each task was progressively increased. In both modes, tasks were presented in such a way that more advanced OLAP functions provided a faster method of moving from one task to the next. For example, participants could go from one *Table Mode* task to another by simply removing a dimension rather than by starting a new table and adding all but one of the dimensions used in the previous task.

In the first six tasks, in both *Table* and *Value Modes,* participants were told which data set to use. However, the seventh task in both modes did not provide participants with the name of the required data set. Instead, the task gave a list of dimensions that would be required to complete the task. This meant participants needed to locate an appropriate data set.

Mixed Tasks were structured so that the first and third tasks were more easily accomplished in *Value Mode,* while the second and fourth tasks were more easily accomplished in *Table Mode*. This was achieved by requiring the participant to locate only one value in the first and third *Mixed Tasks*, but to locate two and three values in the second and fourth *Mixed Tasks*. This organization of tasks gave participants the opportunity to select a mode either on the basis of personal preference or because of perceived efficacy.

RECORDING AND ANALYSIS OF THE RESULTS

A significant amount of data was gathered during the usability testing, but most of it is not relevant to the current study and has been reported elsewhere. The data pertinent to the current study were the various strategies used by participants to complete each task.

Strategies Used

A strategy was defined as a sequence of actions that a participant used to produce an answer to task. This definition has three implications:

- Sequences of actions that only accomplished **part** of a task are not regarded as strategies.

- A sequence of actions that produced an answer is a strategy, even if the answer was wrong.
- Actions carried out in error or recovering from an error were part of a strategy.

Some participants carried out tasks in more than one way, i.e., using more than one strategy. In many cases, a participant would employ some strategy, realize the weakness of the strategy and develop another more successful strategy that resulted in the participant recording an answer. It was decided to record only that strategy which actually gave rise to the participant's answer. This became more of an issue when some participants returned to a task at a later stage, used a different strategy to the original one and altered their original answer. The definition of a strategy was modified to include only that set of actions that led to the participant recording his or her **final** answer. This definition was found to be quite effective and resolved most ambiguities.

MODELLING THE TASK OF RETRIEVING AND ANALYSING ESD

Based on the pilot studies, conducted by Hyland and Hasan (1997) and by Hyland and Gould (1998) and on the results of usability testing in the current study, a more complete, empirical model for the task of ESD use by casual users can be offered and is shown in Figure 4.

The model, shown in Figure 4, does not attempt to describe the use of ESD by experts or how ESD might be manipulated by the entire range of available SIS, e.g., spreadsheets, statistical packages, GIS. Instead, it attempts to model the type of analysis and retrieval tasks that might be carried out by casual users using the less complex functions available in some SIS, including OLAP, obviously.

The model concerns the task of retrieving and analysing ESD, regardless of the type of SIS used to do so. Because of this, the terms used to describe OLAP systems (e.g., dimensions, members) are no longer appropriate. Instead, the model uses the terms "variables" and "values" to describe the same concepts. These terms are used in the statistics literature and in some of the more popular statistical packages. They might not be recognized in statistical database or GIS circles but the usage is reasonably common. The *Abacus* prototype used the terms "variables" and "values" rather than "dimensions" and "members" for the same reasons.

The location sub-task in the proposed task model involves not only finding one or more sets of ESD but also judging the suitability of those sets of data. In a real life situation, a user may have to decide whether a particular source of ESD is reliable, whether the data is sufficiently current and whether the values in the data are likely to satisfy the user's information needs. In the model proposed by Goodhue (1998), these decisions are dealt with in a separate sub-task at the end of the process. When

Figure 4: A Proposed Model for ESD Use Based on Goodhue's Model (1998)

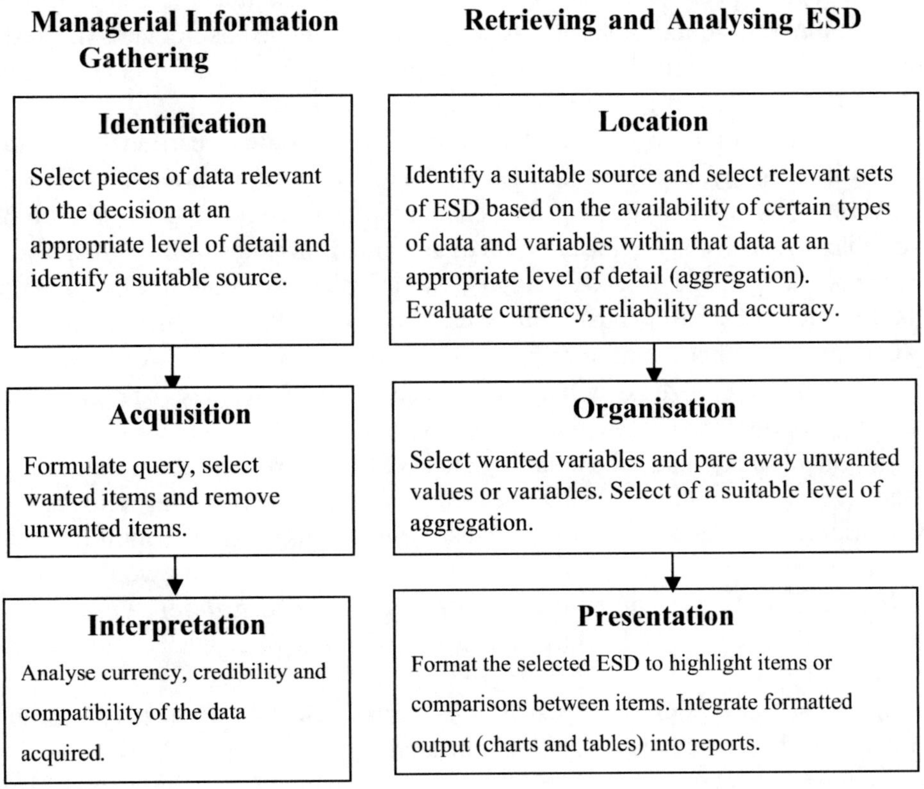

Managerial Information Gathering	**Retrieving and Analysing ESD**
Identification Select pieces of data relevant to the decision at an appropriate level of detail and identify a suitable source.	**Location** Identify a suitable source and select relevant sets of ESD based on the availability of certain types of data and variables within that data at an appropriate level of detail (aggregation). Evaluate currency, reliability and accuracy.
↓	↓
Acquisition Formulate query, select wanted items and remove unwanted items.	**Organisation** Select wanted variables and pare away unwanted values or variables. Select of a suitable level of aggregation.
↓	↓
Interpretation Analyse currency, credibility and compatibility of the data acquired.	**Presentation** Format the selected ESD to highlight items or comparisons between items. Integrate formatted output (charts and tables) into reports.

dealing with ESD, it does not appear that this is a suitable location for these decisions to be made. The organization sub-task is a complex one and it would seem to be foolhardy to spend time and effort organizing ESD that was not sufficiently current or reliable for one's information needs. Consequently, the decision about the suitability of ESD would be better made prior to the Organization sub-task. In practice, however, it is possible that some or all of the sub-tasks will overlap, as originally suggested by Goodhue. It is quite probable these judgemental sub-tasks would also be carried out following the organisation sub-task, as well.

In addition to these considerations, the location sub-task addresses the issue of finding a set of data that contains the required variables and values of those variables, i.e., a user would have to ascertain if a data set contained all of the variables that he or she required and if so, whether the necessary values for each those variables were available. In some SIS, it might be possible to calculate new variables or to calculate new values or group certain values together. If this were the case, then a data set that did not appear to have the required variables or values might be modified to produce the required ones and thus satisfy the user's needs. The user would need to take this possibility into account when selecting the data to be used.

Because the user observation carried out in this study is concerned more with the mechanical aspects of the location sub-task rather than the judgmental aspects described above, little additional detail can be provided about those judgemental tasks at this time. The location sub-task will be described in more detail in a later section of the chapter.

The organization sub-task involves four steps that could be carried out serially or in parallel. Firstly, the user must identify the required variables and include only those variables in the display, i.e., table, chart, map. This could involve the addition of variables to the display or the removal of unwanted variables from the display. It may be necessary at this time to calculate new variables (e.g., combine two or more variables, etc.). The user must then assess the suitability of the default level of aggregation and either zoom in or zoom out on one or more values of the chosen variables. Once again, the user may need to calculate new values or group values together. The final step is the placement of variables and values in such a way as to highlight any features of the data that the user thinks are important. In the case of a table, for example, this might involve locating one or more variables as rows while other variables are placed as columns. In cases where this resulted in multiple rows or multiple columns, the placement of variables in that hierarchy would also be significant. These appear to be the major steps in the organization sub-task in a variety of SIS. These will be discussed in greater detail in three later sections of the chapter.

The presentation sub-task consists of two parts: selecting the display type and the display style. The display type might be a table, chart or map. The decision as to which type of display to use would depend on the amount of data, the level of detail that is necessary and the audience and purpose for which the display is intended. Charts and graphs may be more helpful in showing trends while tables provide more detail. Obviously maps are only appropriate where a geographical dimension is important. The display style would include decisions about fonts, colours, shading, cross-hatching and so on. These can be important factors in determining the usefulness of a display of ESD. Although the *Abacus* prototype supports both tables and charts (but not maps), the tasks completed in usability testing did not involve the use of different display types or the incorporation of such displays into reports or other documents. So, no further details about the presentation sub-task can be determined from the current study.

Details of the Location Sub-Task

One of the aims of user observation was to gather data about the manipulation of ESD by participants and so the tasks were designed so that participants could quickly locate the required data set and begin manipulating it. This was achieved, by telling participants which data set they required, for 16 of the 18 tasks, and simply having them select those data sets. Because the process of locating data sets was also of interest, two tasks were included in which participants needed to locate an appropriate data set. For these two tasks, participants were not told the name of the data set that they needed to use, only which dimensions would be required along with a passing reference to the type of data that would be needed, i.e., whether the data was about people, families or dwellings. The tasks had identical formats and were located at comparable positions in relation to the other tasks. One was the last task in *Value Mode* and required the Dwellings A data set, the other was the last task in *Table Mode* and required the People B data set.

While these two tasks provide an opportunity to study some aspects of the location sub-task, they are only concerned with the process of ensuring that required data exists in a set of ESD, not about the evaluation of the set of ESD, itself. Participants were certainly never required to make judgements about the currency, accuracy or reliability of the data they were using, as they may have to do in real life situations.

The times taken for each location task were recorded for all participants. The results were quite surprising. In the simpler of the two location tasks, participants only needed to look in the first of the sets of Dwelling data, i.e., Dwellings A, to locate the correct data set. Because the task was relatively simple, the minimum time taken to locate Dwellings A was only four seconds and 30 percent of participants completed the task in 10 seconds or less. Surprisingly, 33 percent of participants had great difficulty with the location process, taking a long time to complete the tasks and making many errors during the process. The maximum time taken to complete the first location task was 286 seconds. Even after removing the five longest times, 27 percent of the participants took between 30 and 90 seconds to complete the location task. The behaviour of participants was often quite illogical. For example, some participants ignored the reference to Dwellings in the task, and began by inspecting the People data sets. Other participants repeatedly inspected data sets Dwellings B and Dwellings C but did not inspect Dwellings A.

It should be remembered that the actions being described are only the simplest aspects of the entire location sub-task and only require the participant to confirm the presence of relevant dimensions. The location sub-task would normally require the participant to confirm the presence of appropriate members of those dimensions as well. For example, a user who wanted to know the number of plumbers in a region would not be satisfied with a data set containing an occupation dimension if the lowest levels of aggregation for occupation were tradesmen, managers and professionals. The process of locating a suitable data set would typically require the user to confirm the presence of a number of members for a number of dimensions. Given the difficulty in completing the simple location task in this study, it can be assumed that the more complex tasks of matching members as well as dimensions would be problematic for many users. Moreover, the location sub-task also involves more complex activities such as the evaluation of currency, accuracy and reliability of the data sets. When viewed in its entirety, it appears that this is an extremely complex process.

Based on the data gathered by means of user observation and reflection on the development of the prototype, a normative model of the location sub-task has been developed and is shown in Figure 5. Since the data gathered by means of user observation does not concern the evaluation parts of the location sub-task, the following model deals only with the mechanical aspects of the location sub-task. The terms "variables" and "values" have been used, as these terms are applicable in a variety SIS and would be more widely understood than the terms "dimensions" and "members," which are associated specifically with OLAP and MDDB.

The model provides a *recommended* set of steps for casual users to follow in the location sub-task. In practice, many users would probably vary this process, by

Figure 5: A Proposed Model for the Location Sub-Task

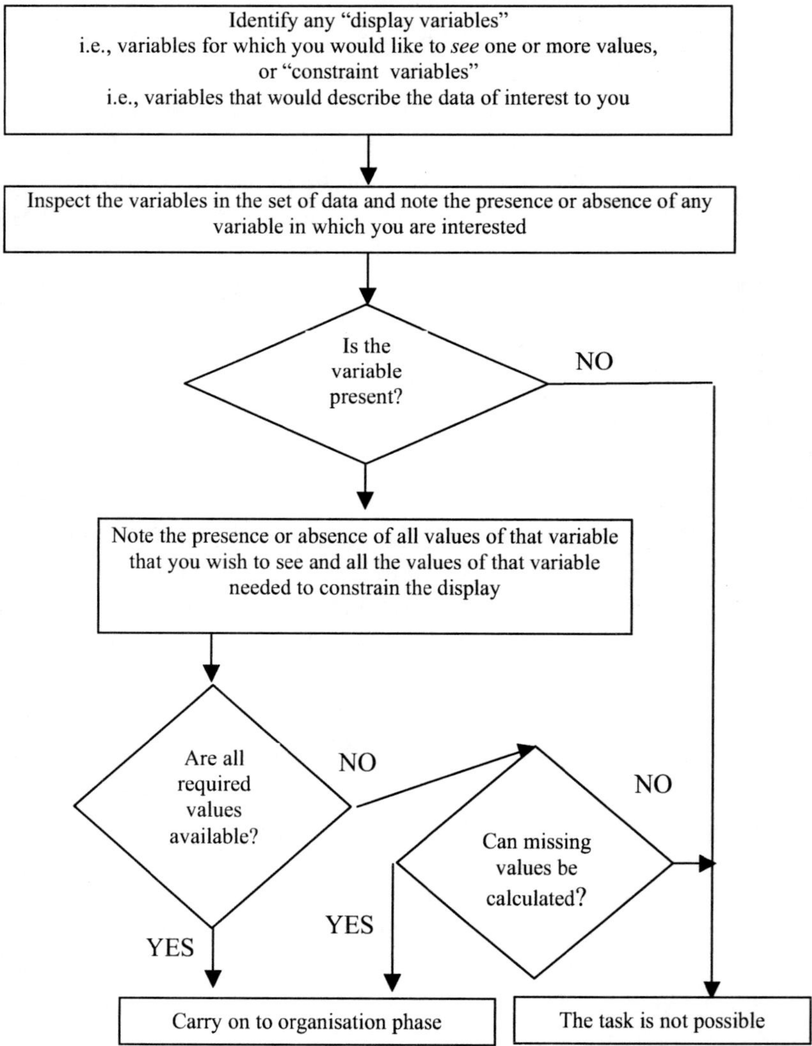

overlapping the location and organization sub-tasks. For example, as soon as a user had located a required dimension, he or she might add the dimension to a table or chart before locating other required dimensions. This is not as efficient as the model proposed above, which ensures that all required dimensions are available before adding any dimensions to the table or chart.

Strategies Used in the Organization Sub-Task

One of the objectives of usability testing was to find out how participants would use the various OLAP functions to complete tasks. Both the training materials and the tasks were deliberately designed to encourage participants to evolve strategies to complete their tasks. Participants did use a significant number of strategies to complete the tasks. Several of these were either unhelpful or idiosyncratic and will be omitted from further discussion.

Strategies Used in *Value Mode*

Because of the highly structured nature of *Value Mode*, only one real strategy was used. The process followed was:

- To clear any existing rules (in one of several ways).
- Then, repeatedly select Define a rule.
- Select a dimension to which the rule would apply.
- Select a member from that dimension.
- Either include or exclude that member from the total being displayed.

This approach was used at least once by all 31 casual participants. Because it was implicit in the organization of the interface, it was used extensively, a total of 265 times in all. Little can be learned from this strategy about the way users might carry out the organization sub-task because the strategy to be used is pre-determined by the interface itself. It can be said, however, the strategy used in *Value Mode* is one that users appear to understand and can adopt quite quickly. In itself, this is useful information.

Strategies Used in *Table Mode*

Only two fundamentally different strategies were observed in *Table Mode*. However, there were a number of interesting variations in the second of these strategies and also in the way participants moved from one task to the next. Each of these variations is indicative of the way the participants were able to employ the available OLAP functions.

In *Table Mode*, the first fundamental strategy was:

- To clear any existing table.
- Then, repeatedly apply slices, one for each dimension described in the task, until the required value is shown on the table.

This strategy does not result in a true table being formed and so participants who used this method were actually in violation of some of the instructions on their task sheets. This strategy was used at least once by ten participants (27.8 percent) and was used to complete a total of 47 tasks. This approach is very fast and many of the participants who used it completed the tasks very quickly as a result. Unfortunately, it is also quite limited in its applicability because it cannot be used when there are two conditions for a single dimension e.g. finding the total number of people who are either widowed or divorced. Despite its limitations, it is a very effective strategy and should be used wherever possible. However, users need to understand its limitations and the use of other strategies to overcome those limitations.

The second fundamental strategy in *Table Mode* was:

- To clear the existing table.
- Then, repeatedly add a dimension as a row or column.
- Zoom in to those dimensions to the required level of aggregation.

This strategy was used at least once by 32 of the participants (88.8 percent). In its simplest form, it was used 167 times. This approach often resulted in a very large table that participants found difficult to use. Faced with such large tables, participants often had to scroll repeatedly backwards and forwards through the table, keeping track of their position by putting their finger on the monitor screen. Despite this difficulty, many users never evolved any other strategy for controlling table size. There were, however, many variations on this method that did solve the problem of table size by combining this fundamental approach with other OLAP functions. These will be described in a moment.

This second *Table Mode* strategy is only effective for simple tables containing one row and one column. In many cases, users might only require such simple tables, in which case, this strategy will serve them well. Table size could still become a problem if one or both of the dimensions on the table had a large number of members. In such cases, or when dealing with more complex tables, one of the variants of this strategy would be far more efficient.

There were three successful variants of the second strategy in *Table Mode*:

1. Do Strategy 2, then, limit the size of the table by defining a rule.
2. Do Strategy 2, then, slice one or more variables not on the table.
3. Add one or more variables to a table then combine slicing, defining rules and zooming.

Having described the strategies and their variations, it is timely to make two comments. First, the majority of participants always used strategy two, without any variation when using *Table Mode*. In fact, the variations on this strategy were only used on about 25 percent (N = 46) of the occasions when it would have been appropriate. Nonetheless, participants did develop significantly complex strategies even during their first encounter with *Abacus*. Second, it must be remembered the training materials only showed participants how to use the OLAP functions, not how to combine them with one another. Consequently, the evolution of the initial strategy and these three variants on that strategy demonstrates that casual users can integrate OLAP functions to produce desired results.

A second set of variations was observed in the way participants moved from one task to another. When moving from one task to the next, most participants would clear the existing table. The generation of a new table at the start of a task may appeal to participants because it returns them to a stable point from which they can follow the same strategy every time. It also ensures that they do not have any residual settings in place from a previous task. However, the tasks themselves were organized in such a way that it was, at times, very inefficient to start a new table. Instead, it was preferable to use some of the OLAP functions to simplify the movement from one task to the next and preserve much of the current table.

The variations on this process included adding new dimensions to an existing table, removing an unwanted member from an existing table or slicing a new dimension rather than adding it to the table. These variations are not necessary to complete the tasks, only to reduce the time taken to complete all of the tasks. It might have been expected casual users would either lack the logical or organisational skills to use such complex variations or be too involved with getting the answers correct to concern themselves with such efficiencies. Judging from the number of such variations developed and the number of individuals who made use of them, this is clearly not the case. For example, one variation was used by 24 percent (N = 7) of the casual participants. The use of these variations was both frequent and widespread.

Extending the Model of the Organisation Sub-Task

Based on the data gathered from usability testing, a normative model of the organization sub-task is proposed (see Figure 6). Since this analysis is not concerned with the location sub-task, the model assumes that all required dimensions and members of dimensions are available.

The model shown in Figure 6 is a normative model in that it represents a set of recommended steps for casual users to follow. Although it is based on a substantial body of empirical evidence, it does not attempt to model all the strategies observed. Instead it represents the results of critical reflection on various strategies and proposes one strategy that appears to produce the required results in a very efficient manner.

Unlike the proposed model of the location sub-task, which would be appropriate for a number of types of SIS, the model of the organization sub-task is only

Figure 6: Proposed Model of the Organization Sub-Task Using OLAP

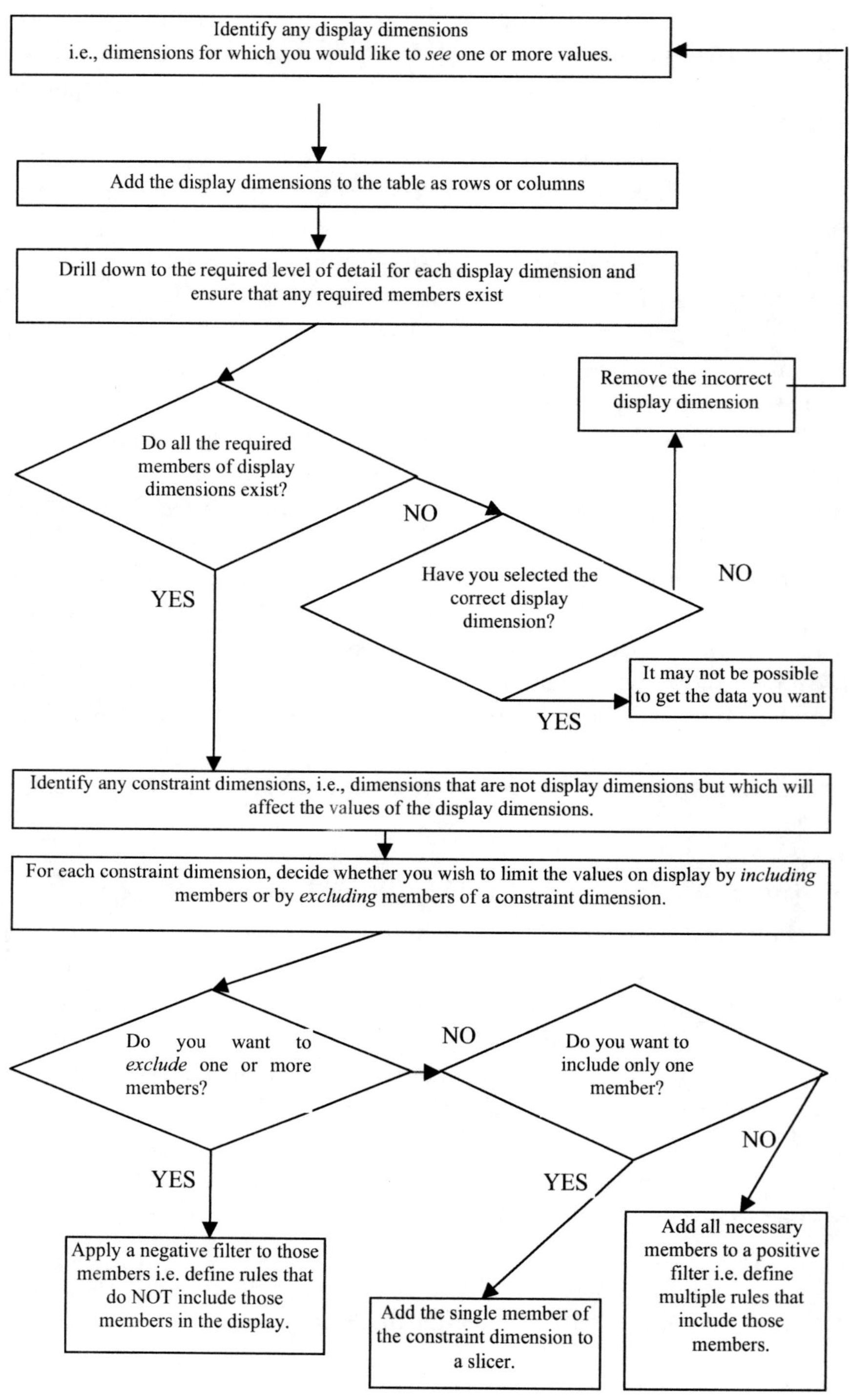

appropriate for SIS having analytical functions similar to those found in OLAP types of applications. The sorts of activities carried out with other types of SIS are extremely varied. For example, the calculation of standard deviations or linear regressions for a set of statistical data is quite a simple task in a statistical package but is not possible in a package such as *Abacus* and may not be possible in many OLAP environments. Similarly, the tasks carried out in a GIS or a spreadsheet might be quite different to those carried out in an OLAP environment. Given the enormous differences in functionality provided by the full range of available SIS applications, it does not appear feasible to produce a single task description for them all.

Concluding Comments on the Development of a Task Model

The data gathered by means of user observation have allowed us to identify and categorize some of the strategies that were employed by casual users when retrieving and analysing ESD. This, in turn, has allowed us to confirm the usefulness of the initial task model and to provide additional detail of some of the sub-tasks suggested in that model.

Although the results described above are interesting and useful, they are subject to a number of limitations. First, the strategies described have been evolved to cope with a specific set of tasks. These tasks may have elicited only a limited set of strategies or pre-disposed users to one strategy more than to another. For example, several users were able to answer all the tasks in *Table Mode* by using only the slicer. However, if any of the tasks had involved two constraints on the same dimension, this technique would have failed and those participants would have been forced to evolve a new strategy.

Second, the strategies above are directly linked to the use of OLAP functions, with which the prototype has been built. A different set of strategies would be found if the prototype had used GIS, for example. Having said this, it is difficult to imagine how users could arrive at the desired result without having some mechanism to control the addition of dimensions (variables), the paring of unwanted members (values) or the aggregation or disaggregation of the data. With this in mind, the above models would still be applicable, to some extent, to other tools that provided similar functions.

Finally, the results of the study do not allow us to reach any conclusion about the efficiency or "learnability" of the strategies that have been evolved. It is possible that one of the strategies described above is more efficient, more intuitive or both, than any of the others. This might not become apparent during a user's first interaction with the prototype but only on subsequent interactions. Of even more concern is the possibility that other highly efficient and learnable strategies exist and that these were not evolved at all. It is a very real possibility that such strategies might be found by other analytical methods and simply taught to users. The normative model, shown in Figure 6, would appear to be one such strategy.

Limitations of the Research

This study has been exploratory in nature and as such it has some inherent limitations.

- The tasks carried out during testing do not cover the entire range of tasks carried out by casual users of ESD. For example, participants only needed to find a single numerical value but casual users frequently need to compare several values. Thus, the testing has not been exhaustive and the use of only one type of task may have skewed the results.
- Because of the amount of data being collected via video-recordings, it was decided to use only one protocol for the collection of data. This protocol does not provide any verbal clues as to the cognitive processes of the participants. As a result, we can only guess about the models of the task being used by participants. Other protocols, such as thinking-aloud, and post-event protocols could be used to provide information about such cognitive processes.
- The only data used in the evaluation of the prototype was census data. It is unclear whether the use of another type of data with which users were less familiar might have affected the performance of participants. Observation of users working with different data sets would be valuable to ascertain the extent of the difference in performance.

FUTURE RESEARCH

Given that the current research is an exploratory study, there are a significant number of areas for future research. A number of variations on the procedures that were followed in this research would be useful. In the current research, the majority of tasks carried out by participants in usability testing required them to locate only a single value. Typical casual users of ESD might carry out a wider range of tasks including complex comparisons of values. It is quite reasonable to expect that even casual users of ESD could be looking for trends or patterns in statistical data and it is unclear whether they would find the *Abacus* prototype suitable for such tasks. Using either the *Abacus* prototype or a prototype developed in another development environment or with a different combination of technologies, the usability testing could be replicated using a more complex set of task.

The current research has given rise to an initial model of the task of ESD use. This model could be tested in a number of ways. For example, a formal experiment could be conducted to measure differences in performance between two groups of users, one having access to the model and the other not. These groups could be required to carry out tasks similar to those in the current study, using *Abacus* or some similar tool.

CONCLUSION

There appears to be a significant number of problems in the use of ESD by casual users and it has been suggested that these problems may be due to a lack of understanding, on the part of ESD providers, of the task of retrieving and manipulating ESD and of the systems required by these users to carry out such tasks. Given that the field of ESD use by casual users has been under-researched, this study attempted to define the major elements of that field, to gather data about those elements and, hence, to provide initial models for these elements.

User observation has led to the proposal of an initial model for the task of ESD use. The model is based on a similar model in the field of MIS use and appears to describe the main sub-tasks adequately. Additional more detailed normative models have been proposed for two of the three sub-tasks in the main model.

REFERENCES

Australian Bureau of Statistics. (1993, April). *A proposal for enhanced ABS client servicing from a corporate marketing and sales program.* ABS Management Meeting.

Ford, A. (1995). Spinning the web: *How to provide information on the Internet*, 1-4. London: International Thomson Computer Press.

Gassler, H., Frohlich, J., & Kopcsa, A. (1996). Selective information on the national system of innovation as an important input for the technology management of firms. *International Journal of Technology Management*, 11(3/4), 329-343.

Goodhue, D.L. (1998). Development and measurement validity of a task-technology fit instrument for user evaluations of information systems. *Decision Sciences.* 29(1), 105-138.

Hyland P.N., & Gould E. (1998). External statistical data: Understanding users and improving access. *International Journal of Human Computer Interaction*, 10(1), 71-83.

Hyland, P.N., & Hasan, H. (1997). The use of external statistical data in local government. *Urban Policy and Research Journal*, 15(4), 279-289.

Latamore, G.B. (1996). Spinning the Web. *Planning,* 62(7), 19-22.

Malmborg E., & Sundgren B. (1994). Integration of statistical information systems - theory and practice. *Scientific and Statistical Database Management - Proceedings of the International Working Conference,* (pp. 80-89).

McQueen, T. (1996). Using on-line technology for community information exchange: City of Nanaimo's experience. *Economic Development Review*, 14(1), 16-18.

Nielsen, J., & Levy, J. (1994). Measuring usability: Preference vs. performance. *Communications of the ACM,* 4(37), 66-75.

Pendse, N. (1999). *The OLAP report: What is OLAP?* Retrieved from the World Wide Web: http://www.olapreport.com/fasmi.htm.

Rogers, C. O. (1987). Information for economic development in Indiana. *Indiana Business Review*, 62(5), 9-11.

Thomsen, E. (1997). OLAP solutions: Building multidimensional information systems. New York: John Wiley & Sons.

Zorn, P. (1996). Use of on-line technology: A GFOA/ MBIA survey. *Government Finance Review,* 12(4), 28-30.

Section III

End User Computing

Chapter VIII

Media Selection and End-User Satisfaction: An Empirical Study of Help-Desk Using SERVQUAL

Sang-Gun Lee
University of Nebraska-Lincoln, USA

Sangjin Yoo
Keimyung University, Korea

Zoonky Lee
University of Nebraska-Lincoln, USA

ABSTRACT

In this paper, we investigate the relationship between the use of different media and customer satisfaction in help desk service. Different dimensions of customer satisfaction were derived based on SERVQUAL: reliability, empathy, assurance, tangibles, and responsiveness. The results support our hypotheses that the use of conventional media (face-to-face and telephone) is related to help desk satisfaction, through reliability and empathy and electronic media (e-mail and Internet), users show higher satisfaction in tangibles and assurance. Also, hybrid media users (multi-media users by task) show a higher level of satisfaction in reliability and responsibility. The results suggest automating help desks should be considered as a way to provide more options to end-users.

INTRODUCTION

Information technology (IT) support for end-users has emerged as one of the leading concerns of organizations. Continuous adapting and updating of new technologies have made development of effective and efficient help desk services challenging for organizations (Whiting, 1997). Organizations must actively search for new ways to provide better help desk services to satisfy growing customer demands and expectations. A number of commercial products using artificial intelligence techniques such as expert systems and case-based reasoning have become popular. Outsourcing the help desk function has also become a viable option for many organizations (Chalos & Sung, 1998). The move to help-desk automation and remote on-line troubleshooting using Internet-based products usually means that more and more help-desk services are computer-based rather than human-based.

Since end-user satisfaction has become the strategic imperative in business, the primary concern here is how to evaluate these new technology-enabled tools (e.g., e-mail and the Internet) with conventional media support (e.g., telephone and face-to-face), in an effort to provide more effective and efficient end-user support.

The main purpose of this study is to investigate the effects of different media on end-user satisfaction in help desk service. More specifically, we will relate the use of different media use along the dimensions of reliability, empathy, assurance, tangible and responsiveness, based on SERVQUAL (Parasuraman, Zenithal & Berry, 1985, 1988, 1991). The major theme of this paper is to show that use of each media is related to different dimensions of customer satisfaction. The results of this study should enable organizations to better design their help desk functions.

REVIEW OF RELEVANT LITERATURE

Most previous studies on media choice have focused on social presence and media richness theory. The researchers define social presence as "the degree to which a medium permits communicators to experience others as being psychologically present" (Fulk, Steinfield, Schmitz & Power, 1987, 1990; Short, Williams & Christie, 1976), or "the degree to which a medium is perceived to convey the actual presence of the communicating participants" (Short et al., 1976). According to social presence theory, communication media are perceived as rating in social presence. Social presence, then, is determined by the degree to which one medium transmits information about facial expressions, directions of looking, postures, and dress, nonverbal and vocal cues. For example, conventional media such as face-to-face and group meetings are perceived as ranked high in social presence. By contrast, electronic media such as e-mail and computer-based written documents are poorly perceived in terms of social presence. Therefore, social presence theorists argued that conventional media are more appropriate for tasks requiring high social presence, whereas electric media and written letters are more appropriate for tasks with low social presence requirement.

Similar to social presence theory, media richness theory focuses on the nature of media characteristics, but in addition it also deems significant their match with task characteristics (Daft & Lengel, 1984, 1986; Hiltz & Turoff, 1981; Hiltz et al., 1986; Lengel & Daft, 1988; Rice, 1984, 1992; Rogers, 1986). This theory is based on task variety and task analyzability: task variety is "the frequency of unexpected and novel events that occur in the conversation process" (Daft & Lengel, 1986, p. 554), and task analyzability refers to "the degree to which tasks involve the application of objective, well-understood procedures that do not require novel solution."

Media richness theorists suggested that rich media, such as face-to-face and telephone, facilitate the immediate exchange of a wide range of communication cues, while leaner media such as e-mail, written roles and regulations, letters, and written notes allow exchange of a restricted range of such cues over a longer period (Daft & Lengel, 1986). Then, the media richness theorists posed that richer media are more appropriate for unanalyzable tasks such as resolving disagreements, making important decisions, generating ideas and exchanging confidential/sensitive information, whereas leaner media are more appropriate for analyzable tasks such as exchanging routine information, clarifying confusing viewpoints, and exchanging urgent/timely information. They suggest, when equivocality is high, organizations allow for rapid information cycles among managers, typically face-to-face and telephone, and prescribe fewer rules for interpretation (Draft & Lengel, 1984; Weick, 1979).

Although these two theories tried to explain end-users media choices, the authors of many empirical studies have suggested that media choice cannot be logically explained or predicted by considering only the inherent richness or social presence of the medium and the characteristics of the task (King & Xia, 1997; Markus, 1988; Rice & Shook, 1990; Trevino & Webster, 1992; Yates & Orlikowski, 1992; Zmud, Lind & Young, 1990). For instance, Ngwenyama and Lee (1997) found that electronic media increase their richness through messenger services such as call and page functions.

Since media richness theory has been only partially supported by empirical research, it is likely that other factors or dimensions might affect end-users' media choices. In order to overcome criticism leveled on media richness theory, we adopted service quality (SERVQUAL), created by Parasuraman et al. (1985), as representative characteristics that are associated with each medium. Parasuraman et al. (1988) developed a 22-item scale consisting of five service quality dimensions. They theorized that regardless of the type of service, customers use basically similar criteria in evaluating service quality and these criteria span virtually all aspects of service. Those dimensions are:

- Reliability is the ability to perform the promised service dependably and accurately.
- Empathy is the provision of caring individualized attention to customers.
- Assurance is knowledge of employees and their ability to inspire trust and confidence.
- Tangible dimensions include physical facilities, equipment, and appearance of personnel.
- Responsiveness is the willingness to help customers and provide prompt service.

HYPOTHESES DEVELOPMENT

To investigate the relationship between media choice and end-user perceptions of help desk functions, a research model was developed as shown in Figure 1 and Table 1. In this model, we used five constructs from SERVQUAL (Parasuraman et al., 1991) that are thought of as being closely related to end-user satisfaction with help desks: reliability, empathy, assurance, tangibles and responsiveness.

We first adopted Kydd and Ferry's (1991) and Daft and Legal's (1986) continuum of communication media, and then developed a new matrix based on SERVQUAL measures. This serves as the basis for our belief that communication media differ in their relative abilities to increase reliability, empathy, assurance, tangibles and responsiveness (see Figure 1 and Table 1). As presented in Table 1, the five media, including conventional and electronic media, offer combinations with various strengths and weaknesses. On the basis of the literature, we derive the relationship between media choice and different aspects of perception of help desk function.

Conventional media provide end-users with the ability to increase reliability and empathy, because they allow end-users to exchange a variety of verbal and non-verbal information (Chidambaram & Jones, 1993). In particular, face-to-face contact has the ability to allow a broad range of communication stimuli and responses, so as to make end-users perceive a personal interest, politeness and attention, get first problem-solving cues, sincere interest and immediate answers without ambiguity. It also permits richer affection than does any form of electronic media. For example, conventional media are often considered as a more natural form of group interaction than comparable non-in person forums (Daft & Lengel, 1986). In other words, electronic media are regarded as less effective media for intense socio-emotional interaction involving heated debates, negotiation and decision-making.

On the basis of the literature reviewed above, we hypothesize that conventional media is positively associated with the perception of reliability and empathy among service quality constructs (see Figure 1). Hence:

Figure 1: Continuum of Communication Media in Help Desk

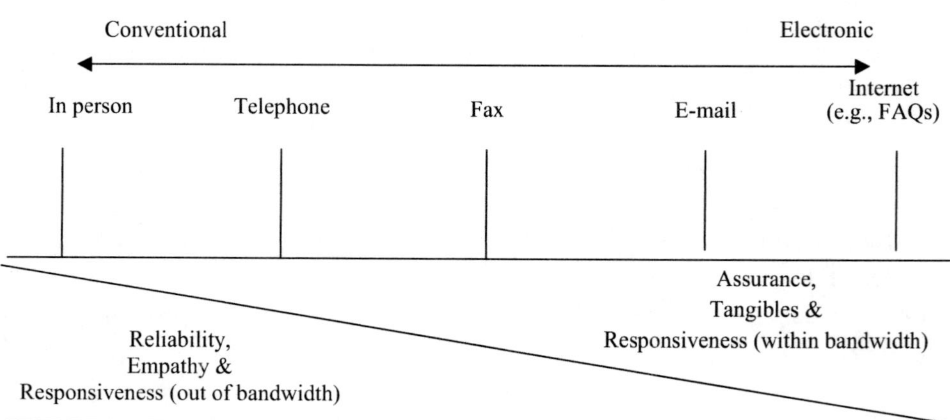

Note: Adapted from Kydd and Ferry (1991), who adapted their framework from Daft and Lengel (1986)

Ha: The use of conventional media is more strongly related to reliability than the use of electronic media.

Hb: The use of conventional media is more strongly related to empathy than the use of electronic media.

We also hypothesize that electronic media increase assurance and tangibles. For example, written documents such as e-mail and Internet (frequently asked questions) help end-users deal with the dual themes juxtaposed by Daft and Lengel (1986). Electronic media allow end-users to focus their idea or problem (Zigurs et al., 1988) and leave evidence of communication. Thus, end-users can obtain confidence, safety, and transaction knowledge.

Hc: The use of electronic media is more strongly related to Assurance than the use of conventional media.

Hd: The use of electronic media is more strongly related to Tangibles than the use of conventional media.

As shown in Table 1, electronic media provide an ability to input comments anonymously and are easy for customers to access (Zigurs, Poole, & De Sanctis, 1988). These characteristics encourage end-users to easily lodge complaints, so they can receive prompt service. However, electronic media have a narrow bandwidth[1]. When electronic media deal with complex problems and out of contents, end-users are faced with more of a time lag than when they use conventional media. Thus, we assume hybrid media users (people who select mixed media determine this based on problems or their own experience) have a higher perception than conventional media users or electronic media users do.

Table 1: Factors Influencing Perceptions of Service Quality: A Comparison of Conventional and Electronic Media

	Communication Media				
	Conventional ◄			►	Electronic
Factors	Face to Face	Telephone	Fax	E-mail	Internet (e.g., FAQs)
Reliability	**1**	**2**	**3**	**4**	**5**
Empathy	**1**	**2**	**3**	**4**	**5**
Assurance	**5**	**4**	**3**	**2**	**1**
Tangibles	**5**	**4**	**3**	**2**	**1**
Responsiveness					
(Within bandwidth)	**5**	**4**	**3**	**2**	**1**
(Out of bandwidth)	**1**	**2**	**3**	**4**	**5**

Note: Adapted from Chidambaram and Jones (1993)
Key qualities of these five media presented in Table 1, the lower, the better

He: The users of both conventional and electronic media will show a higher satisfaction on responsiveness toward help-desk services than conventional media users or electronic media users only.

RESEARCH METHOD AND ANALYSIS

A survey was used in this study. Questionnaires were distributed to 1,000 MBA students in Korea. All of them were part-time students and most were fully employed at the time of the survey. We received 222 usable respondents, a return rate of 22.2 percent.

The initial data analysis showed that most participants were proficient in computer: power-users (11.3 percent), above average (20.7 percent), average (41.0 percent), below-average (18.5 percent) and novice (9.4 percent). In their career paths, the participants were from various fields: manufacturing (20.3 percent), financing/banking (1.4 percent), transportation (12.2 percent), information technology (1.8 percent), retailing (12.0 percent), communications (3.2 percent), education (35.6 percent), health care (5.1 percent), others (7.4 percent) and no response (2.7 percent). The survey utilized a seven-point Likert-type scale to measure respondents' overall perceptions about measurement items. Measurement items per each construct ask respondents to rate the extent to which they feel or agree with the feature described by the statement on a scale of one through seven, where 1 = subjects strongly disagree and 7 = subjects strongly agree.

To test the hypotheses, we first performed a cluster analysis. Cluster analysis is an exploratory data analysis tool for developing meaningful subgroups of individu-

Table 2: Cluster Analysis of End-Users, Media Choice Pattern

media \ mean	Hybrid	Electronic	Conventional
Face to face	**4.58**	1.63	**1.89**
Telephone	**4.93**	4.79	**5.22**
Fax	**4.24**	1.69	1.57
E-mail	**4.55**	**5.38**	2.44
Internet	**5.11**	**5.93**	1.85
Total number	(55)	(95)	(54)

Mean: the extent to which respondents frequently use the media

als or objects. Its object is to sort cases (people, things, events, etc.) into groups, or clusters, so that the degree of association is strong between members of the same cluster and weak between members of different clusters (Hair, Anderson, Tatham & Black, 1998). We grouped the clusters based on face-to-face, telephone, fax, e-mail, and Internet information. Table 2 shows the results of this cluster. We identified three groups of end-users: one group utilizing all of the media, another group using most of the electronic media such as e-mail and Internet, and the other group using mostly telephone and face to face. We named the first group the hybrid group (HG), second group the electronic group (EG), and third group the conventional group (CG). The numbers of end-users were 55, 95, and 54, respectively.

Secondly, we performed factor analysis using measures related to the service perception constructs to assess the reliability of the multi-item scales. Table 3 shows the factor analysis results. These five factors account for more than 78.36 percent of the observed variance. The loading of each of the 15 measures on its respective factor is well over 0.40, and the Eigenvalue of each construct is above one. The results of the factor analysis, therefore, showed convergent and discriminate validity for the measures we used (Campbell & Fiske, 1959; Cronbach, 1971). Also, the reliabilities for the measures were calculated based on Cronbach's alpha, and all five constructs showed strong reliability, with all over 0.75.

Finally, we conducted a one-way ANOVA to detect differences in end-user perceptions among the three groups. In general, our results demonstrate that conventional media users posses a positive perception toward help desks and reliability. However, empathy is not different among the three media-using groups. Electronic media users have significantly more positive perception in terms of tangibles, even though assurance is not statistically significant. The hybrid media user group has more positive perception toward reliability and responsibility than the other two groups (conventional and electronic groups) have (see Table 4).

FINDINGS

Results of the ANOVA partially support the idea that conventional media have more ability as a medium to allow a broad range of communication stimuli and

Table 3: Factors Analysis of Independent Variables

	Tang.	*Resp.*	*Assu.*	*Reli.*	*Empa.*
The medium you use the most will increase visual attention using materials such as pamphlets or public relations.	**.854**				
The medium you use the most makes you feel customer service is visually appealing.	**.838**				
The medium you use the most makes you feel customer service has modern-looking equipment.	**.780**				
The medium you use the most makes you feel customer service is never too busy to respond to your requests.		**.906**			
The medium you use the most makes you feel customer service is always ready to respond your request.		**.813**			
The medium you use the most makes you feel customer service provides a prompt service.		**.774**			
The medium you use the most makes you feel customer service make you feel safe with your transactions.			**.839**		
The medium you use the most makes you feel customer service gives you a confidence about the transaction.			**.784**		
The medium you use the most makes you feel customer service has knowledge about your transactions.			**.598**	.420	
The medium you use the most makes you feel that customer service provides the service promptly.				**.834**	
The medium you use the most makes you feel that customer service will solve the problem right the first time.				**.774**	
The medium you use the most makes you feel that customer service shows sincere interest in the customer.			.447	**.594**	
The medium you use the most makes you feel that customer service is polite.			.454	.476	**.420**
The medium you use the most makes you feel that customer service shows a personal interest.					**.847**
The medium you use the most makes you feel customer service tries to pay personal attention.					**.771**
Eigenvalue	2.506	2.476	2.462	2.404	1.906
Percentage of Variance Explained	16.708	16.504	16.416	16.028	12.705

responses. The results were not consistent with Daft and Lengel's (1986) theory that conventional media are perceived by end-users as the "warmest" media, permitting the exchange of a wide range of socio-emotional communication. However, if we carefully look at the measurements in reliability and empathy, more open-ended communication makes end-users feel personal interest, politeness and attention, and get an immediate problem solving response with an expression of sincerity rather than impersonal ambiguity (Chapanis, Parrish, Ochsman & Weeks, 1972, 1976), even though empathy is not statistically significant.

As shown in Table 5, electronic media partially provides end-users with the ability to increase assurance and tangibles. In hypothesis Hc and Hd, we proposed

Table 4: Results of a One-Way ANOVA by Different Media Choice Group with LSD

			Mean Difference (I-J)	***Std. Error***	***Sig.***
Dependent Variable	(I) Cluster Number of Case	(J) Cluster Number of Case	Mean Difference	Std. Error	Sig.
Reliability	**HG**	**EG**	**2.310**	**.585**	**.001*** **
	HG	**CG**	**1.499**	**.660**	**.011** **
	EG	**CG**	**-0.811**	**.588**	**.089***
Empathy	HG	EG	0.778	.621	.211
	HG	CG	0.810	.702	.250
	EG	CG	0.032	.624	.959
Assurance	HG	EG	0.567	.539	.294
	HG	**CG**	**1.077**	**.616**	**.082***
	EG	CG	0.510	.542	.348
Tangibles	HG	EG	0.351	.613	.568
	HG	**CG**	**1.873**	**.701**	**.008** **
	EG	**CG**	**1.522**	**.617**	**.015** **
Responsiveness	**HG**	**EG**	**1.467**	**.651**	**.025** **
	HG	**CG**	**1.908**	**.740**	**.011** **
	EG	CG	0.441	.655	.502

*** $p < .001$
** $p < .05$
* $p < .10$

that electronic media have higher assurance and tangibles than conventional media. The results of the ANOVA and rank proved that e-mail and Internet FAQ rate higher in tangibles (with statistical significance), even though assurance is not significant. These results indicate electronic media make end-users focus their idea or problem so that end-users can obtain transaction safety, confidence of problem solving and knowledgeable information with evidence of communication. In the case of tangibles, the Internet and e-mail can provide end-users with strong visual performance using figures, tables and prototyping products. Finally, the results indicate that the hybrid group receives prompt service with statistical significance.

In sum, we found an interesting aspect in reliability and responsiveness that the hybrid group, who use various types of communication media, has the highest level of satisfaction. The results of this study imply that organizations should be encouraged to design their help desk with more care and attention.

CONCLUSION

As we expected, customers have different perceptions of various media: higher reliability from conventional media (face-to-face and telephone), and higher tan-

Table 5: Results of Hypotheses

Hypotheses	*Condition* (mean/ranks)	*Hypotheses Supported or Not*	*Statistically Supported or Not?*
Hypo. a (Reliability)	**HG (13.25) EG (10.94) CG (11.76)**	**Yes**	**Yes**
Rank	**1 3 2**		
Hypo. b (Empathy)	HG (11.27) EG (10.49) CG (10.46)	No	No
Rank	**1 2 3**		
Hypo. c (Assurance)	HG (11.14) EG (11.57) CG (11.06)	Yes	No
Rank	**1 2 3**		
Hypo. d (Tangibles)	**HG (11.37) EG (11.02) CG (9.50)**	**Yes**	**Yes**
Rank	**1 2 3**		
Hypo. e (Responsive.)	**HG (12.59) EG (11.12) CG (10.68)**	**Yes**	**Yes**
Rank	**1 2 3**		

gibles and assurance for electronic media (e-mail and Internet). Specifically, the hybrid group indicates higher levels of reliability and responsiveness. These perceptions may lead organizations to prepare different medium for different tasks or use mixed purpose.

The results of this study have some important theoretical implications. First, we applied the concept of media choice to the domain of the help desk service. Second, our research incorporated SERVQUAL theory into media selection mechanism.

The practical implication of our study is that by understanding the types of perceptions customers have for each medium and their behavioral patterns, organizations may be able to provide better help desk service, which is critical in the competitive business world.

REFERENCES

Campbell, D. T., & Fiske, D. W. (1959). Convergent and Discriminant Validation by Multi Trait-Multi Method Matrix. *Psychological Bulletin*, 56, 81-105.

Chalos, P., & Sung, J. (1998). Outsourcing Decisions and Managerial Incentives. *Decision Sciences*, 29(4), 901-919.

Chapanis, A., Ochsman, R. B., Parrish, R. N., & Weeks, G. D. (1972). Studies in Interactive Communication: I. The Effects of Four Communication Modes on the Behavior of Teams during Cooperative Problem-solving. *Human Factors*, 14(6), 487-509.

Chapanis, A., Parrish, R. N., Ochsman, R. B., & Weeks, G. D. (1976). Studies in Interactive Communication: II. The Effects of Four Communication Modes on the Behavior of Teams During Cooperative Problem-Solving. *Human Factors*, 19(2), 101-126.

Chidambaram, L. & Jones, B. (1993). Impact of Communication Medium and Computer Support on Group. *MIS Quarterly*, 17(4), 465-492.

Cronbach, L. J. (1971). Test Validation. In R. L. Thorndike (Ed.), *Education Measurement,* (2nd Ed., pp. 443-507). Washington, D.C.: American Council on Education.

Daft, R. L., & Lengel, R. H. (1984). Information Richness: A New Approach to Managerial Behavior and Organization Design. *Research in Organizational Behavior,* 6(2), 191-233.

Daft, R. L., & Lengel, R. H. (1986). Organization Information Requirements, Media Richness and Structural Design. *Management Science*, 32(5), 554-571.

Fulk, J., Schmitz, J., & Steinfield, C. W. (1990). A Social Influence Model of Technology Use. In J. Fulk, J. Fulk, & C. W. Steinfield (Eds.), *Organizations and Communication Technology,* (pp. 117-140). Newbury Park, CA: Sage.

Fulk, J., Steinfield, C. W., Schmitz, J., & Power, J. P. (1987). A Social Information Processing Model of Media Use in Organizations. *Communication Research*, 14(5), 529-552.

Hair, J. F., Anderson, R. E., Tatham, R. L., & Black, W. C. (1998). *Multivariate Data Analysis*, (pp. 15-16). Upper Saddle River, NJ: Prentice Hall.

Hiltz, S. R., & Turoff, M. (1981). The Evaluation of User Behavior in a Computerized Conferencing System. *Communications of the ACM*, 24(11), 739-751.

Hiltz, S. R., Johnson, K., & Turoff, M. (1986). Experiments in Group Decision Making: Communication Process and Outcome in Face-to-Face Versus Computerized Conferences. *Human Communication Research*, 13(2), 225-252.

King, R. C., & Xia, W. (1997). Media Appropriateness: Effects of Experience on Communication Media Choice. *Decision Science*, 28(4), 877-910.

Kydd, C. T., & Ferry, D. L. (1991). Computer Supported Cooperative Work Tools and Media Richness: An Integration of the Literature. Presented at *The Twenty-Fourth Annual Hawaii International Conference on Systems Sciences*, (Vol. III, pp. 324-332). Los Alamitos, CA: IEEE Society Press.

Lengel, R. H., & Daft, R. H. (1998). The Selection of Communication Media as an Executive Skill. *The Academy of Management EXECUTIVE*, 11(2), 225-232.

Markus, L. (1988). Information Richness Theory, Managers, and Electronic Mail. Presented at the Academy of Management National Meeting, Anaheim, CA.

Ngwenyama O. K., & Lee A. S. (1997). Communication Richness in Electronic Mail: Critical Social Theory and Contextuality of Meeting. *MIS Quarterly*, 21(2), 145-167.

Parasuraman, A., Zenithal, V., & Berry, L. (1985). A Conceptual Model of Service Quality and Its Implications for Future Research. *Journal of Marketing*, 49, 41-50.

Parasuraman, A., Zenithal, V., & Berry, L. (1988). SERVQUAL: A Multiple-Item Scale for Measuring Consumer Perceptions of Service Quality. *Journal of Retailing*, 64(1), 12-37.

Parasuraman, A., Zenithal, V., & Berry, L. (1991). Refinement and Reassess of the SERVQUAL Scale. *Journal of Retailing*, 67(4), 420-450.

Rice, R. E. (1984). Mediated Group Communication. *The New Media: Communication, Research and Technology*, (pp. 129-155). Beverly Hills, CA: Sage.

Rice, R. E. (1992). Task Analyzability, Use of New Media, and Effectiveness: A Multi-Site Exploration of Media Richness. *Organization Science*, 3, 475-500.

Rice, R. E., & Shook D. E. (1990). Relationships of Job Categories and Organizational Levels to Use Communication Channels, Including Electronic Mail: A Meta-Analysis and Extension. *Journal of Management Studies*, 27(2), 195-229.

Rogers, E. M. (1986). *Communication Technology: The New Media in Society.* New York: Free Press.

Short, J., Williams, E., & Christie, B. (1976). *The Social Psychology of Telecommunications*. New York: John Wiley.

Trevino, L. K., & Webster, J. (1992). Flow in Computer-Mediated Communication. *Communication Research*, 19(5), 539-573.

Weick. K. (1979). *The Social Psychology of Organizing.* Reading, MA: Addison-Wesley.

Whiting, R. (1997). Panic at the Help Desk. *Software Magazine*, 17(11), 92-95.

Yates, J., & Orlikowski, W. J. (1992). Genres of Organizational Communication: A Structurational Approach to Studying Communication and Media. *Academy of Management Review*, 17(1), 299-326.

Zigurs, I., Poole, M. S., & De Sanctis, G. (1988). A Study of Influence in the Computer-Mediated Group Decision Making. *MIS Quarterly,* 12(4), 625-644.

Zmud, R. W., Lind, M. R., & Young, F. W. (1990). An Attribute Space for Organizational Communication Channels. *Information Systems Research*, 1(4), 440-457.

ENDNOTES

1 According to Chidambaram and Jones (1993), they referred to bandwidth as an ability of a medium to allow a broad range of communication stimuli and responses.

Chapter IX

End User Support Usage

Robin Munkvold
Nord-Trøndelag University College, Norway

ABSTRACT

This study explores how different end user qualities affect actual use of support sources in organizations. It identifies three qualities: information technology-skills; computer self-efficacy; information technology (IT) -involvement. Sources of support are divided in: formal sources of support; informal sources of support; use of internal documentation and use of external documentation. Hypotheses are tested empirically through a cross sectional study in a large Norwegian organization. The results show end user qualities in varying degree may affect the end users' choice of different support sources. The study also shows access *to a computer expert and giving collegial support might be important factors for explaining the variation in the end users' choices of support services.*

INTRODUCTION

Support services are central elements of any organization. To be competitive, organizations need to optimise the use of the information technology (IT)-resources. The problem is, however, end users tend to spend a lot of their working hours fixing IT-related problems that has nothing to do with their actual work assignments. The employee's expertise and skills in using computer systems have become a critical factor for successful use of information technology in organizations (Cheney, Mann & Amoruso, 1986; Nelson & Cheney, 1987; Mirani & King, 1994). Gartner Group found that about 60 percent of the time end users spend in front of a computer will be to make it work satisfactorily and to learn how to use different programs (Kirwin, 1995). The solutions for solving these problems usually are to offer the employees training, education, assistance or guidance. Do these solutions solve our problems?

Some information systems (IS) researchers have studied the antecedents of variation in the support needs of end users so that these needs can be better explained, predicted and fulfilled (Mirani & King, 1994). Maybe one should look at the end user's actual use of support and make this the basis for figuring out ways to make end users more effective in their daily work.

Why do end users choose different support services? Is it due to variations in end user qualities (i.e., skills, self-efficacy, involvement, etc.)? Is it the qualities of the actual support (context, vicinity, sources, etc.)? Or could it be a result of the end user's relation to the support personnel or the competence of the support personnel that makes the end user choose his source of support? These questions are many that must be answered when searching to find causes of variation in the end user's use of different support sources.

Most literature view end user computing (EUC) support from an overall organizational perspective. Information centre (IC) approaches, generally, do not take into account differences among users, when designing and providing support services (Mirani & King, 1994). To make end users more effective, a useful approach could be to map the causes for the end user's need for different kinds of support. By finding these causes one could improve end user qualities and, therefore increase effectiveness. My focus is on end user qualities, and I aim to find out whether basic end user qualities can affect the way end users choose sources of support or solve their IT-related problems. That is, *are there any basic end user qualities that can be of significance when they choose their sources of support?*

The objective of this study is to identify end user qualities (variables) that may be important for explaining differences in usage of different support sources. I will address three different qualities that might be of significance, when end users solve their problems. These qualities include: IT-skills, computer self-efficacy and IT-involvement.

THEORY, RESEARCH QUESTIONS, CONCEPTUAL MODEL AND HYPOTHESIS

End User Computing Support

To measure the use of different sources of support, EUC needed a more precise definition. Many studies show different perspectives on EUC support (Arnoudse & Oulette, 1986; Bruton, 1995; Doll & Torkzadeh, 1993; Heie & Heistad, 1998; Larsen, 1989; Smith, 1997; Winter, Chudoba & Gutek, 1997).

Through a thorough analysis of the different perspectives on EUC support, a partitioning of EUC support was needed. Doll and Torkzadeh (1993) divides EUC support into three categories. These are:

- Consultation
- Training
- Documentation

This survey seeks to measure ad hoc support needs. The category *Training* is therefore irrelevant. *Consultation* and *Documentation* were singled out as the types of EUC support that would be tested for in this survey. Further analysis showed that Consultation and Documentation could be divided in formal vs. informal sources of support and personnel vs. impersonal sources of support. This resulted in four different types of EUC support sources:

- Personal and informal consultation with colleagues.
- Personal and formal consultation with computer experts.
- Use of external documentation (impersonal and informal).
- Use of internal documentation (impersonal and formal).

Through this review EUC support was defined to be:

All sorts of IT-help that an end user receives or uses in his work to solve arising problems or acquire expertise and skills within IS-use, so that they easier can achieve organizational goals.

This definition limits the perspective on EUC support and makes it somewhat easier to measure.

End User Qualities

As the purpose of this study is to find out whether different end user qualities can explain the differences in their choice of support sources, it is equally important to find these qualities.

There exists some literature on EUC support, but not very much on the end user's choices of support depending on his basic qualities (i.e., skills, etc.). Winter

Table 1: EUC Support Categorization

EUC support	Informal	Formal
Personal	*Consultation with colleagues*, or other non professional IT workers	*Consultation with IS-professionals*
Impersonal	Use of *external documentation* not developed by the local IC. This could be manuals, periodicals, etc.	Use of *internal documentation* developed by the local IC

et al. (1997) concluded in their survey that even though training and support could have improved the end user's computer knowledge, it is clear that it has not lead to high computer knowledge. Their opinion is that it is important for the support personnel to have some knowledge about the end user's computer skills to give them proper support. It then seems reasonably obvious that *computer skills* might affect the end user's choice of different support services. I therefore ask:

Do IT-skills influence the end user's choice of support services?

One would believe that end users with low computer knowledge and skills would need more support than those with high computer knowledge and skills. Øystein Sørebø wrote a paper in 1996 called: *"End-User Computing and the perceived need for support services: Toward an explanation of the independent-user paradox."* The qualities he believed to affect the perceived need for support services include: IT-involvement, computer self-efficacy, and informational influence (from colleagues).

Sørebø questions whether the end user's *IT-involvement* might have a significant influence on the perceived need for support services. Earlier studies have shown that involvement affects information searching (Laurent & Kapferer, 1985; Zaichkowsky, 1986). Finding the solution to computer related problems, through the use of different support sources, could easily be compared with information searching. Zaichkowsky (1986) also points out that an individual's attention towards and experience of what's important in relation to the execution of a specific behaviour will vary with the individual's involvement. In this context, execution of a specific behaviour can be compared with the use of different sources of support and the individual's involvement could be different aspects of the end user's involvement toward the computer.

On these basis one could ask:

Do IT-involvement influence the end user's choice of support services?

Computer Self-Efficacy is an important end user quality. Compaeu and Higgins (1995) argues that this special psychological state will affect the end user's belief about his need for support services. Belief about the need for support services and actual use of different support services are clearly related topics, and therefore my question is:

Do computer self-efficacy influence the end user's choice of support services?

Now I will turn to a more detailed description of each of the three explanatory factors.

IT-Skills

The concept IT-skills is not easily defined. IT is widely used, but often without providing a precise definition. Much work is done on the related concept End User Computing Sophistication. The reason why I have not used the concept, End User Computer Sophistication, is that different authors have defined it differently in different surveys (Blili, Raymond & Rivard, 1994; Huff, Malcolm & Marcolin, 1992; Marcolin, Munro & Compeau, 1993; Rockart & Flannery, 1983; Zinatelli, 1996). It would be difficult to compare the results from the different surveys because of the variations in the definition of the concept.

The subject *skill* is often connected to the subject's *ability*. A few researchers (Cheney & Nelson, 1988; Koohang et al., 1992; Marcolin et al., 1996) have tested end user ability. Both Marcolin (1996) and Koohang (199x) have used Cheney and Nelson's instrument for developing their instruments on end user abilities. Cheney and Nelson identified three clear factors within end user computing abilities: technical abilities, modelling abilities and application abilities. Technical abilities apply to programming, the use of hardware and operating systems. Modelling abilities apply to subjects regarding software engineering. Application abilities apply to skills that are most typically associated with the use of applications systems. All these factors are important for measuring end-users' IT-skills. The aim of this study was, however to measure work-relevant IT-skills. The measure of technical and modelling abilities was therefore less interesting. On this basis, I defined IT-skills to be:

In what degree a person manages to solve different problems with help from different work-relevant information system tools.

IT-Involvement

Earlier research on IT-involvement has mostly been about participator behaviour within IS-development (Ives & Olsen, 1994). The psychological dimension of this participation has been brought to focus in the later years. In spite of Barki and Hartwick (1989), Kappelman (1990) and Kappelman and McLean (1993, 1994) trying to establish a conceptual partitioning between *participation* and *engagement* as two aspects of involvement, it is still common to use end user involvement as a

Table 2: End User Involvement Partitioning

End User Involvement	Related to the Phenomenon	Can be Divided Into:
Situational Involvement (End User Participation)	Behaviour	Process Participation or System Usage
Intrinsic Involvement (End User Engagement)	Psychological State	**Involvement Towards Information Technology, the Computer and Software** or Involvement Towards a Process

description of participant behaviour (Doll & Torkzadeh, 1994; Igbara & Guimaraes, 1994). A solution to this partitioning of behavioural and psychological involvement is to denote them both end user involvement, and to distinguish between the two components *situational involvement* and *intrinsic involvement* (Jackson et al., 1997). One can further divide intrinsic involvement in *a psychological condition* and as *involvement towards information technology, the computer and software or involvement towards a process*. My aim with **IT-involvement** is to measure *involvement towards information technology, the computer and software.* Table 2 shows the partitioning of the concept.

With basis in the work of Barki and Hartwick (1989), I have defined IT-Involvement as follows:

> *The importance and personal relevancy an end user attaches to a computer and the use of it.*

Computer Self-Efficacy

Compeau and Higgins (1995) did a survey on the concept of self-efficacy to prove its usability in the attempt to understand individual behaviour towards computers. The term self-efficacy is future-oriented. It does not deal with what a person has done earlier, but rather with a person's beliefs of what can be done in the future (Compeau & Higgins, 1995b, p. 192).

It is "borrowed" from social psychology, where self-efficacy is said to be the user's beliefs about his capability to organize and execute the courses of action required to manage prospective situations (Bandura, 1996).

Self-efficacy has its origin in the writings of Albert Bandura (1986, 1995). He defines it to deal with: *"peoples judgement of their own capabilities to organize and execute courses of action required to attain designated types of performance. It is concern not with the skills one has, but with the judgements of what one can do with whatever skills one possesses"* (Bandura 1986, p. 391). Thus, Computer Self-Efficacy represents an individual's perception of his ability to use computers in the accomplishment of a task (Compeau & Higgins, 1995a).

The concept has three dimensions (Compaeu & Higgins, 1995a, 1995b). These dimensions are: *magnitude* — the level of computing task difficulty the user can attain; *strength* — whether the conviction regarding magnitude is strong or weak and *generalizability* — the degree to which the expectation is generalized across different software packages and different computer systems.

End users with a high magnitude of Computer Self-Efficacy might judge themselves as capable of operating with less support and assistance than those with lower magnitude of self-efficacy (Compaeu & Higgins, 1995a, 1995b).

Compeau and Higgins (1995b, p. 195) show that support was negatively related to self-efficacy with a regression coefficient of –0,16. The survey thereby showed that the more support given to the end user the less computer self-efficacy he possessed.

Following these research questions, conceptual definitions and discussions, I will utilize the model in Figure 1.

Hypothesis:

H1: The end user's IT-skills will covariate with their respective source of support choices.

H1a: High IT-skills is negatively related to the use of formal sources of support.

H1b: High IT-skills is positively related to the use of informal sources of support.

H1c: High IT-skills is negatively *related to* the use of internal documentation.

H1d: High IT-skills is positively related to the use of external documentation.

H2: The end user's Computer Self-Efficacy will covariate with their respective source of support choices.

H2a: A high degree of Computer Self-Efficacy is negatively related to the use of formal sources of support.

H2b: A high degree of Computer Self-Efficacy is negatively related to the use of informal sources of support.

H2c: A high degree of Computer Self-Efficacy is negatively related to the use of internal documentation.

H2d: A high degree of Computer Self-Efficacy is positively related to the use of internal documentation.

H3: The end user's IT-involvement will covariate with their respective source of support choices.

H3a: High IT-involvement is positively related to the use of formal sources of support.

Figure 1: Research Model

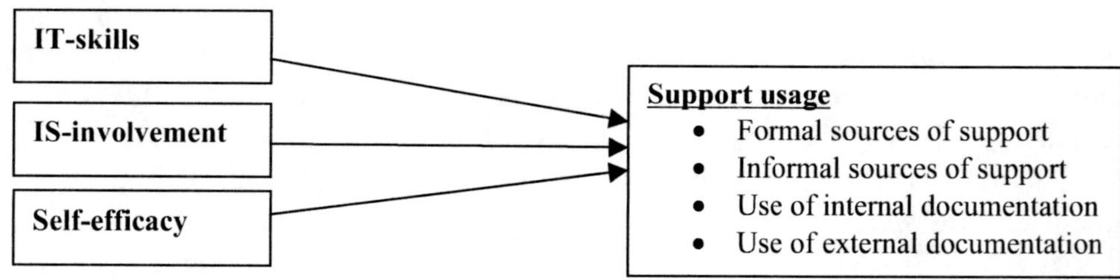

H3b: High IT-Involvement is positively related to the use of informal sources of support.
H3c: High IT-Involvement is positively related to the use of internal documentation.
H3d: High IT-Involvement is positively related to the use of external documentation.

RESEARCH METHOD

With basis in the requirements to causal research models (Bollen, 1989; Churchill, 1995; Frankfort-Nachmias & Nachmias, 1996), a quantitative approach was chosen, with a cross sectional design. To answer the research questions, a questionnaire was developed to measure the different variables. It was important to find a setting where one would surely find variation in end user's choices of different support sources. It was also important to find a setting that was homogeneous. Homogeneity diminishes the danger with alternative predecessors that might create spurious relations (Mitchell, 1985). To ensure a homogenous setting and variation in the end user's answers, a large organization in Norway was chosen (more than 800 employees).

IS-professionals were not included in the survey. The reason was most IS-professionals seldom utilize support personnel. The population was therefore selected to be all non-IS-professionals in the organization.

The Independent Variable (Support Usage):

Through the studies of Lee (1986), Larsen (1989), Delone and McLean; Compeau and Higgins (1995b); Blili et al. (1997), I found three different aspects on the measure of usage: *time spent*, *frequency* and *exploitation ratio.*

Since this research project had a time limit, time spent would be difficult to measure. To measure time spent, one must be sure that the respondents record the time they spend on support usage for a specific period of time. Most end users don't want to be bothered with these things and their answer to such a survey would probably be an estimate anyway. Exploitation ratio measures if a support service is of any use to the respondent. It will not measure in what degree the respondents utilizes different support-services, which was the aim of this study. Therefore *frequency* seemed the best measure to use. Blili et al.'s instrument was changed to fit the aims of the study. The measure was: *How often do you utilize different support sources when using your computer?* Different sources were divided into these categories: *informal support sources, traditional support sources, internal documentation* and *external documentation.* Frequency was measured with five categories, from *less than once a month* to *several times a day.*

Since there is limited research on support usage, and since this instrument never had been tested before, I chose to develop an alternative instrument. This alternative instrument tested for different error situations and asked the respondent *which support source would be his first choice if a specific problem were to arise.*

Pre-tests and later factor analysis showed the alternative instrument was better, and this instrument was chosen to measure the end users' use of different support sources.

Computer Self-Efficacy was measured with Compeau and Higgins's (1995b) instrument. The different items focus on the degree to which the respondent masters the use of new software with different levels of support.

An instrument on IT-Involvement developed by Barki and Hartwick (1994) was pre-tested in the organization. The scale was difficult to translate to Norwegian and the items that were chosen to measure different aspects of the concept were quite similar. A newly developed instrument developed by my mentor Øystein Sørebø was adopted. This instrument measured the importance and personal relevancy an end user expresses towards the computer and use of it.

The IT-skills instrument was developed based on Cheney and Nelson's (1988) instrument. The respondents were asked *to indicate to what degree they used different software* and *to indicate their level of skill within the different types of software*.

In addition to the variables chosen for measuring different end user qualities, three control variables were included. These were *giving collegial support*, *direct access to IS-professionals* and *IC relationship*. The variable *giving collegial support* measures to what degree the respondent gives collegial support to fellow workers. *Direct access to IS-professionals* shows if the respondents have direct access to IS-professionals in the same office location. *IC relationship* defines the respondents' relationships to the information centre on a scale from very good to very bad. Further reviews (through test-respondents) showed that the questionnaire was missing an alternative choice in problem solving. This was *solving the problem themselves*. I, therefore, added this dependent variable to the questionnaire.

The questionnaire was sent to 670 employees. Two hundred and seventy-seven usable questionnaires were returned, which gave a 41.3 percent response rate.

RESULTS

The various sets of variables that are included in this survey have gone through factor analysis, to filter unwanted items that do not measure the variables well enough. Through convergent and divergent validity analysis some items were rejected. This was to ensure the lack of non-redundant concepts.

The results from the analysis supports the following hypothesises: H1a, H1c, H1e, H2b, H2d, H2e and H3a. In addition, *direct access to IS-professionals* seems to correlate positively with the use of *formal support services*, negatively with the use of *informal support services* and negatively with the use of *external documentation*. Also, *giving collegial support* correlates negatively with the use of both *formal* and *informal support services* and positively with the added dependent

Figure 2: Summarizing the Results

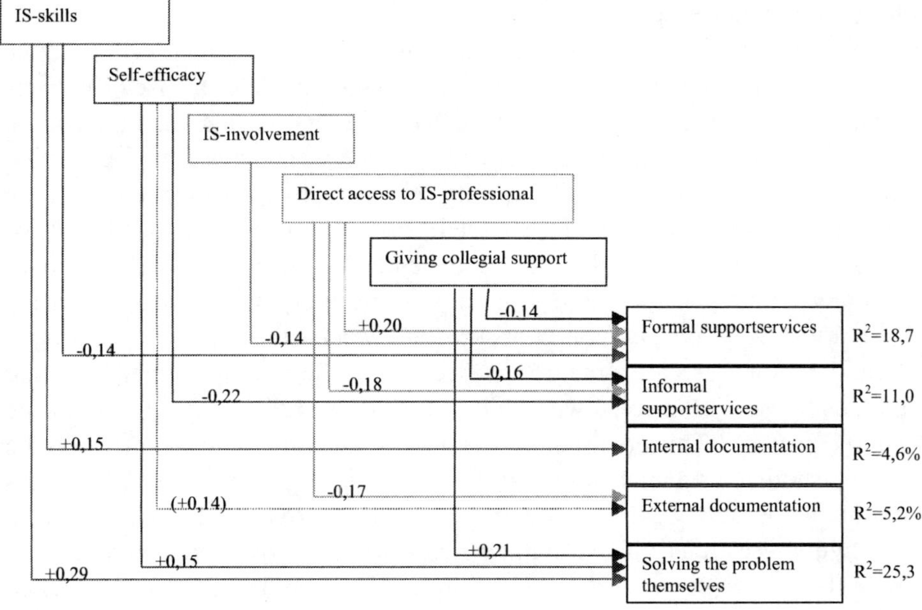

variable *solving the problem themselves*. Figure 2 summarizes the results of the analysis.

The beta (multiple regression) values that are indicated along the arrows apply to the covariance after the inclusion of the control variables. The dashed arrow between Computer Self Efficacy and External Documentation point out there was covariance between the two variables, but this covariance disappeared when the control variables was accounted for. R^2 states explained variance in the dependent variable(s).

IMPLICATIONS, CONCLUSION AND RECOMMENDATIONS

The results show IT-skills might be of importance for the use of formal support services. The negative covariance indicates that formal support services, first of all, would be of use for the novice end users. Earlier discussions point out end users might demand more and better services, from the formal support sources, the higher their IT-skills. My survey does not support these viewpoints. One could expect the enquiries from expert end users would be of such specific nature, the formal support service would not be competent enough to solve such problems. Since I do not have a measure on the actual qualifications possessed by the formal support services in the organization, the answer to this anticipation seems very uncertain. But it might indicate that one, by increasing support qualifications naturally, will be able to help a bigger group of end-users.

The results also show there is a negative covariance between IT-skills and the use of Internal documentation, i.e., the higher IT-skills the less the use of internal documentation. This could imply that the quality of the internal documentation is not good enough. Maybe most internal documents are made for novice users, explaining basic use of different software. The quality of the internal documentation is not measured in this survey, and therefore it will be difficult to point out that documentation quality would impact (indirectly) on the end users' use of internal documentation. Later studies on the subject should therefore contain a measure on the *perceived quality of internal and external documentation.*

An indication that shows the data collected is quite reliable is the result that shows a positive covariance between high IT-skills and the variable *solving the problem themselves*. This covariance is expected, and any other result would be suspicious. Another result that indicates reliability is the result showing the end users giving collegial support negatively covariates with the use of formal support sources.

The hypotheses regarding Computer Self-Efficacy shows a negative covariance towards the *use of informal support sources* (H2b), and a positive covariance towards the *use of external documentation* and towards *solving the problem themselves*. This could imply end users, with a high degree of computer self-efficacy, basically want to solve the problems themselves, either by using external documentation and/or by solving the problems without the use of any support sources. That indicates these end users probably have such high beliefs about themselves they don't see themselves as people needing any help from others. They would expect that no others could solve the problem any faster than themselves anyway.

It is important to notice, when the control variables are included, Computer Self-Efficacy is no longer a valid factor in explaining the use of external documentation. That might indicate a spurious connection. By testing covariance between Computer Self-Efficacy and *access to a computer expert,* I found no covariance. That again might indicate the strong covariance (beta value: -0,17), between *access to a computer expert* and the *use of external documentation,* confounds the effect of Computer Self Efficacy. I would, therefore suggest to test for this in future surveys to clarify the uncertainty around the model.

The results regarding IT-involvement only show covariance with the *use of formal support sources*. Another survey conducted at almost the same time as mine shows the exact same result (Haukedalen, 1998, p. 65). This indicates *end users with a high degree of IT-involvement use formal sources of support more.* The reason why might be, these end users show a bigger interest in computers and computer technology, and therefore are eager to solve IS-related problems. The formal support source might also work as an information channel for these end users.

As their involvement towards IT is higher, they show more general interest for IT, and therefore have the need to get answers regarding information technology.

The results of this survey clearly indicate specific end user qualities affect the end user's choice of support source. I, therefore, recommend organizations to improve these basic qualities of the end user, instead of only providing the traditional support services. Not only should the employees attend training courses to improve these basic qualities, one should also seek to improve the end users' Self-Efficacy and involvement towards computers and computer technology. Especially IT-involvement should be increased. By increasing this quality, one will make the end users use formal support services more often, which again can lead to more effective employees. One must take into mind, although an end-user has high IT-skills and a high magnitude of computer self-efficacy, it does not automatically mean that he/she will solve IT-related problems faster than the formal support group can. For example, if end users feel they are sufficiently qualified to solve IT-related problems, they may well spend days doing exactly this, whereas calling the IT support staff could have solved the problem within minutes.

By increasing end users IT-involvement and by improving quality and increasing availability of the IT support staff, employees would likely become more effective in their everyday work.

In addition, support personnel ought to aim to provide the end users relevant knowledge every time they need help to solve a problem. Bento (1996) talks about *doers* and *facilitators,* when speaking of different types of support personnel. It is not enough that support personnel just solve the problem and leave (doers). They must also transfer the knowledge to the end user, so that the end user more easily can confront the next problem situation they face (facilitators).

It is nevertheless important to notice this survey has been done with data materials from one big Norwegian organization. This does not mean the results and recommendations in this survey would apply to any other arbitrary organization. More research is needed to generalize the conclusions made in this survey.

REFERENCES

Arnoudse, D. M., & Oulette, L.P. (1986). An introduction to the information centre concept. *Information Strategy, 3*(2), 9-12.

Bandura, A. (1986). Social foundations of thought and action: a social cognitive theory. *Series in social learning theory*. Englewood Cliffs, NJ: Prentice-Hall.

Barki, H., & Hartwick, J. (1989, March). Participation and concept of user involvement. *MIS Quarterl,y* 13, (1), 53-63.

Barki, H., & Hartwick, J. (1994a, March). Measuring user participation, user involvement and user attitude. *MIS Quarterly,* 59-82.

Barki, H., & Hartwick, J. (1994b). Explaining the role of user participation in information-System use. *Management Science,* 4(40), 440-465.

Bento, R. F. (1996). Life in the middle: An analysis of information centres from the perspective of their major stakeholders. *Information Management,* 30, 101-109.

Blili, S., Raymond, L, & Rivard, S. (1994). Definition and measurement of end-user computing sophistication. *Journal of End User Computing*, 2(8), 3-12.

Blili, S., Raymond, L., & Rivard, S. (1997). Impact of task uncertainty, end user involvement, and competence on the success of end-user computing. *Information Management*, 33, 137-153. (1998).

Bollen, K., A. (1989). *Structural equations with latent variables.* New York: Wiley.

Bruton, N. (1995). *Effective user support: How to manage the IT helpdesk.* McGraw-Hill Book Company.

Cheney, P.H., & Nelson, R. R. (1988). Brief communication: A tool for measuring and analysing end user computing abilities. *Information Processing & Management,* 24(2), 199-203.

Cheney, P.H, Mann, R.I., & Amoruso, D.L. (1986). Organizational factors affecting the success of end-user computing. *Journal of Management Information Systems*, 1, (3), 65-80.

Churchill, G. A. (1979). A paradigm for developing better measures for marketing constructs. *Journal of Marketing Research*, Vol. XVI.

Churchill, G. A. (1996). Marketing research: Methodological foundations. Dryden Press; c1995. (6th edition).

Compeau, D. R., & Higgins, C.A. (1995a). Application of social cognitive theory to training for computer skills. *Information Systems Research* 6, 2. The University of Western Ontario London, Ontario, Canada N6A 5B9.

Compeau, D. R., & Higgins, C.A. (1995b, June). Computer elf-efficacy: Development of a measure and initial test. *MIS Quarterly*, 189-211

Delone, W. H., & McLean, E. R. (1992). Information systems success: The quest for the dependent variable. *Information Systems Research*, 3(1), 60-95.

Doll, W. J., & Torkzadeh, G. (1988). The measurement of end-user computing satisfaction. *MIS Quarterly*, 2(12), 259-274.

Doll, W. J., & Torkzadeh, G. (1993). The place and value of documentation in end user computing. *Information and Management*, 24, 147-158.

Frankfort-Nachmias, C., & Nachmias, D. (1996). Research methods in the social sciences (5th Ed.). London: Arnold.

Haukedalen, K. (1998). Bruk av brukerstøtte: Hvilke egenskaper for sluttbrukeren kan være av betydning for bruk av brukerstøtte? HiBu – Hønefoss.

Heie, T. H., & Hestad, K. I. (1998). Brukerstøtte: Fra et sluttbrukerperspektiv. HiBu – Hønefoss.

Huff, S.L., Malcolm, C. & Marcolin, B. (1992) Modelling and measuring end user sophistication. ACM.

Huff, S. L., Marcolin, B., Munrow, M. C., & Compeau, D. R. (1994, August).

Understanding and measuring end user sophistication. *Journal of Computing,* 6(1A). The University of Western Ontario, New Zealand.

Igbaria, M., & Guimaraes, T. (1994). Empirically testing the outcomes of user involvement in DSS development. *Omega, International journal of Management Science,* 22(2), 157-172.

Ives, B., & Olson, M. H. (1984, May). User involvement and MIS success: A review of research. *Management Science,* 30(5), 586-603.

Jackson, C.M., Chow, S., & Leitch, R.A. (1997). Toward an understanding of the behavioural intention to use an information system. *Decision Sciences*, 2(28), 357-389.

Kapferer, & Laurent (1985). Measuring consumer involvement for end user computing support. *Decision Science,* 25(4), 481-498.

Kappelman, L.A. (1990). The implementation of computer-based information systems: The respective roles of participation and involvement in information system success. Unpublished doctoral dissertation, Georgia State University.

Kappelman, L. A. (1995). Measuring user involvement with information systems success: The respective roles of user participation and user involvement. *Journal of Information Technology Management*, 3(1), 1-12.

Kappelman, L. A., & McLean, E. R. (1991, December). The perspective roles of user participation and user involvement in information system implementation success. *Twelfth International Conference on Information Systems* (pp. 339-350). New York.

Kappelman, L. A., & McLean, E. R. (1993, October). User engagement in information system development, implementation, and use: Towards conceptual clarity. *Proceedings of the IFIP TC8 Working Conference on Diffusion, Transfer and Implementation of Information Technology* (pp. 199-214). Pittsburgh, PA: North-Holland.

Kappelman, L. A., & McLean, E. R. (1994, January). User Engagement in the development, implementation, and use of information technologies. *Proceedings of the 27th Hawaiian International Conference on the System Sciences*, 4, 512-521. Maui, Hawaii, USA.

Kirwin, W. (1995, March). The true cost of personal computers. Across The Board.

Larsen, T. J. (1989). Managers' use of computers: Middle managers' end-user computing utilization levels and support requirements by level innovativeness. A thesis submitted to the Faculty of the graduate School of the University of Minnesota. University of Minnesota: Minneapolis, MN.

Lee, D. (1986). Usage pattern and sources of assistance for personal computer users. *MIS Quarterly*, 10(4), 313-326.

Marcolin, B. I., Munro, M. C., & Campbell, K. G. (1996). End user ability: Impact of job and individual differences. *Journal of End User Computing*, 3(9), 3-12. Hershey, PA: Idea Group Publishing.

Marcolin, B. I., Munro, M. C., & Compeau, D. R. (1993). End user sophistication: A multitrait-multimethod analysis.

Mirani, R., & King, W. R. (1994a). Impacts of end-user and information center characteristics on end-user computing support. *Journal of Management Information Systems*, 11(1), 141-166.

Mirani, R., & King, W. R. (1994b). The development of a measure for end-user computing support. *Decision Science*, 25(4), 481-498.

Mitchell, T. R. (1985). An evaluation of the validity of correlational research conducted in organizations. *Academy and Management Review,* 10(2), 192-205.

Reve, T. (1985) Validitet i økonomisk-administrativ forskning, i metoder og perspektiver i økonomisk-adminstrativ forskning, 52-72. Oslo, Universitetsforlaget.

Rockart, J. F., & Flannery, L. S. (1983). The management for end user computing. *Communications at the ACM,* 10(26), 776-784.

Smith, A. (1997). Human computer factors: A study of users and information systems. McGraw-Hill Book Company.

Sørebø, Ø. (1996). End user computing and the perceived need for support services: Toward an explanation of the independent-user paradox. Høgskolen i Buskerud, Konferanse: Fifth Edamba Summer School.

Winter, S. J., Chudoba, K. M., & Gutek, B. A. (1997). Misplaced resources? Factors associated with computer literacy among end-users. *Information & Management,* 32, 29-42.

Zaichkowsky, J. L. (1986, December). Conceptualising the involvement construct. *Journal of Consumer Research*, (12), 341-351.

Zinatelli, N., Cragg, P. B., & Cavaye, A. L. M., (1996) "End user computing sophistication and success in small firms." *European Journal of Information Systems,* 3(Vol. 5), 172-181.

Chapter X

Users as Developers — Conditions and Effects of User Systems Development

Anders Avdic
Örebro University, Sweden

ABSTRACT

This chapter presents conditions and effects of User Systems Development using a Spreadsheet Program. It argues that User Systems Development using a Spreadsheet Program is characterized by integration, interactivity and capacity of questioning, which make it possible to control continuous changes in the environment of an organization. Three empirical studies have been carried out using a Grounded Theory influenced approach. The results are presented with the use of the model of generic practice (the ToP model), in order to systemize empirical findings and related theory. The model is used to specify the conditions and results of a specific practice, e.g., a controller practice or an information technology (IT) specialist practice.

INTRODUCTION

In the early days of computers, expertise was needed in order to use computers. As IT tools have become more powerful and user friendly, more and more people have been able to use computers and programs as tools when carrying out working tasks. Nowadays, it is even possible for people without special IT training to construct information systems (IS) that only IT specialists could have done some years ago.

In this chapter the conditions and effects of User Systems Development (USD) using a spreadsheet program (SP) are discussed. USD is performed by a user-developer (UD), a person who acts both as a user and a systems developer. A typical feature of a UD is he/she has a good knowledge of the business and the work related to the IS in question, which is called the user developed application (UDA).

In Figure 1, the difference between Traditional Systems Development (TSD) (1) and USD (2) is outlined in order to demonstrate the nature of USD in contrast to TSD since TSD is familiar to the IS community. To the IT-specialist, knowledge about IS development tools (e.g., methods, program languages) (1a) is in primary focus when developing Tradition Information Systems (TISs) (1c). This is the core of his/her professional knowledge. Knowledge about business (1b) is of course essential but not primary. To the UD knowledge about business (2a) is in primary focus and knowledge about IS development tools (2b) is just a means to accomplish business-oriented tasks, eventually by developing UDAs (2c). The IT-specialist has access to knowledge about IS development tools that is hard to access for non-professionals. Some business knowledge is hard to access to the IT-specialist, since this knowledge is not in the professional knowledge domain of the IT-specialist. The UD on the other hand is the expert on business knowledge. His professionalism depends on his knowledge about business. No one can replace him in this matter. In order to perform USD the UD needs some knowledge about IS development tools. It is not possible though to have access to as much knowledge about IS development tools as the IT-specialist has.

Figure 1: The Relation Between Knowledge and Development

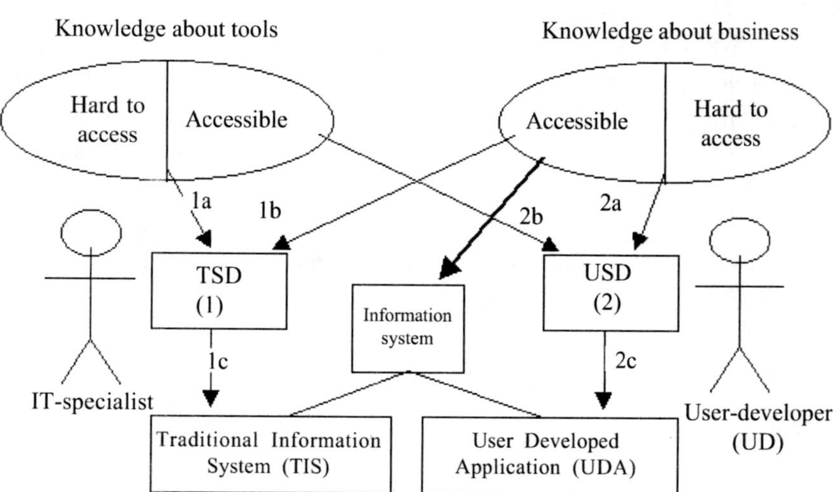

To both the IT-specialist and the UD, both kinds of knowledge are to some degree necessary. In order to make an information system, the most important kind of knowledge is in general knowledge about business, since the information system is about the business. The thick arrow in Figure 1 demonstrates this circumstance.

In order to develop information systems, knowledge about business has to be transferred from business specialists to IT-specialists. This transfer is problematic since people have different frames of references (Alter, 1996; Yourdon, 1989). The entire intention of the sender can therefore not be transferred to the IT-specialist. On the other hand, the IT-specialist cannot fulfill the requirements, since he cannot completely understand the business specialist. Complex systems development tasks still have to be performed through TSD, but as more powerful systems development tools are at hand, the possibilities to perform USD are enhanced from year to year. Spreadsheet programs have properties that give the UD access to IS development features without being an IT-specialist. Other ways to overcome this gap is to perform systems development with an inclusive approach, e.g., RAD (Tudhope, Beynon-Davies, Mackay & Slack, 2001). The systems discussed in this chapter are often small and local and, thereby often not suitable for traditional systems development projects.

With the discussion above in mind, the basic research questions in the chapter are the following:

- What new possibilities can computer users develop in order to perform tasks, when they can develop ISs without help from IT specialists?

The question can be subdivided into the following questions:

- How can UDs take not-easily-formulated knowledge into consideration when performing USD?
- What kind of IS development tool knowledge does a UD need in order to perform tasks?
- What other conditions affect the UD's possibilities to perform USD?
- Which effects are the results of USD?

METHODS

The studies described in the chapter have a strategy that is qualitative, hermeneutic, and Grounded Theory (GT) influenced.

The *qualitative* aspect is manifested through the aim of understanding and interpreting the reality of the UDs (Patton, 1987). A typical feature of qualitative methods is triangulation (Yin, 1994). The methods used are in-depth interviews, studies of SP-UDAs, participant observation and theoretical studies. The *hermeneutic* approach is manifested through the explicit use of the researchers pre-knowledge of USD and of the respondents (Helenius, 1990). Interviews and contacts have been frequent. The researcher's knowledge of USD has resulted in long discussions of different ways to solve specific problems. This has resulted in an atmosphere where the researcher has gained access to the respondents' situation as UD, in a way that would have been impossible if, e.g., survey studies had been performed. This change of perspective is also typical of hermeneutic studies. In the empirical studies, the focus has alternated between product and process (SP-UDA and USD). Another change of focus also closely related to USD is the change of focus between the actual work and UDA-development. While the UD is focused on the tasks at hand, the observer has been focused on the developmental aspect. The research methods can be labeled as *Grounded Theory (GT)* influenced since the empirical research has preceded the theoretical studies (Patton, 1987). Another GT aspect is the aim of an unbiased data collection situation. The choice of both research questions and respondents has been a result of a specific intention, but the data collection has been performed with an awareness of the importance of initially not knowing what really happens when UDs perform USD. The data analysis has therefore been performed according to GT methods (data collection, open coding and selective coding). The coding activities have been aimed at finding a key variable. The variable found is "integration." The importance of this is discussed below.

Three empirical studies have been conducted between 1998 and 2000. Two studies have focused on UDs. Interviews have been conducted with three people in an industry, and three people in a public authority. In the third study, three IT specialists are interviewed about problems related to UDA. The UD-interviews have been open and focused on the systems made by the UDs. Questions have been asked about why the systems were developed, which alternatives and problems there were, how the systems had been developed, how they were used in the UDs work and how the UDs perceived the effects of USD. In depth interviews with each UD have been carried out between three and 10 times, depending on how many UDAs the UD had developed. The interviews have been taped and coded. The analysis has been performed according to GT. The studies are shortly described below.

The industry is a board mill with 750 employees. It can be characterized as a multi-goal, dynamic business, acting in a keen competitive market. The area of board production is technically and chemically advanced and the board machines are very complicated. The customer's quality demands are increasingly detailed and not easily achieved. The three UDs work as controller, production planner and production division manager. The controller is an experienced SP user and the other two are somewhat less experienced.

The 50 employees in the public authority work in building, traffic, environment and maps construction units. The persons interviewed were clerks in different departments. Activities in the authority are characterized by their public nature. This means that business should neither be profitable nor involve a loss. Other important goals are the municipality inhabitants' best interests should always be taken into consideration and activities should be carried out with openness. This demand for openness means the grounds on which decisions are taken should be both available and comprehensible. One of the clerks is a more experienced SP user than the other two.

The three IT-specialists include an IT-manager, a systems developer and a consultant systems developer. Findings show that the IT-specialists perceived problems related to the USD, such as lack of documentation, unstructured applications and limited data processing capabilities in SP. The solutions proposed to these problems included SP training, SP-version upgrading and more structured UDAs.

FRAMEWORK AND RESULT

Since the chapter claims to be GT influenced, studies of related theory have been greatly influenced by the empirical studies. As a framework model, a modified version of the model of generic practice (the ToP model) (Goldkuhl & Röstlinger, 1999) is used in order to systemize empirical findings and related theory. The model can be used to specify the conditions and result of a specific practice, e.g., a controller practice or an IT specialist practice. The modified model consists of a set of conditional categories, *knowledge*, *norms*, and *tools*. The categories that express the specific practice are named *producers* and their *actions*. The last category is the *result* of the practice. When a UD develops UDAs, he acts in at least two types of practices, the primary (e.g., controller) practice and the secondary (developer's) practice. Each practice is related to a profession, e.g., a controller and an IT specialist profession. The model makes it possible to separate the conditions of the different practices. It also makes it possible to discuss which parts of the developer's practice can improve the main practice, without consulting an IT specialist. The nature of the categories is described below, together with presentation of findings from the studies.

Information Systems (Result)

A UDA is an IS and an IS is a result of systems development. The difference between a traditional information system (TIS) and a UDA is mainly a question of how it is built. UDAs are built by UDs with a good knowledge of the business, while TISs are built by IT specialists (Avdic, 1999).

SP-UDAs can be divided into four categories according to the how long learning time the UD need, in order to develop the SP-UDA. The first category is called "Simple SP-system." This rather common UDA consists more or less of structured text. It could be defined as a "pre-stage" to more complex UDAs. The next category is "Small SP-system." Typically it has simple formulas and eventually SUM-functions and simple diagrams. "Large SP-system" has more complex formulas and functions and can be distributed on several spreadsheets. The most complex UDA-system is "Application." It can be very complex and it can include programming code (Avdic, 1999). UDAs in the studies were of small and large types.

User Systems Development (Actions)

TSD can be characterized by the notion of the "life cycle," where tasks are specialized and activities are separated and systemized. User Systems Development (USD) and TSD are profoundly different in many ways. USD actions in the studies were, neither organized nor planned. Specific work related tasks or problems made the UD aware of some information need. USD was looked upon as work rather than systems development by the UD. Compared to TSD, USD is characterized by integration rather than specialization. Still it is systems development.

Success factors of USD have been discussed in the scientific community for more than a decade. The reasons why USD is successfully adapted in an organization have been claimed to depend on the presence of informal channels of communication and how common training on USD tools is (Brancheau & Brown, 1993). Basic conditions (suitable tasks, equipment, knowledge, and certain independence) must be fulfilled to make USD *possible* (Carlsson, 1993). If business and information needs are dynamic, USD can be *justified*. USD is *appropriate* when UDs also have access to well-organized data and get support from management and the IT-department (Auer, 1998). Perceived importance is also claimed to be vital (Blili, Raymond & Rivard, 1998).

When discussing of how to manage and control USD, advocates of *high control* recommend (strict) organization of USD activities (e.g., Andersen, 1994). Advocates of *low control* consider USD as time saving and appropriate because of the lack of detailed monitoring (Speier & Brown, 1997).

The discussion of what factors are determining successful USD is implicitly aiming at organizing USD activities with a certain degree of control. In our study this discussion is not really relevant since the UDs are professional in their respective profession. They have used IT tools, if they have found it relevant, in relation to their work tasks. Since they did not separate USD from running work, they had the same quality demands on the USD result as on the rest of their work. In opposite to some research (Teo & Tan, 1999), our study shows the risk of poor quality in UDA information output should be related to the UDs' professionalism, rather than to design methods or tool properties.

User Developers (Producers)

A UD is a person with a good knowledge of the business who develops UDAs that supports the UD in his work. The UD is primarily a professional (e.g., a controller) who integrates, to some extent, the role of one or more IT specialists, when performing USD. The UD could have good knowledge about IS development tools. This does not disqualify him as a UD; it rather makes him even more efficient.

Knowledge

When performing USD, knowledge is divided between the UD and the tool (SP). Certain kinds of (not too complex) knowledge are formalized into the SP and can be used in the SP-UDA. Other kinds can be formalized by the UD, into the SP-UDA. Some kinds of knowledge (e.g., of critical evaluation of the relevance of formulas) cannot be formalized at all. Still, this kind of not-easily-formalized (sometimes tacit) knowledge can be taken into consideration when using the UDA, since the UD (with business knowledge) is the user of the system. The findings also show that goals, not easily formalized, can be taken into consideration when performing USD.

Knowledge about tools can be used to deepen knowledge about business. UDs in the studies could make tacit knowledge explicit when developing a USD, which in turn made it possible for others to evaluate and criticize the UDA and its output. The UDs were very conscious about that an ongoing change in the company's/ authority's environment made it important to develop not yet known knowledge about conditions and circumstances of their work. Our findings show one important aim of the UD is to articulate knowledge about business and that UDA is one important means to do this.

Norms

Norms and knowledge are closely related and sometimes hard to keep apart. One set of norms that are central in the chapter is professional ethics. Professional ethics are crucial to the UD, since the professionals' activities are monitored not by procedures but by professional and business ethics. Professional ethics, as well a, professional tacit knowledge (se above) cannot easily be transferred to IT-specialists in systems development projects. Therefore, when USD is performed by Uds, professional ethics and tacit knowledge can be taken into consideration in a way not possible in TSD. Findings of the industry study also show that investigations made by the UD, when performing USD, can change organizational norms. Ongoing questioning of business using UDAs can implicitly or explicitly challenge existing models as well as their norms. In the study, the methods of measuring production was questioned, which in turn, resulted in changes in existing models and calculations. In the authority study, changes in the political situation resulted in demands of new models to assess the value of real estate. This does not mean that revolutionary effects take place every time a UDA is developed.

Tools

USD tools are closely related to norms and knowledge, since norms and knowledge are implemented in tools. The main tool, when performing SP-USD, is of course the SP. The SP integrates functions for input, output, storage, processing and presentation. This integration results in interactive development and use. The open nature of the SP can cause different kinds of errors (Panko & Sprague, 1998).

Knowledge of business, tools, and design can prevent some of these errors. Another circumstance that makes SP suitable for UDA is the fact that they are very common. In Sweden almost all employees can have access to a SP.

Because of the integrated nature of USD, learning, using and systems development take place at the same time. Learning applies to both the business and the tool. One conclusion of this is training in the use of a tool can improve the quality of USD, which in turn can improve business. One way for the management to support USD is to initiate and encourage UD-tailored training in the use of tools.

DISCUSSION AND CONCLUSION

SP-USD is characterized by *integration, interactivity and capacity of questioning.* The notion of *integration* can be looked upon in several dimensions:

1. Aspects of ISs — integration of collecting, storing, processing, and distribution of information.
2. Roles — integration of developer, user and manager roles.
3. Roles of actors in systems development — integration of analyst, programmer, database and designer roles.
4. Integration of processing functions of the IS.

The integrated nature of USD results in *interactivity*. Interactivity means the UD can change quickly between developing and using the SP-UDA. During the USD-process, the UD knowledge of the business and USD increases. This is actually the goal of the UD. Since the UD knowledge of the business increases when performing USD, the UD can analyze and also *question* aspects of business (e.g., production measuring methods). The questioning aspect makes it possible to improve business.

SP-USD's can be used as a means of controlling continuous changes in the environment of the organization by changing business with the help of USD. A

Figure 2: Continuous Change and User Systems Development

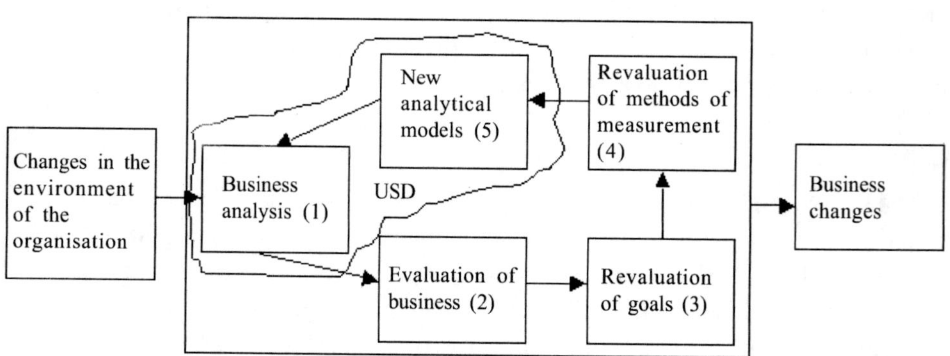

business analysis (1) can result in a revaluation of the business (2), which can result in a revaluation of its goals (3) (and norms), which can result in a revaluation of methods of measurement (4), which can result in new analytical models (5) (UDA), which can lead to a new business analysis (1) and so on. USD is discussed as one way to meet change as a permanent business condition, which differs from traditional methods for systems development.

This way of revaluating organizational goals can be related to double-loop learning as it is presented by Argyris and Schön (1996). This includes not only changes in behavior or strategies, but also means norms of the organization can be changed. The ongoing questioning of business practice performed through USD can imply this form of norm changing.

REFERENCES

Alter, S. (1996). *Information Systems - A Management Perspective.* Menlo Park: Benjamin/Cummings.

Andersen, E. S. (1994). *Systemutveckling – Principer, Metoder Och tekniker.* Lund: Studentlitteratur. [In Swedish].

Argyris, C., & Schön, D. A. (1996). *Organizational Learning II - Theory, Method, and Practice.* Reading, MA: Addison Wesley.

Auer, T. (1998). *Factors Affecting End-User Computing: Skills*, (TUCS Technical Report No. 159). Department of Computer Science, University of Turku.

Avdic, A. (1999). *Användare Och Utvecklare – Om Anveckling Med Kalkylprogram.* Dissertation. Linköping University. [In Swedish].

Blili, S., Raymond, L., & Rivard, S. (1998). Impact of Task Uncertainty, End-User Involvement, and Competence on the Success of End-User Computing. *Information & Management,* 33, 137-153.

Brancheau, J. C., & Brown, C. V. (1993). The Management of End User Computing: Status and Directions. *ACM Computing Surveys,* 25(4), 437-482.

Carlsson, S. A. (1993). *A Longitudinal Study of User Developed Decision Support Systems.* Dissertation, Department of Informatics, Lunds University.

Goldkuhl, G., & Röstlinger, A. (1999). *Expanding the Scope – From Language Action to Generic Practice.* (CMTO Research Papers No. 1999:06). Linköping University.

Helenius, R. (1990). *Förstå och Bättre Veta.* Stockholm: Carlssons. [In Swedish].

Panko, R. R., & Sprague, R. H., Jr. (1998). Hitting the Wall: Errors in Developing and Code Inspecting a 'Simple' Spreadsheet Model. *Decision Support Systems*, 22, 337-353.

Patton, M. Q. (1987). *How to Use Qualitative Methods in Evaluation.* Beverly Hills, CA: Sage.

Speier, C., & Brown, C. (1997). Differences in End-User Computing Support and Control Across User Departments. *Information & Management*, 32, 85-99.

Teo, T. S. H., & Tan, M. (1999). Spreadsheet Development and 'What-If' Analysis: Quantitative Versus Qualitative Errors. *Accounting, Management and Information Technologies,* 9, 141-160.

Tudhope, D., Beynon-Davies, P., Mackay, H., & Slack, R. (2001). Time and Representational Devices in Rapid Application Development. *Interacting with Computers*, 13, 447-466.

Yin, R. K. (1994). *Case Study Research – Design and Methods.* Beverly Hills, CA: Sage.

Yourdon, E. (1989). *Modern Structured Analysis*. Englewood Cliffs, NJ: Prentice-Hall.

Chapter XI

Solving Common Business Problems with Microsoft Office®

Kathryn Marold
Metropolitan State College of Denver, USA

Gwynne Larsen
Metropolitan State College of Dever, USA

ABSTRACT

The authors traced the process of revising and updating a long-existing Micro-Based Software class at the undergraduate level at Metropolitan State College of Denver. The course was designed to allow students to become proficient in end user computing at the operational business level. The revisions were prompted by the increasing sophistication of horizontal microcomputer application programs, the increase in the level of computer literacy among undergraduate School of Business students, and the students' need for experience in problem solving and applying the theory they learned using the Microsoft Office *software suite. A pilot class was taught utilizing the revised curriculum in the Fall of 2001. The revised curriculum involved using Web-based material and regular presentation sessions for solutions to assigned problems. An efficacy survey was administered at the end of the class, to determine student satisfaction with the revised curriculum. The success of the pilot class resulted in implementing the revised content in all sections of the Micro-Based Software class as of Spring semester, 2002.*

BACKGROUND

In today's business environment, most of the commonly occurring daily business problems are solved at the desktop computer, using existing horizontal software applications. Many of the operational level problems are solved using the most popular horizontal application suite, *Microsoft Office*. Some version of *Office* is installed on almost all business computers and is used almost universally throughout the organizational environment. Hence, end user computing proficiency is more important than ever. The central typing pool and the electronic data processing (EDP), or end user support services for problems requiring a short turnaround time, are almost nonexistent anymore. Office staff and lower level managers are responsible for solving daily problems on their own, using the horizontal microcomputer application program with which they are familiar. With current GUI software programs and enhanced Help facilities, including well-designed Search facilities, cascading Windows where Help steps remain on the screen, and social interfaces like the Microsoft *Office Assistant*, the software skills to perform a task is no longer the hurdle. It is actually the problem-solving process that is the challenge. This is an account of how an existing Micro-Based Software course was revamped to include problem-solving elements, so that business school graduates would be better prepared to tackle the daily problems in the office.

Much has been written on end user computing since microcomputers became the *modus operandi* of the business world. More than one journal is devoted entirely to end-user computing, such as *The Journal of End User Computing* sponsored by IRMA and published by Idea Group Publishing. The microcomputer has added a new dimension to end user support by increasing the range of computer information systems and increasing the computer literacy of the end user (Lundgren, 1998).

When hands-on laboratory sessions were introduced into end user computing courses in the 1990s, students were given the opportunity to "learn by doing." The computer provided the vehicle for the learning, where students actually learned concepts while working with the software program. It had become obvious that learning programs should be designed to allow the flexibility that resource-based, self-paced learning could provide (Stoney, 1999). When the hardware could support it, self-paced, resource-based instruction, such as multimedia, provided the links between conceptual and experiential learning (Stoney, 1999). Increasingly, as the program interfaces became totally graphical, many concepts and ideas could not be taught without the aid of technology to represent and manipulate them. Molnar (1997) noted that computers have revolutionized the representation and manipulation of information.

Web delivered courses spawned a new surge in research on micro-based courses. A study was done recently, comparing 94 students in a traditional classroom, with 37 students taking the same course online. It was found the perception of the online students was that they learned as much and had the same quality of instruction as the students in the classroom (Cooper, 2000). This strengthened the premise that end user computing courses could be offered successfully online.

Incorporating problem solving into end user computing courses could be a relatively seamless process. At the undergraduate level, the faculty wants to educate future computer information systems (CMS) professionals, so they will have both the business acumen and the technical skills to solve organizational management problems and provide technical solutions (Rodriguez, 2000). It has been found basic skills are not learned in isolation, but in the process of completing real world tasks that integrate numerous skills (Stoney, 1999). Problem solving could give students practice in applying the theory they learned while using skills obtained from specific application programs.

In the 1960s, Marshall McLuhan (1964) noted that we were witnessing a revolution that was totally new, and changing the very nature of human perception and experience. The electronic environment put us in the world of pattern recognition and out of the world of mere data collection. It took us from an egocentric work environment to a global village; competitiveness no longer depended on just the discovery of new technology. The speed at which knowledge was transmitted through our educational systems created highly skilled workers who could apply their knowledge (Molnar, 1997). We moved from a goods centered work force to an information handling work force. Powerful technologies are now available to augment significantly the skills necessary to convert data into information and transform information into knowledge (Molnar, 1997).

End user computing courses were studied and researched throughout the '90s. Experts agreed an educator must be more than just a "talking book." One way to accomplish this was to use multimedia tools in the classroom, which freed the instructor to enlighten the student's mind" (Luna & McKenzie, 1997). Withrow noted:

> *The 21st century will go down as the age of the mind, the brain and telecommunications. Those who have the skills and knowledge to navigate cyberspace will participate fully in the global village of the future (Withrow, 1997).*

End user computing skills became more important than ever. Courses to teach application programs could be converted into computer-delivered courses. Computer based training (CBT) and Web based training (WBT), if designed correctly, could free both the student and the instructor. Payson noted (1998), "It is pedagogically important in computer mediated instruction to have effective educational programming that can take advantage of new technologies." End user computing was alive and well—just taking on new forms. One distinguishing feature of a CBT is that it is self-sufficient. The student needs little or no outside help beyond the tutorial. The contents of the program and other training management methods motivate the students (Ganger, 1990). Online reference guides are a form of user help on a computer system that allows the user explanatory reference material at the moment it is needed. This reduces the need for instructor interception or more formal training (Ganger, 1990).

Whether the course environment was a new "smart classroom" or the Web, end user computing courses survived. Payson noted the integrated use of several technologies allowed for both synchronous and asynchronous instruction in the most academically sound and cost effective combination for a particular course or program (Payson, 1998). When combined with problem solving elements, the end user computing courses could be even stronger. The state of technology today allows for demonstrations of active problem solving by instructors and interactive problem solving by students during classtime (Niederman & Webster, 1998). With all of the technology available and the presentation equipment that characterizes most college classrooms, students could explain their plans and demonstrate solutions to problems, giving them valuable "real-world" experience. After all, the goal of end-user training is to produce a motivated user who has the basic skills needed to apply what has been learned and then to continue to learn on the job (Niederman & Webster, 1998).

In addition, technology use encourages teacher-as-facilitator approaches. McGrath noted, with technological tools, students show more persistence in solving problems. Technology makes classroom activities feel more real world and relevant, so students take them more seriously (McGrath, 1998). Thus, incorporating problem solving into the end user computing courses was supported by earlier research. We were on established ground with our plans to revise the Micro-based Software course, and the time was right.

Rationale for Revising Existing Class

The authors revised the existing CMS Micro-based Software class to reflect the changes in computing in the last decade, along with the pressing need for business students to solve problems by applying theories learned in the end user computing class. We revised the existing CMS 3270 Micro-based Software class so that it taught School of Business students how to handle the numerous business problems that occur daily at the operational level in all arenas. We called this additional component to the class, "software solutions architecture." This addition reflected our primary goal of allowing students to practice analyzing a problem, planning alternative solutions, committing to one of the possible solutions, and using one or more *Office* components to solve it. That is, the computer skills became secondary to the primary goal of being able to put keystrokes to practice in a "real-life" scenario. In order to parallel the typical business office environment, we stressed solving problems within a team environment. We had students self-select their teams, or in the case of the online sections, we divided them into teams from two to five members.

In the past decade, the level of computer literacy for entry-level School of Business students taking the CMS required beginning information systems class has increased 10 percent (Marold & Fustos, 2001). We concluded that the need for teaching skills of a particular program — in this case *Office* — was not as pressing as it was when Dr. Larsen first designed the course. It is common for business workers at all levels, including those in top management positions, to use computers and software as tools to solve their daily problems: those programs are easier to use than they have ever been, and students are often comfortable with the program interface already. The newly-graduated employee is now much more computer literate and much better prepared to use popular software productivity packages. In most business positions employees are expected to know how to use microcomputers.

Standardizing of End-user Programs

End user computing has matured and become much more standardized in the past decade. Horizontal application software programs are now used in place of the narrower specialized vertical applications of the past. One of the most used is the Microsoft *Office* suite of applications. The tool itself, consisting of *Word, Excel, Access, PowerPoint*, and *Outlook,* is easier than ever before to master, although its functionality has expanded. In addition, the *Windows* computing environment is the standard user interface of today. In other words, all *Windows*-based applications look very much the same; containing the same menu choices in much the same order. We have reached the stage where if a computer user learns the interface of one *Windows* application program, those familiar elements are common to the next program he or she might attempt to learn.

However, developing solutions for problems occurring in daily business situations is still no easier than before. We had noticed an increasing deficiency in student ability to apply theory, despite problem-solving courses in other areas of their undergraduate curriculum. Our premise was that after taking our revised CMS 3270 course, students would be better equipped to solve business problems using the *Office* tools. They would have hands-on experience solving typical operational problems in a team situation and presenting a solution to their peers and instructor.

The Course within a Program

The Micro-based Software course CMS 3270 is the cornerstone course for students minoring in CMS. It is also a major component of our End User Support certificate, popular with students who may already have an older or non-technology degree and want to update their skills. Also, other CMS courses such as Micro User Operating Systems, Analysis of Hardware and Software, and various Internet courses revolve around material taught in this class. Frequently, students from outside the Business School at Metropolitan State College — those in the School of Professional Studies and Language Arts and Sciences — take the course to enhance their personal computing skills and increase their employment opportunities. The course curriculum had not been revised, except for software programs used since it was officially adopted in 1989. It was time to update the course curriculum to better reflect current student needs.

HISTORY OF COURSE

Professors in the CMS department began teaching end-user skills with the advent of the first microcomputers in about 1984. In Micro-based Software, we used the "stand-alone" packages of *dBASE*, *Word Perfect*, and *Framework*. A single integrated package that was powerful enough to include a relational database application was unheard of in the mid-80s. The smaller integrated programs such as *Works* and *FirstChoice* were used in the Introduction to Computers course, but they were not robust enough for serious business applications in our 3,000 level course. The next progression was to *dBASEII, Word Perfect* and *Lotus*. Around 1984, a software package called *Smart* actually combined a database, word processing and a spreadsheet, although the integration was primitive.

A local industry survey (Mawhinney et al., 1999) confirmed our opinion that knowledge of software such as word processing, spreadsheets and database was very important in hiring criteria. During the '90s, we moved from Microsoft's *Office 95*, to *Office 98,* to *Office 2000*, and now are using *Office XP*. Some of our colleagues think it is no longer necessary to teach end user computing in our department, that students are computer literate at an advanced level already, and programs are intuitive, anyway. We think there is a need for a type of self-paced instruction that students can tailor to their needs and learn the required skills in an anytime, anyplace setting (Marold et al., 1999). We believe it is more necessary than ever before, but that end user computing needs to be taught in a way that enhances problem solving and presentation skills, as opposed to just learning keystrokes. The ability to apply the application program skills learned to new situations in a typical business setting is crucial to success for our students — whether they are entering the job market as end user support personnel, or whether they are the end users themselves.

GOALS AND OBJECTIVES OF THE REVISED COURSE

Before beginning the course revision plans and implementing the pilot course in the Fall '01 semester, we solidified some general goals and some measurable objectives. Our main goal was to produce "software solution architects" who could take a problem at the operational business level, design an organized solution process, solve the problem, and implement it within a short turnaround time. The tool — *Office 2000* — used for problem solution, was the same tool many in the business world use today.

Course Objectives

Following are the objectives of the CMS 3270 course known as Micro-Based Software:

- To provide our computer information systems (CMS) majors and minors and those students obtaining a specialized CMS certificate, with business problem solving skills using Microsoft *Office* software.
- To give our students the opportunity to use word processing, spreadsheet, database and presentation graphics programs at an advanced level.
- To assure a level of learning in accordance to Blooms' taxonomy (Bloom, 1956), reflecting the content of a 3,000 level IS course — specifically to apply theory in a problem-solving situation.
- To provide valuable team experience and project management for students in a simulated office environment.
- To emphasize theory and provide for testing concepts gained as a result of skill mastery in current office software applications at the operational level, namely Microsoft *Office.*

Course Revision Specifications

Because this course is also taught online as a Web-delivered course, all of the revisions had to be configured to work in an online environment. Material previously printed, such as class notes, had to be transformed into Web pages and loaded on the Class Website. Problem solving excercises had to be modularized to be delivered at specific intervals on a Forum or Bulletin Board. Solutions to the problems had to be in a form that could be uploaded to a public viewing area, such as a Workspace or Forum, for all the class members to see. Oral presentations at specific class meetings worked fine for traditional classroom sections, but were not appropriate for the online class. Preparing solutions using the *PowerPoint* application allowed for conversion to HTML and subsequent uploading to a public viewing area for all class members to review.

To meet the above objectives, we constructed a series of general business problems at an operational level that could be solved within a short turn-around cycle, either individually or within dyads, emulating operational business environments. We continue to write new problems with each semester's beginning. Not only does this keep "ideal solutions" from miraculously recurring from semester to semester, it keeps the course fresh and the content reflective of the small business world in our locale. Problem assignments often mimic situations that are current in our economy. We design open-ended problems so there are multiple possible solutions. No one solution is the "correct" answer, but students soon decide some solutions are easier and more appropriate for the stated problem. Part of the learning process is to learn to choose the simplest and most appropriate tool for the task at hand. Operational problems typically have very tight turn-around. Refer to the Appendix for samples of typical problem assignments.

METHODOLOGY

Not only have software applications programs changed in the last decade, so have teaching methods. The "chalk 'n talk" lecture sessions and lab demos have given way to smart classrooms and more interactive classes. Sections of almost our entire CMS core curriculum are offered as online Web-delivered courses. The methodology for delivering the CMS 3270 course had to change, too. The traditional classroom sections of the course are delivered in smart, or what we have termed "semi-smart" classrooms, where high-end presentation equipment, including the instructor's laptop, an intranet connection, a sound system, and an overhead projector are available. However, each student does not have to have his/her own computer.

Physical Delivery

The pilot class in the Fall of 2001 was held in a semi-smart classroom, with one session a week in a campus lab, where all students had computers with *Office 2000*, the Web, and a connection to all appropriate campus servers. All lectures, theory discussions, and software demonstrations were delivered in the classroom. The class syllabus was loaded on the Web for all students to access, and printed copies were distributed the first week of class. Hyperlinked within the syllabus page were pertinent materials for the class. So in what Mawhinney and Morrell (1999) termed a WAD — Web augmented delivery — the traditional class became a variety of what sometimes is mistakenly labeled a "hybrid class." (Technically, hybrid classes meet some of the time on the Web, which was not the case here. All class meetings were physical, held in a classroom three times a week.) Instead of overhead transparencies and other more traditional aids, most lecture material was prepared as Web pages, using *DreamWeaver 4.0*. The Web was accessed from within the smart classroom and the material was projected for students as Web pages. Students could use those same Web pages for review, because they were hyperlinked from their syllabus page. Not only did this allow a high-end multimedia presentation of class material and student access ATAP (any time, any place), it also facilitated porting the class material to the Web-delivered section, once the pilot class was successful.

Subsequent classroom sessions were held in smart or interactive classrooms where each student had a computer, as well as the instructor-controlled console. The most successful sessions of the Micro-Based Software class are now held in a special needs lab owned and managed by our School of Business. The classroom setting is an intimate lab with 22 computer stations arranged in a U shape around the instructor station. All student computers are easily monitored from the instructor station, team and instructor presentations use high-end equipment that allows two screens to be projected simultaneously, computer drives are configurable and writable by students, and problem solutions are lively "give and take" sessions, where students learn as much from peer presentations as they do from the instructor.

Problem Solving Component

The students in Micro-Based Software work in a team environment to solve a series of office-type problems, using the *Office* software applications as tools. The students are required to study the problem, determine alternative solutions, decide on a solution, and use presentation software to present that solution to the rest of the class and the instructor. The class as a group then comes to a consensus as to the most effective and efficient solution.

For the pilot classroom section and subsequent classroom sections, the currently assigned problem resides on a campus intranet server for students to view, print, or download. The problems are assigned in two or three-week intervals and students are allowed, and encouraged, to ally with classmates to solve the problem and present the solution in a team environment. They are given the option to solve each problem solo as well, but after the first three problems, almost everyone decides to team up; the barriers to working together are far outdistanced by the benefits of collaborative effort and sharing the workload.

Assessment

Students in the Micro-Based Software class are evaluated by several means, testing both their skills at end user computing and their analytical ability. The following percentages apply:

- Problem solving solutions (50 percent).
- Quizzes and tutorial submissions demonstrating skills in *Office* (15 percent).
- *MOUS* type certification tests for final exam (23 percent).
- Independent papers: non-*Office* software reports (5 percent).
- Final integrated report (7 percent).

Performance and final grades in the pilot class did not differ significantly from the final grades in the non-pilot section of CMS 3270, although the assessment was quite different. Grades in the subsequent offerings of the class show normal distribution.

In the final exam, 23 percent credit consists of achievement scores on the Internet-accessed *SAM (Skills Assessment Manager),* composed of one exam each in Word, Access, Excel, and PowerPoint and published by the Course Technology division of International Thompson Publishing. These *Office* modules simulate the Microsoft Office User Support certificates that are available from official Microsoft vendors for a fee. They are skills-based evaluations of user mastery of *Access, PowerPoint, Excel*, and *Word* application programs at the Core Level or the Expert Level. Students are given tasks to perform in a simulated environment that is timed. There is immediate feedback to the student. The students' scores are automatically entered into an instructor database that reports student results by section, as well. Since the *SAM* testing system is available via the Web and students can have a front-end installed on their own home computers, the exams can be taken on their own time in a semi-proctored situation. From anecdotal feedback from students over three semesters, the *SAM* exams are regarded as one of the most valuable parts of the course. Students appreciate taking exams in an online environment and being exposed to the type of testing they will experience when in a company training program. Microsoft certification is an extremely popular component of employee training in the modern corporate environment.

The individually prepared reports, as well as the tutorials, quizzes, and *SAM* tests balance the course assessments; they reflect the student's proficiency outside of the team problem-solving environment. That is, students must prove they can use the tools at a core level and prepare reports independently. The software report was a holdover from the old curriculum; we originally retained it because we strongly believed it was a very valuable experience. The original idea of having students prepare an independent report on microcomputer software that was not covered in the course was to expose them to various other application programs that are used in business. Many years ago, before the smart classroom was available, these reports were presented orally with the aid of a computer cart. Students showed their classmates a program they knew, and often used in their workplace. This not only gave the class a broad exposure to many programs that we could not possibly cover in the limited 15-week term, it gave the students a perspective on the breadth of applications available for the desktop. It also gave them a recognition level as a result of the "show and tell" presentation by their classmate, and it gave the presenter valuable experience on how to explain a program to the uninitiated computer user. When the interactive lab setting became part of the class, the presentation of these software reports had to be dropped: there was no time for 30 reports within the limited class time. The written reports were then submitted to the instructor. By 2002, when Microsoft applications saturated the desktop environment and the software program that was the subject of the report narrowed to two or three other commonly used programs, we decided to drop this requirement altogether. The final report remains a vital assessment of the student's individual ability to bring together a formal report on a typical business problem.

EVALUATION OF THE COURSE REVISION

In order to evaluate student efficacy as a result of the revised pilot section of CMS 3270 Micro-Based Software in the Fall of 2001, we developed and administered a Student Satisfaction Survey. We personally were satisfied with our revision plans, but what did the students think of the class? Micro-Based Software had always been a popular elective, and we wanted it to remain so. The 10 students in the pilot class had not experienced the previous curriculum, but they did know they were signing up for a pilot class that was a significant revision of what they might have heard 3270 was all about. The section was added and scheduled at a time after the initial offering of the classroom section. Half of the students in the section were Aviation Management majors from the School of Professional Studies. The other five were CMS majors from the School of Business, taking an elective course. All were juniors or seniors at Metro. The instrument was designed to measure the degree to which a student agreed with our main objectives, not as a comparison between the two curricula.

Students in the pilot class in the Fall of 2001 were generally pleased with the revised curriculum and their grades were consistent with grades in the traditional section of Micro-Based Software. The following semester, we incorporated the changes into all sections of the course, including the Web offered section. While there are noteworthy differences in a course taken online and one taken in the classroom, the problem solving scenarios and the assessment of student learning remain the same. Students in the classroom section become very close, and the experience is truly rewarding for the instructor.

The first time the course was taught online presented a few problems in the newly developed problem solving area. We divided the students into six groups of five students each. In our online system, there is a place called Profile for the students to enter their names, phone numbers, and any other information they would like to share. We told the students to be sure to put their phone numbers where they wanted to be contacted and their e-mail address in there. We put the list of group names in the e-mail area called the Forum and told the students the first person on the list was responsible for setting up the meeting times and task allocations. The first problem was posted in a bulletin board type place in the Forum. The students were told what was expected of them as they were in the online class. However, there was no way for them as a group to ask the instructor questions. Some of them asked questions

Table 1: User Satisfaction Survey, n = 8

Question	**(Disagree)**		**Scale**		**(Agree)**	
	0	**1**	**2**	**3**	**4**	**5**
Confident of ability to solve problems				2	5	1
Proficient in advanced WP skills					7	1
Proficient in advanced SS skills				3	5	0
Proficient in introductory DB skills				3	3	2
Proficient in *Office 2000*					5	3
Improved analytical reasoning ability					5	3
Class syllabus and class notes were helpful		1	0	2	4	1
Ability to self-learn new applications				2	2	4
Learned from classmates				5	3	0
Course content too much work	1	1	1	4	0	1
Course content too little work	1	1	3	3	0	0
Expected grade in course (A=5)				2	3	3

Note: Two students from the original 10 dropped out after the September 11 World Trade Center incident. They were Aviation Management majors.

in e-mail and others just worked it out for themselves. The result was not always as satisfactory as it was in the classroom environment, where there was more give-and-take and discussion of what was expected from them. Another major problem is students can decide to drop the course and not participate; an official drop slip does not have to be processed until about six weeks into the semester. Thus, teammates (and instructors) do not know a student has dropped, and someone given an assignment may just not do it and not even tell the team.

Students from the online course were asked to answer in anecdotal fashion three questions pertaining to (1) what they liked about the course, (2) what they did not like about the course, and (3) what they thought could be done to improve the course. Generally, they wrote very favorable comments. They really liked the software tutorial portion of the course and the ability to become more proficient in *Office*. Of course, as in all online courses, they liked the ability to do the majority of work at home. (Two quizzes must be taken at the school's testing center and several of them objected to that. However, our department has adopted a policy that tests cannot be taken online as we want some assurance that the person signed up for the course is doing the work.)

Seventeen students out of 26 answered the survey and six of them objected to the group problems, mostly because of the difficulty of getting together with their teammates. They also felt the group problem scenario was incorporated in enough CMS courses already, and they just wanted to learn *Office*. However, they really liked doing the Microsoft Office User Specialist tests (MOUS) and learning the latest Office software package.

It might take more organization on the part of the instructor to arrange the problem-solving portion, but it *can* be duplicated online, which was one of our major considerations. We do not offer Web courses in CMS that cannot closely approximate the classroom environment, since our administration transcripts do not distinguish between a course taken online and one taken in the classroom. Both environments have the same curriculum and close to the same delivery.

CONCLUSION

We believe, by incorporating problem solving into the existing Micro-Based Software class, it becomes a stronger end user computing course. The area in which students always need more experience — applying the theory they have learned — is added to the curriculum, making the highly practical course even more practical. Tutorials provide instruction in skills and keystroke mastery; solving problems puts those skills to the test. Students enjoy the challenge of solving an operational problem similar to what they would experience on the job, without the pressure of losing a job if the solution is wrong.

The protection of the academic environment gives students the freedom to "test their wings" with operational level business problems within a semester long course.

The instructors, the members of the CMS curriculum committee, and the students who took the course were satisfied with the results of the pilot course, and students continue to be satisfied with the present course offering. We caution that implementing the changes in all future sections of the Micro-Based Software course may not meet with the same success. The planned changes put an added burden on the instructors and require them to be technically savvy with new classroom equipment and proficient with the Web. In addition, students have to work harder than before when there was no test of their ability to apply skills and solve problems in this course. The student satisfaction found in the pilot class may not continue for future classes. Perhaps the excitement of a pilot class appealed to those innovator students who enjoy *any* change from the routine class. Future classes will not always have that population. Nevertheless, after three more offerings of the revised Micro-Based Software class, student satisfaction remains consistent. All of these items dictate more study and cautious optimism toward incorporating problem solving within end user computing courses.

REFERENCES

Cooper, L. (2000). A Comparison of the Output of Computer Applications Between Classroom and Online students. *T. H. E. Journal,* 28(8), 52-54.

Ganger, R. (1990, September). Computer-Based Training. *Human Resource Systems Professionals, Inc. National Conference, Professional Journal.*

Luna, C., & McKenzie, J. (1997, February). Testing Multimedia in the College Classroom. Retrieved February 1997 on the World Wide Web: // www.thejournal.com/magazine/vault/A1543.cfm.

Lundgren, J. (1998). End User Support. *Journal of Computer Information Systems,* 1(XXXIX), 60.

Marold, K., & Fustos, J. (2001, June) A New Model of Hybrid Delivery: Handling the Computer Literacy Requirement for Undergraduate Business Schools. *Proceedings of the Conference of Informing Technology*. Krakow, Poland.

Marold, K., Larsen, G., Robertus, P., & Shaw, K. (1999, April 19). Usability Testing for a Computer Skills WBT Program. *Proceedings of ACM, SIGCPR* (pp. 304-309). New Orleans, LA.

Mawhinney, C., et al. (1999, April 19). Updating the IS Curriculum: Faculty Perceptions of Industry Need. *Proceedings, ACM, SIGCPR* (pp. 219-221). New Orleans, LA.

Mawhinney, C. & Morrell, J. (2000). Hybrid Course Delivery and Internet Courses in the Information Systems Curriculum: A Genesis and Comparison, *Proceedings of the 2000 Western Decision Sciences Institute* (pp. 185-186). Maui, HI.

McGrath, B. (1998). *Partners in Learning: Twelve Ways Technology Changes the Teacher-Student Relationship. Retrieved* on World Wide Web: //www.thejournal.com/magaznine/vault/A1982.cfm.

McLuhan, M. (1964.). *Understanding Media.* NY: McGraw Hill.

Molnar, A. (1997). *Computers in Education: A Brief History*. Retrieved on World Wide Web: //www.thejournal.com/magazine/vault/A1681.cfm.

Niederman, F., & Webster. J. (1999). Trends in End-User Training. *Proceedings CPR Conference.* (pp. 26-28). Boston, MA.

Payson, R. (1998, October). *Affordable Access to High-Quality Electronically Mediated Instruction.* Retrieved on World Wide Web: //www.thejournal.com/magazine/vault/A2045.cfm.

Rodriguez, W. (2000). Web Classroom of the Future: Integrating Course Management Software in a Java-Based Environment. *Interactive Multimedia Electronic Journal of Computer-Enhanced Learning.* Retrieved on the World Wide Web: //imej.wfu.edu/articles/2000/1/07/index.asp, p. 1.

Stoney, S., & Oliver, R. (1999). Can Higher Order Thinking and Cognitive Engagement be Enhanced with Multimedia? *Interactive Multimedia Electronic Journal of Computer-Enhanced Learning.* Retrieved on World Wide Web: //imej.wfu.edu/articles/19999/2/07/index.asp.

Withrow, F. (1997). *Technology in Education and the Next Twenty-Five Years.* Retrieved on the World Wide Web: //www.thejournal.com/magazine/vault/A1680.cfm.

APPENDIX

Problems for Office Software Class

Review of Basic Problem Solving Process

Define the problem
Identify possible alternative solutions
Choose the best solution
Prepare (or identify necessary) documents to execute the plan
Analyze the results (or proposed results)

File Management

You are the director of User Support Services for a medium-sized ABC Manufacturing Company with only one physical location. You and your subordinates have prepared a multimedia presentation for the Marketing Department. The 400 MB program needs to be delivered to the Marketing Director for approval and use. Plan how to deliver the program to Marketing from your development machines in the IT department.

Assumptions:

- IT has the latest microcomputer hardware and software.
- The company is networked and is an ISP for the Internet.
- The Marketing Department employees are computer literate, and have Pentium III microcomputers purchased in 1999.
- The company runs *Windows 2000* as an operating system.

Prepare an operational plan for delivery of the program and send it to me on a floppy disk and a hard copy printout. I will choose two or three and put them in the Forum.

Managing Resource Cuts

Your company is experiencing recent budget cuts for travel and marketing. You have just been informed that there will not be two individuals, but only one, traveling to the New Products and Software Symposium and Trade Show in New York City next week. You have prepared a *PowerPoint* slide show for your booth in the Exhibition Hall, featuring your newest Human Resource Management and Employee Tracking software program. You now will be the only person manning the booth for the 12 hours a day the Exhibition Hall is open during the five-day symposium. Plan how to cover many curious potential clients' inquiries about your new software, plus maintaining contact with already established clients who own your other software products.

Assumptions:

- The reserved booth is assigned and set up, including power connections and security, by the convention hall management company.
- You are bringing your own laptop computer, the *PowerPoint* presentation, and a personal projection system.
- All hardcopy brochures, handouts, bulletins, booth backdrop, and so forth are shipped already, and will be set up at your booth by the convention hall management company.

Demonstrate a solution to this problem and present to the class (10 minutes) at the designated due date. Turn in hardcopies of your planned solution. The class will discuss the various team plans and come to a consensus as to the most efficient and practical plan.

Small Business Need

You are the director of Westminster Recreation Center and manage an aquatics program for school age children. You need to develop a way to manage the swimming accomplishments of the participants, and issue certificates of participation when appropriate. The swimmers are divided into age groups in several non-competitive loosely organized "sessions" each year. Six teenage Water Safety Instructors at the center will track accomplishments of the swimmers..

Assumptions:

- The center has adequate computers with hardware and software for employee use.
- The Water Safety Instructors are computer literate, but are by no means software developers.
- The Water Safety Instructors turn in hard-copy printout summaries of swimmer accomplishments to you, in a standardized format, and issue certificates to swimmers at the end of each session.
- No permanent long-term records need to be kept of swimmers and their accomplishments for each session.
- Each Water Safety Instructor has two age groups of swimmers in six sessions a year; each session lasts six weeks.
- Employee turnover for the WSI's is high (25 percent).

Data:

Facility Name: Westminster Recreation Center; Westminster, CO

Swimming Pool length: 25 meters

Swimmer Age Groups (both boys and girls): 8 and under
9-10
11-12
13-14
15-18

Swimming Strokes and Milestones:

Free style	200 meters	400 meters	800 meters	1 mile (66 laps)
Backstroke	"			"
Breast Stroke	"			"
Butterfly	"			"
Individual medley	"			"

Prepare a solution to this problem and give the results to me as before — hard copy and on a disk. I will choose two or three of the best and put them in the Forum.

Project Management Problem

You are the Project Manager for the annual national meeting of District Sales Managers for national retail division of Yeti Mountain Bike Sales. Solution to this problem involves preparing the appropriate documents for the Project Notebook and presenting the plans to the Executive Committee for review and approval.

Assumptions:

- There are 15 district sales managers.
- You have two administrative assistants who can devote part of their time to this project.
- The meeting will cover three days at the corporate headquarters in Boulder, CO.
- You have a budget of $30,000 for the entire project (sales managers cover their own travel and lodging expenses from their division budgets).
- You will need a minimum of:
  - Work breakdown schedule of tasks and roles.
  - A project schedule with roles, tasks, milestones.
  - An itemized budget.
  - Agenda of activities for the meeting.
  - Contracts for organizations whose service you engage.
  - Record of planning notes and important documents.
  - Wrap up report of meeting outcomes, bound and presented to managers at their departure.

Prepare the Project Management Notebook with all materials as complete as you can make them without physically executing the project. The class will serve as the Executive Committee when the Notebook is turned in on the due date. The class will discuss the various team plans and come to a consensus as to the most efficient and pleasing notebook.

IT Desk Problem

You are the coordinator of User Support Systems for the IT Department of a large financial consulting firm. You manage a Help Desk for incoming requests from 3,000 employees in all departments — from CEO to Marketing to Human Resources to Accounting. You need to develop an Office-based Help Desk Scheduler application to handle the recordkeeping for incoming requests, schedule responses to each call in the most expedient manner by a qualified IT user support employee, and record the action taken by the employee and the satisfaction of the end user with the solution provided him/her.

Assumptions:

- The annual performance evaluations of Help Desk employees and the funding received by the IT Department for User Support Services is dependent upon these records.
- The Help Desk operates on a 24-7-363 schedule — with skeleton staff on weekends.
- The records must be accurate and must be retained for a minimum of five years.

- An annotated and categorized log of what action was successful for each problem will be available to Help Desk employees to review before completing their calls.
- The employee that performs the help call is responsible for entering data into the log.
- The company's strategic plan is to double their business within five years.

Plan the solution to this problem and be prepared to present the plan to the Chief Information Office by the appropriate date assigned. Nothing can be executed without the CIO's approval, so completing the Help Desk Schedule application is not required; a well-thought out feasible plan is.

Selective Group Communication

State University has a series of annual scholarship awards for students who meet GPA and total hours requirements. The Office of Academic Affairs (OAA) needs to notify those qualifying individuals to invite them to apply for the various awards. Some of the awards have further gender, ethnicity, or residency requirements. That is, all students do not qualify for all awards. In a general pool, the OAA has an *Outlook* e-mail system *Contact* list of State University senior level students who have a 3.2 or better GPA. The list contains only the school e-mail address of each student, in a comma-delimited text file.

Assumptions:

- Every student in the e-mail list qualifies for at least one of the annual awards.
- The school is networked among all departments.
- All of complete official student records are stored in an *Oracle* database on the university Hitachi mainframe.
- The OAA has permission to access mainframe records for viewing purposes only.
- Written invitations must be issued, using the United States Postal system.
- There are six categories of awards:
  - GPA of 3.6 or better with service and leadership documented
  - Female gender with GPA of 3.5 or better
  - Native American or Hispanic ethnicity, of either gender
  - Documented disability, with GPA of 3.2 or better
  - Colorado students (male or female) who graduated high school from a Metro Denver area secondary school system.
  - Nontraditional students over 28 years of age who are degree seeking.
- An administrative assistant is available to accomplish the communication within a two-week period.

Prepare an operational plan to formally notify each group of students for the appropriate scholarship and invite them to apply by a specific due date. You should define the most expedient solution, since time and resources are limited. Present your plan to the class on the designated date. The class will discuss the most efficient and practical plan, and come to a consensus as to the best solution.

Section IV

Information Technology and the Organization

Chapter XII

Changing a Business School Corporate Culture: Teaching in the 21st Century on a Different Blackboard

Jennifer Paige Nightingale
Duquesne University, USA

ABSTRACT

This chapter introduces the concept of an Academic Management System, which is designed to enhance communication among faculty, staff, students, and administration. Using an Academic Management System, built within a Course Management System, has the potential to improve communication, reduce administrative costs, and allow 24-hour access to information. The experience of one university that integrated these technologies has had a positive effect throughout campus and, as a result, several other programs are now developing similar sites for their faculty, staff, students and administration.

INTRODUCTION

On January 8, 2002, President George W. Bush signed the *No Child Left Behind* Act into law, launching a new era in American education. *No Child Left*

Behind focuses on how teachers and students can learn to use technology, where previous federal programs focused on increasing access to more technology. The goals of the *No Child Left Behind* Act are to (1) improve student academic achievement using technology in elementary schools and secondary schools; (2) assist students to become technologically literate by the time they finish the 8th grade; and (3) ensure that teachers are able to integrate technology into the curriculum to improve student achievement (Kozberg, 2002). It is critical that this model of standardization be adopted throughout America's education system in order to enhance learning and student achievement.

The Duquesne University School of Business in Pittsburgh, Pennsylvania, has created an online community called the School of Business Administration Network (**SOBA-Net**) to enhance communication between faculty, staff, students, and administration. Using a Course Management System (CMS), Blackboard®, as the underlying technology or framework, developers can build an academic management system (AMS).

SOBA-Net is quickly becoming an information source on which students, faculty, and staff depend. The motivation for developing SOBA-Net was to establish a virtual community where students, faculty, adjunct instructors, and staff can work together to achieve a common goal — improve student achievement and produce quality graduates. This paper presents the effects SOBA-Net has had on the School of Business, and discusses the growing user base.

THE IMPACT OF TECHNOLOGY

Technology clearly has had, and will continue to have, a major learning, administrative, and business impact on education. Many institution segments are moving transactions and shared information to the online environment, such as the Internet. According to the U.S. Department of Education (1999), the percentage of students using computers in colleges and universities has increased from 55.2 percent in 1994 to 64.7 percent in 1997; and has nearly doubled for students using computers at home for schoolwork from 23.1 percent to 40.8 percent.

Greene, Cattagni and Westat (2001) found that e-mail, the Internet, and Websites are rapidly becoming core components of postsecondary instruction for students in the United States. A fall 1998 survey reported in *The Condition of Education 2001* showed that 97 percent of full-time faculty and staff had access to the Internet, 69 percent used e-mail to communicate with students, and 40 percent used a course-specific Website.

The demand for online teaching and learning resources has already reached a significant high; Web-based and Web-enhanced courses are already popular e-learning platforms in higher education today. According to *Student Monitor*, 90 percent of college students used the Internet and 6 percent were connecting once a day or more. According to *Campus Computing*, over 53 percent of college courses used e-mail last year, almost 39 percent used Internet resources, and almost 28 percent used Web pages for class materials and resources (Vallone, 2000).

As education and technology continues to fuse and evolve at rapid speed, institutions will find an enormous array of effective solutions to augment their educational offerings and build deeper relationships with current and prospective students, alumni, and administrators (Blackboard® Incorporated, 2001). CMSs are one solution that is modifying the way instructors circulate information. Green (2001) found a growing number of campuses identify CMSs as "very important" in their institutional information technology (IT) planning and approximately one-fifth (20.6 percent) of all college courses now use course management tools, up from 14.7 percent in 2000. In addition, a leading e-Learning industry analyst firm projects that the higher education e-Learning market will grow from $4 billion in 2000 to $11 billion by 2003 (Stokes, 2000).

THE HISTORY OF SOBA-NET

There is no doubt that technology has had a major impact on our daily lives. Currently, there are several CMSs on the educational market, and in the summer of 1999, Duquesne University adopted Blackboard®. Like Blackboard®, the others — WebCT, TopClass e-Learning Suite™ and eSocrates Knowledge Exchange™ to name a few — offer faculty essentially the same features and functions. For example, an instructor can use a CMS course site simply and easily for increasing the availability of course materials, assignments, resources, and/or grades. In addition, an instructor can make use of the CMS's communication, assessment, and management tools to extend the course beyond its physical, spatial, and temporal confines.

In an effort to meet student and faculty demands of improved communication throughout the school, a Blackboard® site was created to encourage students to take an active role in their academic career. The creation of SOBA-Net has taken the foundation of a CMS and altered it to become an AMS. It services nearly 2,000 undergraduate and graduate students, along with their academic advisors and departmental organizations, and provides them with curriculum, school, and professional information. In addition, it has promoted communication among the business school faculty, staff and students, while greatly increasing faculty familiarity with Blackboard® and, thus the use of it in their teaching. As a result, several other Duquesne University programs are now developing similar Blackboard® sites for their students and faculty.

What is a Course Management System?

A CMS is a course shell created for faculty to use to enhance a traditional face-to-face course or to deliver a course entirely online. A CMS provides a password protected Internet site with the web interface or framework necessary for instructors to make course materials of various types readily accessible to students on the Internet, conduct online discussions and communications with and among students, and create and disseminate assessments and surveys of various types.

A CMS is only a tool that enables faculty to use the Internet to disseminate course content and instruction — the content, methodology, and purpose should always remain separate — while eliminating the need to have advanced level Website creation and management skills to facilitate their teaching and enhance student learning.

Why Blackboard®?

Blackboard® makes it relatively easy to provide students with course materials in Web page, PDF, Word, or PowerPoint formats. It provides student home page creation, built-in chat and online discussion capabilities, e-mail, collaborative or group work facilitation and management areas, assessment creation and automatic grading, grade book distribution, class management features (such as calendaring or tasks), and a digital drop box for students to submit assignments. Course sites are password-protected and available only to registered students.

Although Duquesne University supports both WebCT and Blackboard® CMSs, Blackboard® was selected because of its low learning curve, visual appeal and secured environment. In addition, some of the school's faculty participated in training when Blackboard® was initially implemented campus-wide in summer 1999, bringing a familiarity component into play, and encouraging faculty involvement during construction and implementation.

SOBA-Net reinforces both Duquesne University and the School of Business's directive of integrating technology across the curriculum. For many faculty members, the shear thought of integration can be greatly intimidating. By using Blackboard® as an AMS, faculty members can observe how a CMS is used to aid in distributing materials and communicating with students. In moving from observing to participating, the intimidation can be significantly reduced. In addition, students can become familiar with the mechanics and feel less anxious when they participate in a Web-enhanced course.

What Were the Initial Objectives?

It was first thought academic advisors would benefit most, as they constantly searched for a better method of communicating with the students and distributing information relevant to their academic career. Thus, they embraced and encouraged this improvement and, rather than merely adding to the student's knowledge bank, the objective was to set students up for success by requiring them to take an active role in their education. Students and advisors would be able to work smarter and more efficiently, help improve overall communication between faculty, staff and students, validate concepts taught throughout the business curriculum (i.e., teamwork, planning, and communication), and greatly reduce the paper trail.

METHODOLOGY

Choosing the Technology

Tomei (2002, p. 5) explains that to succeed in technology implementation, we need to understand that the technology itself is not the goal. In deciding what technology will support the objectives or if a CMS can satisfy determined needs, consider the following:

- The benefit of a CMS to faculty and an institution is that it should provide instructors with a pre-made course web template, which they can easily put, especially if they possess the computing skills and knowledge identified above, their course materials and activities.
- A CMS should service the majority of instructors and their curriculum needs and yet be flexible enough to provide advanced users with the basics upon which they can then add further functionality and meet the needs of special and unique requests.
- A CMS should be cost-effective for the institution in terms of operating and support costs and resources.
- Not only are developer skills and understanding important, an institution must commit to effective infrastructure and strategic support of the CMS by ensuring that adequate support for users exists and that resources are available for hardware and software improvements and maintenance necessary for reliable operation of the CMS.

Currently, Blackboard® has been able to meet the above criteria, and as its increased use by faculty and programs across campus indicates, it has become the preferred CMS at Duquesne University. Regardless of which technology you choose, you must realize the implementation is an ongoing process that demands time, attention, and dedication.

Getting Started

Before documents and information are uploaded, specific objectives and guidelines must be established. White and Weight (2000, p. 185) have used technology as a tool to enable human relationships, and have found that people are the real reason for success in any online learning environment. This environment requires a value-added approach, where technology is used to enhance the complex private and social activities of the learning process (p. vii). In this stage, three factors must be considered:

- **Content Management.** What should be online? Who will provide it? Who will maintain and update? How will it be organized? Is security an issue? What areas of the CMS should be enabled or disabled?
- **Interactivity.** What limitations will be imposed? Do all users have the ability to participate in threaded discussions? Should specific guidelines and standards be established and posted?
- **User Management.** Who will manage the users and passwords (if applicable)? Should different security settings exist for different types of users (i.e., faculty, staff, students, etc.)?

Building the Virtual Community

Once guidelines are established, the construction can begin. This is the longest part of the process and obtaining the information can be a challenge. Consider holding CMS training sessions to involve the faculty and staff—your colleagues can add valuable feedback and offer assistance to feel like a valuable part of the process. After all, the virtual community encompasses the entire school, so demonstrate the need for and value of teamwork from its inception. In addition, draw an initial layout of the AMS before uploading the content (see Diagram A). It is critical the content is organized and easy to navigate, or users will not return.

If You Build It, They Will Come

That is not exactly correct. The overall marketing and enthusiasm generated will determine its success, and like the implementation phase, marketing the AMS is an ongoing process that demands time, attention, and dedication. To generate interest and maintain momentum, remember behavior breeds behavior — if you are excited about the AMS, then others will follow suit. Users must have a reason to log in — offer incentives or hold contests to create initial excitement. The results indicate that both the faculty and academic advisors proved to be a valuable communication medium and significant marketing resource.

Diagram A: Snapshot of SOBA-Net's Structure

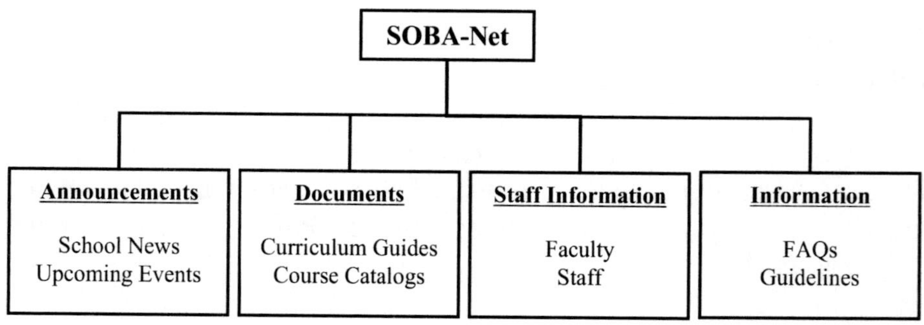

Leading Edge Versus the Bleeding Edge

Several lessons were learned during the creation of SOBA-Net. Developers must be realistic that 100 percent of the users will not log in or become regular users of the system. The means to build a large user base is to target key people in the school — faculty and academic advisors are obvious resources because of the quantity of students to which they are exposed. In addition, administration must "buy in" to this idea. Not all schools will have the resources at hand, leading to the possibility of requiring and requesting funding. If they cannot be convinced of the value of an AMS, why should anyone else? Third, two key factors must exist for this venture to be successful — the developer must possess strong organizational skills and a basic marketing plan must be developed. Lastly, developers must be realistic. It will take time to obtain and organize the information, as well as uploading it to the AMS. This is not something that can be created in a week.

RESULTS

To assess SOBA-Net's success, the data was manipulated in two ways: (1) a survey was posted on SOBA-Net and student users were asked to respond; and, (2) the total logins and users' activity were tracked. The survey's correlating message explained its purpose, indicated that it would not take more than five minutes to complete, and offered several give-away items as an incentive. The resulting sample was 211 completed questionnaires, a 14.4 percent response rate.

The questionnaire consisted of both close-ended and open-ended questions. The close-ended questions asked about login instructions, ease of navigation, and usefulness of information. The open-ended questions allowed the respondents to indicate their answers in their own words and inquired about items that could be added to improve SOBA-Net. In addition, it included an area for additional thoughts if the respondent wished to express.

Table 1 illustrates the fall 2001 semester's basic results of SOBA-Net users, average hits per day, and the percentage of users who have logged in, as compared to the overall user base. The figures do not equal the *Current Total* because summer activity is not reflected in the table. The formal implementation was September 2001. In considering adoption of this initiative, statistics show that 1,035 users out of 1,683 potential users, or 61.5 percent of all potential users, had accessed SOBA-Net as of January 7, 2002. Of the potential users, 1,470 are students, (87.3 percent of all potential users), 46 are full-time faculty (2.7 percent of all potential users), 63 are adjunct instructors (3.7 percent of all potential users), 16 are administrators (.95 percent of all potential users), and 88 are staff (5.2 percent of all potential users).

Over 28,000 user logins were recorded as of end December 2001, with an overall average of 222 hits per day. Of the potential respondents, 1,035 users (61.5 percent) have logged into SOBA-Net, and as documented in a recent survey, 54

Table 1: SOBA-Net Statistics for Fall 2001 Semester

	Total Users	Total Logins	Unique Logins	Average Hits/Day	Ratio: Users vs. Potential Users
September 2001	1,364	5,943	523	198	38.3%
October 2001	1,439	10,797	670	348	46.6%
November 2001	1,678	3,992	380	133	22.6%
December 2001	1,680	3,435	356	111	21.2%
Current Total	1,683	28,217	1,035	222	61.5%

percent of those student users cited "professor or instructor" in response to the question, "How did you learn about SOBA-Net?"

Table 2 illustrates the basic results of SOBA-Net users during the 2001-2002 academic year, average hits per day, and the percentage of users who have logged in as compared to the overall user or potential user base. In considering adoption of this initiative, statistics show that 1,341 users out of 1,708 potential users, or 78.5 percent of all potential users have accessed SOBA-Net. Of the potential users, 1,495 are students, 46 are full-time faculty, 63 are adjunct instructors, 16 are administrators, and 88 are staff. Nearly 50,000 user logins were recorded by the end of May 2002, with an overall average of 206 hits per day. Research is currently being pursued to determine characteristics of regular users, occasional users, and infrequent or non-users. The infrequent or non-users will be surveyed for needs analysis and improvement of SOBA-Net.

SOBA-Net serves its main purpose as a means of school-wide communication medium through its ease of use, high percentage of users, and variety of user options. In terms of ease of use, 92 percent of respondents found login instructions easy to comprehend and follow, while 75 percent reported navigating through SOBA-Net was simple.

FUTURE PLANS

We are in *Phase 2* of SOBA-Net, which involves moving the information that was on Blackboard® to the School of Business Website (http://www.bus.duq.edu/current.asp). At the time SOBA-Net was developed, we did not possess the technical skills to construct it directly on our Website. Its success, along with improved technical resources and knowledge during the past year, has enabled us to centralize the information.

Table 2: SOBA-Net Statistics for 2001-2002 Academic Year

Total Users	Total Logins	Unique Logins	Average Hits/Day	Ratio: Users vs. Potential Users
1,708	49,728	1,341	206	78.5%

Regardless of which technology is used, it is important to understand how the fundamental concepts, through the construction and use of an AMS, will aid in building relationships and enhancing communication skills.

CONCLUSION

SOBA-Net provides connectivity via the Internet, preserves the School of Business, Duquesne University, and meets President George W. Bush's initiative for technology integration and enhancement, and appeals to the students' desire for online resources. The data illustrates that many potential users are taking advantage of this communication medium from internal job postings to scholarships geared toward business students.

While it may be too early to determine its long-term potential of improving communication, reducing administrative cost, or allowing 24-hour access to information, SOBA-Net has encouraged students to become more self-sufficient and assume some responsibility and accountability for their educational outcomes. In addition, there has been a notable increase in faculty use of Blackboard® in their classes, and students are encouraging those who do not use it to adopt it. The School of Business's experience has had a positive effect not only school-wide, but also throughout campus and, as a result, several other programs are now developing similar sites for their faculty, staff, students, and administration.

REFERENCES

Blackboard® Incorporated. (2001). Course and portal solutions: Blackboard 5. Available on the World Wide Web: http://products.Blackboard.com/cp/bb5/index.cgi.

Green, K. (2001, October 29). 2001 national survey of information technology in U.S. higher education. *Educause 200.* Indianapolis, IN.

Greene, B., Cattagni, A., & Westat, E.F. (2001). U.S. Department of Education, National Center for Education Statistics. *Internet access in U.S. public schools and classrooms: 1994- 2000* (NCES 2000-071), (Washington, DC: U.S. Government).

The Internet, Distance Learning & the Future of the Research University, Presented to the Subcommittee on Basic Research, Committee on Science, U.S. House of Representatives. (2000, May 9) Testimony of Carol Vallone, President and CEO, WebCT). [Online]. Available on the World Wide Web: http://www.house.gov/science/vallone_050900.htm.

Kozberg, L. (2002, January 8). *Paige joins President Bush for signing of historic no child left behind act of 2001: Bold new federal law to improve student achievement.* [Online]. Available on the World Wide Web: http://www.ed.gov/PressReleases/01-2002/01082002.html.

Stokes, P. (2000, June). *E-learning: Education businesses transform schooling.* Eduventures.com, [Online]. Available on the World Wide Web: https://www.eduventures.com/pdf/doe_elearning.pdf.

Tomei, L. A. (2002). *The technology façade: Overcoming barriers to effective instructional technology.* MA: Allyn & Bacon.

U.S. Department of Education, National Center for Education Statistics. (1999) *Digest of Education Statistics 1999* (NCES 99-036). Washington, DC: U.S. Government, 1999.

U.S. Department of Education, National Center for Education Statistics. (1999). The context of postsecondary education. *The Condition of Education 2001* (NCES 99-036). Washington, DC: U.S. Government, 1999.

White, K.W., & Weight, B.H. (2000). *The online teaching guide: A handbook of attitudes, strategies, and techniques for the virtual classroom.* MA: Allyn & Bacon.

Chapter XIII

The Role of the Organizational Context in the Use of a Workflow System: Lessons from a Case Study

Anabela Sarmento
ISCAP-IPP, Portugal

ABSTRACT

This chapter discusses the role of the organizational context in the use of a workflow system. It argues there are organizational factors such as structure, power, people, technology and culture, that constrain and enable the use of workflow systems. The author hopes that, by presenting a case study of a Portuguese organization, which implemented and used a workflow system, it will help to identify those organizational factors, which could affect implementation, and to understand how they can influence the success, or failure, of such a system. Finally, the results will contribute to a better management of the process of change.

INTRODUCTION

The macroeconomic environment, where organisations actually operate, can be characterized by several changes. We witness the globalisation of markets, the disappearance of geographic borders and an increase in commercial exchanges (Quinn, Baruch & Zein, 2002). To cope with these changes, challenges and opportunities, organisations are adopting new models of social organisation, oriented towards work teams, with a flatter hierarchical structure, where information is playing an important and decisive role in the competitiveness of the organisation.

The adoption of such changes is accompanied by the implementation of new information technologies (IT) that allow them to process the necessary information with speed and accuracy. Included in these IT solutions are workflow systems (WS). These systems are defined as proactive computer systems, which manage the flow of work among participants, according to a defined procedure consisting of a number of tasks. They co-ordinate user and system participants, together with the appropriate data resources, to achieve defined objectives by set deadlines (Hales & Lavery, 1991). The focus of these systems is on the way work usually flows, i.e., on the process, and not on the information contained in the support documents. These systems present themselves as one solution able to improve the efficiency and management of organizational processes. They provide communication tools, allowing collaboration, information and knowledge sharing and coordination of work. They also support organizational processes and work teams, providing tools to facilitate informal communication, automation and reduce the time taken to complete the task, allowing the realisation of work in a more efficient, effective and creative manner (Jablonski, 1996; Khoshafian, 1995).

Based on Systems Theory (Bertalanffy, 1940), an organisation and its environment can be considered as an open and dynamic system of complex, interrelating and interdependent parts. It is the relationships and the processes that make up the organizational context, rather than the separate entities or the sum of the parts. This means that a change occurring in one part of the system implies changes in all the others, including the environment.

Besides, the adoption of any technology always means change. According to Laudon and Laudon (1998), "information systems (IS) and organisations have a mutual influence on each other. (…) IS affect organisations and organisations, necessarily, affect the design of systems" (p. 75). Thus, the adoption of an IS is mediated by factors that "influence the interaction between IT and organisation" (p. 75).

As WS is a recent technology[1], the organizational impacts are not yet very clear (Boersma, 1994; Holm & Hedman, 1997; Kueng, 1998; Ljungberg, 1997). Besides, the research about these systems has focused on the phase of its development and implementation, forgetting its organizational impact. Also, care has been taken to address the technological issues of the system neglecting the characteristics of the organization where it has been implemented and the users that will work with it. Yet, we know that much of the success of the adoption of a system depends, not on the technology but on the context in which it is used.

Aware of this fact, this paper tries to fill this gap, identifying several contextual factors that influence the use of a WS. The structure of the chapter is as follows: first, some models already used in the study of the impact of IT in organisations are described. After a brief critical analysis on them, and considering its strengths and weaknesses, another model is presented. This one is applied to a case study. Finally, results are presented and discussed.

FRAMEWORK OF ANALYSIS OF THE IMPACT OF TECHNOLOGIES IN ORGANISATIONS

The adoption of an IS by different organisations does not always give rise to the same changes. These depend on the interaction between the characteristics of the organisation, together with those of the system adopted. The context where the IS is implemented and used will act as an enabler or a constrainer of the changes that will arise. In the following sections some models already in existence, and used to study the impact of IS on organisations, are presented as well as a critical analysis of them. The section is completed by presenting a framework of analysis that aims to fill in the gaps of these models.

Models Already in Existence

The search of the literature revealed the existence of models for further analysis. Leavitt (1965) explained the relation between technology and organisation using four variables: technology, people, structure and tasks. These variables are interdependent, so if one changes, the others change too. This model is considered to be too simple and abstract (Shimada, 1991) and, as the variables are interdependent, the model does not assume a beginning or an end and does not focus on change but on equilibrium. Scott Morton (1986) presents another model based on the Leavitt's but instead of people he uses "individuals and roles" and instead of structure he uses "structure and organizational culture." He also adds other variables such as process management, planning, budgeting and rewarding. Also, as with Leavitt's, this is an abstract model.

In 1986, Danziger and Kraemer used a model, which considered only three variables: organizational environment (organisation and environmental issues related to the use of the technology in the organisation), technology (technology's characteristics, hardware and software, people and organizational arrangements) and user's characteristics (education, training, motivation, roles, tasks) (Danziger & Kraemer, 1986).

Shimada (1991) proposes another model in which the organisation recognises its external environment and designs its business strategy to adapt to this environment. As a result, technology becomes an absorbed factor, affecting its strategy, organizational behaviour and organizational culture. When the organisation adopts technologies, its organizational performance changes according to the technology used, with the kind of attitude taken — active/leading or passive/following — and the methods of integration of business systems and information systems attempted.

In 1998, Laudon and Laudon (1998) proposed a model with three variables: structures, tasks and people. This model has been used by Kueng (1998) to study the impact of WS.

Critical Analysis of the Models Above

All these models seem to be valid. However, they seem to ignore the power relations and the organizational culture. Scott Morton (1986) considers culture at the same level as structure. According to them, structure and culture act in the same way. Schein (1993, 1996) disagrees with this point of view, stating that culture can act as an inhibitor or facilitator in the adoption of a technology; as such, it should be considered independently. Shimada (1991) considers culture as a contingency factor but he does not see power as a conditioning factor regarding impact. The results of Pinsonneault and Kraemer (1993, 1997) assert power should be taken as a contingency factor as well as the others.

Framework Proposed

As we have seen, in the previous section, the models already used to study the impact of IS on organizations have strengths and weaknesses. None of them simultaneously consider, technology, structure, people, politics, and culture. They focus in some of these factors, but none considers them all. An analysis of the impact of IS on an organization considering only some of these factors would always be incomplete. Furthermore, taking into consideration the outcomes of the research of Bertrand and Guillemet (1988) and Bolman and Deal (1997), the organizational factors able to influence the use of a WS, are:

1. Technological factors, including the characteristics of the technology to be adopted and the technology already existing in the organisation.
2. Structural factors, meaning the organizational design, the complexity, the number of hierarchical levels, the number of departments, the centralisation or decentralisation of power and decision-making, the coordination of tasks, the formalisation of procedures, the design of tasks and jobs and the degree of specialisation.
3. Social and individual factors, embracing the multidisciplinary work teams, their distribution in time and space, their education, training, work satisfaction, skills and individual characteristics.
4. Political factors, meaning that decides on the kind of technology to adopt, its design and implementation, who is going to use it, its purposes and objectives.

Figure 1: Framework of Analysis

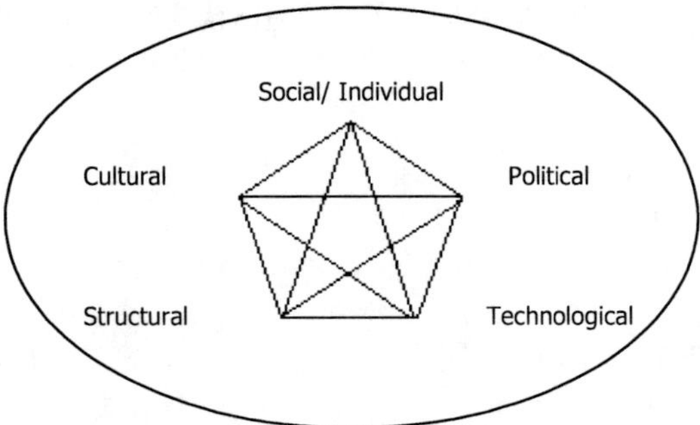

5. Cultural factors, referring to culture, norms, rules and the reaction to change as well as knowledge and organizational learning capacity.

Figure 1 presents the relationship that can be settled among these factors. They cannot be analysed in isolation. They interact with each other, influencing the effects of the adoption and use of new IT. Furthermore, it is not possible to say that one factor is more important than the other because the result of an interaction depends on the relation established among them, over a period of time. For example, if people, in the organization feel that the adoption of new IT will cause them to lose power, they will create obstacles to its use. Furthermore, in an organisation with a proactive culture that stimulates change, the adoption and use of new IT will be easier.

CASE STUDY

Data Collection and Analysis

This framework was applied to a Portuguese company that implemented a WS. This was a longitudinal study, where I accompanied the enterprise from initial implementation of the system, until some nine months following its full operation.

Data collection was done between May 1999 and March 2001. I used multiple techniques to gather data and collected several documents about the enterprise, including the process where the WS was going to be implemented. I observed meetings and training classes, as well as people at work. I also conducted more than 20 semi-structured interviews, each about half an hour in length, with some participants being interviewed more than once over the period of study. The interviews were done at three different stages. The first occurred before the adoption of the system. The purpose of these interviews was to know how people worked, their vision of the enterprise and their expectations regarding the system. The second and third stages occurred after one month and between six and nine months, respectively, of the installation of the system. The objective of these interviews was to know what kind of changes people had identified and the reasons behind these changes.

The interviews spanned all levels of the company and all the potential users of the system. They were fully recorded and transcribed. I used qualitative techniques to analyse data (Miles & Huberman, 1994), and whenever necessary used the NUD*IST[2] program.

The Organization

Fieldwork was conducted with the Alpha Corporation (pseudonym). This organization was incorporated in December 1985 and is located in the north of Portugal. In the early days, the business was mostly concerned with the microfilming of hospital radiological images. Later, in 1996, the company re-oriented to consulting and programming activities in Electronic Documentation Storage. In 1998, the company developed a Document and Database Filing System, which is part of a proprietary Electronic Document Management System (EDMS). Although it started as a family business, this company currently employs 45 workers, whose average age is 28 years old. The staff is now distributed in a linear and functional hierarchical structure with three levels that comprise the following departments: administrative and financial (AFD), commercial, quality, research and development (R&D), marketing, SAP, technical support and production. This growth was due to increased market demand in the area of microfilming and digital archive and also to the development and success of their EDM System.

In 1999, for strategic reasons, Alpha Corporation decided to adopt a WS. Their objectives were to understand the process of development and implementation of this system. Such knowledge would help them to incorporate it into their EDMS and to maintain (and possibly increase) their market share. They also needed this to comply with the requirements of Quality Process Certification.

Each department has only one or two employees, except production, which has more than half of the employees of the firm. The top of the hierarchy is composed of three partners to whom all the departments report.

In technological terms, the company is well-equipped. There is almost one computer per person. Employees are familiar with technology and are confident in the use of their equipment.

As for human factors, almost all the employees have a college degree, except two members: one from AFD, who has completed secondary school, and the production director, who has a ninth-grade education. Both will be the members of staff who will use the new system most regularly. Everyone does regular training in his or her field of work. Generally speaking, the employees of this firm are interested, committed and are willing to learn. They help each other whenever the need arises, and do not seem afraid of showing lack of knowledge or expressing their difficulties in any situation.

Power and decision-making are concentrated in the top of the hierarchy. Other members of staff do not have much autonomy to act on their own initiative.

As there are only 45 employees working in the same building, internal communication is facilitated. Informal ties are very important, sometimes replacing formal relationships.

The word that best describes the culture of this firm is technology. This is supported by the area of business, the architecture, the available technologies, the existence of an R&D department, the employees' backgrounds and training and by the general attitude towards the development of the company and the drive to improve the company's market share.

The Workflow System

The system adopted was the *Metro* from *Action Technologies*, which is based on the work of Medina-Mora, Winograd et al. (1992). The system is based on the language/action perspective which is a four-step action workflow protocol[3] (see Figure 2).

This system is Web based, which means the environment where the employees work is similar to an Internet site. This system was chosen mainly because *Action Technologies* is a business partner of this corporation, and so access to the material and information needed to develop and implement the system was considerably eased. People can see the status of previous orders and check information regarding purchase behaviour, that is, when and how many internal orders he/she has placed, and the most ordered items.

The Process

The process chosen to incorporate the WS was the purchase process and, in particular, the stationery material. For administrative employees, this refers to paper, pens, pencils, archive files, etc. For production, it includes all the material necessary to microfilm and digitalise the client's documents.

Figure 2: Model of WS Based on the Language/Action Approach

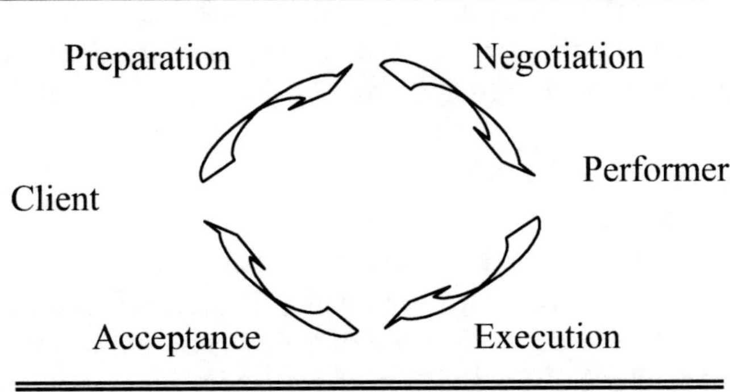

Source: Schael, 1998

The process is composed of two sub-processes: one concerns the internal demand and the other the order to the supplier. To better understand the influence of some of the organizational factors, concerning the use of the system, I will start by describing the process before and after the adoption of the WS.

Before the WS

Sub Process of Internal Demand

The applicant fills in the internal demand in MSWord and prints it (or he/she prints the form and fills it by hand). This document is then signed and delivered by hand to an employee of AFD. Usually, when the product arrives, the applicant is informed orally. Between delivering the internal demand to the AFD and the moment of the material arriving, the applicant does not know the status of his/her demand.

Sub Process of Order to the Supplier

Applicant delivers the internal order to an employee of the AFD. Based on these forms, the AFD person phones the supplier and asks for supply of the material. When the material arrives, the employee in the AFD notifies the applicant, in person or by phone. At the end of the month, he/she gathers all the internal demands, organizes them by date and fills in a formal order that is delivered to the supplier. There is no control of orders. Despite the existence of a written document to support the process, it is not easy to know how many orders are issued by month, by department or by person. The process, before the implementation of the WS, was considered by the employees to be slow and bureaucratic, with some redundant tasks (e.g., to print and fill in the form by hand, instead of sending, for example, an email to the colleague or phoning) (see Figure 3).

The following paragraphs describe the process as it became after the adoption of the WS.

After the WS

Sub Process of Internal Demand

When someone wants to make an internal demand, he/she only has to open the Internet browser and go to the site corresponding to the purchase process. After filling the internal demand, with the material requisition, it is sent electronically to the AFD (see Figure 4).

Sub Process of Order to the Supplier

Daily, the employee of the AFD opens the page of the purchase process and sees if there are any internal demands to process. If so, she fills the order to the supplier by opening MS Word. At the beginning, this operation was not so easy, as the computer of this employee did not have enough memory, blocking constantly. The

Figure 3: The Process Before the Adoption of the WS

Process		Purchase Process (Stationery Material)		
Sub Processes		Internal Demand	Order to the Supplier	
Activities		Internal Demand	Order to the Supplier	Receipt of the Material
Tasks	Supplier			Order; Give to supplier
	Manager of the Process		Receive demand; Phone supplier	Deliver order; Collect internal demand; Arrange orders by date; Fill formal order
	Internal Applicant	Open computer; Print demand; Fill demand; Sign demand; Deliver demand		Inform material arrival

Figure 4: The Process After the Adoption of the WS

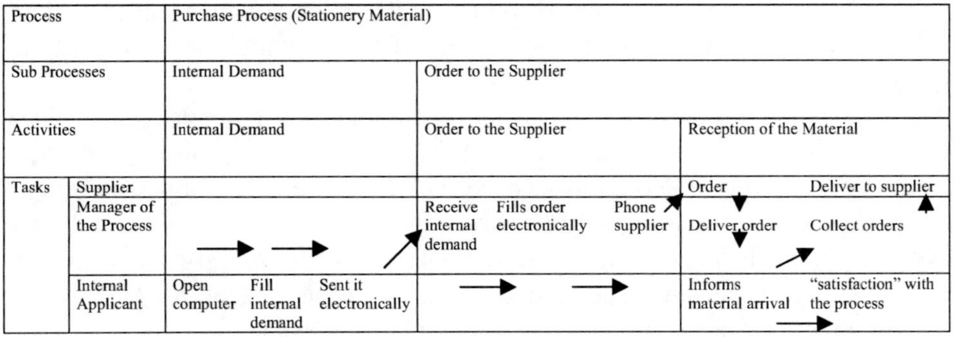

Process		Purchase Process (Stationery Material)		
Sub Processes		Internal Demand	Order to the Supplier	
Activities		Internal Demand	Order to the Supplier	Reception of the Material
Tasks	Supplier			Order; Deliver to supplier
	Manager of the Process		Receive internal demand; Fills order electronically; Phone supplier	Deliver order; Collect orders
	Internal Applicant	Open computer; Fill internal demand; Sent it electronically		Informs material arrival; "satisfaction" with the process

order is passed to the supplier by phone. The formal document, containing all the items ordered, is only given to the supplier at the end of each month. The material ordered is delivered almost immediately after being ordered (for most of the items it can be one or two days; for some unusual items it can be longer).

When the material arrives, the requester is informed electronically or by phone. After picking up the material, the requester needs to open the original demand and record receipt of the material (see Figure 4).

After nine months of full use of the new system, there were 73 internal demands and, consequently, 73 orders. Approximately 75 percent of these internal orders were made by two employees — the person in AFD and the Production Director. All other users made only two or three internal demands, during the same period.

PRESENTATION AND DISCUSSION OF THE RESULTS

In this section, the organizational factors that conditioned the use of the system are going to be identified. This will take into consideration the framework of analysis described above.

Structural Factors

One of the aspects that influenced positively the use of the WS was that the process and the flow of work did not change significantly following the adoption of the new system. Implementation of the system was achieved using existing procedures. There was no attempt to rethink or redesign the process. However some tasks were eliminated, for instance, the printing of the internal demand and its delivery to the AFD. With the new system, all these tasks can be performed from each employee's desk.

Furthermore, some effort was made to present the electronic forms so they looked as similar as possible to those in paper support. Although this was not a core process, nor involved a large amount of paper circulating or needing to be filed, some employees said that, as they do not need to print the internal demand anymore, the system has streamlined the amount of paper in circulation and the volume of the archiving file.

As for completion time, opinions are not unanimous. Some employees consider the time is reduced. This reduction is due to the fact that tasks can now be performed from each person's desk. People do not need to be circulating in the organization and wasting time waiting for attention. However, there are two employees that do not agree task accomplishment time has been reduced. On the contrary, they state the new process is slower and takes longer to be performed. One of these is the production director. He complains that before the new system, on some occasions he could order the material directly from the supplier; now this is not possible. Furthermore, he has shown some difficulties in using the new system, needing to be helped in the filling of the internal demand. The other employee was the person in AFD. Her complaints are related to the fact her computer did not have enough memory and blocked each time she wanted to fill in the order to the supplier. According to her, this contributes to a slower process, as she states:

> *"It is when I print. I am on the Internet and then I open the MSWord and fill in the order. I print and there is an error. I have too many applications opened. I have to call in technical support and then I take a long time to perform the task."*

However, at the end of the case study (nine months after full use), these two people considered that the application has helped to reduce the task accomplishment time. They now see themselves as experts in the use of the system. This seems to be due to the regularity of the tasks. A task performed sporadically requires a bigger effort from the performer. An employee, required to execute sporadic tasks, not related to the core business, might need help (memory, colleagues, handbooks, etc.). This is precisely the case with these demands. The internal demands concern, for most of the employees, the necessary material to execute daily administrative tasks, which means that there is no need to order it regularly. To production, it concerns the material needed to prepare the client's documents to be microfilmed and digitalised, meaning this department may need to place orders more often, for that kind of material. To make things worse, the WS is only used in this process. This means, to make an internal demand, employees have to open the application and fill in an electronic document. But as they request material sporadically, they do not feel completely at ease in its use, which brings new problems. Each time the employee needs to order something he/she does not remember all the steps to be followed.

Another factor that contributed to stimulate the use of the application was the fact all the events were registered, not allowing the user to forget something. As one employee said:

> *"Sometimes I arrived there and delivered my order to the girl that works there; then I left and it was forgotten. When I called to ask the status of my order, she would look for the papers to give me an answer but this was not always possible; the order was already in the trash. These are situations that do not happen anymore."*

Finally, all internal demands are standardised, i.e., the support document is the same for everybody.

Political Factors

The majority of people didn't attempt to see if they had more information available after the use of the WS. Only the person in AFD did this. I am not surprised by these results, as the process involved is of minor importance to the main activity of the enterprise. The information available now has no immediate interest for employees. Besides, as the use of the system is sporadic for the majority of people (except for the person in AFD and the production director), the information available has no direct relevance for them.

Nevertheless, there is one exception, the person in AFD who now uses the system quite often and consults the information available out of curiosity.

> *"I was curious; I now know how many internal demands are made."*

Human Factors

As for human factors, one of the aspects that seemed to have influence in the use of the system was the literary qualification of the employees. In this enterprise, the majority of people have a degree, some in the area of engineering or in information systems. The knowledge acquired, as well as the attitudes and competencies developed during their education might have helped in the use of the application and in the acceptance of change. Though, these are precisely the employees that use the system sporadically, they do not display difficulties in its use.

However, there are two users that do not have a degree. They are the person in AFD and the production director. They showed more difficulties at the beginning. As for the production director, he states:

> *"I am afraid of damaging something. If I do make a mistake, I get worried; that is why I do not go further. I am afraid of doing something wrong."*

These difficulties might be the consequence of some gaps in his educational background. However, they are also connected with his lack of knowledge about the use of computers in general. What he knows was learned in this enterprise, with the help of his colleagues. He knows the minimum necessary to perform daily tasks.

As for the person in AFD, her difficulties are related to technical problems with the equipment. This person also reveals, in the beginning, she didn't like using the system, perhaps because she didn't understand the flow of work very well. However, at the end of the study, she shows great enthusiasm for learning and using the system; she also shows initiative and curiosity about the added potential of the application.

Another aspect that might have had some influence is the fact the users are young. It seems to be natural that young people manifest a facility and appetite for using the new technologies.

Furthermore, the system did not interfere with the informal communication channels between colleagues. It allowed for the inclusion of social interactions when filling in the internal demands, notably when a colleague expressed doubts or difficulties.

Finally, I refer to the training necessary to teach employees to use the system. This was undertaken by the leader of the project and was carried out on site. There was a session with all the potential users, when the leader of the project showed how the system worked. At the end of the demonstration, the person in AFD volunteered to try the system to see what kind of difficulties she would have. The leader also asked the Production Director if he wanted to try but he was unwilling, in front of all of his colleagues. During the first days of use, the project leader was available to answer all doubts arising and to help to perform tasks, whenever necessary. One of the employees mentioned helping the production director with his first internal demand:

> *"We made the first demand together. He was going to fill in the paper version of the form. I asked if he needed anything and said, "let's use the workflow system." Everything went well. He already had his pen in his hand but I said, "let's see how the workflow works."*

Technological Factors

As mentioned above, this system follows the approach of Action Technology based on the language/action perspective. This means, to finish the process, the client must record the demand has been satisfied, on the system. The performance of this step has already brought out some problems. The applicants receive the material demanded and this seems to represent to them the end of the process. They do not see any advantage in having to return to the system, open the page and record receipt. However, the application requires, after receiving in person the material ordered, the applicant must record receipt. Usually, the employees forget to do so and the internal demands remain unsatisfied, as far as the system is concerned.

> *"I think that the application does not need so many steps. Action Technology obliges us to go through these steps because of their approach. Someone has drawn my attention, again and again, to the internal demand. I did half of it but I should have gone back to validate. I usually forget and so the demand remains there; employee XXX cannot work on it because I haven't validated it."*

Some employees also reported the application really conditions the process design.

> *"The flow could have fewer steps. We don't use the system daily; if we had other applications, I believe that things could become easier. As I always have Outlook open, I could also have Action and could see if I had tasks to perform. At the moment, I only open Action to fill in internal demands."*

The technologies already existing in the organisation also appear to hinder the full use of the WS. The adoption of an application, installed with technology that does not support, or does not profit from it, constitutes an obstacle to its use.

> *"It takes me a lot of time. I take almost an hour to do an order to the supplier. I think that is because of our system. It is always breaking down. I need to call in the technical support quite a lot."*

But the fact the system breaks down didn't prevent this employee from enjoying the application. As she says:

> *"I like the application. I like it but the breakdowns trouble me. I have to call in the technical support and then it takes me a long time to perform my tasks."*

None of the other employees showed dissatisfaction with the new system. This situation is not strange as it is only the employee of AFD that needs to have MS Word, Internet and *Metro* opened at the same time.

Finally, I would like to report that some of the characteristics of the new system pleased the users, since some redundant tasks were eliminated, tasks were performed from each employee's desk, there was better control of the process and all the events were registered. Nevertheless, these characteristics do not concern this application in particular but all WS.

Cultural Factors

As far as these factors are concerned, this is an enterprise that appears to be up-to-date in technological terms, namely in microfilming and electronic document management. This company has already lived through some periods of change and innovation, as a result of the research and development carried out. The adoption of a new system cannot be considered as a novelty. Employees are encouraged to regularly attend new courses of training.

The top managers describe the organizational culture as being *"young, aggressive and technological."* They have never considered the use of the system as compulsory. They state that they do not use the system.

Table 1 summarises the organizational factors described above. They are presented as constrainers, which mean the ones that influenced negatively, and enablers, which mean the ones with a positive influence on the use of the system.

As we can see, this is a small enterprise, specialised in the area of microfilming and digitalisation of documents. Its mission is to offer solutions of document management and optical archiving. Employees are young and have high academic qualifications. They have also lived through some changes and developed an EDMS, internally. I can say this is a technological organisation, which manifests itself in the solutions offered, in the training of employees, in its departments and even in the architecture of the building and existing equipment. Its market is also technological; in order to maintain and increase its market share, they need to develop new solutions. The organisation, including the employees, is imbued with a spirit of innovation and change, which reflects in the daily routine and in the development of new projects.

FINAL COMMENTS

It should be noted the factors described above are not isolated but interdependent. Moreover, we cannot say one is more important than the other, as they interact constantly. For example, although some of the existing technologies were obsolete and prevented the employee of the AFD from performing her job adequately, she was curious and committed enough to overcome her difficulties, even though her educational background is not as good as some of her colleagues. On the other hand, even those with a degree experienced some difficulties in performing their tasks and learning how to use the application, probably because these tasks were infrequent, rather than familiar routine. This problem was in turn exacerbated by the *Metro* application requiring users to register their satisfaction with the process before ending it, which, in such a small and simple process as this, constituted a constraining factor.

Although there was some dissatisfaction with the new application, the perceived predominant ethos of the company, which favours and encourages change, enhanced their willingness to adopt the new system and seems to have helped the

Table 1: Summary of the Organizational Factors that Enabled or Constrained the Use of the WS

Organizational Factors		Enablers	Constrainers
Structural Factors	Process	Some employees consider that the process is faster now. Elimination of redundant tasks. Reduction of paper volume (reduction in file volume). Better management of each employee's time. Forms are explicit.	Person in AFD and Prod. Dir. consider that process is slower now (new tasks and problems with the equipment).
	Tasks	Tasks can be performed from each employee's desk. AFD and Prod. Dir. – tasks are done regularly contributing to a routine of work.	
	Coordination and Control	All movements are registered. Process is clearer as well as responsibility. Forms are standardised.	
Political Factors	Information	AFD – tried to see what kind of information she had available after the use of the new system.	
Human Factors	Literary Qualifications	The majority of the employees have a degree.	AFD and Prod. Dir. does not have a degree.
	Knowledge about Computers	Good knowledge about computers (business and educational background of the employees).	AFD and Prod. Dir. does not have good knowledge about computers. Their knowledge was acquired in the daily routine of work.
	Age	Average age of 28 years old.	
	Training	All the employees have regular training. The project leader did train to use the system in the enterprise.	
	Personality	Employees are curious and have a will to learn and to overcome difficulties.	Prod Dir. admits being afraid of touching the application.
	Informal Communication	The new system seems not to have influenced the informal relationships	
	Social Interactions	The difficulties of some employees were overcome by collaboration.	
Technological Factors	Existing Equipment		AFD – at the beginning the equipment blocks constantly. It has insufficient memory.
	Application Characteristics	Application is easy to use; it allows the registration of events, the control of the internal demands and the elimination of tasks redundancy. Tasks can be performed without employee's displacement.	Need to record receipt at the end of the process.
Cultural Factors	Symbols	Enterprise is updated in technological terms. They have already lived through other organizational changes and Information Systems adoption.	Top managers do not use the system. Its use is not compulsory.

Figure 5: The Interaction Between the Organizational Factors

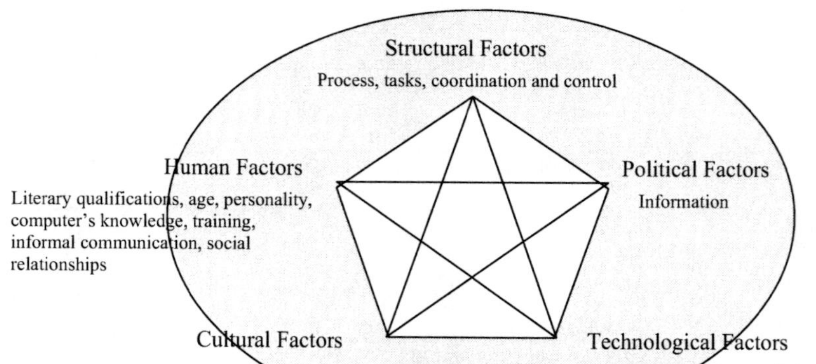

staff overcome their difficulties. Any expressed dissatisfaction was counteracted by the unanimous recognition that the new WS did reduce paper volume, a welcome change.

Figure 5 represents the initial model used to study the impact of the WS on organisations presented in the first sections of this paper, and improved. It shows, not only the general factors that influence the use of a WS, but also the specific ones that mediated use in this particular case.

Thus, for instance, in structural factors, it should be taken into consideration the process involved, the characteristics of tasks as well as the coordination and control. For human factors, we have the literary qualifications, the age, the personality, the information literacy, the training and the relationships. As far as political factors are concerned, the access to information should be considered. In the technological factors, the use of a new technology can be influence by the characteristics of the existing technologies as well as those of the new system adopted. Finally, culture should also be considered, namely the symbols and the way the enterprise generally reacts towards change.

These factors, as shown in Figure 5, are interrelated and the results of such interaction evolve over time. Change is a process rather than an event (Orlikowski, 2002).

CONCLUSIONS

This paper describes a framework designed to assess the impact of the adoption of a WS in a company and its application to a case study. Results showed the organizational factors that constrained or enabled changes in this case were: the frequency of performance of the task; the characteristics of the WS adopted; the existing technologies; the employees and the culture of the organization. These factors are interdependent, being the outcome of the adoption of a WS and the result of the interaction between them. Being aware of which factors might interact beforehand will contribute to a better management of the process of change.

REFERENCES

Bertalanffy, L. (1973). *General Systems Theory.* Harmondsworth, UK: Penguin Books.

Bertrand, Y., & Guillemet, P. (1988). *Organizations: A Systemic Approach.* (in portuguese language) Lisbon: Instituto Piaget.

Boersma, P. (1994). *Experimental Research into Usability of Organizational Impact of Workflow Software.* Department of Computer Science and Section Ergonomics, Master Thesis, Twente, University of Twente.

Bolman, L., & Deal, T. (1997). *Reframing Organizations: Artistry, Choice and Leadership.* San Francisco, CA: Jossey-Bass Publishers.

Danziger, J., & Kraemer, K. (1986). *People and Computers: The Impact of Computing on End Users in Organizations.* New York: Columbia University Press.

Hales, K. & Lavery, M. (1991). *Workflow Management Software: The Business Opportunity.* OVUM.

Jablonski, S. B. (1996). *Workflow Management: Modelling Concepts, Architecture and Implementation.* London: International Thomson Computer.

Khoshafian, S. B. (1995). *Introduction to Groupware, Workflow and Workgroup Computing.* New York: John Wiley.

Kueng, P. (1998). Impact of Workflow System on People, Task and Structure: A Post Implementation Evaluation. *Proceedings of the 5th European Conference on the Evaluation of Information Technology*, UK, (pp. 67-75).

Laudon, K.C. & Laudon, J.P. (1998). *Management Information Systems: New Approaches to Organization and Technology.* New York: Prentice Hall.

Leavitt, H. J. (1965). Applied Organizational Change in Industry: Structural, Technological and Humanistic Approach. In J. G. March (Ed.), *Handbook of Organizations,* (pp. 1144-1170). CA: Irwin.

Ljungberg, J., Holm, P. & Hedman, A. (1997). Information Technology and Organizational Effects: Supporting the Sales Process with Workflow Technology. *Proceedings of the SIGCPR'97*, (pp. 171-179).

Medina-Mora, R., Winograd, T., et al. (1992). Action Workflow Approach to Workflow Management Technology. *Proceedings of the Conference Computer Supported Cooperative Work (CSCW'92)*, (pp. 281-288).

Miles, M. & Huberman, M. (1994). *Qualitative Data Analysis.* London: SAGE Publications.

Orlikowski, A. (2002). Improvising Organizational Transformation Over Time – A Situated Change Perspective. In J. Yates & J. Maanen. (Eds.), *Information*

Technology and Organizational Transformation – History, Rhetoric and Practice, (pp. 223-275). London: SAGE (appeared in 1996, *Information Systems Research*, 7(1), 63-92).

Pinsonneault, A. & Kraemer, K. (1993). The Impact of Information Technology on Middle Managers. *MIS Quarterly*, 17(3), 271-292.

Pinsonneault, A. & Kraemer, K. (1997). Middle Managers Downsizing: An Empirical Investigation of the Impact of Information Technology. *Management Science*, 43(5), 659-679.

Quinn, J., Baruch, J. & Zein (2002). Intellect, Innovation and Growth. In J. Henry & D. Mayle (Eds.), *Managing Innovation and Change,* (pp. 5-22). London: SAGE Publications.

Schael, T. (1998). *Workflow Management Systems for Process Organisations.* Berlin: Springer-Verlag.

Schein, E. (1993). On Dialogue, Culture and Organizational Learning. *Organizational Dynamics*, 22(2), 40-51.

Schein, E. (1996). Culture: The Missing Concept in Organization Studies. *Administrative Science Quarterly*, 41(2), 229-240.

Scott Morton, M. (1991). *The Corporation of the 1990's: Information Technology and Organizational Transformation.* Oxford: Oxford University Press.

Shimada, T. (1991). The Impact of Information Technology on Organizations in Japanese Companies. In E. Szewczak, C. Snodgrass & M. Khosrowpour (Eds.), *Management Impacts of Information Technology: Perspectives on Organizational Change and Growth,* (pp. 298-329). Hershey, PA: Idea Group Publishing.

ENDNOTES

1 The first reference found for Workflow Systems is dated 1990. The second appears in 1992 and the majority of references to these systems only occur in 1997.

2 NUD*IST — Non-numerical Unstructured Data Indexing Searching and Theorizing — it is a computer package designed to help to handle non-numerical and unstructured data in qualitative analysis, by supporting processes of coding data in an index system, searching text or searching patterns of coding and theorizing about data.

3 In phase one (preparation) the customer asks for a service or product. In the second phase (negotiation), the supplier promises to fulfil a specific condition. In the third phase (execution), the supplier fulfils the work, which leads to the delivery of the requested service or product. The final phase (acceptance) closes the loop and involves the customer's acknowledgment or formal

declaration of satisfaction (or non-satisfaction), after the customer receives the service or product (Schael, 1998).

Chapter XIV

Strategic Models for the Delivery of Personal Financial Services: The Role of Infocracy

Steven Gordon
Babson College, USA

Paul Mulligan
Babson College, USA

ABSTRACT

The growth of the Internet and the rapidly evolving regulatory climate in the United States and abroad have radically altered the environment of the financial service industry. This chapter focuses on integrated personal financial services (IPFS) — the integration of services such as banking, insurance, and investing for the end consumer — in this new, networked economy. It identifies three different business models for the delivery of IPFS. It explores the concept of an infocracy, a form of organization in which information provides the underpinning of structure and the basis of individual power, and addresses its implications for the management and success of the alternative IPFS business models.

INTRODUCTION

In recent years, two factors — a relaxed regulatory environment and the growth of the Internet — have changed the competitive landscape of the personal financial services industry. Prior to the mid-1990s, active federal enforcement in the United States of the 1933 Glass-Steagall Act prohibited joint ownership of banking, insurance, and securities trading companies. Similar laws hindered horizontal integration in the industry abroad. As the regulatory environment eased in the late 1990s, mergers, such as that between Citibank and the Travelers Group, occurred as financial service companies sought to increase their market reach. But it was not until 1999 that the passage of the Financial Modernization Act finally allowed bank holding companies, securities firms, and insurance companies to combine operations. Subsequently, consolidation in the industry accelerated as businesses prepared to take advantage of potential economies of scale and reach and the promise of providing an integrated financial environment for their customers.

The growth of the Internet has also changed the delivery of personal financial services. People are beginning to trust the Internet with their money and are not afraid to use it for banking, investment, and insurance. Pure Internet banks have emerged, and traditional banks have endeavored to design effective strategies for integrating Internet and conventional channels, also known as bricks-and-clicks.

It is natural to assume advances in the Internet and other information and communication technologies might affect how financial service companies address the potentiality of horizontal integration subsequent to deregulation. Had financial regulation eased 10 years ago, most companies would have had little choice but to pursue a strategy of acquisition and merger to attain the capacity for providing integrated financial services and to preserve market share. However, the Internet creates opportunities to build organizations, real and virtual, based on the control of information rather than the ownership of assets. Through this means, the structure of financial organizations in the post-Glass-Steagall world has begun to reflect their strategy, their origins, and their beliefs regarding the role of information in organizational control.

In the following section, we first review the literature to understand how researchers believe information technology (IT) affects the structure of organizations. We then address what an ideal world would look like from the perspective of the consumer of personal financial services. We also analyze how businesses are leveraging information technology to transform themselves to satisfy this ideal. We examine the concept of an infocracy — a form of organization proposed by J.G. Clawson, in which the basis of power is information — and show how it applies to the alternatives for financial service organizations in the coming decade. Finally, we examine the managerial and research implications of this concept.

HOW IT AFFECTS ORGANIZATIONAL STRUCTURE: A HISTORICAL PERSPECTIVE

Researchers have widely observed that information technology plays an important role in shaping organizations and molding the nature of work (Bartezzaghi et al., 1981; Benjamin & Levinson, 1993; Drucker, 1988; Huber, 1990; Malone & Rockart, 1993; Wang, 1997; Whisler, 1970). Naturally, this role is indirect: changes in technology affect information flow and the potential for information flow, and these, in turn, affect organizational structure.

Nearly half a century ago, Leavitt and Whisler (1958) proposed advances in information technology would allow large industrial organizations to centralize control and decision making and it would radically alter the nature and organization of middle management jobs. The authors theorized that top executives would be less dependent on subordinates, because computers would allow these top executives to recognize and react to everything of importance that occurred, even in the most dispersed and complex organizations. Middle management tasks would become routine and business groups would be merged. Roughly 10 years later, when the predicted trend toward re-centralization failed to materialize, Dearden (1967), responded that although computers might centralize logistics, top management lacked both the time and the expertise to centralize all but the most important decisions. Lawrence and Lorsch (1967) noted increased differentiation of departments or data necessitated an increase in integration mechanisms, but allowed for decentralization of task and structure. With the further development of communication infrastructure and computer networking in the early 1980s, Leavitt and Whistler's argument seemed to reassert itself. Researchers argued, for example, information systems could extend the control of headquarters over foreign subsidiaries that would otherwise distance themselves from the home office as they matured (Prahalad & Doz, 1981).

The computer's role in automation was also recognized as affecting the organizational structure of manufacturing firms (Bartezzaghi et al., 1981). Clutterback (1979) hypothesized that the increasing power of information processing would narrow the distinction between blue-collar and white-collar workers and could reduce or eliminate the need for middle management. Attewell and Rule (1984), in a meta-study of research addressing the impact of computerization on factors such as job satisfaction, unemployment, inter-occupational change, and work redesign, found the impact of IT is inconclusive.

Wide area networks made possible inter-organizational information systems, which increased the opportunities for competitive alliances crossing organizational boundaries (Cash & Kosynski, 1985). By the late 1980s and early '90s, information technology was blamed for industry trends towards decentralization and downsizing (McDowall, 1985), and praised for enabling efficiencies through business process redesign (Brynjolfsson et al., 1994; Hammer, 1990). Later, researchers argued the widespread acceptance of client server computing precipitated movement from a command-and-control structure to decentralized authority and growth in teamwork and team-based management (Hitt & Brynjolfsson, 1997).

Clayton Christensen has popularized the term "disruptive technology" as one that enables innovative companies to create new business models that alter the economics of their industry (Christensen, 1998; Christensen & Tedlow, 2000). The technology of electronic commerce is clearly such a force in many industries. It has not only changed business models, but in so doing, it has also affected the structure of companies competing in this environment.

The concept of the virtual organization (Davidow & Malone, 1992) predated, but anticipated, the widespread use of the Internet for electronic commerce. Other models, such as the creative Web (Conklin & Tapp, 2000), e-network (Davenport, 2000), value net (Brandenburger & Nalebuff, 1997; Nalebuff & Brandenburger, 1997), and e-lance structure (Malone & Laubacher, 1998), although differing in details, share the concept of a dynamic, flexible structure with blurred organizational boundaries.

HOW IT AFFECTS ORGANIZATIONAL STRUCTURE: A THEORETICAL PERSPECTIVE

There is a significant body of research that examines the relationship between structure and technology, but the *mechanism* by which information technology affects organizational structure remains scantily studied and poorly understood. One theory holds that organizational hierarchy is affected by the human inability to attend to more than a few bits of information at once (Simon, 1973). Central to this theory is the idea that organizations obtain or generate more data than any one person can assimilate to make informed decisions. As information flows to the tops of organizations, this "attention bottleneck," as it is called, becomes narrower and narrower. Information technology can theoretically loosen this bottleneck by processing, summarizing, and indexing the information. By contributing to managers' abilities to process more information, IT increases their potential span of control and flattens the management structure.

Bolton and Dewatripont move this theory out of its hierarchical context by proposing that firms organize to minimize the costs of processing and communicating information among its members (Bolton & Dewatripont, 1994). Specialized agents (human or computer) process data creating information with more specificity and relevance to the decision maker. The organizational structure, then, reflects returns to specialization and a trade-off between specialization and communication. This may, in part, explain why Leavitt and Whisler's (1958) centralization forecast has not materialized. As deregulation propels industry consolidation and customer demands fuel horizontal integration, organizations are forced to maintain divisionally localized processing capabilities to effectively manage their expanding product scope. Information technology affects organizational structure by decreasing the cost of creating or automating specialization agents and decreasing the cost of communication and integration.

Another theory holds that information technology affects organizational structure by changing the differential between internal and market transaction and coordination costs (Malone & Laubacher, 1987). The theory is based on the hypothesis that market coordination costs are higher than internal coordination costs. As information technology reduces the costs of market coordination, market transactions should become more desirable relative to internal transactions, thereby reducing firm size and the degree of vertical and horizontal integration.

The implication of these theories is the growth of the Internet should enable partnerships and other virtual organizational forms, and improve their viability relative to more hierarchically controlled structures. As the relative costs of coordination, transaction support, communication, and agent automation change, we would expect to find evidence of structural change among firms in the financial service industry.

INTEGRATION OF PERSONAL FINANCIAL SERVICES — THREE MODELS

The response of the financial service industry to deregulation is predicated, in part, on the will of companies to respond to consumer expectations and preferences. Pundits in the industry believe consumers will demand a full integration of personal financial services. They believe, for example, the consumer of the not-too-distant future would like, at a single Web site, to pay her bills, check her account balance, add money to her smart-cash card, check her credit card balance, check the current value of securities in her portfolio, buy and sell stocks and bonds, buy insurance, and issue instructions to reallocate the investment mix of payroll-deducted deposits into her 401K plan.

The quality of the integrated service experience will depend not only on the quality of the user interface, but also on the completeness of information and access to all the user's financial resources and on the features provided. Ideally, every financial instrument owned by a customer will be internally liquid and appear to be centrally located and controlled, restricted only by the legal and financial parameters of the instrument.

Three pure models and hybrids of these models can characterize the strategies of companies that have begun to offer integrated personal financial services (IPFS). The first model, which we call the Unified IPFS, describes companies that provide all or most of the services a consumer might want within a single corporate structure. Today, most Unified IPFS companies exist as holding companies, and, while their services are not yet well integrated, they are attempting to achieve a more seamless service delivery system through expanded investments in information technology. Unified IPFS providers currently differ in their degree of integration and the extent to which they can provide a full range of financial services.

The second model, which we call Allied IPFS, describes companies that provide diverse services through inter-organizational alliances. These companies focus on one primary area, such as banking, but provide a broad range of services through alliances with other companies. An example of such a company is Sovereign Bank, which provides, for example, investment products through their partner Lantern Investment Services and annuity products through IFS Agencies, Inc.

The third category, which we call Portal IPFS, describes companies that provide no direct, transactional services of their own but act as portals through which consumers can manage all of their financial services. An example of such a company might be Quicken, with its relationships with Ameritrade for brokerage services and Firstib.com for banking services. Although Quicken does not currently provide the seamless integration that we expect from the Portal IPFS firm of the future, it clearly hints at what this future might be.

Hybrid IPFS models are possible. For example, a company that appears to be a Unified IPFS provider might outsource some of its low volume products or services to companies that specialize in providing them. The result would be a company that is dominantly Unified, but selectively Allied. A Portal could also provide its own banking or brokerage services, creating a Portal/Allied or even a Portal/Unified hybrid.

Table 1 summarizes from the consumer's perspective the relative advantages, disadvantages, and risks of dealing with businesses pursuing each of the three IPFS strategies. Table 2 compares the strategies from the supplier's perspective as to competitive advantage, competitive focus, required core competencies, information technology focus, and service focus. It also provides some examples of organizations that are pursuing each strategy. The remainder of this section elaborates on each strategy.

Unified IPFS

A distinct advantage of the Unified approach is that a single corporate entity captures all revenues and maximizes its 'share of wallet' with the customer. A Unified company can increase the market share of each of the services it provides by cross selling. Such a company aims to "own" a customer from "cradle to grave,"

Table 1: Customer Perceptions

	Unified	**Allied**	**Portal**
Customer value proposition	One stop shopping Lifetime relationships	Best in class Flexibility	One stop viewing Unlimited providers
Perceived competitive vulnerability	Lost focus Exposure to niche players	Complex customer service Coordination/run costs Revenue sharing	Customer service Brand Ambiguous revenue model
Sources of customer resistance	Lack of diversity (performance) Perceived eggs in one basket	Customer servicing Limited choice in service providers	Security Privacy Permission granting

Table 2: Organizational Components

	Unified	Allied	Portal
Anticipated competitive advantage	Cross-selling Brand development Integration options Full revenue capture	Internal focus Provider diversity Reduced start-up costs	Flexibility Lowest start-up costs Integration of non-financial data
Competitive focus	Share of wallet	Share of customer	Share of information
Core competencies	Intra-organizational integration	Inter-organizational integration	Cross-industry integration
IT focus	Information management	Information transfer and integration	Screen scraping and presentation
Service focus	Service bundling	Service matching	Service aggregation
Examples	Schwab; Fleet; Citigroup	Sovereign Bank; Trustmark Bank	Quicken; InsurBank; Yahoo

providing banking for the young, investment and retirement planning services for the middle-aged wealth accumulator, and trust management and reverse mortgage services for the elderly wealth distributor. The opportunity to establish brand recognition is also a benefit for a Unified IPFS provider.

The major disadvantage of the Unified IPFS strategy is the potential for a loss of corporate focus. The current diversity in investment products and continued advances in information technology make it difficult to be best in class, for all products and services. The Unified providers compete directly with each other, but also compete with more focused allied and portal players who, by incorporating product specialists into their networks, seek to provide premier service in a single product or market. From the consumer's perspective, the limitations in service and product options and choices, and the thought of putting all one's financial "eggs" in a single basket, can be problematic.

The ability of Unified IPFS providers to offer a seamless integration of accounts may sway customers to opt for a single provider. However, if an Allied or Portal IFPS company can offer both integration and a choice of providers, the Unified IFPS provider may find itself at a disadvantage.

Allied IPFS

The primary benefits of the Allied approach are internal focus and external provision of choice to consumers. The enhanced focus gained by concentrating on a limited product-market offering eliminates resource deployment conflicts that may arise in more diverse Unified organizations. The firm can acquire, develop, and deploy human, capital, and technological resources in the development of a narrower set of competencies that are specific to their core business.

Proponents of the Allied model often boast of its apparent flexibility. Stronger partners can simply replace poor performing alliance members. However, this benefit is more illusory than real. Removing a partner for the alliance is extremely difficult unless all consumers opt to shift to the new alliance member. Adding a new member to provide alternatives to weak partners may violate contractual agreements or create confusion for customers. One cannot help but be reminded of the old cliché: "a chain is only as strong as its weakest link."

The Allied model's major weakness for consumers, relative to the Unified strategy, is the challenge of providing a seamless integrative experience for the customer. Unified providers may find crossing internal *functional* boundaries difficult but the Allied firms face greater obstacles when crossing *organizational* boundaries. The coordination costs inherent in these relationships may impact financial performance by either shrinking margins, if prices are fixed, or compromising competitive position if the alliance raises prices to preserve margins. The goal for alliance members is to leverage focus, such that the cost savings from internal operating efficiencies and excess returns earned by product specialists outweigh the added coordination costs.

Portal IPFS

The advantage of the Portal IPFS provider is the choice of provider rests with the customer, as opposed to the Allied model in which the dominant provider pre-selects alliance partners. Furthermore, the portal model allows for multiple providers for the same product-service, which maximizes consumer freedom of choice. Portal IPFS providers also have the capability to incorporate non-financial services, such as frequent flyer accounts, news, and e-mail.

The major challenge for Portal providers is to placate consumer anxiety regarding privacy and security. The account consolidation benefits delivered by the Portal model also raise fears about identity theft. Customer servicing and accountability are also significant issues for this model. Today's Portal providers are not capable of providing customers service for such things as account registration changes, address changes and problem resolution. The technical standards imposed by the Internet enable this model, but further establishment and maintenance of business process standards will be necessary to facilitate delivery on the Portal concept's full potential.

The Portal model is the newest of the three and currently services the smallest customer base. However, adoption rates continue to accelerate (Torris et al., 2001) as service levels improve and privacy concerns dissipate. The true power of the Portal will be realized when providers fully integrate account processing and augment transactional services with comprehensive add-on services.

THE COMING INFOCRACY

Science fiction writers have long used the term "infocracy" to describe a Cyborghian or Gaia society composed of beings that have no concept of self, other than as a component of a functioning community. The term seems to have first been used to describe organizational forms by Zuurmond, who defined it in a government setting as the virtualization of bureaucracy (Zuurmond, 1996). Zuurmond's infocracy describes an organization that appears to have become flat, lean, less hierarchical, more open, and more flexible, but only because its bureaucratic structure, rules, and standards are translated into and enforced by information systems. Zuurmond's infocracy retains a bureaucratic structure.

Clawson popularized another definition of infocracy — a form of organization in which the basis of power is information (Clawson, 1999, 2000). Clawson observes that the industrial revolution generated a shift in the dominant management paradigm from aristocracy to bureaucracy. He suggests the information revolution is spawning a similar shift from bureaucracy to infocracy (see Table 3). In an aristocracy, with power derived from gender and lineage, decisions are made by those entitled to do so by birth. In a bureaucracy, decision-making authority is vested in those at the highest organizational levels; these office holders are assumed to know the most and to be best able to effect wise decisions. In an infocracy, decisions are made by those best equipped to interpret the relevant data, rather than those empowered to make decisions by dint of their positions. Clauson calls the people with the right information and knowledge "node interpreters."

The transition from bureaucracy to infocracy could have significant implications for how organizations operate. For example, Clawson hypothesizes the most effective leadership styles will be those relying on information based persuasion rather than command and control behavior.

Clawson suggests the transition from bureaucracy to infocracy will proceed faster than the move from aristocracy to bureaucracy. Bureaucracies, while designed to control information, are largely structured around the physical assets of the underlying organization. An infocracy has no comparable physical restrictions, which may explain the faster rate of transition. We believe the information-intensive nature of financial services and lessening importance of associated physical assets positions this industry to be an early adopter of infocratic principles.

Table 3: Clawson's Management Paradigms

	Aristocracy	**Bureaucracy**	**Infocracy**
Period	Pre Industrial Revolution (18th century and before)	Post Industrial Revolution (19th and 20th centuries)	Information Age (Now and future)
Power source	Gender and lineage	Office and gender	Node Interpreter*
Assumption	"Father Knows Best"	"Boss Knows Best"	"Node Interpreter Knows Best"

* *Node interpreter: Person who has access to relevant and current data and the education and experience necessary to interpret and act upon them*

Clawson was not the first to predict the demise of bureaucracy as an effective management structure. As early as 1966, Bennis had forecast the "coming death of bureaucracy" (Bennis, 1966). Bureaucracies, with their functional divisions, and hierarchical structures, seemed too slow to compete at the speed of information.

Yet, there remains considerable research that affirms the value of bureaucracy in providing direction, structure, stability, and control (Adler, 1999), even in turbulent conditions (Perrow, 1970; Schellenberg & Miller, 1998). Despite predictions to the contrary, identifying any reduction in the bureaucratic structure of today's industry has proved to be devilishly difficult (Collins, 1998).

The internal adoption of and transition to infocratic organizational structures and processes does not ensure market acceptance. Many consumers accept, and perhaps derive assurance from, bureaucratic structure and policy. The movement to infocracy-supported channels and services will require firm investment in new skills for customer-facing employees and the acceptance of new rules of engagement for consumers. Service providers will require training, perhaps even licensing, in a broader set of products. Consumer education must address comfort and trust levels necessary to support increasingly disintermediated single-point-of-contact service encounters. Well-trained, efficient representatives will be needed to accelerate the development of consumer comfort and confidence.

HYPOTHESIS DEVELOPMENT

It is reasonable to hypothesize a fit between a company's product strategy and its organizational structure. A Unified IPFS might be expected to have a divisional structure, probably based on product rather than functional units, with responsibility and power delegated to those in charge of each division. Although some matrix structures might be necessary to motivate and control cross-selling and joint product development, the overall organizational structure is likely to be highly bureaucratic. An Allied IPFS would seem to require a more dynamic structure to respond to and nurture the inter-organizational fluidity inherent in its strategy. While each of the individual partners in the alliance might be somewhat bureaucratic, the governance of the alliance, as a whole, must have power both within and across organizational boundaries and must be sufficiently democratic to satisfy its respective partners. One might expect an Allied IPFS to exhibit a semi-bureaucratic or adhocratic structure, with distributed decision-making, some degree of democracy, and less control than one would find in a bureaucracy. A Portal IPFS, built solely on the flow of data with little to no control over its customers, would seem to require an infocracy if its internal structure, leadership, and decision making parallels the face it presents to the consumer. Thus, our null hypotheses:

H1: Companies following a Unified strategy are more bureaucratic and less infocratic than those following other IPFS strategies.

H2: Companies following a Portal strategy are more infocratic and less bureaucratic than those following other IPFS strategies.

Yet, it is also reasonable to argue for the opposite hypothesis. A Portal IPFS might demand a bureaucratic structure to counterbalance the fluidity of its customer/supplier relationships by tightly controlling procedures and management oversight. A Unified IPFS might need to operate as an infocracy to become nimble enough to compete with a Portal IPFS. Thus, the truth of these hypotheses needs to be verified empirically.

Testing these hypotheses is complicated by three significant problems. First, the concept of IPFS is relatively young, as is the technology to achieve cross-organizational coordination. As a result, few Allied IPFS providers and even fewer Portal providers exist. Whether more will arise as time passes and technology improves remains to be seen. Second, the concept of infocracy has only recently been proposed. To the best of our knowledge, it has never been operationalized, and no instruments exist to measure it. Finally, it is likely to prove difficult even to identify a company's IPFS strategy. We are beginning to see hybrid strategies, with Unified companies, for example, outsourcing some products to selected Allies, while attempting, at the same time, to provide some Portal functions. These problems give rise to opportunities for future research.

DIRECTIONS FOR FUTURE RESEARCH

The current research has motivated several directions for future research. First, as a prerequisite for study in this area, techniques are needed to classify company strategies as Unified, Allied, or Portal. Although the pure strategies are easy to classify, mixed strategies will likely prevail. What percentage of a company's functions should be in-house for it to be classified as Unified? What percentage should be provided by an ally in order for it to be classified as Allied? Should company IPFS strategy be measured on a continuum?

Second, the concept of an infocracy must be operationalized. How can the degree of infocracy be measured? Can one develop a scale on which an organization can be rated as somewhere between bureaucratic and infocratic? Or, is infocracy, to some extent, orthogonal to bureaucracy, so that it is possible to incorporate both within an organization?

Finally, research needs to be done on the relationship between strategy and structure. Hypotheses H1 and H2 can be tested and their implications examined.

REFERENCES

Adler, P.S. (1999). Building better bureaucracies. *Academy of Management Executive*, 13(4), 36-49.

Attewell, P., & Rule, J. (1984). Computing and organizations: What we know and what we don't know. *Communications of the ACM*, 27(12), 1184-1192.

Bartezzaghi, E., et al. (1981). Computers, management and organization: Reflections on a pilot study. *Information & Management*, 4(5), 239-258.

Benjamin, R., & Levinson, E. (1993, Summer). A framework for managing IT-enabled change. *Sloan Management Review*, 23-33.

Bennis, W. (1966). The coming death of bureaucracy. *Think Magazine.*

Bolton, P., & Dewatripont, M. (1994). The firm as a communication network. *The Quarterly Journal of Economics*, 109(4), 809-839.

Brandenburger, A.M., & Nalebuff, B.J. (1997). *Co-opetition : 1. A revolutionary mindset that redefines competition and cooperation; 2. The game theory strategy that's changing the game of business.* Doubleday.

Brynjolfsson, E., et al. (1994). Does information technology lead to smaller firms? *Management Science*, 40, 1628-1644.

Cash, J.I., Jr., & Kosynski, B.R. (1985). IS redraws competitive boundaries. *Harvard Business Review*, 63(2), 134-142.

Christensen, C.M. (1998). Why great companies lose their way. *Across the Board*, 35(9), 36-41.

Christensen, C.M., & Tedlow, R.S. (2000). Patterns of disruption in retailing. *Harvard Business Review*, 78(1), 42-45.

Clawson, J.G. (1999). *Level three leadership: Getting below the surface.* Upper Saddle River, NJ: Prentice Hall.

Clawson, J.G. (2000, May/June). The new infocracies. *Ivey Business Journal*, 76-82.

Clutterback, D. (1979). The future of work. *International Management*, 34(8).

Collins, D. (1998, March). Knowledge work or working knowledge? Ambiguity and confusion in the analysis of the knowledge age. *Journal of Systemic Knowledge Management.*

Conklin, D.W., & Tapp, L. (2000). The creative Web: A new model for managing innovation. *Ivey Business Journal*, 64(5), 60-68.

Davenport, T. (2000). Davenport on...: Nets upon nets. *CIO*, 13(12), 54-56.

Davidow, W.H., & Malone, M.S. (1992). *The Virtual Corporation: Structuring and Revitalizing the Corporation for the 21st Century.* Harper.

Dearden, J. (1967, January/February). Computers: No impact on divisional control. *Harvard Business Review*, 51-56.

Drucker, P.F. (1988, January/February). The coming of the new organization. *Harvard Business Review*, 45-53.

Hammer, M. (1990, July/August). Reengineering work: Don't automate, obliterate. *Harvard Business Review*, 104-112.

Hitt, L.M., & Brynjolfsson, E. (1997). Information technology and internal firm organization: An exploratory analysis. *JMIS*, 14(2), 81-101.

Huber, G.P. (1990). A theory of the effect of advanced information technologies on organization design, intelligence, and decision making. *Academy of Management Review*, 15(1), 47-71.

Lawrence, P., & Lorsch, J. (1967). *Organizations and environment: Managing differentiation and integration*. Boston, MA: Harvard University Press.

Leavitt, H.J., & Whisler, T.L. (1958, November/December). Management in the 1980s. *Harvard Business Review*, 41-48.

Malone, T.W., & Laubacher, R.J. (1998). The dawn of the e-lance economy. *Harvard Business Review*, 76(5), 144-152.

Malone, T.W., & Rockart, J.F. (1993). How will information technology reshape organizations?: Computers as coordination technology. In S. P. Bradley, J. A. Hausman, & R. L. Nolan (Eds.), *Globalization, technology, and competition: The fusion of computers and telecommunications in the 1990s,* (pp. 37-57). Boston, MA: Harvard Business School Press.

Malone, T.W., et al. (1987). Electronic markets and electronic hierarchies. *Communications of the ACM*, 30(6), 484-497.

McDowall, D. (1985). Restructuring the organization: Sharp cuts and new directions. *Canadian Business Review*, 12(3), 34-36.

Nalebuff, B.J., & Brandenburger, A.M. (1997). Co-opetition: Competitive and cooperative business strategies for the digital economy. *Strategy & Leadership*, 25(6), 28-35.

Perrow, C. (1970). *Organizational analysis: A sociological view*. Belmont, CA: Wadsworth.

Prahalad, C.K. & Doz, Y.L. (1981). An approach to strategic control in MNCs. *Sloan Management Review*, 22(4), 5-14.

Schellenberg, K., & Miller, G.A. (1998). Turbulence and bureaucracies. *The Journal of Applied Behavioral Science*, 34(2), 202-221.

Simon, H.A. (1973). Applying information technology to organization design. *Public Administration Review*, 268-278.

Torris, T., et al. (2001). *Exploiting finance portals*. Amsterdam: Forrester Research, Inc.

Wang, S. (1997). Impact of information technology on organizations. *Human Systems Management*, 16(2), 83-90.

Whisler, T.L. (1970). *The impact of computers on organizations*. New York: Praeger.

Zuurmond, A. (1996). From bureaucracy to infocracy: Towards management through information architecture. In J. Taylor, I. Snellen, & A. Zuurmond (Eds.), *Beyond BPR in public administration. Institutional transformation in an information age*. Amsterdam: IOS.

Chapter XV

Role of Behavioral Factors in Strategic Alliances

Chong Kim
Marshall University, USA

Purnendu Mandal
Marshall University, USA

Dale H. Shao
Marshall University, USA

ABSTRACT

The number of strategic alliances formed between organizations has increased dramatically and are projected to continue increasing over the next few years. Behavioral and cultural factors play a major role in the success (or failure) of a strategic alliance between partners, but many managers pay little attention to this aspect while in the process of negotiations. This paper highlights a number of human and organizational culture issues, which played a major role in the process of developing a strategic alliance between a major telecommunications organization and several retail electricity organizations. A framework for strategic alliance was developed for this new market situation, which helped the organizations involved understand the future informational requirements and dependence of the partners on one another.

INTRODUCTION

Strategic alliances are a mutual agreement between two or more independent firms to serve a common strategic (business) objective (Bronder & Pritzel, 1992). Senior managers in U.S. banking industry believe alliances between companies are having a substantial impact on organizations and will continue to increase their influence (Gonazlez, 2001). Alliances have had a growth rate of 25 percent and are projected to have a value of $40 trillion by the year 2004 (Parise & Sasson, 2002). The "make versus buy" decision is becoming the "make versus buy versus partner decision" (Parise & Sasson, 2002).

A successful alliance should not imply an imposition of one organization's culture over another. Rather, it should create a new culture that brings together the best elements of each. Unfortunately, "creation of a new culture" is rarely practiced, as alliances are often viewed solely from a financial perspective, leaving the human resource issues as something to be dealt with later and without a great deal of effort (Adler, 2001). The creation of a new culture involves operations, sales, human resources management, technology, and structure among other issues. It is undoubtedly expensive and time consuming to create a new culture, but, in the end, employees become contented and more productive.

For an organization to exploit the benefits of alliances, human factors and information technology (IT) factors must be the basic components for any analyses and plans. The case of a telecommunication company is presented here to highlight the major considerations in human and IT issues which resulted from strategic alliances with new business partners. The telecommunication company identified a new market opportunity as a result of changed market conditions. The company is in the traditional business of telecommunications and information services, but identified a new market opportunity in the retail electricity distribution business that became apparent as a result of market deregulation in the electricity industry. The firm's own strength in IT areas, its strong market position, and the opportunities in forming alliances with other business partners in the electricity industry, were the main considerations for this strategic move. The company, however, neglected to consider the business-cultural differences that existed between TEL (Telecommunications Organization) and potential partners in the electricity business.

DEVELOPING A STRATEGIC ALLIANCE

Conceptual Viewpoint

Strategic alliances focus on combining resources of various organizations through acquisition, joint venture, or contracts. The main purpose of an alliance is to create one or more generic advantages such as product integration, product distribution, or product extension (Pearlson, 2001). In alliances, information resources of different organizations require coordination over extended periods of time.

Bronder and Pritzl (1992), suggest a strategic alliance exists when the value chain between at least two organizations (with compatible goals) are combined for the purpose of sustaining and/or achieving significant competitive advantage. Four critical phases of strategic alliance, namely, strategic decision for an alliance, alliance configuration, partner selection, and alliance management are shown in Figure 1. These four phases provide a basis for a continuous development and review of the strategic alliance, which increases the likelihood of the venture's success.

The details of activities included in various phases are described below:

Phase I — Strategic Decision — Is this Strategic Alliance Justified?

1. Situation Analysis — Are we presently set-up for this strategic alliance?
   a. Globalization
   b. Deregulation
   c. New markets
   d. Developments in technology
2. Identification of Strategic Cooperation Potential — Are we compatible?
   a. Internal trends
   b. Own strengths
   c. Own weaknesses
   d. Time as a competitive weapon
3. Evaluation of Shareholder Value Potential — Is the cost/benefit worth it?
   a. Contribution to free cash flow
   b. Value drivers

Figure 1: Strategic Alliance Phases (Bronder & Pritzl, 1992)

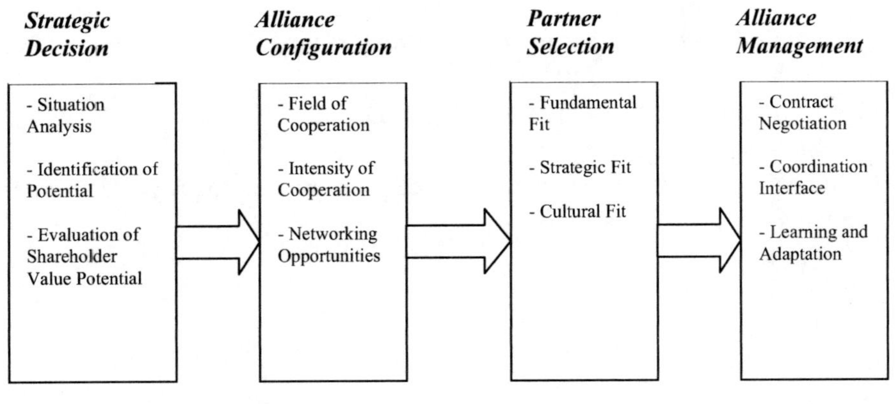

Phase II — Configuration of a Strategic Alliance — How Should We Set-Up the Alliance's Structure?

1. Field of Cooperation — What direction of cooperation and value chain activities should be involved?
   a. Horizontal, vertical or diagonal direction
   b. Research and development, marketing and sales, production and logistics, procurement and recycling
2. Intensity of Cooperation — How deep should our alliance be?
   a. Time horizon
   b. Resource allocation
   c. Degree of formalization
3. Analysis of Opportunities for Multiplication — How deeply should the alliance infiltrate our network?
   a. Systems
   b. Processes
   c. Products/services
   d. Competencies
   e. Brands

Phase III — Partner Selection — One of the Most Important Success Factors of the Strategic Alliance

1. Fundamental Fit — Do the company's activities and expertise complement each other in a way that increases value potential?
   a. Common intention
   b. Compatible vision
   c. Balanced positions of power
   d. Mutual gains
   e. Controlled risks
   f. Potential for increasing shareholder value
2. Strategic Fit — Do our strategic goal structures match?
   a. Harmony of business plans
   b. Common specification of appropriate configuration
   c. Similar planning horizons
3. Cultural Fit — Is there a readiness to accept the geographically and internally grown culture of the partners?
   a. Pluralism
   b. Assimilation
   c. Transfer
   d. Resistance

Phase IV — Managing a Strategic Alliance — How do We Continually Manage, Evaluate, and Negotiate Within the Alliance to Increase the Odds of Continued Success?

1. Contract Negotiations — How do we protect ourselves and still allow enough freedom for the venture to work?
2. Coordination Interface — Who and what do we need to put in place to keep the alliance working properly?
3. Learning, Adaptation, and Review — How do we deal with conflicts and opportunities that arise from the alliance relationship?

Bronder and Pritzl (1992) suggest the development process of a strategic alliance should be considered a strategic problem that utilizes a structured analysis. Their framework provides a way to conceptually analyze a strategic alliance opportunity.

Before an organization commits to a strategic alliance, they should have a management plan developed to deal with the human behavior aspects of the new organizational unit. Once a strategic alliance is a "done deal," the organizations must manage the alliance. Parise and Sasson (2002) discuss the knowledge management practices organizations should follow when dealing with a strategic alliance. They break the creation of a strategic alliance down in to three major phases:

- *Find* — making alliance strategy decisions and screening and selecting potential partners.
- *Design* — structuring and negotiating an agreement with the partners.
- *Manage* — organizations should develop an effective working environment with the partner to facilitate the completion of the actual work. This phase includes collecting data relating to performance and feedback from both partners on how they think the alliance might is progressing. Managing relationships and maintaining trust are particularly critical during the Manage Phase.

Parise and Sasson (2002) stress knowledge management techniques are especially important for a successful alliance. They discuss the need to develop a systematic approach for capturing, codifying and sharing information and knowledge, a focus on building social capital to enable collaboration among people and communities, an emphasis on learning and training, and a priority on leveraging knowledge and expertise in work practices. They also state their study indicates easy access to information and knowledge is a recurring theme in successful alliances.

Parise and Sasson (2002) provide what they call the building blocks of alliance management. Four of their building blocks relating specifically to human behavior factors are:

- *Social capital.* Building trust and effective communication with the partner are necessary ingredients for an effective relationship.
- *Communities.* Communities of practice allow for the sharing of personal and experiences and tacit knowledge based on a common interest or practice. Communities can be realized using electronic meeting rooms and forums or more formal alliance committees.
- *Training.* Companies that rely heavily on strategic alliances should have formal training for managers and team members.
- *Formal processes and programs.* Alliance know-how should be institutionalized. An example of this is Eli Lilly, a leading pharmaceutical firm, created a dedicated organization, called the Office of Alliance Management, responsible for alliance management.

Companies that use alliance management techniques that stress knowledge management are more successful than those who do not. Parise and Sasson (2002) stress that leveraging knowledge management across a company's strategic alliance is a critical success factor for partnering companies.

Practitioner's Viewpoint

Gonzalez (2001) suggests the following practical steps in developing strategic alliances, which are based on the planning, implementation, and evaluation processes:

1. Set-up an alliance strategy — What is the vision and strategy for the partnership, including analyses of our market potential, competition, organizational strengths and weaknesses, and organizational culture?
2. Select a partner — Are we strategically aligned and culturally compatible?
3. Structure the alliance — How should we set-up our financial and legal obligations?
4. Manage the alliance — How do we make the alliance work on an ongoing basis? What should be addressed in our implementation plan?
5. Re-evaluate the alliance — How do we determine if our alliance is work? What do we measure and how do we make adjustments, if necessary?

Gonzalez also lists several common pitfalls experienced by companies developing strategic alliances:

1. Many organizations do not have an alliance strategy that addresses the gaps in their business strategy.
2. Many organizations do not develop an explicit joint strategy with their partners.
3. Too often, a disproportionate amount of attention is paid to the financial aspects of the deal at the expense of — and sometimes neglect of — the strategy and the focus on implementation.

4. Lack of ongoing commitment to the alliance by different parties, which would derail the alliance.
5. Lack of realistic expectations and assessment of efforts.

Gonzalez recommends the above steps, as they have been successful in partnership formation in Canada, the U.S., Asia, and Mexico. Her experiences show the steps work well regardless of the industry or type of business. She believes strategic alliances are the best way for companies to succeed in the global economy.

CULTURAL ASPECTS IN ALLIANCES

As discussed in the preceding sections, alliances among firms naturally would result in many organizational changes. Leavitt (1965) concluded there are four types of interacting variables to consider when dealing with organizational change, especially in large industrial organizations: task variables, structural variables, technological variables, and human variables. He proposed structural, technological, and people approaches to organizational changes, which derive from interactions among the four types of variables mentioned above.

The four variables are highly interdependent so that a change in any one variable usually results in compensatory changes in other variables. The introduction of new technological tools — computers, for example, may cause changes in structure (communication system), changes in people (their skills and attitudes), and changes in performance and tasks. Therefore, it is imperative to consider all areas that might be affected when a company plans to introduce change to an organization.

Pre-existing people related problems at a target company, often cause many alliances to fail to reach their full financial and strategic potential. Numerous case studies report failure of alliances due to lack of consideration for the potential impact of behavioral and structural aspects (Burrows, 2000; Numerof & Abrams, 2000). To build an effective alliance, institutions must pay particularly close attention to cultural, personality and structural incompatibilities. Leaders from alliance institutions need to recognize the personality differences in their managers, as well as, the demands required by the life cycle stage of their organizations (Segil, 2000). It has also been demonstrated that successful alliance partners share many strong similarities regarding performance and relationships (e.g., people skills) (Whipple & Frankel, 2000). Understanding potential incompatibilities gives institutions contemplating alliances a solid foundation on which to explore the feasibility of joint projects. It also increases the likelihood the alliance will operate successfully (Whipple & Frankel, 2000).

Successful alliances are impeded, when the culture of one or both associations highly differ in value. "High control value" is inconsistent with the toleration for ambiguity and the "willingness to compromise" often required for strategic alliances.

Maron and VanBremen (1999) suggests the use of William Bridges' Organizational Character Index, which can be a useful tool for analyzing the cultural differences between two associations to determine how well they might work together. It promotes better understanding between two associations; fosters an appreciation for what both partners could bring to an alliance; and identifies underdeveloped qualities in both associations that could inhibit the success of an alliance.

IT ISSUES IN ALLIANCES

Long term IT considerations, such as IT architecture, is a major consideration. A strategic consideration, such as new alliances, would require visioning of a different IT architecture. Applegate, McFarlan and McKenney (1999) view IT architecture as an overall picture of the range of technical options as well as business options. "Just as the blueprint of a building's architecture indicates not only the structure's design but how everything — from plumbing and heating systems, to the flow of traffic within the building — fits and works together, the blueprint of a firm's IT architecture defines the technical computing, information management and communications platform" (p. 209).

Figure 2 brings out the dynamic nature of the IT architecture development process. The technology part, shown by dotted oval, is concerned with design, deployment and how it is used. This part is the core of IT architecture and a huge proportion of IT professionals' time is devoted to these activities. Consideration of business options, which feed to various technology options, is a higher-level activity

Figure 2: Forces Affecting Overall IT Architecture

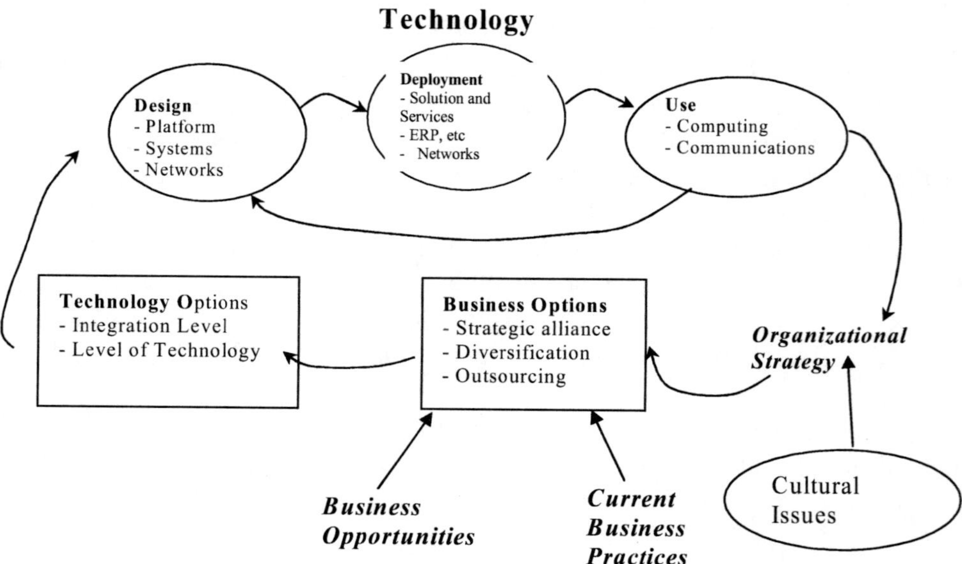

in the IT architecture development process. Business options, such as strategic alliances, mergers and acquisitions, outsourcing, diversification, etc., are influenced by major internal as well as external factors, such as current business practices, business opportunities, and organizational strategy. There is a direct link between technology and organizational strategy. The technology (with its operational and technical settings) exerts a strong influence on the organization's future strategic direction. Thus, one can observe (as shown in Figure 2 through connecting lines), a close link between technical and other business factors, and, like ever changing business, the IT architecture is a dynamically evolving phenomena.

An alliance can exist between any number of organizations. For example, telecommunication organizations could form an alliance for international joint ventures, or an alliance can be established between a banking organization and an IT supplier. The notion of developing a strategic alliance suggests an organization's performance can be significantly improved through joint, mutually dependent action. For a strategic alliance to be successful, business partners must follow a structured approach to developing their alliances and should include as part of this process, strategic planning, communication, efficient and effective decision-making, performance evaluation, relationship structure, and education and training.

Strategists have often suggested organizations should consider entering into similar or somewhat related markets sectors to broaden their product/service portfolios (Henderson & Clark, 1990; Markides & Williamson, 1997). Both the dimensions of market [customer and product as per Ansoff (1986)] in a related market can easily be identified and strategies formulated for deployment. The main advantage of adopting such a strategy is an organization can easily use its competencies and strategic assets in generating a strategic competitive advantage (Markides & Williamson, 1997). Determining the design and the requirements of a new information system (IS) is a relatively simple task. In contrast, diversification into a significantly different market for an IT/IS organization is a very challenging task, which needs considerable evaluation of IT infrastructure and human relations.

THE NEW ENVIRONMENT — WITH AN ALLIANCE

The telecommunication organization (TEL) discussed in this chapter provides services to its customers through its own telecommunications network and would like to improve its customer base by forming a strategic alliance with the retail electricity distribution organizations. As large telecommunication organizations exhibit structural inertia, generating a competitive advantage in a new market poses an enormous challenge (Henderson & Clark, 1990). An organization must make a distinction between a new product and the means to achieve that new product. The recent merger between American On-line and Warner Publishing clearly demonstrates that it is not too difficult for an IT organization to offer new products in an existing market. Considering this point, strategic alliances and partnerships could be a way for an IT organization to enter into a completely new product market. From a systems development perspective, alliances may result in the development of new interfaces to the existing ISs or alternatively a new integrated IS.

As per the deregulation rules, a retail distributor must make financial settlement with other suppliers of the electricity industry supply chain. This needs to cover the cost of electricity from the wholesale electricity market, tariffs for distribution of the same by the transmission and distribution service providers, and meter data collection from meter providers (MPs) and meter data agents (MDAs). The processes and systems therein must be able to interface with retail energy distributors accounting and billing, service activation and service assurance processes and systems.

To conduct business as a market participant, TEL must purchase wholesale electricity and services for the physical delivery and metering to the customer. There are two clear options available to TEL to purchase electricity:

- By *direct participation* and trading in the national electricity market (NEM). This means TEL would perform all electricity trader functions, including the act to bid and settle wholesale purchases in the national electricity market from its own resources and carry all market and prudential risks and responsibilities.

Figure 3: Energy Trading Risks

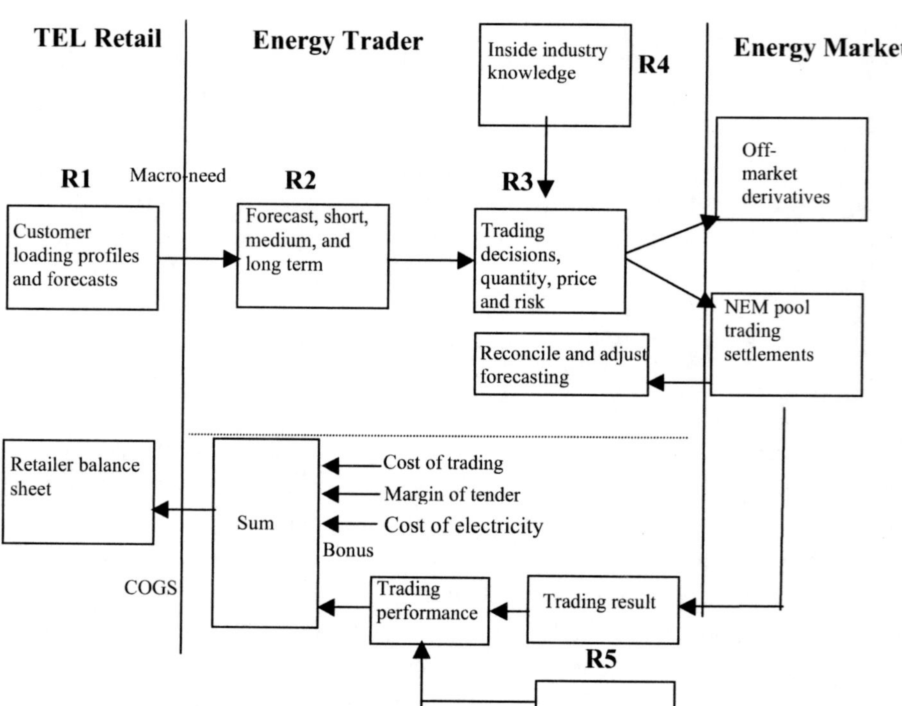

Table 1: Risk Allocation for Energy Trading

Risk	Description	Risk Allocated to
R1	Customer numbers/market share not achieved.	Retailer
	Mix of customer profile types is not as expected	Retailer/Trader
R2	Load/Purchasing forecasts are not accurate	Trader
R3	Trading decisions are flawed	Trader
	Market price risk	Retailer/Trader
R4	Industry development expectations are incorrect	Trader
R5	Incorrect or unrealistic performance expectations are set	Joint - Retailer/Trader

- By *engaging an existing specialist energy trader*. This means TEL would form a close and long-term relationship with one (or more) existing trader(s) who would operate all market trader functions and processes on TEL's behalf. This would be an outsourced supply arrangement. The sharing of risk and responsibilities is a matter for specific agreement with the trader.

Figure 3 and Table 1 identify the risks associated with the Energy Trader functions for various participants in the national electricity market.

COMPLEXITY IN NEW INFORMATION SYSTEMS DEVELOPMENT

The management of TEL must first realize the complexity and limitations of their IT infrastructure, before they venture into the new business. TEL follows a standard procedure called Product Development Operational Model (PDOM) for any IT product development and this procedure was also applied in developing its IT architecture design. PDOM is very similar to standard Systems Development Life Cycle (SDLC) (Kendall & Kendall, 1995).

Figure 4 shows the relationship between TEL and the third parties that it must reconcile.

Reconciliation with these third parties is critical to ensure the following items are accurate for customers: charges, dates (i.e., customer's start and end dates), rates, services received, usage and loss factors. Reconciliation is also necessary to ensure that payments are settled for the correct dollar amount, and are on time. The third parties with whom TEL will be required to settle with are National Electricity Market

Figure 4: Relationships Between TEL and Third Parties

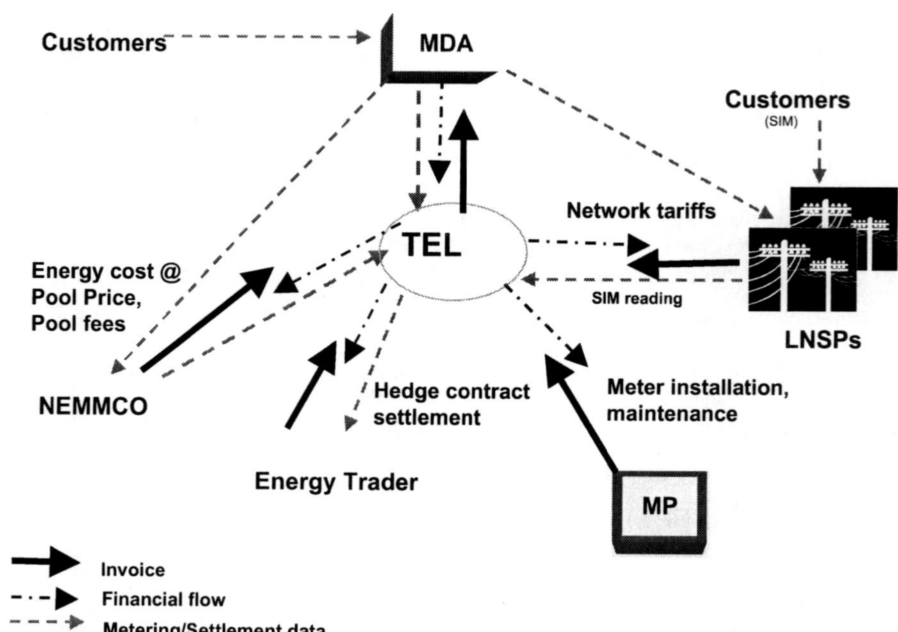

Management Company (NEMMCO), Local Network Service Providers (LNSPs), MDAs, MPs, Energy Traders, and other retailers.

For the proposed alliance to become effective, TEL will be required to develop a number of third party relations with electricity retailers. These relationships are shown in Table 2 below.

To forge a meaningful alliance, TEL would be required to make a number of major business decisions, which would influence their overall IT architecture. These decisions would form the core of the IT system and partnership relations and are presented in Table 3.

If these alliances are to eventuate, the existing processes and systems will be used to generate reports to partner sales and commissions. TEL would be required to provide a lot of technical support to potential strategic partners, since partners in the electricity retail business in general do not have well developed information systems. In fact, most electricity retailers had manual settlement systems. This would be a serious limitation to full-scale system integration.

CULTURAL FIT BETWEEN TEL AND ITS PARTNERS

Table 4 shows there are significant differences between TEL and the other partners. A strategic alliance in this situation would require a careful evaluation of

Table 2: Electricity Retailers and Third Party Relationships

Retailers	Relationships
Electricity Sourcing	TEL will need to contract energy traders to purchase electricity in the national electricity market. TEL will be required to settle periodically with these organizations for services rendered.
NEMMCO	Tel will be required to settle periodically with National Electricity Market Management Company (NEMMCO) for wholesale electricity purchases. NEMMCO will provide billing reconciliation data.
MDA	TEL will contract with NEMMCO accredited MDAs for the collection and provision of customer electricity usage data for billing purposes. TEL will be required to settle periodically with MDAs for services rendered.
MP	TEL as an RP, will have a relationship with MPs in the provision and maintenance of meter installations and TEL will be required to settle periodically for services rendered.
LNSP	TEL will enter into service agreements with each Local Network Service Provider (LNSP) for the use of their distribution network and for the connection and supply of electricity. TEL will be required to settle periodically with LNSPs in terms of distribution fees for network use.
NEMMCO and State Regulators	TEL will pay fees to NEMMCO and state regulators for operating licenses and other regulatory charges.
Generators	TEL may contract with generators (outside of the spot market) for long term energy requirements.
TEL Partner sales commissions	TEL could potentially enter into sales partnerships and pay appropriate commissions.

the strengths and weaknesses of each firm, and detailed planning of what the reorganized alliance would look like. The IT architectural planning would not only present the overview of future challenges, but would also provide the chief information officers (CIOs) a summary of the nature of human related activities they would be faced with once the alliance became a reality.

Before companies agree to participate in the strategic alliance, they should first determine if their organizations can work together harmoniously. To determine whether they can work well together, each company should attempt to determine what type of organization it is, i.e., what is TEL's unique personality or culture? As

Table 3: Major Business Decisions TEL Must Make

Decision
TEL will require a customer signed application form before the Retail Transfer process can commence.
TEL will not enter into and conduct a customer transfer under the BETS process.
The company will negotiate contracts with a LNSP, which will ensure that LNSPs will connect customers to their network at a customer nominated date and time or within a reasonable time. Noteworthy each LNSP will perform service location work for the electricity connection.
TEL will appoint only registered to read meters at agreed customer start date and times.
An MP will install and remove electricity meters only with company's written instructions.
Each LNSP is responsible for fault rectification and maintenance of their electricity distribution network in their local area. TEL will hand off to the appropriate LNSP for fault calls made to TEL. TEL will pay the relevant service fee, but if the customer is culpable for the fault, the onus will be on the LNSP to recover costs.
MDAs are to provide all customer electricity usage to the Retailer for billing purposes, typically daily overnight for smart meters. MDAs will employ manual meter readers to read SIMs at a minimum interval of monthly regardless of the billing cycle.
TEL will settle with MDAs, LNSPs, MPs, energy traders and the Pool for electricity energy cost of goods sold.
TEL must provide energy forecasts to energy traders so they can determine the amount of energy to hedge.

shown in Table 4, both TEL and its partners exhibit a different cultural setting, and this observation suggests further investigation to make the proposed alliance effective.

Though not utilized in this case study, we advocate the deployment of organizational character index (OCI) tool (Bridges, 1992) to TEL and its partners to investigate the cultural fit issues. To determine whether they should work together on possible strategic alliances, the American Society of Clinical Pathologists (ASCP) and the College of American Pathologists (CAP) wanted to discuss their organizational cultures in a "nonthreatening and nonjudgemental way," and felt the OCI tool would be an effective measurement tool for this situation (Maron & VanBremen, 1999). Bridges (1992) explains how OCI can be used to categorize organizations, similar to the way the Myers-Briggs Type Indicator describes the characteristics of

Table 4: Structural and Behavioral Differences

Factors	TEL	Partners
Company organizational structure/ size	Very complex and large in sales volume	Small to medium size, relatively simple structure
Employee work habit	Flexible work hours	Relatively rigid work hours
Customer relations	Good relations with existing customers – excellent customer services	Indifferent to customer complaints
Employee training	Good opportunity for skill upgrading	Reasonable opportunity to technical skill development
IT system compatibility	Highly developed IT system	Manual or primitive IT systems
Employee satisfaction	Highly motivated, well paid work force.	Competent, but low paid work force
Employee turn over	High turn over	Relatively low employee turnover

the individual. OCI, a public domain tool, consists of a written questionnaire that takes 10 to 15 minutes to complete. Bridges stresses that there are not right or wrong types of organizations; it merely brings out organizational personalities. OCI categorizes organizations for the following types (Maron & VanBremen, 1999):

- Its orientation or source of energy (extroverted or introverted).
- How it gathers information or what it pays attention to (sensing or intuitive).
- Its way of processing information, how it judges situations, and how it makes decisions (thinking or feeling).
- How it deals with the external world (judging or perceiving).

The OCI tool was most useful in its ability to stimulate constructive discussions about the two company's cultural differences. Using the OCI tool ASCP and CAP accomplished the following objectives:

- It promoted better understanding between the two associations.
- Fostered an appreciation for what both partners could bring to an alliance.
- Identified "underdeveloped" qualities in both associations that could inhibit the success of an alliance.

The OCI provides valuable insights into difficulties organizations, with certain characteristics might face, in a joint venture such as a strategic alliance. It also highlights the underdeveloped qualities of an organization. These qualities might then be improved. Improving on the qualities can increase the likelihood that a joint venture will be successful.

Maron and VanBremen (1999) stress the "OCI is not a definitive diagnostic tool. It is best used as a way to stimulate discussion, largely because it helps potential partners better understand and articulate their own, and each other's values and expectations."

To use the OCI tool, the following set of simple steps could be followed:

- Administer the OCI questionnaire.
- Tabulate the responses.
- Use the results as the basis for discussion by volunteer leadership and staff.

The OCI could assist the organizations in determining whether their organizational cultures might work well together, but there are other human factors to consider. Burrows (2000) discusses problems he encountered after he became involved with a joint venture and was given the responsibility for handling the people issues.

He quickly realized the joint venture had no real chance of success and discovered the following problems:

1. Reticence on the part of local or senior management to permit one-on-one meetings with employees was determined.
2. Employees were fearful about talking openly about what it was like to work at the company.
3. Employees felt no significant affiliation with, or affection for, the company.
4. The owner of the company and employees were vague or evasive when asked specific questions about the on-site operations manager.
5. Management at all levels did little to build trust and a sense of framework.
6. Management was concerned about safety, but only because accidents were expenses that lowered profitability.
7. Turnover was high.
8. Employee relations were non-existent.
9. The attitude regarding new hires was sink or swim.

Burrows stresses the importance of understanding the "people situation at the target company," if a successful long-term relationship is to result. One of the situations he highlights are "pre-existing people problems." He indicates most companies misunderstand, ignore, or minimize these problems. He states, once the joint ventures are created, man problems reveal themselves, which undermine value-creation opportunities, jeopardize relationships with customers, and reduce productivity.

Burrows provides positive outcomes associated with fully investigating the target company:

1. Substantiate a discounted offer you might make to acquire the company, based on potential people problems.
2. Help keep target management honest.
3. You are able to discover both the target company's people problems and strengths.

Dixon and Marks (1999) provide many reasons why partnerships fail. Three reasons related to human behavior factors are:

- *Inattention to the human resources issues.* Make a conscious effort to retain top managers. Explicitly let them know they are an important part of the organization.
- *Organizations fail to plan for other human resources issues.* Employee consideration, including the process of aligning benefits plans and related legal/actuarial, asset management and plan design factors. Factor in training for new systems and procedures. Allocate time for the employees to transfer their identity and loyalty to the new organizational unit.
- *Poor communication.* Develop a communication system that allows the employee access to information regarding what is happening regarding the merging of the two organizations. Attempt to minimize confusion and uncertainty. Treat employees with respect.

Three ways to increase the odds the partnership work:

- *Build the culture.* Attempt to develop a plan to minimize the shift from the old to the new organization.
- *Create a learning environment.* For the employees to feel comfortable with the new firm, opportunities for learning must be available. The fast pace associated with mergers, acquisitions, and alliances do always allow for formal training, but it should allow time and opportunities to learn during the conversion to the new organizational unit. The company leadership should stress a "learn at all times" mentality.
- *Balance achieving results with concern for people.* If employees do not feel they are an important part of the organization, they will have little motivation to assist with the success of the new organization.

DISCUSSION

In today's competitive business environment, new methods of evolution from independence to interdependence are continuing to unfold — strategic alliances are one of those methods that can be used to achieve competitive advantage. In the process of developing a strategic alliance, IT architecture and human factors play important roles. In addition to considering the projected information systems the organization will require, information officers should focus on the human factors of its organization to increase the odds that an alliance will be successful. IT planning highlights major weaknesses and incompatibilities with information systems of various parties within an organization. Those incompatibilities, however, can intensify further due to operational and work practices in partner organizations.

Though this case study pertains to a telecommunications company, the concepts can be applied to any business, which contemplates diversifying its operation. The development of an IT system and the serious consideration of human issues would lead to practical improvements in the way most organizations approach strategic alliance development planning.

REFERENCES

Adler, L. (2001). Merger Mess. *Business Mexico*, 11(7), 24-25.

Ansoff, I. H. (1986). *Corporate Strategy*. London: Sidwick and Jackson.

Applegate, L. M., McFarlan, F.W., & McKenney, J.L (1999). *Corporate Information Systems Management: Text and Cases*. Boston: Irwin McGraw-Hill.

Bridges, W. (1992). *The Character of Organizations: Using Jungian type in Organizational Development*. Palo Alto, CA: Davies-Black Publishing.

Bronder, C., & Pritzl, R. (1992). Developing Strategic Alliances: A Successful Framework for Co-operation. *European Management Journal*, 10(4), 412-420.

Burrows, D.M. (2000). How People Problems Can Sap Value From a Deal. *Merger and Acquisitions*, 35(9), 36-39.

Dixon, D., & Marks, M. (1999). Making Mergers, Acquisitions & Alliances Work. *Health Forum Journal*, November/December, 30-33.

Gonzalez, M. (2001). Strategic Alliances: The Right Way to Compete in the 21st Century. *Ivey Business Journal,* September/October, 47-51.

Henderson, R., & Clark, K. (1990). Architectural Innovation: The Reconfiguration of Existing Product Technologies and the Failure of Established Firms. *Administrative Science Quarterly*, 35, 9-30.

Kendall, K.E., & Kendall, J.E. (1995). *Systems Analysis and Design*, (3rd Edition). NJ: Prentice-Hall International.

Leavitt, H. J. (1965). Applied Organizational Change in Industry: Structural, Technological and Humanistic Approaches. In J. March & R. McNally (Eds.) Handbook of Organizations, 1144-1170.

Markides, C. C., & Williamson, P .J. (1997). Related Diversification, Core Competencies and Corporate Performance. In A. Cambell & K. Sommer Luchs (Eds.), *Core Competency-Based Strategy*, (pp. 96-122). London: International Thomson Business Press.

Maron, R. M., & VanBremen, L. (1999). The Influence of Organizational Culture on Strategic Alliances. *Association Management*, 51(4), 86-92.

Numerof, R. E., & Abrams, M. N. (2000). Subtle Conflicts that Wreck Merger Visions. *Mergers and Acquisitions*, 35(3), 28-30.

Parise, S., & Sasson, L. (2002). Leveraging Knowledge Management Across Strategic Alliances. *Ivey Business Journal*, March/April, 41-47.

Pearlson, K. E. (2001). *Managing and Using Information Systems*. New York: John Wiley & Sons.

Segil, L. (2000). Understanding Life Cycle Differences. *Association Management,* 52(8), 32-33.

Whipple, J., & Frankel, R. (2000). Strategic Alliance Success Factors. *The Journal of Supply Chain Management: A Global Review of Purchasing and Supply,* Summer, 21-28.

Section V

The Human Side in IT Research

Chapter XVI

Building a Custom Client-Side Research Tool for Online Web-Based Experiments

Stu Westin
University of Rhode Island, USA

ABSTRACT

This chapter describes a general software-based approach to conducting online Web research through the development of a custom research tool. Specifically, the tool is an Internet Explorer-like Web browser that can be designed to deliver experimental treatments and to collect experimental data with great precision and flexibility. The purpose of the manuscript is to introduce this approach to Web-based research, and to discuss the most salient issues, techniques, and problems that are involved in the development and use of such a research instrument.

Programming custom event handlers, for a preexisting software object called the WebBrowser Control, constitutes a major part of the research approach. Event handling techniques having to do with downloading and navigation, with browser interface emulation, and with window and session control are presented. Other relevant issues such as cache management, keyboard handling, and accessing HTML page elements through the Document Object Model are also presented.

INTRODUCTION

Research studies involving the use of the World Wide Web are becoming increasingly common in disciplines such as MIS, marketing, and e-commerce. The focus of these studies is quite varied and may involve issues of human factors (e.g., how does download time impact Web use?), issues of information processing (e.g., what search strategies are employed in various situations?), issues of information content (e.g., how much detail should be provided in the initial product description in an e-commerce application?), or a myriad of other questions. Regardless of the issue being studied, data collection for online Web research often proves to be a vexing problem, and ideal research designs are frequently sacrificed in the interest of finding a reasonable data collection mechanism. Similarly, the administration of experimental treatments under precisely controlled conditions is hardly a trivial exercise when the Web is involved. The researcher is often forced to sacrifice external validity in an attempt to obtain a reasonable degree of internal validity in these experiments.

This chapter describes a general software-based approach to conducting online Web research through the development of a custom research tool. The purpose of this discussion is not to describe a specific research design, or to detail a particular research methodology. Rather, the motivation is to introduce this rather atypical approach to the research area, and to discuss some of the salient issues, techniques, and problems that are involved. Much of the material contained herein was developed as the author struggled with this very topic. It is hoped the reader will be provided with some valuable insights into what to expect from the custom research tool, and how to proceed with its development.

BACKGROUND

Understanding the Problem

Server-side data collection mechanisms based on active server page (ASP) scripts or the like can prove useful in some research circumstances. Consider, for example, the situation where you want to investigate the impact of download time on user satisfaction. Using ASP scripts, a delay mechanism can be easily built into a Web page so that the server will delay serving the requested page to the client until some precise, predetermined time has passed. Different experimental treatment levels are accomplished by merely manipulating the delay time that is scripted into the Web page. Here, the experimental subject, using an ordinary browser, will have the perception that the page is slow to download because of the delay between when the page is requested (e.g., by clicking a hyperlink) and when the page is available in the browser. As another example, consider the situation where you want to study the end user's Web search strategy by recording which pages are accessed, along with the sequence of page access. In this case, we need to record the so-called "click-stream data." Again, ASP scripts in the Web pages could provide a simple data collection mechanism by logging each page request (page ID, server timestamp) in a server database. In both of these research scenarios, standard Web browser software such as Internet Explorer (IE) can be used in the experiment.

In considering the above research problems, it is obvious client-side data collection mechanisms can be constructed just as easily. In both cases, Java applets, Java scripts, or VB scripts can be embedded into the HTML pages to handle the required tasks, and, again, standard browser software can be used. The only difference in this client-side approach is that the data collection is being handled by the client rather than the server machine. Neither approach provides any obvious benefits over the other, although in the client-side approach, the Web pages could be stored locally and thus Web access, or even network access is not required.

One flaw in all of these research scenarios lies in the fact the experimental domain must be restricted to a limited set of Web pages that have been appropriately scripted for data collection. If the experimental subject is allowed to "wander" beyond this limited set of pages (an activity that is quite fundamental to the nature of the Web), then these user actions will not be recorded, and the validity of the experiment will be nullified. There will simply be no data collection scripts to execute. Related to this is the fact that all Web pages used in the experiment must be developed and maintained by the investigator — a task which can be quite labor intensive if a large number of pages are to be made available. Obviously, the experimental pages should usually be large in number and professional in appearance, if external validity is to be maintained.

In some situations the research data can be collected without the use of client- or server-side scripting. Click-stream data, for example, can sometimes be gleaned through the use of standard network management software, or through so-called "network sniffers" that can be configured to monitor Internet requests and/or page downloads. In this case the experimental treatment can involve pages other than those created specifically for the research study, and, again, standard browser software can be used for the experiment. The problem here is in the precision or in the format of the data, as the software was not designed for this purpose. Pages containing multiple frames, for example, may be logged as individual (frame) downloads in some circumstances and as a single page download in others. Client requests that are satisfied through the local cache will not be logged at all.

A problem that underlies all of the data collection methodologies discussed thus far is they suffer from a lack of experimental control. This lack of control comes from the fact the instrument with which the experimental subject is interacting (a standard Web browser such as IE) is not designed to be used as a research tool.

Consider the situation where we wish to study Web use behavior through analyzing click-stream data. There are ways of gathering data on page requests or page downloads, as noted above. However, there is no means, short of direct observation, of recording *how* a particular page was requested. The page request could have come in the form of a click on a hyperlink, but the request could just as easily have been generated automatically, through a dynamic action on the page (e.g., meta refresh), or through the Back or Forward buttons in the browser interface. Normal click-stream data will not distinguish between these circumstances, so the precise behavior or intentions of the experimental subject cannot be determined.

Another problem relates to the occurrence of multiple windows. Many Web sites open hyperlinks in new browser windows, and the savvy experimental subject can even cause this to happen himself (shift-click in IE). The problem here is normal click-stream data cannot reflect which of the open windows is active when subsequent actions occur, or even that there are multiple windows in use. Again, the data cannot capture, or misrepresents the behavior in question; true "streams" cannot be traced.

Yet another problem relates to the browser cache. Beyond setting the size of the cache, the experimenter has little control over how or when the cache is used in responding to subjects' page requests. (Note that the cache in IE cannot be fully disabled.) In some circumstances this can introduce systematic error into the data and thus can have a negative impact on the data analysis.

Toward a Solution

When faced with these and other related problems in a Web-based study, this author set out to find a solution. It was determined, for maximum flexibility and experimental control, the experimental manipulations (treatments) and the data collection mechanisms should be as close to the experimental subject as possible. That is, they should ideally be embedded in the browser itself. This led to the development of a custom IE-lookalike browser for use in Web-based experiments. As it turns out, this is not as complex an undertaking as it might first appear.

With custom browser software there is no need to depend on scripts or applets in experiment-specific Web pages to administer experimental treatments or to record user actions. Consequently, there is no need to restrict the experimental domain to a limited set of custom Web pages. With this approach, the experimental domain can include the entire Web. The custom software can be built with the ability to precisely record user activity and to preempt or modify actions that could be harmful or inappropriate for the experimental context. Experimental control and experimental manipulation can be integrated into the browser itself.

The software that we know as Internet Explorer (IE) is essentially a software interface surrounding a set of dynamic link libraries (DLL) that provide the requisite Internet processing functionality. The main "guts" of IE is a DLL called SHDOCVW.DLL. This is supported by other DLLs such as MSHTML.DLL, which is responsible for the rendering of HTML documents in the browser window (Microsoft, 2002a). Microsoft, in its Visual Studio suite of software development products, provides a software object called the *WebBrowser Control*. The object is actually stored as the aforementioned SHDOCVW.DLL that governs the behavior of IE (Cornell & Jezak, 1998, p. 80). This control can be employed in Visual Basic

(VB) or in C++ programs to add Web browsing functionality to software applications. The *WebBrowser* object works with the standard event-based model of Windows computing. The fundamentals of this model are described next.

Windows software objects (e.g., the *WebBrowser Control*) communicate with their environment by sending out "messages." Messages, also known as events, are how an object tells the environment what is happening (including all relevant details), and when. The process of sending a message is called "firing an event." If a programmer wants her software to react to a certain event, then she can code an "event handler" for the event. An event handler is simply a special subroutine that is bound to the firing of a particular event. The specific details surrounding an event are manipulated as arguments of the event handler subroutine. If an event handler contains no code at all, then that event is, for all intents and purposes, ignored; the event still happens, but nobody cares. If, on the other hand, an event handler does contain program code, then the lines of code detail what will occur at the time of the event.

The *WebBrowser Control* fires events for all of the major occurrences in an Internet session. For example, events are fired when a request to navigate to a page is made, when a page has completed downloading, and when a request is made to open a new window. Essential details such as URL, Target Frame, and Page Title are available with the *WebBrowser* events. Coding event handler subroutines for these *WebBrowser* events is the key to building a customized IE-lookalike browser for Web-based research.

In some cases, Internet actions can be altered or preempted through a *Cancel* argument in the event handler. One important example of this is the *BeforeNavigate2* event handler. This routine fires *after* a navigation has been requested by the user, but *before* the request is fulfilled. This allows the custom software to inspect and evaluate the situation, and to possibly modify or cancel the request before it is allowed to proceed.

Properties and methods of the *WebBrowser* object can be used to dynamically emulate all of the visual and behavioral features of the IE interface such as the status bar, the browser window caption, and the standard buttons (Back, Forward, Stop, Refresh, Home, etc.). In short, an emulation of IE can be built with the inclusion of as few or as many features of the IE interface as are needed in the experimental context. IE features that might corrupt the experiment can be left out or can be monitored by the custom software.

Figure 1 shows a snapshot of a custom browser that was created by the author for a recent research project. This browser is not IE, but rather is a Visual Basic software application hosting a *WebBrowser Control* object. The *Title Bar Control* at the top of the VB form programmatically displays the title of the current browser page (as does IE). Similarly, the *Status Bar Control* at the bottom of the VB form always shows the URL of the currently selected hyperlink. The *Button Controls* on the VB form (Back, Forward, Stop, etc.) are controlled by the software to emulate

Figure 1: Snapshot of a Custom Browser that was Created by the Author for a Recent Research Project

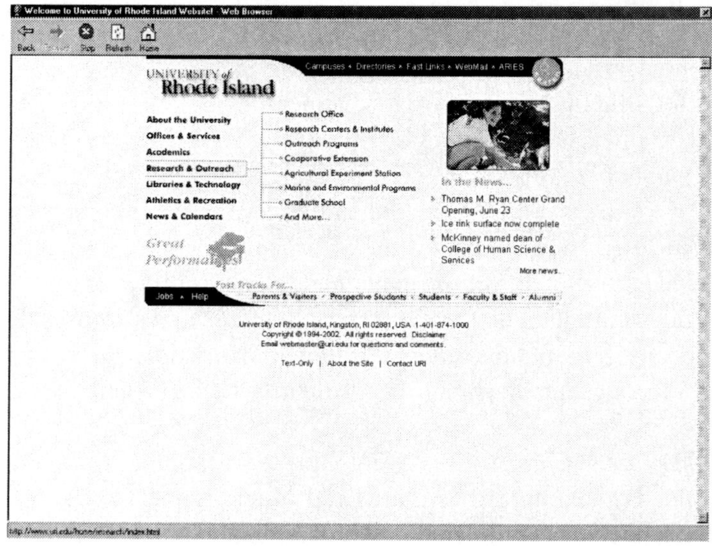

their IE counterparts unless a particular action would be detrimental to the experiment. Noticeably absent is the URL entry area through which the user could normally enter a URL target. This feature was left out as part of the experimental design.

In this application the VB form is programmed to fill the entire screen, including the Windows Control Bar, at all times. The Windows Close Button, at the top right, is for show only. It is programmatically disabled so that only the researcher can close the application through a special key sequence. Through these features (and some special keyboard handling techniques), the experimental subject is effectively locked into this application for the duration of the experiment.

Figure 2 shows the record structure for one of the data files, named MAIN.DAT, from this same research project. This is provided to illustrate the rich, detailed nature of data that can be captured through this approach. This particular file contains one record per URL downloaded by the browser. The file captures the so-called click-streams of the user. Note that this data was captured from the general Web, rather than from a limited set of research-specific pages.

The purpose of the first two fields, Subject_ID and URL_Sequence are obviously provided for record sorting and identification purposes. The purpose of the final field, Full_URL, is also obvious. The Target_Frame field holds the name of the page frame (if any) in which the URL was displayed. This is an important aspect of a click-stream since each URL download operation does not necessarily translate into a unique page as seen by the user. This information, which was captured through the *BeforeNavigate2* event (above), is frequently missing from click-stream data.

Figure 2: Record structure for a data file

MAIN.DAT (one record per URL)
Subject_ID
URL_Sequence#
Target_Frame (if any)
URL_Start_Time (since session began)(E^{-2} sec)
URL_Duration (E^{-2} sec)
User_Action (Click, Back-Button, Forward-Button, Home-Button, Automatic)
Full_URL

The URL_Start_Time field measures the time of the experimental subject's mouse click, within the context of the experimental session (rounded to the hundredth of a second). This item is easily captured since the *WebBrowser Control* fires a *DownloadBegin* event. The URL_Duration field is a measure of the time until the subsequent download.

The information in the User_Action field is difficult, if not impossible, to capture through alternative experimental approaches. Beyond recording *what* URL was downloaded, we are often concerned with *how* that download was initiated. That is, what were the intentions and motivations of the experimental subject? Intentionally navigating through previous pages via the Back button is clearly different from exploring new pages through hyperlinks. Some URLs are downloaded automatically through scripts or through a meta refresh on other pages. With a custom browser, the software surrounding the *WebBrowser Control* can analyze the mouse clicks and the button presses of the experimental subject to determine how each URL is requested and can record this information along with the click-stream data.

By developing a custom browser research instrument, the investigator is free to include (covertly) all of the requisite mechanisms of experimental control and data monitoring into the browser itself, no external scripting or network monitoring is needed. Timers to precisely control the duration of the experiment or the occurrence of experimental treatments can be easily embedded into the browser software. Experimental treatment randomization can also be built in.

User activity down to the keystroke or mouse-click level can be monitored and recorded with millisecond accuracy if needed. Certain events can also be blocked or modified if necessary. For example, an attempt to open a page in a new window can be intercepted (the *NewWindow2* event of the *WebBrowser Control*) and the page redirected to the initial window. With this approach, no special (i.e., scripted) Web pages are needed, but attempts to "wander" to irrelevant sites or inapposite protocols (e.g., "mailto:," "ftp:," etc.) can easily be halted if desired. The cache can be controlled programmatically through calls to the Windows API. Perhaps best of all, once the basic system is developed, modifications and new features are a fairly simple to effect.

MAJOR ISSUES AND TECHNIQUES

In this section, I will discuss some of the more important programming issues and techniques, and the key *WebBrowser* events that are involved in building a customized browser for Web-based experiments. Code snippets are shown in bold and use the syntax of VB. When the event handler subroutine formats are presented, only the relevant arguments are provided. The ellipsis symbol (...) is used to indicate that additional arguments exist, but are left out of this presentation.

Windows programming skills (VB, C++, J++, etc.) at the intermediate level are needed to actually build a satisfactory tool, but the reader who possesses such a skill set should be pushed well along the learning curve by this material. This author has already struggled through the too-sparse documentation and convoluted technical papers. It seems the reader should be spared the need to reinvent the wheel.

Events of the WebBrowser Control

With the release of Internet Explorer Version 6, the *WebBrowser Control* (i.e., SHDOCVW.DLL — the "guts" of IE) works with 37 unique events. Luckily, only a handful of these are vital to this application. These more important events are now discussed. The subset is broken down into categories for the purpose of the discussion. The categories relate to (1) navigation and downloading issues, (2) browser interface emulation, and (3) window and session control.

The first category of *WebBrowser* events has to do with navigation and downloading activities. Experience has shown a significant portion of the processing for this application should appear in these event handler routines. Perhaps the most important event for this application is named *BeforeNavigate2* (the '2' suffix is just a means of differentiating this event from its deprecated predecessor, *BeforeNavigate*). This event fires after navigation has been requested (e.g., when the user clicks a hyperlink), but before the navigation action is attempted by the browser software. The event handler subroutine has the following format: **BeforeNavigate2 (URL as Variant, TargetFrameName as Variant, Cancel as Boolean, ...)**. If the *Cancel* argument is set to TRUE before the event handler subroutine ends, the navigation request is completely ignored by the browser. The beauty of this event handler is it gives the programmer the ability to analyze the request and to possibly cancel or to even modify the request before any action is taken. The *URL* and *TargetFrameName* arguments (these can be treated as string data) provide the details necessary to make this decision.

In the application considered here, the custom browser program could contain a list of inappropriate URL targets or a list of heuristic rules against which the request could be compared. For example, a few lines of code can parse the *URL* argument and identify the protocol portion. Requests containing irrelevant protocols such as "mailto:" or "ftp:" can be halted. The programmer even has the ability to cancel the original request (**Cancel = TRUE**), and to covertly send the browser to a totally different location. This action can be accomplished with the *Navigate2* method of the *WebBrowser Control*. The code would look something like this: **myBrowser.Navigate2(newUrlString)**.

Individual navigation activities can be monitored through the two *WebBrowser Control* events, *DownloadBegin* and *DownloadComplete*. These fire for every *BeforeNavigate2* event that is not cancelled — even if a navigation error occurs. Beware that *DownloadComplete* is a somewhat misnamed event. A page is not really available for processing by the user or by your application until the occurrence of the *DocumentComplete* event. This latter event does not fire in the case of a navigation error. The *DocumentComplete* event subroutine is probably the best place to manage the timing and recording of click-stream data. The format is as follows: **DocumentComplete(URL as Variant, ...)**.

A few words of warning are warranted at this juncture. First, when frames are involved, the navigation-related events fire for each frame element. With the *BeforeNavigate2* event handler, testing the *TargetFrameName* argument against the null string can determine whether the navigation is for a frame element. Second, the value of the *URL* argument in the *BeforeNavigate2* event handler may differ from that of the subsequent events. This is because this first event uses the original URL specification that initiated the navigation process (e.g., the actual HREF attribute coded in an HTML Anchor element). Subsequent events use the canonicalized, fully qualified version of the URL.

The second category of events to be discussed for this application has to do with emulating the behavior of the Internet Explorer interface. I will discuss how to emulate the IE Title Bar (at the top of the window), the IE Status Bar (at the bottom of the window), and the standard IE navigation buttons (Back, Forward, Stop, etc.). The Title Bar is handled quite easily through the *TitleChange* event handler of the *WebBrowser Control*. The format is **TitleChange(Text as String)**. The event fires each time the title of an IE session would change. The single argument, *Text*, contains the title that IE would display. Emulation of the textual portion of an IE Status Bar is correspondingly simple. The relevant event handler is as follows: **StatusTextChanged(Text as String)**.

The graphical download-progress animation of an IE Status Bar is easily emulated with the help of the *ProgressChange* event. This fires whenever the system updates the progress of a download process. Numeric arguments indicate the degree of progress achieved. The *DownloadBegin* and *DownloadComplete* events indicate, respectively, when an animated Progress Bar should be made visible or should be hidden.

The *WebBrowser Control* object maintains a URL history list that can be used to emulate standard Back and Forward buttons. Two methods of the control, *GoBack* and *GoForward*, invoke, respectively, navigation to the previous and to the subsequent URLs in the list. Handling the dynamic of the enabled-state of these emulated buttons is a bit more complex, however. For example, the Back button in

IE is enabled as long as there is at least one prior page in the history list; it is disabled otherwise. The IE Forward button is enabled, if and only if, there is at least one subsequent page in the list. This particular dynamic can be handled with the *CommandStateChange* event. This event fires whenever the enabled-state of either of these buttons should change. The two arguments of the event handler indicate (1) which button is affected, and (2) what the new state should be.

Emulation of the remaining IE buttons is quite simple, indeed. The *WebBrowser Control* has methods named *GoHome*, *GoSearch*, *Refresh*, and *Stop* that can be tied to the click of button objects on the form container. The meanings of these actions are obvious. Note, however, the *GoHome* and the *GoSearch* methods are tied to the respective settings, Home Page URL and search configuration, in the Internet Explorer program (these are actually stored in the Windows Registry). In the research application considered here, you would most likely want to send the experimental subject to experiment-specific pages, so these two method calls may not be suited for this research context. Use appropriate *Navigate2* method invocations instead.

The final set of *WebBrowser* events to be discussed deals with session control and window control. When experimental subjects are allowed to roam freely on the Web, there is no telling what type of scripts and software routines might be encountered. A particularly vexing problem in this research context has to do with multiple windows. Hyperlinks are often designed to display the navigation target within a new window, causing multiple windows to be open simultaneously. With click-stream data, this translates into a situation where simultaneous streams are being formed. The research problem stems from the fact there is no way of determining which stream is the focus of the user's attention at any particular time. This author's solution is to preempt the new window creation and to redirect the navigation to the initial window. The *NewWindow2* event is the key to this approach.

The *NewWindow2* event of the *WebBrowser Control* precedes the creation of a new window (new browser instance). The handler for this event has the following format: **NewWindow2(ppDisp as Object, Cancel as Boolean)**. The *ppDisp* argument can be thought of as a reference to a yet-to-be-created new browser object. By modifying this reference within the event handler routine, you can redirect the action to a known browser object as long as the *Cancel* argument remains FALSE. Redirecting this action directly to the initial *WebBrowser* can be problematic, so my solution redirects to a preexisting, yet hidden, buffer *WebBrowser Control* (e.g., **Set ppDisp = Me.myBufferBrowser.object**). The *BeforeNavigate2* event handler of this buffer browser then cancels this navigation request and navigates back to the original browser (**myBrowser.Navigate2 URL: Cancel = TRUE**). The end result is all Web navigations are presented in the initial browser window. For an alternative approach, see Microsoft Knowledge Base Article #Q185538 (Microsoft, 2001a).

Web pages, designed to be displayed in new windows, often contain "close" buttons that run scripts to close the (new) window (e.g., **window.close** in JavaScript).

Since a new window was not created in our application, we cannot allow this to happen in our custom browser. The effect would be to close the single main window and to terminate the Internet session. The *WindowClosing* event of the *WebBrowser Control* provides a simple solution to this problem. This event fires when the *WebBrowser Control* is about to be closed through a script action. The event handler is **WindowClosing(Cancel as Boolean, ...)**. Just set **Cancel = TRUE** to circumvent the action. Optionally, you can invoke the *GoBack* method to simulate closing the window by returning to the prior page in the history list.

While automatic pop-up windows and banner ads are annoying to the normal Web user, they can really raise havoc in a Web-based experiment, where control over the stimuli is needed. These can be extinguished by merely setting **Cancel = TRUE** in the *NewWindow2* event handler discussed above. The problem here is not all new browser windows should be cancelled – only the automatic pop-up ones should. My solution to this dilemma is to extinguish any new window that is generated automatically (i.e., not resulting from a button or hyperlink click action) and whose dimensions are below some critical threshold. The *ClientToHostWindow* event simplifies this decision. The event fires when a new window is opened through scripting. The event handler subroutine format is **ClientToHostWindow(CX as Long, CY as Long)**. *CX* and *CY* are, respectively, the width and height of the window in pixels, as prescribed by the scripted invocation. In my experience, 600 pixels work well as a threshold for both height and width.

Other Special Techniques

In this section, I will discuss some of the remaining programming issues and techniques that are somewhat unique to this research context. Topics include (1) how to control browser-caching activity, (2) how to manage keyboard and mouse activity, and (3) how to extend the reach of the custom browser to include the minute details of the HTML pages.

Control over caching behavior can be critical in Web-based experiments. Page caching in the *WebBrowser Control* is managed according to the Internet Explorer settings stored in the Windows Registry. For consistency across sessions, I advise that caching be controlled programmatically, from within the custom browser application. Specifically, I suggest the cache be flushed with each URL downloaded. This action can be invoked within the handler for the *DocumentComplete* event. At first glance, programmatic cache flushing appears messy, involving a half dozen API function declarations. Luckily, Microsoft Knowledge Base article #Q262110 (Microsoft, 2001b) provides cut-and-past code for this task that can be used with little modification.

My experience with this application indicates effective control over keyboard behavior, and to a lesser degree, control over mouse behavior, pose one of the biggest programming challenges. The *WebBrowser Control* recognizes neither the *KeyPress* event nor the *KeyUp/KeyDown* events, so a custom keyboard handler must be built from scratch. Similarly, the *MouseUp/MouseDown* events do not fire, so a custom mouse handler is also necessary. These tasks are best handled through subclassing techniques and callbacks. The intricacies of these software techniques is beyond the scope of this discussion. Help can be found in Microsoft Knowledge Base articles #Q168795, #Q170570 and #Q177992 (Microsoft 2002b, 2001c, 2001d), and in Appleman (1999).

Internet Explorer responds to over 60 keyboard shortcuts (Microsoft, 2001e). By default, the *WebBrowser Control* responds similarly to these same keycodes. Many of these can potentially corrupt the integrity of your Web-based experiment, as can several standard Windows shortcuts. These harmful key sequences should therefore be ignored by this software application. To accomplish this, your keyboard handler should *always* trap and extinguish the Escape key, the Applications key, the left and right Windows keys, all function keys, and the Shift-Enter key combination. In addition, any key combinations containing the Control key or the Alt key should be killed. For general external validity, the following basic browsing keys should be retained in all cases: tab, shift-tab, home, end, enter, page up, page down, up arrow, and down arrow. A simple, conservative approach to keyboard handling is to extinguish all keys *except* for this final set.

With regard to mouse activity, IE, and thus the *WebBrowser Control*, responds to a right mouse click by displaying a context-sensitive pop-up menu. Pressing Shift in conjunction with the left mouse button requests a hyperlink be sent to a new window. Your custom mouse handler should therefore ignore these mouse actions. Only the simple left click is needed in this software application.

The *WebBrowser Control* has yet another capability that holds great potential in this research context. Your custom browser can gain access to, and can even interact with, all aspects of any current HTML page. Access is provided through the *Document* property (e.g., **myBrowser.Document**) which exposes the full content of the HTML Document Object Model (DOM). The DOM is a fairly complex structure, and it will not be presented here (see http://www.w3.org/DOM/ for full details). As an illustrative example, though, your application can access the cookie object of the current HTML page with the following simple reference: **myBrowser.Document.cookie**. As another example consider that timestamp information for each visited page can be captured with **myBrowser.Document.lastModified**. You can even unobtrusively analyze the entire set of *unvisited* links on a page by processing the **myBrowser.Document.links( )** array. This feature can indeed add great power and flexibility to your custom research instrument.

SUMMARY

This chapter has presented the key issues surrounding the development of a custom Web browser for conducting Web-based experiments. By using this client-side (vis. server-side) approach, to administering treatments and collecting data, the researcher is afforded a high degree of experimental control and precision. The behaviors of the experimental subject can be analyzed and recorded at the level of the mouse click or individual key press. Treatments and measurements timed to the millisecond are easily attained. Flexibility is provided by the fact the software can be customized to meet the specific needs of the research context. The software can be programmed to analyze navigation requests and, in the case of inapplicable requests, to preempt or modify the Web action before the navigation takes place. This allows for experiments to involve the general Web, rather than being restricted to a limited set of experiment-specific pages. Thus, external validity can be greatly increased.

The chapter presented many of the details surrounding the use of the *WebBrowser Control*, and described the specifics of programming custom handlers for several of the key *WebBrowser* events. Specifically, event handlers having to do with (1) navigation and downloading activities, (2) emulation of browser interface behavior, and (3) window and session control were discussed.

Beyond these topics, the chapter presented a discussion of some other special software techniques that are pertinent to this research context. Many of the requirements of a custom keyboard handler for this application were detailed, as were those of a custom mouse handling routine. Programmatic control over browser caching behavior was also discussed. Finally, it was illustrated how the custom browser tool can gain access to detailed elements of the HTML page by processing the DOM structure. This technique has the potential to add even more power, flexibility and control to your custom software tool.

REFERENCES

Appleman, D. (1999). *Dan Appleman's Visual Basic Programmer's Guide to the Win32 API*. Indianapolis, IN: Sams Publishing.

Cornell, G., & Jezak, D. (1998). *Core Visual Basic 5*. NJ: Prentice Hall.

Microsoft (2001a). *HOWTO: Cause Navigation to Occur in Same WebBrowser Window (Knowledge Base Article #Q185538)*. http://support.microsoft.com/default.aspx?scid=kb;en-us;Q185538.

Microsoft (2001b). *HOWTO: Clear Cache When Your Application Hosts a WebBrowser Control (Knowledge Base Article #Q262110)*. http://support.microsoft.com/default.aspx?scid=kb;en-us;Q262110.

Microsoft (2001c). *HOWTO: Build a Windows Message Handler with Address Of in Visual Basic (Knowledge Base Article #Q170570)*. http://support.microsoft.com/default.aspx?scid=kb;en-us;Q170570.

Microsoft (2001d). *HOWTO: Intercept Keyboard Input from Visual Basic (Knowledge Base Article #Q177992)*. http://support.microsoft.com/default.aspx?scid=kb;en-us;Q177992.

Microsoft (2001e). *Internet Explorer Keyboard Shortcuts (Knowledge Base Article #Q306832)*. http://support.microsoft.com/default.aspx?scid=kb;en-us;Q306832.

Microsoft (2002a). *Reusing the WebBrowser Control*. http://www.msdn.microsoft.com/workshop/browser/Webbrowser/Webbrowser.asp.

Microsoft (2002b). *HOWTO: Hook Into a Window's Messages Using Address Of (Knowledge Base Article #Q168795)*. http://support.microsoft.com/default.aspx?scid=kb;en-us;Q168795.

Chapter XVII

Towards a Sociopragmatic-Constructivist Understanding of Information Systems

Boris Wyssusek
Technical University Berlin, Germany

Martin Schwartz
Dr. Glinz & Partner, Germany

ABSTRACT

Contemporary understanding of information systems (IS) is flawed by fundamental problems in information systems research and practice. In this chapter, we claim that philosophical presuppositions have a great influence on our understanding of IS. Reflecting on the modernism-postmodernism debate and its methodological consequences for IS research, we derive the need for a paradigmatic foundation of IS research. Referring to Kuhn's concept of "paradigm," we develop a framework for the conceptualization of "paradigms of inquiry." We use the notion of "model," which we believe to be pivotal for the understanding of IS, to illustrate the implications of the adoption of a "paradigm of inquiry." In response to a criticism of both the positivist and the radical-constructivist paradigms, we develop a paradigm called "sociopragmatic constructivism" (SPC). Presupposing that human inquiry relies on social contextualization, common practice and cultural history, we propose an agenda for upcoming IS research grounded in SPC.

INTRODUCTION

Recurring failures in the development of information systems (IS) (Boustred, 1997), the persistence of the "software crisis" (Gibbs, 1994; Naur & Randell, 1969), as well as the "productivity paradoxon" (Attewell, 1994; Brynjolfsson, 1993; Strassmann, 1997) indicate that information systems research (ISR) — in spite of all progress made at the methodic level — did not proceed very far in developing a methodological foundation for the understanding of these problems. Their persistence gives rise to the question of the appropriateness of today's presuppositions in IS research and practice, and provides a practical motivation for engaging in more fundamental, methodological reflections. Consequently, these exceed today's known boundaries of ISR, and extend to disciplines like philosophy of science, anthropology, sociology, and psychology.

Furthermore, a review of the publications in major outlets of the ISR community makes quite obvious that methodological considerations as well as underlying philosophical presuppositions are rarely explicated. This (prevailing) negligence of philosophical considerations has severe consequences for IS research *and* practice. As Collier (1994) states:

> *"a good part of the answer to the question 'why philosophy?' is that the alternative to philosophy is not no philosophy, but bad philosophy. The 'unphilosophical' person has an unconscious philosophy, which they apply in their practice — whether of science or politics or daily life" (p. 17).*

In the early days of ISR, Gorn (1958) writes to the editor-in-chief of the *Communications of the ACM* (CACM) that "philosophy has served some of its most important functions to the world of communication in the society by [...] critical evaluations of the fundamental concepts of the arts and sciences." He concludes the "general subject matter of the letters-to-the-editor department should include, then, the philosophy of computing" (p. 2). As can be observed in editions of the CACM ever since, Gorn's idea did not result in much change yet.

As a reason for this lack of transdisciplinarity in ISR, McFarlan (1984) states:

> *"...many IS researchers, although they possess strong technological skills, lack the tools and perspectives necessary for cross-disciplinary work. Further, even if they have such skills, IS scholars are often not intellectually inclined to undertake these complex studies" (p. 2).*

Twenty years later, this assertion is still true, as can be seen — with some exceptions — in current curricula, conference programs, and the table of contents of many journals in the IS domain.

A cause for this dissatisfying methodological situation of ISR can be traced back in its historical development. Because ISR is rooted in disciplines like cybernetics, general management and industrial engineering, various theories, concepts, and methods as well as their underlying presuppositions are transferred to ISR, mostly without prior methodological reflection.

Some consequences of this unreflected transfer became obvious in areas such as artificial intelligence (AI) and business process reengineering (BPR). With AI's roots in cybernetics, information theory and cognitive psychology, the adopted assumptions about human nature and the human mind that become most obvious in the *computational theory of mind* (e.g., Putnam, 1975), led to ideas and visions concerning the possibilities of AI which, from today's point of view, would be regarded as illusionary or science fiction at best (e.g., Dreyfus, 1972, 1992). In BPR, failure can also be traced back to unrealistic assumptions about human nature. It is commonly known that about 70 percent of all BPR projects failed in one way or another (Hammer & Champy, 1993), mostly due to the negligence of social and cultural aspects of work. This negligence is rooted in the widespread mechanistic view of the human being, which has no room for the social and cultural conditionality of humanness.

For our purpose, philosophical considerations in the context of ISR are important for two reasons: they affect the nature of research itself, and they are fundamental for the understanding of information systems. Viewing information systems as tools of mediated human inquiry and trying to understand the implications of this view for the development and use of information systems requires a prior understanding of human inquiry.

As various analyses have revealed, positivism is the dominating concept of inquiry in ISR (Klein & Hirschheim, 1987; Orlikowski & Baroudi, 1991; Ridley & Keen, 1998). This epistemological position is based on presuppositions of human inquiry already being criticized for a longer time in disciplines like organization theory and sociology (Hassard, 1993; Dahms, 1994). These disciplines (should) have considerable impact on theories of design, development, and use of information systems, since social institutions provide the context for their use.

The development of *postmodern* concepts, within the field of organization theory since the 1980s, has led to application and further elaboration of interpretive approaches towards human inquiry. The (now) competing positivistic and interpretive approaches lead, due to their fundamental character, not only to different understandings of organization, but of information systems as well. Therefore, any discussion about information systems as tools of mediated inquiry is inevitably integrated into a discourse about epistemological positions.

Several authors have already addressed this problem (Hirschheim, Klein & Lyytinen, 1996; Iivari, 1991; Falkenberg et al., 1998). Their emphasis, however, is more on methodological considerations of IS research and development, and less on consequences of philosophical presuppositions for the understanding of information systems. Nonetheless, a trend towards more discussion of philosophical questions and an increasing critique of positivist approaches can be noticed (Fitzgerald & Howcroft, 1998).

In this chapter, we try to substantiate the need for a philosophical foundation of ISR, as a basis for a well-founded understanding of information systems. Focusing on issues of methodological pluralism, we provide a short outline of the modernism-postmodernism debate that is taking place in the social sciences. Most importantly, we further elaborate on its methodological consequences for ISR. From this we derive the need to ground research in well-defined and explicated philosophical suppositions. Referring to Kuhn's (1996) concept of a paradigm, we describe a framework for the conceptualization of the so-called "paradigms of inquiry," allowing a systematic description of existing approaches and the development of new approaches to human inquiry. Being unsatisfied with existing approaches, we also find the need for a new paradigm of inquiry. After providing an outline of our paradigm, referred to as "sociopragmatic constructivism," we describe a research agenda which serves both as a basis for the further development of our approach and as a framework for IS research and practice.

PRELIMINARY CONSIDERATIONS ABOUT HUMAN INQUIRY

In this section, we start off by describing some implications of cultural development on the understanding of human inquiry, which have been largely discussed during the last 30 years within the modernism-postmodernism debate. Especially in response to the "anything goes" debate, we use Kuhn's (1996) concept of a paradigm to develop a framework for the conceptualization of different paradigms of inquiry, which will be applied in the following sections.

Winds of Change: From Modernism to Postmodernism

Societal and cultural influences play a major role when we try to understand human inquiry and science in general. Organizations are cultural constructs. Nature, wherever it occurs in the range of human consciousness, is already culturally 'coated.' Technology, being a result of cultural achievements, is permanently — while it evolves — becoming a part of culture.

Culture can neither be regarded as a temporal nor as a spatial constant. However, historically culture's influence upon human cognition was ignored most of the time. With his famous dictum "homo mensura," Protagoras gave us a first hint on the cultural conditionality of human cognition. But it took until the beginning of the 20th century for cultural anthropology and philosophy of culture to emerge.

With modernism and postmodernism, two cultural epochs are differentiated. This difference is of interest especially with respect to their corresponding conceptions of human inquiry.

In general, modernism may be regarded as a framework for the epoch of the industrialized society, or in philosophical terms, the "age of the enlightenment." Even if there is no identifiable 'starting point' of modernism, there are five developments which are regarded to be constituent for the modern age: the emergence of the nation state, the advent of science, economic and technological progress, the rise of the West, and the secularization and democratization of society (Allen, Braham & Lewis, 1992; Hall & Gieben, 1992). Scientific development led to an intellectual revolution with subsequent rejection of superstition, tradition and also religious authority. Technological advances together with the economic transformation of the 18th and 19th centuries introduced a period of self-sustaining growth. Growth was also supported by the rise of the West as the main economic and political power through worldwide exploration, colonization and exploitation of resources.

The fundamental assumption of modernism is, thus, basically positivist in connection with a naïve ontological realism and epistemological objectivism. Until the end of the 19th century, the mechanization of the world was, at least to most researchers, the foundation for the explanation of virtually any problem. Technology improved production and living conditions; belief in progress dominated questions on development of society or science.

Along with all progress made during modernism, most industrialized societies went through a structural change the economists call the "three-sector-hypothesis" (Fourastié, 1954). The service sector is becoming more important today. However, due to this change, the former modern workforce is confronted with entirely different problems, to which their modern world view (with its assumptions and attributes listed above) does not provide the appropriate answers to anymore. Many of the basic assumptions of modernism no longer hold in our world today. This led philosophers to question modern issues using a different framework: postmodernism.

Postmodernism, which has its origins in a fundamental criticism of modernism, is first found in arts and architecture at the beginning of the 20th century (Bell, 1962; Pannwitz, 1917). From there, three concepts of the postmodern evolved, which, according to Gmür (1991), can be summarized as (1) the postmodern as the opposite of the modern, (2) postmodern as a standstill in progress, and (3) postmodern as a new, radical modern. The differences between many postmodern views do not always become clear. Science itself is evolving. Postmodern concepts of science break with the modern ideas like "truth" or "unity of science" and encompass "multi-methodological approaches" which are highly dependent on social and cultural context (Bell, 1926; Hassard, 1993; Rosenau, 1991). Cultural and scientific developments, influenced by the postmodern turn, also have adapted to a different view on human inquiry and knowledge. Classic (i.e., modern) concepts of "knowledge," which regard it as an objective entity, are superseded by postmodern concepts, which view knowledge as culturally determined, subjective or social. As a consequence, epistemology, the classic field of philosophy dealing with human inquiry and concepts of "knowledge," now also discusses these new concepts (Lyotard, 1984; Rorty, 1991; Sorri & Gill, 1989).

In summary, postmodern critique signifies a general process of de-legitimization. In the scientific sphere, a loss of confidence in rational theory, the safeguards of rigorous research methods, the capacity for objective knowledge, and the promise of steady progress in the growth of knowledge can be asserted (Gergen, 1996) — be it under the 'postmodern label' or not. However, developing a sound philosophical foundation of human inquiry and knowledge has not become easier, since there is a multitude of positions to chose from, as we will see in the following sections.

The Concept of "Paradigm of Inquiry"

Being in favor of intellectual diversity supported by postmodern conceptions of science, but afraid of "anything goes" in its literal meaning, we argue that researchers must specify the (pre-)suppositions their work is based on and can be judged on. This demand does not necessarily preclude the simultaneous use of different methods and methodologies. But a mixture of methodologies based on incompatible ontological, epistemological or anthropological presuppositions has to be denied. Otherwise, due to their incommensurable (pre-)suppositions, multimethodological approaches will allow no unequivocal interpretation of the results obtained, rendering their declaratives arbitrary.

Grounding research programs within a specific discipline is of limited use because such 'local' concepts hinder transdisciplinary research. We argue the foundation has to be laid on a meta-scientific level. With reference to philosophy of science and drawing on the concept of "paradigm" developed by Kuhn (1996), we propose the use of a framework for the conceptualization of so-called "paradigms of inquiry." While philosophers mostly desist from classifying positions, we want to use the framework for a classification — even if reductionistic. This framework does not only allow the positioning of paradigms relative to each other, but also supports the conceptualization of new ones. Thus, it serves descriptive as well as prescriptive purposes. We are well aware of the fact that all frameworks have one problem in common: the dimensions used for their composition are arbitrary and the 'borders' imposed by the categories chosen may implicate distinctions which are not always appropriate to make, as we will see when describing sociopragmatic constructivism.

An unspecified reference to Kuhn can be considered problematic, since Kuhn himself used the term "paradigm" in at least 21 different definitions (Masterman, 1970, p. 61). This makes it necessary to take a closer look at the concept of "paradigm" used.

Kuhn's concept of "paradigm" is the result of an analysis of both history and sociology of science. It concludes in a rejection of induction and falsification as driving forces in the development of science. Thereby, the thesis of continuity in science, in the sense of cumulative scientific progress or a constant growth of knowledge available to mankind, is negated. Rather, scientific development (and development of knowledge along with it) is seen as characterized by revolutions that are followed by phases of relative stability, and so forth.

According to Kuhn, the development of a science starts with a pre-scientific, pre-paradigmatic phase, which is characterized by a non-systematic search and analysis of facts (observation data) and, for the most part, an absence of theory. What may look like endless freedom at a first glance, for example, choosing the object or methods of research, appears at a closer look as being limited and framed by existing social and cultural experience (Fleck, 1935). Possible ways out of this phase are strongly influenced by the concept of the "scientific community" which, through interaction between participating scientists, leads to the development of different "schools" (de Solla Price, 1963). In each of these schools over time a consensus on different aspects of their science forms, which is then communicated in more or less formal ways. As Kuhn (1996) writes:

> *"A scientific community consists [...] of the practitioners of a scientific specialty. To an extent unparalleled in most other fields, they have undergone similar education and professional initiations; in the process they have absorbed the same technical literature and drawn many of the same lessons from it. Usually the boundaries of that standard literature mark the limits of a scientific subject matter, and each community ordinarily has a subject matter of its own. There are schools in the sciences, communities, that is, which approach the same subject from incompatible viewpoints" (p. 177).*

The increasing structuring of research topics and research methods opens the paradigmatic phase in a science. Pre-science becomes normal science, "firmly based upon one or more past scientific achievements, achievements that some particular scientific community acknowledges for a time as supplying the foundation for its further practice" (Kuhn, 1996, p. 10). Kuhn (1996) has not given an unequivocal description of the function of a paradigm in normal science, which leads to intense debates on this issue (Banville & Landry, 1989; Lakatos & Musgrave, 1970). Masterman's (1970) attempt to classify the different uses of these terms by Kuhn differentiates three concepts of "paradigm": metaphysical, sociological, and construct paradigm (pp. 65-68).

The metaphysical paradigm represents the most extensive consensus possible within a science: a worldview or Weltanschauung. Worldview, as understood by Kuhn, thereby implies that perception is influenced by experience. In this sense it is like a 'lens' through which we perceive the world. Changing one's worldview from one to another is no continuous process, but rather a radical shift. It is impossible to view the world through one or the other 'lens.' The world, as seen with the old worldview, has a different 'Gestalt' than the one seen with the new one. The two cannot be compared; they are incommensurable (Kuhn, 1996, pp. 111-117).

The sociological paradigm encompasses "the entire constellation of beliefs, values, techniques, and so on shared by the members of a given community" (Kuhn, 1996, p. 175) and is a concretion of the metaphysical paradigm. Taking the social dimension into consideration in describing science emphasizes the subjectivity of their self-conception. At the same time, the concept of "objectivity" in science has to be dismissed. Instead, they are to be considered socio-cultural phenomena, which can only be interpreted with respect to their social, historical and cultural background. Theories, based on the idea of a cumulative development of science and knowledge, are unable to explain fashions and recurrent ideas in science, as Kuhn (1996) illustrated with several examples from history of science.

The construct paradigm is the most concrete form of a paradigm. It refers to the methodical layer of science, to specific tools, instruments, and procedures for producing and collecting data. Many authors have criticized Kuhn's (1996) thesis of a single dominating paradigm within normal science (p. 19), criticizing it as 'monistic' (Banville & Landry, 1989, p. 49). Questioning Kuhn's argument, they tried to prove the existence of multiple paradigms in science, just as Culnan (1986) does for the field of management information systems. Masterman (1970) differentiates between single paradigm and multi paradigm sciences, the former applying to the natural sciences, the latter to the social sciences (pp. 73-76). Kuhn (1996) revises his paradigm concept, describing it as "constellations of group commitment" (p. 181). In order to avoid further terminological problems, he proposes the term "disciplinary matrix." Main elements of this matrix are "symbolic generalizations," "common beliefs," "shared values," and "shared exemplars" (pp. 182-187).

Postulating, as we do, a paradigmatic foundation of research, is also being criticized. Banville and Landry (1989) assert, "one should not distract researchers from their daily activities and ask them to try to set up a set of rules to be called a paradigm; rather, one could observe how these researchers proceed, elaborate a model and propose it as a paradigm" (p. 50). But this view is questionable itself, if we take Kuhn's (1977) characterization of normal science into consideration: "Normal scientists never examine their paradigm critically, in particular the paradigmatic theory. They simply use the theory uncritically as an instrument for puzzle solving" (p. 141).

This description of missing reflection in science can equally be taken as an explanation for the missing philosophical foundation of ISR. Normal research within a paradigm never questions its own basic assumptions. But even if someone wants to make a conscious choice between paradigms, e.g., in a crisis situation, things do not get easier: the existence of several adoptable paradigms in a research field poses the question to the researcher which paradigm or which 'school' she/he should follow. The decision in favor of one certain paradigm should be well considered, since its consequences have a fundamental impact on all following work. As Lincoln (1990) states:

> *"The adoption of a paradigm literally permeates every act even tangentially associated with inquiry, such that any consideration even remotely attached to inquiry processes demands rethinking to bring decisions in alignment with the world view embodied in the paradigm itself" (p. 81).*

The consequences of adopting a paradigm result in several advantages and disadvantages:

> *"For example, research paradigms facilitate the practice of a community of scholars by providing shared assumptions about the nature of phenomena, a vocabulary for representing such phenomena, and criteria for evaluating scholarly work. On the other hand, frames are constraining when they reinforce unreflective reliance on established assumptions and knowledge, distort information to make it fit existing cognitive structures, and inhibit creative problem solving" (Orlikowski & Gash, 1994, pp. 176-177).*

For this reason, Kuhn (1996, p. 178) emphasizes the importance of concurrent or sequential affiliation to different scientific communities, resulting from an "enlargement of the horizon" aimed at by inter- or transdisciplinary research.

Postmodern concepts of science challenged the modern monoparadigmatic concepts, accompanied by an increasing propagation of antipositivist epistemological positions, which reject ontological realism. Giving up the idea of an objective reality, the problem of "missing ontological unity" (Kanitschneider, 1991) can be interpreted in a new way. Research results no longer have to claim absolute truth or absolute insight, but instead have to be evaluated on the basis of their pragmatic value. Because goals of research result from individual or social demands, research becomes increasingly subjective. Therefore, postmodern concepts of science support multi-paradigmatic approaches. These do not completely eliminate the above-mentioned 'framing'-problem, but ease the problem by allowing multiple perspectives through different paradigms.

Our position is not a general rejection of multi-paradigmatic approaches. We postulate, however, that research paradigms (and their corresponding methodologies) have to be consistent in terms of themselves. The analysis and evaluation of the results obtained have to take place within a dedicated methodology (endogenous criticism). This proposition is absolutely reconcilable with Mingers' (2001) critical pluralism. He proposes a critical, yet multi-methodological approach to achieve a base of methods as needed in the particular research situation. Thereby one is not restricted by a single paradigm. It will, in any case, be necessary to assign methods to a certain paradigm of inquiry, because without this assignation the results will relapse into the already mentioned "anything-goes"-pluralism.

Our concept comprises the categories ontology, epistemology, anthropology and methodology. Frameworks similar to this concept have been used for example in sociology (Guba, 1990), organization theory (Burrell & Morgan, 1979; Morgan & Smircich, 1980), and information systems research (Iivari, 1991; Orlikowski & Baroudi, 1991).

This concept of "paradigm of inquiry" can be interpreted as a morphological box (Zwicky, 1969), whose possible instances are restricted by several constraints. For example, a naïve ontological realism is not compatible with a radical constructivist epistemology, which itself is not compatible with a concept of the "human" as being deterministic, and a nomothetic methodology. From the perspective of cognitive science, paradigms of inquiry can also be viewed as frames (Minsky, 1975), or schemata (Rumelhart, 1980), hence as prototypical forms of conceptualization, guiding the process of inquiry. The concept of "paradigm of inquiry" is bound to a corresponding theory of culture (e.g., modernism, postmodernism), since it provides the holistic background of our conception of the world (Weltanschauung). With the advent of postmodern organization theories, the impact of theories of culture on paradigms of inquiry has become obvious in a discipline closely related to IS research.

Figure 1: Framework for the Conceptualization of Paradigms of Inquiry

Category	Relevant Questions	Debate(s)
Ontology	What is the nature of the "knowable"? What is the nature of "reality"? Is reality external to the individual and imposing itself on the individual consciousness or a product of individual cognition?	Realism vs. Nominalism Realism vs. Idealism Realism vs. Anti-Realism
Epistemology	What is the nature of the relationship between the knower (the inquirer) and the known (the knowable)? What are the grounds of knowledge? What is truth?	Positivism vs. Anti-Positivism Objectivism vs. Subjectivism Empirism vs. Rationalism
Anthropology	What is "human nature"? What is the relationship between human beings and their environment?	Determinism vs. Voluntarism Primacy of the Individual vs. Primacy of the Society
Methodology	How should the inquirer go about finding out knowledge?	Nomothetic vs. Ideographic

In the next paragraphs we provide a non-comprehensive description of issues of the categories chosen to constitute the framework depicted in Figure 1. Since there is a host of definitions available in the literature, our description serves also as an explication of our understanding of these categories.

Ontology

In the 17th century, the concept of "ontology" was developed to describe a branch of philosophy dealing with the nature of being, even if early Greek philosophers were already concerned with ontological problems.

In the Middle Ages, the ontological debate was concerned with the nature of universals (as opposed to particulars) and is characterized by the two distinct positions of *realism* and *nominalism*. Realists believe that universals have an existence independent of mind. For nominalists, universals are just signs or names referring to single objects or sets of objects. Thus, they are dependent on the mind and have no existence themselves. Generalizing the two positions, one can say, realists assume the existence of a structured world, with the structure being independent from mind. Nominalists, on the other hand, deny the existence of a structured world. Structure, and names referring to it, are the results of cognitive processes and, thus depending on the mind.

Ontology changed dramatically with Kant. According to his criticism, ontology "presumptuously claims to supply, in systematic doctrinal form, synthetic *a priori* knowledge of things in general" (Kant, 1787, B303). In his argument, he opposes realism to idealism: *realism* means that we perceive objects whose existence and nature are independent of our perceptions, whereas *idealism* means that they are dependent on our perception. Unsatisfied with both positions he argues:

> *"Thoughts without content are empty, intuitions without concepts are blind. It is, therefore, just as necessary to make our concepts sensible, that is, to add the object to them in intuition, as to make our intuitions intelligible, that is, to bring them under concepts. These two powers or capacities cannot exchange their functions" (Kant, 1787, B75).*

Kant reversed the classical view of cognition, known as "Copernican turn" in philosophy. Instead of understanding knowledge as conforming to objects, we have to understand the objects as conforming to the conditions of the possibility of our knowing. Thus, human knowledge is limited to appearances; we are not able to know of the "things-in-themselves."

For Kant (1787), the "scandal of philosophy" is that no proof has yet been given of the "existence of things outside of us" (Bxl). Whereas for Heidegger (1962, p. 249) the scandal is "not that this proof has yet to be given, but that such proofs are expected and attempted again and again," thus making the question for the nature of reality of the external world a pseudo-problem.

Heidegger (1962) conceptualizes "being" as "Dasein" which means essentially "in the world." He understands "world" similar to Husserl's (1986) concept of "life-world" as "everyday world," which is disclosed to us by pre-scientific experiences. These experiences are gained from using entities in the world as "tools" that are ready to hand. Only when tools fail we engage in theoretical cognition, thereby entering the scientific world. When we acquire knowledge about entities in the world we are always seeing entities in a "context of significance," in which these entities are related to each other and gain their meaning. Thus, entities do not have an existence themselves, but are always dependent on the existence of other entities.

Epistemology

Early Greek philosophers were already concerned with the nature of knowledge, but the concept of "epistemology," as we understand it today, was developed only in the second half of the 19th century to describe not only a theory of knowledge but also a theory of science (Köhnke, 1986, p. 58).

The central question of epistemology is concerned with the relation between the knower and the knowable. This question is based upon an assumption, which has been canonized by Descartes (1998) in his distinction between "res extensa" (i.e., body) and "res cogitans" (i.e., mind).

Another question of epistemology is concerned with the status of knowledge. Going back to Plato's distinction between knowledge and belief, knowledge has been characterized as "justified true belief." This characterization leads to the question, how can we justify our beliefs in order to gain knowledge? The central criterion to this justification is truth, which again raises questions about truth.

There are two distinct positions in epistemology: *empiricism* and *rationalism*. Empiricism is based on the assumptions that all knowledge is derived from our experiences. While observing the world around us, information about the world is being perceived as sense-data by our senses and imprinted on the mind. Therefore, the mind is understood as "tabula rasa" or "white paper" (Locke, 1959, II.i.2).

According to empiricists, the criteria for truth and thus for knowledge generally is being described by the "correspondence theory of truth," which holds that we have gained true knowledge about the world if our perceptions are in correspondence with it. In other words, propositions about the world are only true, if they are in correspondence with the facts. 'Correct' perceptions can therefore be understood as perfect mappings of some domain of the world into our minds. Thus, a problematic issue of empiricism is, it cannot explain the knowledge we have of things that cannot be found in experience (e.g., quarks).

Rationalists question the idea of sense-data being the source of knowledge. For them knowledge can only be derived from reason. In its most radical form, rationalism is based on Plato's concept of "innate ideas." In his famous cave analogy, Plato argues, that while observing the world, we actually perceive only the shadows of the real world. Only with reason we are able to remember the innate ideas, which provide us with true knowledge about the real world.

Dismissing the concept of "innate ideas" rationalists are confronted with the problem of finding other criteria of true knowledge. With his famous dictum "cogito ergo sum" (I think, therefore I am), Descartes (1998) provides us with such a criteria: the reason itself. He argues, that even the most radical skeptic has to admit, that to be skeptical about something requires the existence of reason. However, denying sense-data as some source of knowledge has to be regarded as a questionable proposition, since it cannot explain the existence of knowledge that cannot be gained without experiences mediated through our senses (e.g., language).

The argument provided by Kant, in his criticism of ontology, stating that "thoughts without content are empty, intuitions without concepts are blind" (op. cit.), is thus equally true for epistemology. In order to gain knowledge about the world, we have to have some access to the world and we have to have some faculty allowing us to structure our experiences. With Kant's (1787) words: "The understanding can intuit nothing, the senses can think nothing. Only through their union can knowledge arise" (B75).

With advances in neurophysiology and cognitive psychology, a new epistemology called "radical constructivism" (Glasersfeld, 1996; Watzlawick, 1984) has gained popularity, also in information systems research (Floyd, Züllinghoven, Budde & Keil-Slawik, 1992). Radical constructivists argue we cannot acquire knowledge about our environment, since the sensory input does not inform us about the qualitative nature of the stimuli. Our nervous system and the mind have only access to information about perturberations in our sensory organs. Consequently, all our knowledge about the 'world' is fictitious, is a construction of our mind. The concept of "truth" has therefore been dismissed and substituted by the concept of "viability" (Glasersfeld, 1996). Mental constructions are considered knowledge, if they help us to deal with our environment. It does not matter, if knowledge is in correspondence with the environment or not. Even if it is, we would not be able to realize it.

Whereas radical constructivism is an individualistic approach, social constructivism (Berger & Luckmann, 1966), developed in sociology of knowledge and thus not necessarily to be considered an epistemology, explains knowledge as a result of social interaction. There are no objective criteria for knowledge. Rather the concept of "truth" is based on the consensus theory of truth, which holds that within a certain community a proposition is considered as being true, if a consensus about its truth has been attained.

Anthropology

The concept of "anthropology" in the sense of a science of human nature was developed in the 16th century. Casmann (1594) describes human nature as dualistic: "Anthropologia est doctrina humanae naturae. Humana natura est geminae naturae mundanae, spiritualis et corporeae, in unum hyphistamenon unitae, particeps essentia."

The early understanding of anthropology was that as of a natural science, having the goal to explain human nature on the basis of biological or physiological concepts. But soon philosophers discovered *reason* as a feature that distinguishes human nature from the nature of all other beings, could not be explained in terms of natural science. The resulting distinction between humans rational and empirical nature has led to the classical body-mind dualism, which has been dominating anthropology ever since.

Kant, emphasizing the complementarity of the empirical and rational nature of humans, introduced anthropology as a philosophical problem, but only in the early 20th century, with writings by Scheler (1928), Plessner (1928) and Gehlen (1940), philosophical anthropology has been inaugurated as an independent discipline.

Already in Plato's "*Republic*" and Aristotle's "*Politics*," we find an understanding of human nature which goes way beyond the classical body-mind dualism, and stands contrary to the still dominating individualistic anthropology — the understanding of human nature as a result of man's cultural embeddedness. Social and cultural anthropology, thus, try to explain human nature on the basis of man's always already given social and cultural context. This effort is based on the assumption, that a human being without social and cultural context is not imaginable, a sole human being would not be a human being.

From a methodological point of view, individualistic anthropology seeks to explain human nature on the basis of the sole individual, whereas social and cultural anthropology seek to explain human nature by considering culture and society as primary sources of human nature.

In the early 20th century, a new approach towards the understanding of human nature was developed. Cassirer (1967, p. 23) refers to concept of "functional circle" (Funktionskreis) (Uexküll & Kriszat, 1934), which describes the anatomical basis of organisms' interaction with their environment as two coupled systems — "Merknetz" (receptor system) and "Wirknetz" (effector system). He argues humans are different in a certain respect: receptor and effector system are extended by a symbolic system, which adds a new dimension of reality. In addition, Vygotski (1978) writes in the early 1930s: "The use of auxiliary signs breaks up the fusion of the sensory field and the motor system and thus makes new kinds of behavior possible" (p. 35). Man does not just live in a merely physical universe, but lives in a symbolic universe. He cannot "confront reality immediately; he cannot see it, as it were, face to face. Physical reality seems to recede in proportion as man's symbolic activity advances" (Cassirer, 1967, p. 25). Thus, the resulting understanding of human nature is based on the understanding of man as "animal symbolicum" (Cassirer, 1967, p. 26).

Methodology

The fact we have to follow a certain path to reach a destination is the idea behind the concept of "method." In other words, a (scientific) method is a certain procedure we have to follow in order to pursue a certain goal (usually to gain knowledge), and methodology is the science concerned with methods. Its interest lies in the development of descriptive or prescriptive theories about methods, and in the determination of the requirements that have to be fulfilled in order to make a certain method applicable in certain situations. The last task is especially important for the sciences because the concept of the methodic foundation of knowledge developed by Plato can still be regarded as the most crucial criteria for scientificity. Prescriptive methodology, therefore, provides frameworks for scientific work, on which the quality of research can be judged. Such a framework does not only comprise propositions about the methods themselves, but also about the underlying ontological, epistemological, and anthropological presuppositions, as well as their implications for using the methods. Methodology can thus be regarded as encompassing our concept of "paradigm of inquiry."

Within methodology we can distinguish two different strands: the nomothetic and the ideographic. Nomothetic methodology is the foundation of quantitative research and natural science. It is explanatory, focused on 'hard' methods, deductive, ahistoric, and seeks to discover universal (natural) laws. The latter implies the assumption of their objective existence and that the researcher has no impact on the research findings. Ideographic methodology, on the other hand, is the foundation of qualitative research and, thus, mostly applied in the social sciences and humanities. It is explorative, focused on 'soft' methods, inductive, historic, and seeks to understand and to make sense of the phenomena under investigation. The latter implies, for example, experiences, knowledge, and values held by the researcher have an impact on the research findings.

From the beginnings of science in the history of mankind, science was characterized by monomethodological approaches: there was only one single way to gain knowledge. In his now famous book "Against Method," Feyerabend (1972) questions this monism and argues in favor of methodological pluralism. With the rise of postmodern concepts of science, drawing heavily on the ideas of Feyerabend, methodic and methodological pluralism has gained increasing popularity, especially in the social sciences (Guba, 1990; Hassard, 1993; Rosenau, 1991). As we already have stated above, multimethodological approaches are due to their foundation in incommensurable ontological, epistemological, and anthropological (pre)suppositions prone to the fallacies of an unreflective "anything goes" attitude. This leads to the necessity to develop criteria for the scientificity of multimethodological approaches. An overview on issues of multimethodology has been given by Mingers and Gill (1997).

HUMAN INQUIRY AND INFORMATION SYSTEMS

We regard information systems as instruments of human inquiry. Within the process of inquiry, these instruments serve as a medium, providing the user with information on matters of interest. The instrumental view on information systems puts them close to other instruments like microscopes, observatories, and the like.

The use of instruments in the process of inquiry and interpreting the results obtained are both influenced by philosophical (pre)suppositions. For example, from the viewpoint of positivism, these instruments do not have any effect on the way we perceive the reality, thus the objective status of the inquirer is not affected by the use of tools. From the viewpoint of radical constructivism, the use of tools is bound to theories the inquirer holds about them. Human inquiry is therefore guided by theories.

Morgan and Smircich (1980) have provided an overview of paradigms of inquiry in the social sciences (see Figure 2). The paradigms have been arranged along a spectrum with objectivism and subjectivism as the endpoints. Even if this overview is quite reductive, it illustrates the fundamental issues and some of their consequences when a researcher selects a paradigm of inquiry.

In the following, we present two paradigms, positivism and radical constructivism, which are positioned on opposite ends of a whole spectrum of possible paradigms of inquiry, some of which have been described in the framework depicted in Figure 2. We use these paradigms to illustrate the implications of the adoption of a paradigm for the understanding of information systems.

In order to illustrate the impact of an adopted paradigm of inquiry on the understanding of information systems, we use the notion of "model," referring not to the mathematical but to the general notion of model (Stachowiak, 1973).

With different paradigms of inquiry, there are different interpretations of the notion of "model." These depend on ontological, epistemological, and anthropological positions because they determine the interpretation of "representation" — one of the essential features of models.

Figure 2: Paradigms of Inquiry in Social Sciences (Morgan & Smircich, 1980, p. 492)

	Subjectivist Approaches to Social Science					Objectivist Approaches to Social Science
Basic Ontological Assumptions	Reality as a projection of human imagination	Reality as a social construction	Reality as a realm of symbolic discourse	Reality as a contextual field of information	Reality as a concrete process	Reality as a concrete structure
Basic Assumptions About Human Nature	Man as a pure spirit, consciousness, being	Man as a social constructor, the symbol creator	Man as an actor, the symbol user	Man as an information processor	Man as an adaptor	Man as a responder
Epistemological Stance	To obtain phenomeno-logical insight, revelation	To understand how social reality is created	To understand patterns of symbolic discourse	To map contexts	To study systems, process, change	To construct a positive science
Some Favored Metaphors	Transcendental	Language game, accomplish ment, text	Theatre, culture	Cybernetic	Organism	Machine
Research Methods	Exploration of pure subjectivity	Hermeneutics	Symbol analysis	Contextual analysis of Gestalten	Historical analysis	Lab experiments, surveys

The Notion of "Model" in Positivism

The paradigm of positivism, dominating the field of IS research, is characterized by a realist ontology: reality exists independently of the human mind, and is driven by natural laws and mechanisms. The positivist epistemology is empiricism. It is objective and the inquirer has 'direct access' to nature. He performs a non-interactive inquiry process, biasing factors are thereby excluded from influencing his findings. This epistemology is based on a correspondence theory of truth. From an anthropological perspective, the positivist has a mechanistic worldview, he sees humans in a behavioristic fashion as stimulus-response mechanisms. Consequently, the methodology used is nomothetic. Questions or hypotheses are stated in advance in propositional form and subjected to empirical tests (falsification) under carefully controlled conditions.

From the positivist point of view, a model is regarded as a representation (mapping) of the 'true' reality. This representational notion of "model" presupposes a direct relationship between the model (the representation) and the model source (the original). A model is "good" or "true," if it corresponds with reality — the essence of the correspondence theory of truth. The simplification (abstraction) of the representation is realized by intentionally neglecting 'objective' properties of the part of reality under investigation. Applied to information systems, the positivist notion of "model" assures that what we perceive through the use of information systems is an 'objective' representation of reality. Subsequently, the use of information systems does not make any difference to the direct perception of reality.

The Notion of "Model" in Radical Constructivism

The ontology of radical constructivism is relativistic. This means that realities exist in the form of multiple mental constructions, which are dependent on their form and content on the person who holds them. The epistemology of radical constructivism is rationalism. It is subjective, the inquirer and the inquired subject are fused into a single (monistic) entity. The resulting findings are literally the creation of the process of interaction between the two; the concept of "truth" is substituted by the concept of "viability" (Glasersfeld, 1996). Anthropologically, humans are seen as "creators of realities." A radical-constructivist methodology would then be ideographic; individual constructions are elicited and refined hermeneutically.

Constructivists generally question the direct relationship between a model and reality. For them, models do not have an existence independent of a human using it as a model. Since radical constructivists assume there are as many realities as individuals and realities are subjective, then models are therefore subjective as well. Research findings, as well as models, are the result of the interaction between the inquirer and the inquiring situation. The research findings and models are influenced by the knowledge, attitudes, and values of the inquirer. Applied to information systems, the constructivist notion of "model," as opposed to the positivist one, allows a very different interpretation of the function of information systems within the process of inquiry. Information is no longer considered to provide an objective account of reality, but is subject to the context-dependent interpretation of the individual.

Methodological Implications

Since computer-based information systems in organizations usually incorporate models of the organization, we can use abstract models of organizations for the illustration of methodological implications of the notion of "model" adopted.

Referring to our conceptualization of paradigms of inquiry, an organization theory can be viewed as an ontology, constituting and describing the nature of an organization. Adoption of an organization theory can therefore be regarded as a selection of an ontological position. Since ontological, epistemological, anthropological, and methodological positions are not independent of one another, we claim that the adoption of an organization theory is highly influential on the adoption of a certain paradigm of inquiry (and vice versa). This subsequently has a major impact on the way individuals perceive and interpret information about an organization provided by an information system. With an epistemologically bound ontology, the adoption of an organization theory not only determines what has to be considered as information, but also the relation between information, the organization (what the information is about), and the user of the information system. Since models and information are fundamental to the conception, development, and use of information systems, all aspects of the notion of "model" discussed above apply to information systems as well. Thus, the adopted notion of "model" and the adopted paradigm of inquiry, all must be taken into consideration when we try to understand the role of information systems within the process of human inquiry, ultimately to understand information systems.

SOCIOPRAGMATIC CONSTRUCTIVISM

At the latest with Hegel's "Phenomenology of Spirit" (Phänomenologie des Geistes) (Hegel, 1979), the role of community or institutions as constitutive elements of cognition have become the subject of philosophical investigations. This thought resumed with cultural philosophy at the beginning of the 20th century (Cassirer, 1953; Rickert, 1910), phenomenology (Husserl, 1986) and hermeneutics (Dilthey, 1946; Heidegger, 1962), as well as the philosophy of living (Lebensphilosophie) (Bergson, 1896). On the sociological side symbolic interactionism (Blumer, 1969) and the sociology of knowledge (Berger & Luckmann, 1966) can be found. Following materialistic ideologies, a reconsideration of approaches like philosophy of language and action theory (Davidson, 1980; Dewey, 1929; Quine, 1960) took place. Despite the ongoing discussion of the role of community in the approaches mentioned above, the relation between individual and community, as well as the interaction processes in between are still not sufficiently clarified. Since we regard the processes of cognition as constituted by communities, it is our conviction a paradigm of inquiry must be supplied, which takes this fundamental prerequisite into consideration.

Sociopragmatic constructivism (SPC) is — in a positive sense — an eclectic approach towards a paradigm of inquiry. In its development we draw on several sources and are confronted with some common problems. As Albert (1985) expresses in his "Münchhausen Trilemma," any attempt to articulate foundations for paradigms of inquiry leads "to a situation with three alternatives, all of which appear unacceptable" (p. 18). The trilemma forces one to choose between:

- An infinite regress, because the propositions that serve as a foundation need to be founded themselves.
- A logical circle that results from the fact that in the process of giving reasons, one has to resort to statements that have already shown themselves to be in need of justification.
- Breaking off the attempt at a particular point, by dogmatically installing a foundation.

At the same time the problem arises, in developing such a *metaphysical* paradigm of inquiry, one always already has to refer to a paradigm of inquiry. Therefore, the development of SPC is self-referential; while developing the elements of SPC, we have to understand these elements in terms of SPC and vice versa — a phenomenon well known as "hermeneutic circle." As Heidegger (1962, p. 195) explains: "What is decisive is not to get out of the circle but to come into it in the right way". For the understanding of any paradigm of inquiry, this assertion leads to the conclusion that one has to participate in the hermeneutic circle.

Following the same conceptualization of paradigms of inquiry developed above, we describe our concept of SPC in the following paragraphs. As will become clear in the outline of this paradigm of inquiry, the arbitrary chosen categories are at odd with holistic approaches. The categories draw distinctions between issues which, from the perspective of SPC, should not be separated. In spite of this drawback, we deem the systematicity of the conceptual framework to be helpful in the understanding of paradigms of inquiry.

Ontology

Sociopragmatic-constructivist ontology is relativistic, since:

> *"...facts are not given, but constructed by the questions we ask of events. All researchers are constructing their object of inquiry out of the materials their culture and their research paradigm provides; additionally, values play a central role in this linguistically,*

> *ideologically, and historically embedded project that we call science" (Lather, 1990, p. 317).*

Hence, the ontology of SPC is epistemically bound. The idea behind sociopragmatic-constructivist ontology is also influenced by Heidegger's (1962) "epistemological analysis of existence" (Daseinsanalytik) and "throws" the individual into a common context always already given. This "context of significance" is characterized by an understanding of being (Sein) developed in the course of the mankind and a specific worldliness (Weltbezug). This is in line with Cassirer's (1967) observation that man is not able to perceive the world directly, but only mediated through his symbolic system. Reality and cognition of reality therefore have to be regarded as a result of symbolic interaction between socially contextualized humans and their environment. We do not assume an isolated subject perceiving or constructing objects, but a common, socially and culturally mediated construction of world, containing both objects and subjects. Collaborative action takes place on the basis of symbolically constituted worlds of meaning which, being rooted in practical needs of human life, are constructed not always with the individual's consciousness. Interactive communication by symbolization modifies both individual and common worlds of meaning, thus modifies reality.

Epistemology

Sociopragmatic constructivism rejects the classical epistemological subject-object dichotomy and describes cognition as a phenomenon of common practices within a community. A phenomenon is thereby not something given by sensual experience (positivism), and also not a solipsistic construct ex nihilo (radical constructivism). It is an experience, which is influenced by cultural-historical experiences of the relevant community that are manifested in its specific symbolism. Sociopragmatic-constructivist epistemology has its roots in radical constructivism (Glasersfeld, 1996; Watzlawick, 1984), cultural symbolism (Blumer, 1969; Cassirer, 1953), and social constructivism (Berger & Luckmann, 1966). Radical constructivism serves as explanation for the physiological basis of cognitive processes, but it does not account for their social and cultural prerequisites, which only make processes like knowledge creation and knowledge 'exchange' possible. Therefore, we draw also on cultural symbolism and social constructivism, which provide a sound basis for the explanation of the symbolic nature and social dimension of knowledge. The very idea of social construction within SPC must be understood in the sense of a socially, pragmatically oriented description of intersubjective processes, within which humans create, stabilize, share, and modify their knowledge. The construction of knowledge is thus only to be explained on the basis of cultural history. The criteria for the truth of knowledge is based on the concept of "viability" and on the consensus theory of truth, which we deem to be in a reciprocal relationship. Knowledge can only be true within a community if there is a consensus about it, but a consensus will only be reached if the knowledge is viable, and vice versa.

Anthropology

The anthropology of SPC does not regard human nature as something given. Human nature is constantly evolving by shared common practice and influenced by its cultural history. There are no constant human features; there are always synchronous as well as diachronous differences. The dialectics of general and specific knowledge, theory and practice, individual and society have to be explored, with their mutual dynamic relations in mind. Human nature, the very essence of our existence, can only be understood if we try to understand dynamic cultural systems. The descriptions of human beings and of the prerequisites of becoming human have to be developed on the basis of a theory of social interaction. We, therefore, draw on cultural symbolism, viewing the human being as an "animal symbolicum" (Cassirer, 1967). Knowledge, any 'exchange' of knowledge, and any intellectual interaction between humans are bound to the use of symbols. But we also draw on social constructivism:

> *"There is only human nature in the sense of anthropological constants (for example, world-openness and plasticity of instinctual structure) that delimit and permit man's socio-cultural formations. But the specific shape into which this humanness is molded is determined by those socio-cultural formations and is relative to their numerous variations. While it is possible to say that man has a nature, it is more significant to say that man constructs his own nature, or more simply, that man produces himself" (Berger & Luckmann, 1966, p. 67).*

Any effort to gain an appropriate understanding of human nature therefore must consider culture and society as primary sources of human nature.

Methodology

Sociopragmatic constructivism is committed to the phenomenological method (Heidegger, 1962; Husserl, 1986), with the consequence that no longer the condition — the "what" — of circumstances is the issue, but the "how" — how these circumstances appear in the existence of humans. The phenomenological question is about the understanding of existence and being, and all derivable connections, statuses, processes, and structures. For SPC, ontology and phenomenology are therefore not two different disciplines (beside other philosophical ones), but determine both subject-matter (Gegenstand) and method (Heidegger, 1962). Sociopragmatic-constructivist methodology is therefore ideographic. We do not try to discover universal laws, but to make sense of phenomena with respect to the socio-

Figure 3: Paradigm of Sociopragmatic Constructivism

Ontology	Relativist; realities are developed by shared language and common practice, embedded in their cultural history; reality is a result of interaction between the social contextualized humans and their environment
Epistemology	Constitution of knowledge -- what humans want to know and why -- is to be explained on the basis of their cultural history; consensus theory of truth; viability
Anthropology	Human nature is a result of human practice, embedded in their cultural history
Methodology	Transdisciplinary analysis of culture in the sense of an analysis of human practice; ideographic

cultural context in which they appear. The inquirer is thus always part of the research situation, her/his values, experiences, and his/her enculturation have a substantial impact on research findings. In turn, these cannot simply be transferred from person to person, but are themselves subject to the process of 'exchange' by shared common practices.

In Figure 3, we have summarized our outline of sociopragmatic constructivism according to our framework for the conceptualization of paradigms of inquiry.

Examining this description of SPC makes it clear the categories of our framework are based on somewhat arbitrary distinctions, because the four categories are obviously dependent on one another; understanding human nature is not possible without an understanding of man's cognitive capabilities. On the other hand, the understanding of these capabilities requires an understanding of human nature. The same is true for the relationship between ontology, epistemology, and methodology. An essential feature of SPC is all categories of the framework are intertwined. We can only understand one category with respect to all the others, and vice versa — a hermeneutic circle.

Sociopragmatic Constructivism and Information Systems (Research)

The notion of "model" in SPC differs in various aspects from the notions of "model" in other paradigms of inquiry, and consequently the developed understanding of information systems will be different.

The major difference between the sociopragmatic-constructivist notion of "model" and the notions of "model" in radical constructivism or positivism consists in the introduction of a social context representing "the world." The assumption of an "external world" is rejected. "World" is rather embedded in a social context with social practices. Experience of the world is therefore a social phenomenon. Social practices not only determine forms of representation, but also *what* is to be represented, since the "what" is neither an objective fact, in the positivist sense nor something created *ex nihilo* in radical constructivist sense.

With respect to sociopragmatic-constructivist ontology, the model source is not something given. Due to the fact that models are models of something, that is representations, the questions are raised: what does a community regard as worthy of representation and what is actually represented? This means one has to practically provide analytical results that clarify what is 'really' represented, or one has to enter an interactive process and find common models via participation in a common language.

A similar idea is true for the understanding of "abstraction" in the process of modeling. Models do not map all properties of the original they represent, but only those properties that seem to be relevant for the designers and/or the users of a given model. From a sociopragmatic-constructivist point of view, one has to trace the appropriate "horizons of meaning" and the appropriate contexts in order to explicate the preferences of the internalized "customary given" interpretation modes, of both the users and the designers of a model. Moreover, it is important to explicate (via common practical action and explicatory interaction) what needs to be neglected in the given case, in order to integrate the various model interpretations in the process of modeling.

Models do not stay in a one-to-one relation to their origins, rather they have a substitution function for certain subjects that is bound to certain situations in a given temporal space and with regard to given imagined or real operations. At this point, it is possible to intervene only by means of communicative interaction and participation in a practice. These are forms of the mutual acknowledgment of the "horizons of meaning" of both the designers and the users of models.

Consequently, applying the paradigm of SPC to the development of an understanding of information systems, the function of information systems within the process of human inquiry has to be analyzed from the perspective of shared human practice. This idea can also be found in the concept of "action research." "In action research, the emphasis is more on what practitioners do than on what they say they do" (Avison, Lau, Myers & Nielsen, 1999, p. 96). Thus, phenomenologically framed action research seems to be a reasonable starting point for developing an appropriate method of information systems research. Transdisciplinary analysis of culture, being the most general concept of "method" in SPC, allows us to overcome the shortcomings of reductive approaches.

RESEARCH AGENDA

Having described our approach to human inquiry, we consider the current status of sociopragmatic constructivism, with respect to Masterman's classification, as both a "metaphysical," depicting a "Weltanschauung" — a consensus reached within our research group on the most fundamental issues of human inquiry —, and a "sociological paradigm," encompassing "the entire constellation of beliefs, values, techniques" (op. cit.) shared by our research group. In order to turn the current status of our paradigm of inquiry into a viable methodological framework for research, we must develop a "construct paradigm," which provides us with methods, tools, instruments, and procedures for gaining insight into the subject under consideration.

Finally, we will now describe our developing research agenda. This will be an iterative, heuristic process, during which we will have to go back and forth between the actual development and the meta-scientific level as we encounter fundamental problems. Thus, the development of the research agenda will actually not be preceded, but accompanied by the evolution of the paradigm of inquiry used (which in our case will be sociopragmatic constructivism). In the following paragraphs we present the next tasks to explore the field of information systems. The categorization is arbitrary and the problems addressed may even overlap, but we believe the categories chosen facilitate an understanding of a workable research agenda and what IS research could look like.

1. Refinement of sociopragmatic constructivism as a research paradigm.
   As we outlined above, we do not assume SPC to become a quasi-static paradigm, which once developed and defined, will just serve as a stagnant framework for further research in IS. Rather, it will have to be refined on an ongoing basis. This means we will have to continuously question its basic assumptions, and redefine properties of SPC accordingly. This redefinition will be guided by objectives like the practical relevance of the properties and their viability in a certain context, which of course depends on this very context as well as on the people applying such a paradigm in that context.
2. Practical application of sociopragmatic constructivism.
   In order to enable people to apply the paradigm of sociopragmatic constructivism, we will need to develop practical guidance for the application of SPC in conception, development and use of IS. Again, practical relevance and viability will be our essential objectives. Participatory approaches are prototypical examples that provide a frame of reference for the development of a practical applicable SPC.
3. Implications of sociopragmatic constructivism for IS research.
   The developments we describe will, on the basis of SPC as a research paradigm, necessarily have several implications for the understanding of IS research. We therefore have to take care of the following issues:
   a. *Foundations of IS*, i.e., methodological considerations become necessary when talking about information systems. A shift from methodical to methodological considerations will have to take place as we start questioning basic assumptions taken for granted in contemporary IS research.
   b. *Explication and further refinement of fundamental concepts* like "information" or "model," which depend on the paradigm of inquiry chosen. By

adopting a new paradigm, sociopragmatic constructivism, we will also have to develop means for the explication of concepts for an appropriate analysis of our presuppositions.

c. *Transdisciplinarity* will be pivotal for understanding IS as socio-technical systems and instruments of mediate inquiry. We regard the disciplines listed in the following paragraphs as being most influential on the understanding of information systems:

i. *Cultural Theory.* The impact of this discipline on IS research would include most of the results of the modernism-postmodernism debate, as well as newer results from cultural philosophy and organization theory, which will have an ongoing impact on IS research too.

ii. *Philosophy of Science.* The consideration of the philosophical foundations of IS will also have a continuous impact, if only due to the fact the epistemological position to be taken in IS research is not clear by now.

iii. *Sociology.* Getting to know and becoming able to explain the social processes constituting an information system will be an important issue for the whole project to succeed.

In summary, by developing SPC along with this research agenda, we strive to understand more of the background of "doing IS research" and "developing information systems." In doing this, we realize that we need to take other research disciplines into consideration. The fact that most of the topics addressed here seem to be in a flux, is, in our view, "not a bug, it's a feature!" — because 'the world' is continuously evolving.

CONCLUSION

Persistent problems in IS research and practice give rise to a reconsideration of the prevailing presuppositions of human inquiry. The lack of a philosophical foundation of IS research and its negligence of methodological advances in disciplines like organization theory and sociology can be regarded as a major cause for many of the recurrent problems in the conception, development, and subsequent use of information systems. An analysis of contemporary literature in the fields of organization theory and IS research, as well as philosophy of science provides a host of relevant material to be considered influential for the conceptualization of new paradigms of inquiry, which we regard as appropriate in the current state of IS research.

Our reflections on the modernism-postmodernism debate and its methodological implications for IS research have led us to the conclusion that a well-defined "paradigm of inquiry" is necessary as a foundation for further work in this field. We have criticized positivism, the dominating paradigm of inquiry in contemporary IS research, as being ignorant about the subjectivity of human efforts — therefore also about the subjectivity of human inquiry. On the other hand, radical constructivism, as an emerging paradigm of inquiry in IS research, has also been criticized because of its explanation of reality construction on the basis of the cognitive performance of a sole individual. Since all human inquiry relies on social contextualization, shared language, and common practice, we believe these aspects have to be taken into consideration in pursuit of a conceptualization of a new paradigm of inquiry.

With the proposed paradigm of sociopragmatic constructivism, we are striving to overcome the deficiencies of the criticized paradigms of positivism and radical constructivism. Focusing on social contextualization, shared language, and common practice as constituents of human inquiry, SPC can be regarded as a response to fundamental problems in IS research and practice. It provides a different view on model, information, information systems, and on the function of information systems in the process of human inquiry.

Based on our paradigm of inquiry "sociopragmatic constructivism," we have developed a research agenda, which we believe to be appropriate for tackling the fundamental issues in IS research and practice. With the research agenda developed we pursue three main goals:

- Refining sociopragmatic constructivism, not only as a paradigm of inquiry, but also as a research paradigm, taking the individual as well as its social and cultural context into consideration.
- Testing of the viability of the sociopragmatic-constructivist approach, by continuously building "communities of practice," both while engaging in theoretical reflection and working in practical IS projects.
- Describing and discussing implications for IS research, thereby taking the perspectives of fields like philosophy, sociology, or organization theory into consideration in order to foster transdisciplinary research.

Developing a paradigm of inquiry and a research agenda based on this paradigm seems to be quite ambitious. However, we believe that trying to solve the persistent fundamental problems in IS research and practice with the means provided by classical paradigms of inquiry seems to be even more ambitious. It is our conviction that SPC will provide us with a conceptual framework for developing an appropriate understanding of the function of IS in the process of human inquiry. Sociopragmatic constructivism, being rooted in the "life-world" (Lebenswelt), will also provide us with a methodology that is implementable in the form of a sociopragmatic-constructivist practice. Applying this methodology in IS research and practice will eventually help us to find answers to questions raised by the persistence of fundamental problems in IS research and practice.

REFERENCES

Albert, H. (1985). *Treatise on Critical Reason.* Princeton: Princeton University Press.

Allen, J., Braham, P., & Lewis, P. (Eds.). (1992). *Political and Economic Forms of Modernity.* Cambridge, MA: Polity.

Attewell, P.A. (1994). Information Technology and the Productivity Paradox. In D. H. Harris (Ed.), *Organizational Linkages: Understanding the Productivity Paradox* (pp. 13-53). Washington: National Academy Press.

Avison, D., Lau, F., Myers, M., & Nielsen, P.A. (1999). Action Research. *Communications of the ACM, 42*(1), 94-97.

Banville, C., & Landry, M. (1989). Can the Field of MIS be Disciplined? *Communications of the ACM, 32*(1), 48-60.

Bell, B.I. (1926). *Postmodernism and Other Essays.* Milwaukee, WI: Morehouse.

Berger, P.L., & Luckmann, T. (1966). *The Social Construction of Reality: A Treatise in the Sociology of Knowledge.* New York: Anchor Press.

Bergson, H. (1896). *Matière et mémoire. Essai sur la relation du corps à l'esprit.* Paris: F. Alcan.

Blumer, H. (1969). *Symbolic Interactionism. Perspective and Method.* Englewood Cliffs, NJ: Prentice-Hall.

Boustred, C. (1997). ATSI Seminars. In K. Liu (Ed.) (2000), *Semiotics in Information Systems Engineering* (p. 3). Cambridge: Cambridge University Press.

Brynjolfsson, E. (1993). The Productivity Paradox of Information Technology. *Communications of the ACM, 36*(12), 67-77.

Burrell, G., & Morgan, G. (1979). *Sociological Paradigms and Organisational Analysis – Elements of the Sociology of Corporate Life.* London: Heinemann.

Casmann, O. (1594). *Psychologia Anthropologica; Sive Animae Humanae Doctrina, Methodicé Informata.* Hannover: Fischer.

Cassirer, E. (1953). *The Philosophy of Symbolic Forms.* New Haven: Yale University Press.

Cassirer, E. (1967). *An Essay on Man. An Introduction to a Philosophy of Human Culture.* New Haven: Yale University Press.

Collier, A. (1994). *Critical Realism: An Introduction to the Philosophy of Roy Bhaskar.* London: Verso.

Culnan, M. J. (1986). The Intellectual Development of Management Information Systems, 1972-1982: A Co-Citation Analysis. *Management Science, 32*(2), 156-172.

Dahms, H.-J. (1994). *Positivismusstreit. Die Auseinandersetzungen der Frankfurter Schule mit dem logischen Positivismus, dem amerikanischen Pragmatismus und dem kritischen Rationalismus.* Frankfurt am Main: Suhrkamp.

Davidson, D. (1980). *Essays on Actions and Events.* New York: Oxford University Press.

De Solla Price, D.J. (1963). *Little Science, Big Science.* New York: Columbia University Press.

Descartes, R. (1998). *Discourse on the Method for Conducting One's Reason Well and for Seeking Truth in the Sciences.* Indianapolis, IN: Hackett.

Dewey, J. (1929). *The Quest for Certainty: A Study of the Relation of Knowledge and Action.* New York: Minton, Balch and Co.

Dilthey, W. (1946). *Die Philosophie des Lebens: eine Auswahl aus seinen Schriften 1867-1910.* Frankfurt am Main: Klostermann.

Dreyfus, H. (1972). *What Computers Can't Do.* New York: Harper and Row.

Dreyfus, H. (1992). *What Computers Still Can't Do.* Cambridge, MA: MIT Press.

Falkenberg, E. D., et al. (1998). *A Framework for Information Systems Concepts (FRISCO Report).* Geneva: International Federation for Information Processing.

Feyerabend, P. (1972). *Against Method: Outline of an Anarchistic Theory of Knowledge.* London: Verso.

Fitzgerald, B., & Howcroft, D. (1998). Competing Dichotomies in IS Research and Possible Strategies for Resolution. In R. Hirschheim et al. (Eds.), *Proceedings ICIS '98* (pp. 155-164). Atlanta, GA: ICIS Administration Office.

Fleck, L. (1935). *Enstehung und Entwicklung einer wissenschaftlichen Tatsache. Einführung in die Lehre vom Denkstil und Denkkollektiv.* Basel: Schwabe.

Floyd, C., Züllinghoven, H., Budde, R., & Keil-Slawik, R. (Eds.). (1992). *Software Development and Reality Construction.* Berlin: Springer.

Fourastié, J. (1954). *Die große Hoffnung des 20. Jahrhunderts.* Köln: Bund-Verlag.

Gehlen, A. (1940). *Der Mensch. Seine Natur und Stellung in der Welt.* Berlin: Junker und Dünnhaupt.

Gergen, K. (1996). Organization Science in a Postmodern Context. *Journal of Applied Behavioral Science, 32*, 356-378.

Gibbs, W.W. (1994). Software's Chronic Crisis. *Scientific American, 271*(3), 86-95.

Glasersfeld, E. von (1996). *Radical Constructivism.* New York: Routledge.

Gmür, M. (1991). *Managementlehre: Post- Oder Noch Modern? — Abschiedsvorstellung eines Teilprojekts der Moderne.* Working Paper No. 2/91, University of Konstanz.

Gorn, S. (1958). Letters to the Editor. *Communications of the ACM, 1*(1), 2-4.

Guba, E.G. (Ed.). (1990). *The Paradigm Dialog.* Newbury Park: Sage.

Hall, S., & Gieben, B. (1992). *Formations of Modernity.* Cambridge: Polity.

Hammer, M., & Champy, J. (1993). *Reengineering the Corporation: A Manifesto for Business Revolution.* New York: Harper Business.

Hassard, J. (1993). *Sociology and Organization Theory. Positivism, Paradigms and Postmodernity.* Cambridge: Cambridge University Press.

Hegel, G.W.F. (1979). *Phenomenology of spirit.* New York: Oxford University Press.

Heidegger, M. (1962). *Being and Time.* New York: Harper and Row.

Hirschheim, R.A., Klein, H.K., & Lyytinen, K. (1996). Exploring the Intellectual Structures of Information Systems Development: A Social Action Theoretic Analysis. *Accounting, Management & Information Technology, 6*(1/2), 1-64.

Husserl, E. (1986). *Phänomenologie der Lebenswelt. Ausgewählte Texte II.* Stuttgart: Reclam.

Iivari, J. (1991). A Paradigmatic Analysis of Contemporary Schools of IS Development. *European Journal of Information Systems, 1*(4), 249–272.

Kanitschneider, B. (1991). Unification as an epistemological problem. In G. Schurz, & G. Dorn (Eds.), *Advances in Scientific Philosophy* (pp. 255-264). Amsterdam, Rodopi.

Kant, I. (1787). Critique of Pure Reason. Retrieved July 14, 2002 from the Hong Kong Baptist University Web site: http://www.arts.cuhk.edu.hk/Philosophy/Kant/cpr/cpr-open.html.

Klein, H.K., & Hirschheim, R.A. (1987). A Comparative Framework of Data Modeling Paradigms and Approaches. *The Computer Journal, 30*(1), 8-15.

Köhnke, K.C. (1986). *Entstehung und Aufstieg des Neukantianismus: die deutsche Universitätsphilosophie zwischen Idealismus und Positivismus.* Frankfurt am Main: Suhrkamp.

Kuhn, T.S. (1962). *The Structure of Scientific Revolutions.* Chicago, IL: University of Chicago Press.

Kuhn, T. S. (1977). *The Essential Tension.* Chicago, IL: University of Chicago Press.

Lakatos, I., & Musgrave, A. (Eds.) (1970). *Criticism and the Growth of Knowledge.* Cambridge: Cambridge University Press.

Lather, P.A. (1990). Reinscribing Otherwise — The Play of Values in The Practices of the Human Sciences. In E.G. Guba (Ed.), *The Paradigm Dialog* (pp. 315-332). Newbury Park: Sage.

Lincoln, Y.S. (1990). The Making of a Constructivist. In E.G. Guba (Ed.), *The Paradigm Dialog* (pp. 67-87). Newbury Park: Sage.

Locke, J. (1956). *Essay Concerning Human Understanding.* New York: Dover.

Lyotard, J.F. (1984). *The Postmodern Condition: A Report on Knowledge.* Minneapolis, MN: University of Minnesota Press.

Masterman, M. (1970). The Nature of a Paradigm. In I. Lakatos & A. Musgrave (Eds.), *Criticism and the Growth of Knowledge* (pp. 59-89). Cambridge: Cambridge University Press.

McFarlan, F.W. (1984). Introduction. In F.W. McFarlan (Ed.), *The Information Systems Research Challenge – Proceedings* (pp. 1-6). Boston, MA: Harvard Business School Press.

Mingers, J. (2001). Combining IS Research Methods: Towards a Pluralist Methodology. *Information Systems Research, 12*(3), 240-259.

Mingers, J., & Gill, A. (Eds.). (1997). *Multimethodology.* Chichester, UK: Wiley.

Minsky, M.L. (1975). A Framework for Representing Knowledge. In P.H. Winston (Ed.), *The Psychology of Computer Vision* (pp. 211-277). New York: McGraw-Hill.

Morgan, G., & Smircich, L. (1980). The Case for Qualitative Research. *Academy of Management Review, 5*(4), 491-500.

Naur, P., & Randell, B. (1969). *Software Engineering: A Report on a Conference Sponsored by the NATO Science Committee, 7–11. October 1968, Garmisch.* Brussels: NATO Scientific Affairs Division.

Orlikowski, W.J., & Baroudi, J.J. (1991). Studying Information Technology in Organizations: Research Approaches and Assumptions, *Information Systems Research, 2*(1), 1-28.

Orlikowski, W.J., & Gash, D.C. (1994). Technological Frames: Making Sense of Information Technology in Organizations. *ACM Transactions on Information Systems, 12*(2), 174-207.

Pannwitz, R. (1917). *Die Freiheit des Menschen; Buch 1: Die Krisis der europaeischen Kultur.* Nürnberg: Carl.

Plessner, H. (1928). *Die Stufen des Organischen und der Mensch. Einleitung in die Philosophische Anthropologie.* Berlin: de Gruyter.

Putnam, H. (1975): The Meaning of "Meaning." In K. Gunderson (Ed.), *Language, Mind and Knowledge. Minnesota Studies in the Philosophy of Science* (vol. 7, pp. 131-193). Minneapolis, MN: University of Minnesota Press.

Quine, W. v. (1960). *Word and Object.* Cambridge: The MIT Press.

Rickert, H. (1910). *Kulturwissenschaft und Naturwissenschaft.* Tübingen: Mohr.

Ridley, G., & Keen, C. (1998). Epistemologies for Information Systems Research: A Study of Change. *Proceedings of 9th Australasian Conference on Information Systems* (vol. 2, pp. 520-533). Sydney, Australia: The University of New South Wales.

Rorty, R. (1991). *Objectivity, Relativism, and Truth.* Cambridge: Cambridge University Press.

Rosenau, P.M. (1991). *Post-Modernism and the Social Sciences: Insights, Inroads, and Intrusions.* Princeton: Princeton University Press.

Rumelhart, D.E. (1980). Schemata: The Building Blocks of Cognition. In R.J. Spiro, B.C. Bruce, & W.F. Brewer (Eds.), *Theoretical Issues in Reading Comprehension* (pp. 33-58). Hillsdale: Erlbaum.

Scheler, M. (1928). *Die Stellung des Menschen im Kosmos.* Darmstadt: Reichl.

Sorri, M., & Gill, J.H. (1989). *A Post-Modern Epistemology: Language, Truth and Body.* Lewiston: Mellens.

Stachowiak, H. (1973). *Allgemeine Modelltheorie.* Wien: Springer.

Strassmann, P.A. (1997). *The Squandered Computer.* New Canaan: The Information Economics Press.

Uexküll, J. von, & Kriszat, G. (1934). *Streifzüge durch die Umwelten von Tieren und Menschen. Ein Bilderbuch unsichtbarer Welten.* Berlin: Springer.

Vygotsky, L.S. (1978). *Mind in Society. The Development of Higher Psychological Processes.* Cambridge: Harvard University Press.

Watzlawick, P. (1984). *Invented Reality – How Do We Know What We Believe We Know?* New York: Norton.

Zwicky, F. (1969). *Discovery, Invention, Research.* New York: Macmillan.

ACKNOWLEDGMENTS

We would like to thank Jane Ivory Ernstthal and Rene Vidmer for their patience while helping us translate German English into American English.

About the Authors

Steven Gordon is an associate professor of information systems and technology at Babson College, USA. He is a co-author of the textbook *Information Systems: A Management Approach.* Dr. Gordon's research and consulting interests focus on two areas: organizational structure for the delivery of information technology services and e-commerce in the financial service industry. His research appears in the *Communications of the ACM*, *Information & Management*, *Journal of Global Information Management*, *Information Systems Management*, the *International Journal of Service Industry Management*, and other academic journals. He is a global associate editor of the *Journal of Information Technology Cases and Applications* and serves on the editorial review board for the *Journal of End User Computing*.

* * * *

Anders Avdic was born in 1950 in Arboga, Sweden. His accomplishments include: seaman, boring-machine operator, and bachelor of systems science. He was a lecturer at Örebro University, Örebro, Sweden, 1985. Licentiate thesis 1995, *Systems development using a Spreadsheet Program;* doctoral thesis 1999, *User and Developer, User Systems Development;* senior lecturer, Örebro University, Örebro Sweden 1999. He is a member of the VITS research group Linköping, Sweden. Research interests include: end user computing, local systems, and knowledge management.

Yuan Gao is an assistant professor of information systems at the School of Information Systems at Ramapo College of New Jersey, USA. His research interests include systems design and consumer behavior in hypermedia, user acceptance of information technology, and e-commerce strategy and implementation. He earned an MBA and a PhD in Business from Zicklin School of Business, Baruch College-The City University of New York (CUNY).

Jeffrey Hsu is an assistant professor of information systems at the Silberman College of Business Administration, Fairleigh Dickinson University, USA. His research interests include human-computer interaction, e-commerce, groupware, distance learning, and data mining. He is the author of six books, including numerous papers and articles, and has professional experience in the IT industry. Hsu holds a Ph.D. in management information systems from Rutgers University, several master's degrees, and various professional certifications. Dr. Hsu is always interested in discussing opportunities for research and other scholarly activities, and can be reached via e-mail at jeff@fdu.edu.

Peter N. Hyland is a senior lecturer in the School of IT and Computer Science at the University of Wollongong, Australia, where he has worked for nine years. Peter is a member of the Decision Systems Laboratory and his research covers OLAP and emerging database technologies, HCI issues in the use of such databases and the development of Enterprise Information Portals, particularly in government agencies. Peter's current projects include the usability of electronic medical records, the development of an information architecture for the NSW State Emergency Service and the implementation of an Enterprise Information Portal by the NSW Police.

Chong Kim is professor and head of the division of management and marketing, Lewis College of Business, Marshall University, West Virginia, USA. He holds a BA in English from Yonsei University, MBA from Miami University, and PhD in Organizational Behavior from Ohio State University. Besides his 25-year career at Marshall, he also taught at Rider University. He published numerous articles in professional refereed journals and trade journals, and presented in national and international conferences. Dr. Kim is also a grand master instructor of Taekwondo, and he has been teaching the martial arts over 49 years.

Gwynne Larsen has co-authored several textbooks on DOS, Novell Netware, introduction to computers, the Internet, Microsoft Works, Microsoft Office and Word Perfect. From 1997 until 2002, Dr. Larsen has been listed in Marquis' Who's Who in the World, America, and in the West. She belongs to several international information systems organizations and serves on the editorial review board for two of those organizations. Dr. Larsen started teaching courses online in 1997 and now offers Introduction to Computers, Micro Based Software, and The World Wide Web. She received an MBA and PhD from the University of Denver.

Sang-Gun Lee is a PhD candidate in MIS at University of Nebraska-Lincoln, USA. He received a BA in business administration and an MBA from Sogang University. He also had studied doctoral work at Waseda University in Japan. His research interests are e-SCM, e-business model, computer security, and development of object-oriented systems. He has published some articles in the *International Journal of Management Science, Korean Journal of Management Information System*, and *International Journal of Production Research* (forthcoming), and presented more than 20 refereed papers in HICSS, AMCIS, IRMA, DSI, IDSI, APDSI and WDSI.

Zoonky Lee is an assistant professor of information systems at the University of Nebraska-Lincoln, USA. He holds a PhD from the University of Southern California. He received a master's degree from the University of Michigan in Statistics and from Carnegie Mellon University in Social and Decision Sciences. His teaching interests include e-business, database design, systems analysis and design, and integrated enterprise systems. His research interests include designing IT infrastructures for organizational learning, electronic business, and IT support for knowledge workers. His dissertation was a finalist in the 1999 ICIS Dissertation Competition. He has published in various journals including *Information and Management*, *Journal of Organizational Computing and Electronic Commerce, Electronic Markets*, *Journal of Information Technology*, *Communications of the ACM*, *Computer and Security* and *Journal of Business Strategies*.

Susan K. Lippert is an assistant professor of management information systems in the Department of Management at Drexel University, Philadelphia, Pennsylvania, USA. Her current research interests include use and management of information technology. Her special interest is in the exploration of technology trust. Dr. Lippert received her PhD in MIS and an MBA in logistics, operations, and materials management from The George Washington University, Washington, D.C. She has taught undergraduate and graduate courses most recently as a visiting assistant professor at The George Washington University. Professor Lippert has published in the *Journal of End User Computing*, the *Journal of Management Education*, the *Journal of Mathematics and Science Teaching* and the *Annals of Cases on Information Technology*.

Purnendu Mandal is an associate professor of MIS in the Department of Management and Marketing, Lewis College of Business, Marshall University, West Virginia, USA. He is currently teaching courses on principles of MIS, database management, electronic commerce and strategic MIS. He taught in England, India, Singapore, Australia and the USA. He published over 100 refereed journal and conference papers. His works appeared in *EJOR, IJPOM, IJQRM*, *Industrial Management and Data Systems, Intelligent Automation and Soft Computing:*

An International Journal, Logistics Information Management, etc. Dr. Mandal serves in a number of professional bodies and currently is in the editorial board of three international journals.

Kathryn Marold is a professor of computer information systems at Metropolitan State College of Denver, USA. She teaches courses in GUI programming, information systems, micro-based software, and multimedia. Dr. Marold helped develop several online Internet versions of her department's courses. She has co-authored several books on computer software. Dr. Marold currently teaches classes in the Visual Basic programming language, Computer Applications for Business, and Micro-based Software. Her first love is the classroom, but she also enjoys research and writing. For recreation and relaxation, she enjoys biking and hiking in the beautiful mountains of Colorado and in the surrounding Southwest.

Paul Mulligan is an assistant professor in the management division at Babson College, USA. He teaches cross-functional courses that integrate the study of information technology and operations in the core curriculum of Babson's MBA program. He also teaches graduate and undergraduate electives in service industry management. He is co-author of organizational change and operations strategy papers that appear in *California Management Review* and *Long* Range *Planning.* His most recent publications focus on the interaction between information technology and service delivery systems in financial services. Findings from this research appear in *Information and Management*, *Strategic Finance* and *The International Journal of Service Industry Management.* He is currently researching the impact of Internet technology on industry and organizational structure in the financial services.

Robin Munkvold was born in Harstad, Norway, in 1972. He moved to Steinkjer, Norway in 1986 and has been living there since. Munkvold was educated at Nord-Trøndelag University College (Norway) and Buskerud University College (Norway). He is now an assistant professor at Nord-Trøndelag University College (1998 - present) and teaches different subjects within information technology.

Jennifer Paige Nightingale received her bachelor's degree from the University of Pittsburgh and two MS degrees from Duquesne University in education and information systems management. She began her appointment on the business school faculty at Duquesne University, USA, upon receiving her second master's degree. She has over 13 years management and training experience and presently teaches courses in management information systems, serves as the business school's webmaster, and owns her own retail business. She is listed in *Who's Who Among America's Teachers* (2002). Her goal is to complete her doctoral studies. E-mail: nightingale@duq.edu.

Victor Perotti is an assistant professor of management information systems at Rochester Institute of Technology, USA. Dr. Perotti has been honored for both his teaching and research. His research interests include the business application of complex systems and electronic commerce. He was awarded the Richard and Virginia Eisenhart Provost's Award for Excellence in Teaching. In 2000, he and co-author Dr. Tom Pray were awarded the "Best Paper Award" at the ABSEL conference for their work, *Visual Modeling of Business Simulations*. Currently he is working with colleague Dr. John Ettlie on a large sponsored research grant to examine Web-based new product development tools.

Anabela Sarmento is a professor at the Institute of Administration and Accountancy (ISCAP)/Polytechnic School of Porto (Portugal). She is also an invited researcher at the Algoritmi R & D Center, Information Systems Group, at the University of Minho (Portugal). She lectures courses related to business communication, information society, and interactive marketing. Her primary area of research is the impact of information systems on organizations, namely in the domain of communication, knowledge and organizational learning, as well as in the role of the context in the use of information systems. She is also interested in knowledge management and its relation with information systems. She received her doctorate in information systems from the University of Minho (Portugal) in 2002.

Martin Schwartz has a master of business and engineering with a focus on logistics, industrial information technology, manufacturing, marketing, and controlling. His diploma thesis was on "Executive Information Systems for Inventory Management." From 1996 to 1998, he was a research affiliate at the Department of Computer Science, Technical University Berlin, Germany, in the project "Enterprise Knowledge Medium," which was performed in cooperation with University St. Gallen. Research interests include: management information systems, customer relationship management, knowledge management, and philosophical foundations of information systems. His doctoral thesis was on "Design of Information Systems for Customer Relationship Management." Since 1998, Schwartz has been a consultant with Dr. Glinz & Partner; a Duesseldorf consulting company specialized in customer relationship management.

Dale H. Shao is an associate professor of management information systems at the Marshall University Elizabeth Lewis College of Business, USA. His primary interests of teaching and research are in the areas of management information systems, network security, enterprise resource planning, and supply chain management. He regularly presents scholarly research at national academic meetings and has an extensive research record. Currently, he is a member of many national academic organizations. He has extensive teaching experience in various areas of information systems and network planning.

Adrie Stander is currently a senior lecturer in information systems at the University of Cape Town, South Africa. He obtained his BSc degrees in Information Systems and Psychology from the University of South Africa and an MTech from Cape Technikon. He has over 20 years experience in the South African IT industry. He has a keen interest in the human side of IT and has done research in many related areas such as mobile usability, cultural aspects of user interfaces and gender issues in the IT industry. He has spoken at conferences in Africa, Europe and the USA.

Rawiwan Tenissara obtained a master's degree in applied statistics and computer science, and completed a PhD in instructional systems technology at Indiana University Bloomington. She currently is a lecturer at Information Systems Education Center, National Institute Development Administration, Bangkok, Thailand. Her research interests are human computer interaction, instructional and interface design, and database design.

Nata van der Merwe is currently a lecturer in the Department of Information Systems at the University of Cape Town, South Africa. She has qualifications in linguistics, education and information technology, with her highest qualification being an MA from the University of Stellenbosch, South Africa. Nata has 15 years experience in the IT industry and IT-related academic environments. She is currently leading a study looking at issues around the retention of women in the IT industry.

Stu (Wes) Westin is a professor of information systems at the University of Rhode Island, USA. He has published articles in a variety of national and international academic journals, including *MIS Quarterly*, *Journal of Database Management*, *Information & Management*, *Behaviour & Information Technology*, and *Telematics and Informatics*. Dr. Westin is also associate editor of the *Journal of End User Computing*, and a contributing author to several academic books on computers and information technologies. In addition, he has developed numerous custom software systems for research and educational applications. He has lectured in the US and in Europe on the topics of information systems and information technology

Boris Wyssusek has a master's degree in computer science and business administration from Technical University Berlin, Germany, with a focus on systems analysis, enterprise information systems, organization theory, and marketing of innovations. His diploma thesis was on Case-based Reasoning (computer science) and Organizational Epistemology (business administration). From 1997 to 2002, he has been a research affiliate and PhD student at the Department of Computer Science, Technical University Berlin, with a doctoral thesis on "Methodological Aspects of Organizational Modeling." Research interests include: organizational modeling, participative systems analysis, knowledge management, and philosophical foundations of information systems.

Sangjin Yoo is a professor of MIS at Keimyung University in Daegu, Korea. He received a PhD in MIS from the University of Nebraska-Lincoln. Before taking his current position, he was an assistant professor of MIS at Bowling Green State University in Ohio, USA. He has published more than 50 papers in national and international journals including *California Management Review, Long Range Planning, Organizational Dynamics, Journal of MIS Research,* and *Korean Management Science Review.*

Index